Governance in the Twenty-first Century: Revitalizing the Public Service

Edited by B. Guy Peters and
Donald J. Savoie

Canadian Centre for Management Development
Centre canadien de gestion
McGill-Queen's University Press
Montreal & Kingston • London • Buffalo

© Canadian Centre for Management Development/
Centre canadien de gestion 2000
ISBN 0-7735-2129-1 (cloth)
ISBN 0-7735-2130-5 (paper)
Legal deposit fourth quarter 2000
Bibliothèque nationale du Québec

McGill-Queen's University Press acknowledges
the financial support of the Government of
Canada through the Book Publishing Industry
Development Program (BPIDP) for its activities.
It also acknowledges the support of the Canada
Council for the Arts for its publishing program.

The opinions expressed are those of the authors
and do not necessarily reflect the views of the
Canadian Centre for Management Development.
An abridged version of chapter 8 was published
in the *International Review of Administrative
Sciences* (Vol. 66, No 1, March 2000, 45-55).

Printed in Canada on acid-free paper

Canadian Cataloguing in Publication Data
Main entry under title:
Governance in the Twenty-first Century:
revitalizing the public service
(Canadian Centre for Management Development
series on governance and public management)
Co-published by Canadian Centre for
Management Development.
Includes bibliograhical references.
ISBN 0-7735-2129-1 (bound)
ISBN 0-7735-2130-5 (pbk.)
1. Public administration. 2. Civil service reform
I. Peters, B. Guy II. Savoie, Donald J., 1947-
III. Canadian Centre for Management
Development. IV. Series.
JF1601.G68 2000   351   C00-900765-2

Contents

Preface

This volume, the third in the Canadian Centre for Management Development's series on Governance and Public Management, offers the reader an international perspective on some important challenges facing governance in this new century. It is no easy task to offer guidance on how to revitalize our public services in this new context, but some most authoritative authors from Canada, New Zealand, Sweden, the United Kingdom, and the United States drew on their expertise to provide well-informed and insightful analyses about important issues which politicians, public servants, and citizens will need to consider in seeking to ensure progress. As underlined by one of the peer reviewers, new insights are provided on a wide range of public sector issues: the role of the nation-state in governance, the role of political leadership in public service reform, new human resource management challenges, relations (or "bargains") between politicians and public servants, fundamental questions about performance measurement, challenges relating to information and communication technology in government, intergovernmental relations and citizen engagement, organization patterns, privatization, and accountability. A concluding chapter examines key questions which emerge from this attempt to look into the future with regard to the role of government, its future effectiveness, the instruments it will need, and more particularly the type of public service which will be needed in the emerging model of governance.

Both this volume and its two predecessors, *Governance in a Changing Environment,* and *Taking Stock,* are the outcome of a pioneering approach at the Canadian Centre for Management Development (an agency of the Government of Canada) that aims to bring together the insights of academic specialists and senior practitioners of public administration. All three projects involved two intersecting networks, an international network of distinguished researchers together with a similar network of senior Canadian public service executives. In each case the research agenda and topics for exploration were established by the executive network. As they met monthly to explore each topic over the period from January 1997 to November 1998, the executives were assisted in their reflections through presentations from and dialogue with individual researchers. This dialogue also helped the researchers to deepen their own understanding of key issues in public administration. A roundtable in the fall of 1998 provided an opportunity for the international research team to compare perspectives and approaches and to exchange views with leaders of the Canadian Public Service.

Through such interactive approaches and other similar methods – such as action research round tables – the Canadian Centre for Management Development seeks to involve practitioners directly in the research process, and to undertake research in a manner that is relevant to researchers and executives alike and that produces both knowledge and action outcomes. At CCMD we like to say that our objective is to undertake research not just for public service executives and leaders but with them also. We believe that these approaches offer models that may well be of interest to other learning and research organizations in the public sector, and elsewhere too. An excellent example is the Citizen-Centred Service Network, which won the 1999 Gold Award for Innovative Management of the Institute of Public Administration of Canada.

The success of this process of reflection, dialogue, and refinement is due in large measure to the initiative and inspiration of Ralph Heintzman, the CCMD Vice-Principal for research at the time, and of David Holdsworth, who was Assistant Secretary to the Cabinet (Management Priorities and Senior Personnel), at the Privy Council Office, as well as to the leadership and guidance of the volume's co-editors, B. Guy Peters and Donald J. Savoie, both of them leading scholars of comparative public administration and Senior Fellows of CCMD. I am grateful to them for the knowledge, wise counsel, and leadership they provided throughout the development of the program and in bringing the work to completion. I am also grateful to the senior public servants who participated in different ways as the program took shape and who offered many unique and valuable insights from the practitioner's perspective. Finally, I extend my warm thanks to the distinguished international team of research collaborators for their outstanding contribution to this volume and dedicate the latter to the memory of Vincent Wright, a member of the group who passed away before it could be published.

Governance in the Twenty-first Century: Revitalizing the Public Service is the outcome of the third in a series of three research programs. The first looked at the changing environment for governance and public administration. *Taking Stock* looked back over a decade or more of public sector reform and attempted to draw lessons and insights from experience in many countries and jurisdictions. This third program looked forward and explored the conditions and requirements for revitalizing the public service in the decades to come. The whole research program attempted to position the public service in the context of a changing public policy environment, rapid technological change, and a more involved and demanding public.

CCMD's new long-term research agenda will focus on modernizing governance. A research plan has been developed around four sub-themes: citizens and citizenship, changes affecting representative democracy, the future role of government, and future public service reforms. I look forward to sharing the results of this future research with practitioners, researchers, and students in Canada and around the world as soon as they become available during the years 2000-2001.

MAURICE DEMERS
Director General,
Strategic Research and Planning
Canadian Centre for Management Development

Acknowledgments

The production of a substantial volume such as this involves the skills and dedication of many different people, both at the research stage and during the publication process. I am grateful to all those at the Canadian Centre for Management Development who have devoted so much of their time to bringing this ambitious project, the third volume in our series on Governance and Public Management, to a successful conclusion. In particular, I would like to thank Ralph Heintzman's assistant, Ginette Turcot-Ladouceur, for her invaluable assistance in managing the many arrangements associated with the research program, including the meetings of practitioners and the contributors to this volume. I also extend my warm thanks to my own assistant, Anne Morin, to Ginette Benoît at the Université de Moncton and to Michèle Renaud, our publications assistant for liaison with the authors and publishers and for assistance in seeing the final texts through the publication process.

Finally, I am grateful to Philip Cercone and his team at McGill-Queen's University Press for their commitment to promoting and publishing CCMD's Governance and Public Management series and the professionalism they have shown in bringing this third volume to completion.

MAURICE DEMERS

PART ONE

INTRODUCTION

Introducing the Topic

DONALD J. SAVOIE

Without doubt, national civil services in most Western countries have been subjected to more reform measures during the past twenty years than any comparable political or administrative institutions. This is new. Indeed it has often been said that civil servants favour the status quo, that many have a well-honed capacity to give the appearance of change while, in fact, moving very slowly or even standing still.

The signs of real change, however, are now everywhere. Many national civil services are – at least as traditionally defined – smaller than in the past; appointments to senior positions no longer go to those who have come up through the ranks of a department; new organizations to deliver services have been established. The list goes on. This is not to suggest for a moment that civil servants themselves have been the force behind all the changes. In many instances the impetus came from the political leadership, starting with Margaret Thatcher. Still, in some countries like Australia, Britain, and New Zealand, many far-reaching changes have been implemented by civil servants.

The past twenty years have clearly demonstrated that civil servants can embrace change, even the kind of change that can hardly be described as being in the interest of their institution. Yet it is still not at all clear what works, what does not work, and which change offers the most promise to strengthen the government's policy advisory capacity and its ability to deliver services.

3

There was no grand design to begin with, so national civil services were left to try various approaches, to see what might work.[1]
To be sure, we know why the political leadership wanted
change. A difficult fiscal situation, along with a strongly held
view that the machinery of government was in serious need of
repair, spoke to the need for change. However, what was less
clear is precisely what the political leadership had in mind for
their national civil services.

Although the first wave of reforms came from right-wing governments, the new political leaders promoting a different ideology (i.e., from Bush to Clinton, Major to Blair, and Mulroney to
Chrétien) still want change – and it is not at all clear what they
expect from their national civil services. No doubt they want
them to be responsive to their policy preferences and to manage
government programs as efficiently as possible. But that is no
different from what was expected of them, say, thirty or fifty
years ago. The political manifestos or platforms of parties currently in power shed little light on the role of the civil service,
except that it should be different from what is currently the case.
Beyond the standard generalities about the need to improve
government operations and services to the public, not much else
is said. Certainly, one would be hard put to find in these documents anything that would qualify as a "vision" for the future
role of the civil service. It appears that some things never change.
Party platforms have been – and remain for the most part – content simply to say that things inside government will be better if
only the right party (their party) is elected to power.

While this book does not attempt to define a vision for the
national civil service, it does seek to make a contribution through
a discussion of the changes that have been introduced in recent
years and their implications for the future. As well, it looks ahead
to potential challenges and offers advice on how they can be met.
In short, the book's objective is to explore the conditions and
requirements for revitalizing the public service.

This is the third book in the series on the broad theme "Governance
and the Civil Service." The first, *Governance in a Changing Environment,* sought to understand the ways in which governance

and public administration were being reshaped and rethought. The second, *Taking Stock: Assessing Public Sector Reforms,* looked back over a decade or more of public sector reforms to draw lessons and insights from experience in several countries. Both books were the result of a collaboration between practitioners and researchers. Senior federal government managers were involved in reviewing the issues and drafts of the papers and in promoting a debate between themselves and the authors on the issues.

Ralph Heintzman, former Vice Principal of Research at the Canadian Centre for Management Development, described the process in his preface to *Governance in a Changing Environment.* He wrote that three steps were involved. The first was to bring the research team together for extended exchange and debate at the beginning and near the end of the process. The second was to create an opportunity for dialogue between the researchers as a group and similar groups of senior public managers: this was accomplished by joint meetings. The third step was to arrange encounters or interviews between the individual researchers and senior public managers (Peters and Savoie, 1995).

We adopted essentially the same process for this book. The one difference is that practitioners were directly involved very early on in setting the research agenda and in deciding what papers ought to be prepared. Senior staff members of the Canadian Centre for Management Development met with fifteen senior practitioners to map out in some detail the issues to be reviewed and the chapters to be prepared. It is important to stress that practitioners themselves identified the need for all of the chapters in this book. In this sense, it is their book.

Once the practitioners had agreed on the issues to be reviewed, we recruited an outstanding international team of scholars to produce the papers. Interviews and meetings of one kind or another were also held between practitioners and many of the scholars at various stages in the preparation of the book.

A number of the same practitioners and scholars were involved in all three books; thus, there has been some continuity in the three exercises. As a result, many chapters in this book again deal with broad governance issues and continue to take stock of various public sector reforms undertaken during the past fifteen years or so. Efforts are made, however, to look ahead and offer suggestions on ways to strengthen the public service. Much like the two earlier books, this one also provides a comparative perspective.

In many ways this book was the most difficult but also the most rewarding of the three to produce. It was the most difficult because looking ahead to explore the conditions and requirements for revitalizing public service is not easy at the best of times – that is, when stability reigns. One would hardly now describe as stable the public sector in the countries surveyed for this book. In addition, scholars are hesitant to speculate on what might be. Practitioners, as our consultations with them revealed, are also for the most part more interested in reviewing past efforts and current challenges than in speculating on what the future may hold. This book was the most rewarding because it brought senior practitioners and scholars together to identify the key challenges and issues confronting the Canadian civil service and to discuss possible ways of strengthening it.

The main difficulty of course was that there are too many variables, too many forces at play, and too many unknowns for either scholars or practitioners to feel sure about what the future may hold for the civil service. If recent history is a guide, then about all that we can say with any degree of confidence is that there will be still more changes designed to "fix" government operations and the civil service yet again. Despite this difficulty, the authors have made every effort to tackle the issue and explore the conditions and requirements for revitalizing public service.

THE CHALLENGES AHEAD

Though it may not be clear what the future holds for government operations and the civil service, the main challenges confronting Western countries are fairly clear. The Organization for Economic Cooperation and Development (OECD) states that "an increasingly open international economy puts a premium on national competitiveness and highlights the mutual dependence of the public and private sectors. Citizen demand is more diversified and sophisticated and, at the same time, the ability of governments to deal with stubborn societal problems is being questioned. The policy environment is marked by great turbulence, uncertainty and an accelerating pace of change. Meanwhile, large public debt and fiscal imbalances limit governments' room for manoeuvre" (OECD, 1995). To the OECD's list of challenges we could add demographic changes, greater global and regional economic integration, and the growing interdependence between various sectors in society, not least between the public and the private and between the different orders of government. All of this at a time when many voices are increasingly calling for a diminished role in society for the nation state.

Of particular interest to us is the need to protect, or better yet, to strengthen the capacity to govern and to deliver public services. The various reforms of the past fifteen years do not appear to have brought government closer to the public it serves or to have increased the confidence that citizens have in their governments. Joseph S. Nye opens his 1997 essay on governance with the sentence, "Confidence in government has declined." He reports: "In 1964, three-quarters of the American people said that they trusted the federal government to do the right thing most of the time. Today (i.e., 1997) only a quarter admit to such a trust." Nye is quick to add that "the United States is [not] alone. Canada, Britain, Italy, Spain, Belgium, the Netherlands, Norway, Sweden, and Ireland have also seen some decline of trust in government" (Nye, 1997). It is important to note, however, that the decline in public confidence in government has been concomitant with sharp declines in confidence in virtually all institutions, including large businesses and the media.

What is remarkable is that Nye wrote his essay following nearly two decades of a never-ending parade of government reform. No sooner had one been unveiled, offering all kinds of promise, than a new one was presented. These ranged from new financial management information systems, new approaches to expenditure review exercises, contracting out, make or buy, Total

Quality Management, the empowerment of managers and their front line workers, clients, and politicians to the restructuring of the machinery of government, notably the establishment of executive or special operating agencies. The list goes on. Yet, by all accounts, our "confidence in government" had diminished.

It is important to stress that the politicians who have set out over the past twenty years or so to fix government started from the premise that bureaucracy was the problem. It is revealing to note that political institutions, at least when compared to civil services, have remained largely intact. The Canadian Parliament, for example, has not been "downsized" or "restructured." The same can be said about the American Congress and Presidency. We have not sought to contract out parliamentary functions. Similarly, relationships between Parliament and the executive in British parliamentary systems or between the President and Congress have not been overhauled.

The reforms that have transpired, however, have taken a toll on civil servants, on how they perceive their institution and their own contributions. The various reforms which were implemented have been anything but "intellectually consistent." Indeed, many were "often inherently incompatible."[2] But if there were an underlying theme to them all, it is that the private sector is, by definition, superior to the public sector. Thus, the view has grown (widely held among the political elite) that the best way to fix government bureaucracy was to adopt private sector practices. Of course, the impact of this view has been dispiriting to the civil service. A number of students of government in Britain, the United States, and Canada have written about a morale problem and a crisis of confidence in their civil service.[3] The former Clerk of the Privy Council and Secretary to the Cabinet, Canada's top civil servant, commented on the morale problem in the fourth annual report to the prime minister on the public service of Canada. She wrote about a "quiet crisis" in the public service. She explained that some former public servants "after an exemplary career, would not advise their children to follow in their footsteps" and that "some students would not consider a career in the public service if presented with other options."[4] And it is not just politicians who take a dim view of the civil service. Ordinary Canadians, Australians, Americans, and others appear to share the negative assessment. A senior bureaucrat in Australia recently observed that "the main challenge facing the public service is the lack of esteem in which it is held."[5]

The above suggests that those who wish to put forward suggestions to revitalize the civil service should do so with great care. There is always the risk that the cure will be worse than the disease. The political leadership that led the first wave of civil service reforms – Thatcher, Reagan, and Mulroney – ought not to be surprised to hear that morale is low in the civil service.

The purpose of their reforms was not to strengthen morale, but to bring the bureaucrats to heel. Indeed, Thatcher was convinced that it was the senior civil servants who had undermined Britain's economy. Reagan, during his 1980 presidential campaign, described the federal bureaucracy as "overgrown and overweight," and pleaded to bring "corruption fighters" into government. Mulroney, meanwhile, promised to give "pink slips and running shoes to bureaucrats" once elected to office. He also declared that since "coming to Ottawa from the private sector, I have been appalled by the waste of time and talent in government." They all, by turn, spoke about the need to "deprivilege the civil service" and the need to "drain the swamp" (Savoie, 1994).

It is necessary to understand the reasons for the decline in confidence in government if we are to identify the means to protect or strengthen the capacity to govern and deliver public services. It would be unfair to claim that responsibility lies solely with Margaret Thatcher et al. To be sure, their message, repeated time and again, that government had become part of the problem rather than part of the solution had an impact. When politicians and the media repeat as conventional wisdom that government is inept, then perception can become reality. Nye draws a parallel between the message that government cannot do anything right to "demarketing campaigns" found in the private sector where "consumers are urged not to buy certain products" (Nye, 1997).Politicians no longer run solely against the party in power. They also run against government. We are told, for example, that since Jimmy Carter's 1997 campaign, politicians tend to run against Washington (Nye, 1997). But there are other reasons why governments no longer enjoy the kind of confidence and even deference they once had.

It may well be that expectations of what governments could accomplish had to be adjusted and that this is what has happened over the past twenty years. Governments proved that they were equal to every challenge they faced during the Second World War when they got involved in virtually every sector of the economy. By the end of the war, the British, Australians, Canadians, and Americans believed that their governments could meet any new challenge. After all, they had mounted a successful war effort, the Allies had won the war and the war economy had run well. Unemployment had fallen to zero, and yet prices had been held down. The Second World War also bequeathed a creative and smooth-running machinery of government in their countries. Certainly, government was the place to be in post-war society if you were fresh out of university, bright, ambitious, and preoccupied with the public interest. In Britain, Archbishop William Temple had promoted, with considerable success, the concept of the welfare state in contrast to Hitler's warfare state. Being a direct participant in building the welfare state could be every bit as exciting for the young university graduate as had been being part of the war effort.

We discovered during the war years that government can be very effective, focused and ultimately successful when pursuing an overriding objective, such as defeating Hitler. But things are different in less dramatic times when equally valid objectives are competing for limited fiscal resources, when the political leadership is uncertain about which one it wants to pursue or for how long. Then when an unforeseen political crisis crops up, everything else is put aside. Watergate taught us that there is always a constant stream of political crises or potential crises waiting to be unearthed. The media, as is well known, are less deferential and more critical of government than they were in the pre-Watergate days. The breathtaking speed of modern communications, especially television, is putting enormous pressure on government to make decisions quickly for fear of appearing indecisive and not in control. Television gave its viewers a ringside seat during the Gulf War, for example. The modern media are global, increasingly critical, and widely accessible, even to the illiterate class.[6] Within minutes, they can zero in on any issue anywhere in the world and compare virtually any given situation in one country to a similar one in another. Above all, the media have a capacity to intrude into the political arena and the operations of government and to inform the public quickly, visually, and with considerable impact about what is not working. That said, it is important to recognize that though the publics in different nations are almost certainly better informed than in the past, this does not mean that they are well informed. Clearly, there is still a great deal of work to be done on this front.

To be sure, the media have had a great deal to report on. Gone are the days of small government and the luxury to pursue a limited number of highly visible objectives with single-minded determination. The immediate post-war years provided reconstruction, strong economic growth and a new economic doctrine (Keynesian economics) that captured the treasuries of virtually every Western government. Government expanded in all directions. Before too long, governments, particularly the political leadership, suffered from an "overload" problem. There were simply too many issues and too many policies and activities to oversee for presidents and prime ministers and their cabinets to cope with. Some issues were handled very well, particularly when the political leadership of the day decided to pursue them, but others were allowed to drift. Senior civil servants, unable to secure firm policy direction from the only ones who could give it – the political leadership – tried as best they could to keep things on an even keel. Before too long, however, they stood accused of favouring the status quo and of having too much influence over policy.

Meanwhile, some government programs began to work at cross purposes. Governments proved especially inadequate at coordinating policies and pursuing a goal or even a series of goals. The classic example here is the u.s. Department of Agriculture, which encourages tobacco farmers, while the Surgeon General is busy promoting antismoking campaigns. There are countless such examples in economic-development policy, environmental protection, social policy, and government procurement policy. All in all, few government organizations can define their tasks on the basis of clearly stated goals in legislation or as resulting from policy reviews. Government, by its very nature, speaks to different objectives and policies, not always compatible with one another. Goals even within government departments and agencies are often vague, at times deliberately so. This explains why senior government officials often tend to be cautious administrators rather than daring managers. To change course or to sort out conflicting objectives requires a huge wrench of the wheel. In any case, only political leaders can do this and all too often they are too busy pursuing their own "pet" priorities or managing the latest political crisis to take the time to do so.

Governments are also dealing with a better informed and, by ricochet, a more demanding public than was the case forty years ago. The media, particularly television, is one reason, but there are others. For one thing, citizens today are better educated and more knowledgeable about government policies and operations. For another, dramatic advances in information technology have made information about government intentions, programs, and activities more accessible. New communications technology and easier access to government information provide outside groups and individuals a capacity to develop positions on a whole range of policy issues and to challenge government policy.

The OECD points to globalization and the need for nation states to be competitive as a key challenge in the years ahead. But, ironically perhaps, there is a flip side to this challenge. Historically marginalized groups, cultural groups, regional and local communities are gaining prominence on the political agenda. We are seeing a veritable "explosion of ethnicity" together with a "politically focused cultural pluralism" in many advanced industrial countries.[7] This, in turn, has given rise to a radically different type of cleavage in society that is putting new pressures on the structures of government. Individuals are bypassing political parties in voicing their opinions and concerns. They increasingly do so through interest groups or under the banner of "individ-ual" or "charter" rights. Those that cast their views or demands in terms of "rights" do so under the "most powerful of moral considerations" and are usually in no mood to abide by a con-sensus or even to negotiate (Pocklington, 1982).

All of the above makes the point that there is no shortage of challenges facing national governments and their civil services. It is in this context that measures to revitalize the civil service must be developed.

REVITALIZING MEASURES

How are nation states responding to those challenges? How do they propose to revitalize their civil services? At the risk of sounding repetitive, efforts thus far have been largely directed only at the civil service.

The OECD reports, much as our *Taking Stock* did, that different countries are responding differently. It adds, however, that "although there is no single best model of public sector manage-ment, common trends can be identified. Some have been inspired by best private sector practice, adapted to public sector needs. The objective is fundamental change, transforming behaviour and attitudes" (OECD, 1997). Looking to the future, the OECD insists that "the pressures to make public services more responsible and cost-effective will not abate." It predicts that "in the decades to come, the well-performing public sector will be radically different in appearance and behaviour. Typically, it will be less involved in direct service provision; concentrate more on providing a flexible framework within which economic activity can take place; regulate better, with more complete information about likely impacts; continuously evaluate policy effectiveness; develop planning and leadership functions to respond to future economic and social challenges; and take a more participative approach to governance" (OECD, 1997). Peter Self outlines what he describes as a "powerful new paradigm" which squares with how the OECD sees the future. He writes that this "paradigm holds that governments should in general do less; ... that they should privatise public services or their delivery wherever practicable; and that they should reform their own operations in accordance with market concepts of competition and efficiency" (Self, 1993).

On the face of it, one is tempted to conclude that national civil services are in line for more of the same. Indeed, during the past twenty years or so, many have sought to be radically different in both appearance and behaviour – that is why, for example, executive or special operating agencies have been established, performance pay measures have been introduced or strengthened, as has contracting out, and why a new emphasis has been placed on responding better to the needs of clients.

Still, practitioners involved in shaping the scope of this study and in defining the key issues for individual chapters in this book raised the same concerns as did OECD. They too spoke about the impact of globalization on their departmental policies and day-to-day work. They also mentioned government overload and asked how policy coordination could coexist with independent operating agencies. More to the point, they asked how does one direct self-steering interorganizational networks?

They spoke to a need to rethink the role of government and the boundaries of public service. There are now limits to the role of national governments, ranging from international trade agreements to a new focus on citizen engagement and participation. What are these limits and where are the new boundaries, they asked? They also raised concerns about the agency model, maintaining that this model has limits that we have not explored. When, they asked, should the agency model be adopted? What are the implications for accountability, public service values, and ethics?

They raised very few objections to making government more client- or performance-oriented. For the most part, they acknowledged that increasing market discipline in the public sector has already demonstrated that it holds promise. They also have no objection to competition. They see wider application of market-type mechanisms in the future, including contracting out, user charges, and the development and promotion of internal markets.

But, they add, this can never represent the complete picture. Government will still deliver services and civil servants will continue to generate policy advice. How will we know, they asked, how effective is the civil service, and how can we tell? Past efforts, they point out, have been directed at identifying opportunities for contracting out, all the while assuming that what is contracted out will be better managed. We may well have lost sight of what it is the civil service does well or better than the private sector. But, they argue, we need to know how this can be determined.

They attached a great deal of importance to performance measurements and evaluation. They argue that performance measurements in future ought to be designed for two groups – internal managers and external examiners, including citizens interested in the program. They add that new efforts should be made to encourage outside groups, notably parliamentary committees, to develop a keener interest in performance measurements and in evaluating programs and the quality of public services.

Practitioners insist that many future efforts to revitalize the public service should be undertaken "through people." The future of national civil services, they argue, depends on how civil servants feel about their institution and their work and how they are treated. Various downsizing exercises of the past have had an impact. There is a view, strongly held by some practitioners, that there is a general decline in loyalty towards the institution of the civil service. They also suggest that downsizing reinforced this trend and in fact may well have accelerated it.[8]

The "people factor" in turn raises a number of questions. Practitioners argue as to whether attempts should be made to strengthen loyalty within the civil service. If so, by whom and how? Should the civil service be a more or less unified institution than at present? Some believe that it will need to be more unified in some ways than it is now (e.g., policy formulation) and less unified in other ways (e.g., personnel). In what ways, and with what consequences? Should government departments and agencies, for example, all enjoy separate employer status?

Management development and training will become even more important in the years ahead. A civil service removed from direct service delivery will need to be accomplished in the management of partnerships and performance contracts; in the playing of brokerage, networking, and advisory roles; and in the management of intergovernmental relations. Canada's former Clerk of the Privy Council and Secretary to the Cabinet argues that governments and organizations are probably misadapted to deal with an increasing number of policy issues, since the more important ones are now horizontal and do not respect boundaries or fit neatly within areas of jurisdictions. The solution, she writes, calls for "a shared sense of priority, shared not only across ministries but across governments as well. Again, our ability to make the necessary alliances is central to our ability to meet the challenges presented by horizontal issues. The machinery can be adapted to support the priority of the day but without a shared view on the importance of the issues, organizational change alone will not help" (Bourgon, 1993). It is for this and other reasons that management development and training will become indispensable.

Practitioners also said that we need to revisit the relationship between politicians and civil servants. Although it has changed in recent years, everyone goes on as if the old rules still apply – mainly because we have not developed new ones. Ministers now, as a matter, of course, bypass their officials when seeking policy advice, preferring to consult their own partisan staff, lobby groups and lobbyists, and think tanks. No less important a development is the trend towards greater public visibility for civil servants, a trend that will likely continue. This could well lead to a different civil service, one in which bureaucrats become political actors or take policy positions before the media or parliamentary committees. This, in turn, will have an impact on accountability and the long-standing implicit contract between Cabinet and the civil service. Some practitioners asked if one could still establish a clear distinction between "political" and "bureaucratic" accountability?

Other practitioners reported that there are inherent contradictions in the reform measures already introduced and that these should be sorted out before bringing new ones on board. Task forces of senior officials in Ottawa have been reporting of late that the links between policy and operations are too weak and growing weaker still.[9] Yet, the government has embraced, however tentatively in some instances, the agency model. It is this model that is responsible for the weaker links. How then, practitioners asked, can governments delegate managerial authority and retain a capacity at the centre to coordinate policies and think strategically?

Practitioners pointed to information technologies as a major new development shaping the civil service of the future. They saw great potential in the application of information technologies, arguing that they could increase efficiencies in government operations, promote greater participation in policy making, strengthen the delivery of public services, and promote greater job satisfaction. New information technologies question the relevance of the traditional model of program and service delivery and lessen the need for a large physical infrastructure. This in turn means that the physical presence of government will become less visible to citizens. How, they asked, will politicians react to this development? New information technologies certainly allow a greater geographical spread of offices, thus bringing services closer to citizens or clients. They also provide options for organizational design that were not available in the past. They can transform the civil service, making clerical workers redundant. Rather, the new civil service will become a place for knowledge workers who require a vastly different organizational and management culture from clerical workers. They expect more than just a job and a pay cheque. How can the civil service attract and retain people of this calibre?

These, then, are some of the concerns practitioners voiced during various meetings to discuss the issues for this book. The scholars responded by presenting papers to a round table held in Ottawa in late 1998. Practitioners, in turn, responded to the draft papers with new questions and suggestions for improvements. This process has resulted, we believe, in an integrated set of papers that address the principal issues facing national governments and offer some suggestions on how the civil service could be revitalized.

Role of National Governments

B. Guy Peters reviews the growing literature on governance and argues that the nation state remains and will continue to remain the dominant actor in setting goals for society. He challenges a number of ideas found in the recent literature and considers the various roles national governments are being asked to play. He contends that they must continue to resolve conflicts if only because there is no other legitimate actor available to do so. Too often, he adds, we assume that what is true in one sector will also be true in another. Globalization, for example, is having an impact on the role of government in setting economic policies. But the impact is much less clear in social policy.

The debate about the role of the nation state, he insists, should not boil down to an either/or scenario. Rather, the debate should be over how best to organize the governing of nation states, what new tools to introduce and old ones to discard and what mechanisms for proper public accountability should now apply. He concludes by looking ahead and suggesting ways to strengthen the governance of nation states.

Rethinking the Boundaries

David Cameron and Richard Simeon review recent changes in Canadian intergovernmental relations and suggest that a new federalism – collaborative federalism – is emerging. They then cast intergovernmental relations in a broader setting: the perspective of democratic citizenship. What kind of implications, they ask, do intergovernmental relations hold for such democratic values as accountability, transparency, and citizen participation?

They do not limit their investigation to Canada, but include other countries with a federal system, on the grounds that a comparative perspective can provide lessons that may well apply in more than one country. They go further still, by pointing out that multi-level governance issues have replaced federal–provincial ones. The Canadian civil servant is expected to deal with new institutions at home (i.e., emergent aboriginal government structures) and abroad (i.e., international tribunals). All these developments pose new challenges not just to government officials but to democratic citizenship.

The future, they argue, will be a world of multilevel governance. This raises a number of questions: how will accountability requirements apply in future? Where will the proper home for finding political answers be located? How will civil servants operate when problems and potential solutions they are expected to deal with are "simultaneously local, regional, national, and international"?

Chris Pollitt answers the question "how do we know how good public services are?" by explaining that many OECD countries use measurement. The move towards targets and quantified measures has been especially evident in Anglo-American democracies and transcends political ideology or parties.

Pollitt identifies a number of problems inherent to "measured governance." For one thing, there are limits, if only because many government decisions are by definition political decisions. If they were not, we could conceivably establish targets and performance indicators for every government activity and then put the decision-making process on automatic pilot. Things can never be that simple in a politically charged environment when finite means always come face-to-face with infinite wants. There are other problems as well, ranging from motivation to technical difficulties.

Still, as Pollitt argues, many countries are now firmly on the measurement road and they are not likely to turn back. He makes two important suggestions to strengthen the measurement culture in the public sector. The first is that good data sets require uniformity and stability. That is, to the extent possible, data need to be produced in well understood and widely shared formats. Second, governments need to recognize that performance measurements or data have met with limited political interest and that they should intensify their efforts to push performance measurements "outwards."

Vincent Wright discusses the current transition period, in which the role of government is being redefined. He writes that the line dividing the public and private sectors is increasingly blurred and that there are important consequences in store for public administration. Still, he believes that there has probably never been a period in history when the public and private sectors were able to operate in hermetically sealed jurisdictions or space. The difference is that today the two sectors flow into one another with less and less distinction between them. One ought not, he cautions, assume that this can take place without significant consequences. He reviews in some detail the impact on governance.

Wright maintains that it is not possible to return to the status quo ante. The changes have been too numerous and too profound to turn back the clock. Still, he argues, any attempt to revitalize must include, as one of its key element, a restatement of some public sector values, such as integrity, fairness, and accountability. In addition, it is very important for a revitalized public sector to provide a clear reassertion of the proper role of public servants in making and implementing public policies.

Christopher Hood outlines the "public service bargain" struck between politicians and civil servants over their respective duties to review their mutual state of relations. He reviews a number of recent changes in public administration that have had an impact on the bargain, including the agency model and the trend towards political management based on public opinion surveys and focus groups. These and other developments have strained the bargain. Hood turns to "the Prisoners Dilemma" to describe some incentives motivating both sides to cheat on the bargain.

The public service bargain, Hood argues, has had a number of unintended effects. Changes intended to improve management practices can promote the reverse behaviour. Executive agencies in Britain, for example, may have empowered people to "count things" rather than to manage things.

He speculates on the possibility of revising or abandoning the public service bargain. What, he asks, would happen if we were to replace it by ad hoc hiring or firing arrangements? A more likely scenario, he admits, is that the public service bargain will evolve, but it will not be scrapped. Career civil servants will continue to serve and continue to operate under its aegis. However, they may well have to learn to work alongside others, such as pollsters and consultants, who will operate under a far different set of rules.

Ignace Snellen maintains that new information technologies will continue to have more impact on government than on the private sector because the core of government operations is about assembling, storing, processing, transporting, and providing information. The delivery of government programs has the potential to be automated to the point that there may be no need to delegate authority or to empower the street-level bureaucracy. However, new information technologies hold the promise of establishing a single point of service for "clients" or "citizens," given that files and databases on individuals can be fully integrated.

Information technologies can promote greater citizen participation in government policy and decision making. Some even suggest that they constitute the tools to promote direct democracy. But, as Snellen points out, there has been thus far no spectacular growth in direct democracy or for that matter much change in the shape of democracy. There are few cases, for example, of politicians using web sites to consult citizens.

The impact of information technologies is already being felt inside government departments. The judiciary, according to Snellen, is next in line. The legislative branch will be the last to exploit new technologies and there are strong reservations as to whether democratic bodies will ever turn to them to strengthen their position.

Peter Aucoin and Ralph Heintzman look at accountability, one of the most important and controversial issues in public administration in recent years, particularly with the advent of the New Public Management school. Much of the debate or controversy, they write, rests on a misunderstanding, confusion, and even myths about the meaning of accountability in a democratic political system. They maintain that we ought not to lose sight of the very purpose of accountability – to control for the abuse and misuse of public authority, to provide assurance in respect to the use of public resources, and to promote learning in pursuit of continuous improvement in public management.

There are a variety of forces now at play making accountability in government more difficult or challenging. For one thing, there are greater demands for accountability for performance on the part of a better educated and less deferential citizenry and more assertive and better organized interest groups. In addition, there are strong demands for a greater degree of devolution or debureaucratization in government. There is also pressure to move to a greater degree of shared governance and collaborative management in public administration. Lastly, governments are increasingly expected to address demands for results and for recording or demonstrating performance.

The authors conclude by arguing that improving accountability for performance constitutes an important agenda for revitalizing the public service. They insist that the important issue, as some have suggested, is not about any inherent tension between accountability and performance. If it were so, they point out, then the democratic principles of accountability would somehow be antithetical to the pursuit of efficiency.

Jonathan Boston reports on various efforts in OECD countries to develop alternative service delivery mechanisms. The reasons for experimenting with new forms of delivery are as varied as there are forms of delivery. Governments have turned to them to cut costs, to improve management, and service, to encourage innovation, to promote greater democratic control, to empower and motivate employees, and so on. Boston does not attempt to provide a formula to determine which service delivery model should correspond to given circumstances. It depends, he argues, on the case in question and on the objectives being pursued.

Instead of reviewing the various forms of alternative service delivery, Boston concentrates on two models – the agency model and contracting out. Both have strengths and weaknesses and he reviews them in some detail.

Looking to the future, he writes that efforts to identify and promote alternate forms of service delivery will continue. He offers some words of caution and advice. He urges governments to review every case on its own merit if only because, in many instances, improvements can be secured without changes in the formal structure or legal status of the organization. He also urges the politicians to recognize that, if the goal is to make public agencies more creative in service delivery, there will be fiscal and political risks.

Jon Pierre writes that the most important government reforms in recent years have been at the operating or program level. There is a view, now widely held, that public services no longer always need to be produced by government organizations. Customer choice – not political decisions – should now determine what services ought to be delivered and by whom. He outlines various models to define or establish the boundaries of the public service. Whatever model one looks to, Pierre argues, as others in the book have, we are witnessing a blurring of lines between the public and private sectors.

But where does this leave the desire to have citizens participate more fully in the affairs of their governments? The question becomes more relevant as citizens are less and less inclined to turn to membership in political parties as a vehicle to participate in the affairs of state. Public–private partnerships and the shift to the agency model also appear to be less susceptible to democratic and political control than do standard government departments and programs.

Vision of Public Service

Recent public sector reforms have raised a number of questions about the civil service as an institution. Some have asked whether security of tenure is still necessary to maintain the values of service. Others have sought to explore more fully the continuing role of career service in protecting the public interest.

Donald J. Savoie and Jacques Bourgault carried out in-depth interviews with fourteen senior Government of Canada officials to identify the key questions and the areas of concern for those managing at the top of public organizations. They also consulted the relevant literature, in particular OECD and government documents from abroad, to compare experiences and lessons learned.

Managing at the top requires some different skills than was the case, say, fifteen years ago. There is less and less willingness to rely on "vertical structures of command and control," new information technologies are changing relationships between senior managers and their employees, and issues are now increasingly "horizontal." These developments will continue to shape managing practices in future. But there will be other important requirements. Senior managers of the future will want to hone their capacities to manage "up," "down," and "out." They will need to motivate knowledge workers, which requires different skills than those required to motivate clerical workers. But this constitutes only part of the solution. Politicians and political institutions also need to change; they need to evolve to enable public organizations to function better. Failing this, senior permanent officials will continue to play at the margins, trying as best they can to reform their institution.

Patricia Ingraham, B. Guy Peters, and Daniel Moynihan review the most important developments in national civil services in recent years. They report on downsizing, government restructuring, including the shift to flatter organizations, and changes in labour–management relations. They also ask a number of questions, notably whether governments now have the right people for the tasks in hand. They seek to answer this and other questions by reviewing reforms in human resources management and by describing the new civil service, particularly its composition.

Looking to the future, they consider which skills and expertise will be needed. They also review some fundamental issues that may not have received the attention they deserve. They ask, for example, if public organizations start to resemble and act like private ones, do they still carry the responsibility to reflect the democratic concerns of representativeness and equity?

NOTES

1 See, among others, Donald J. Savoie, *Thatcher, Reagan, Mulroney: In Search of a New Bureaucracy*. Pittsburgh: University of Pittsburgh Press, 1994.
2 See, among others, B. Guy Peters, *The Future of Governing: Four Emerging Models*. Kansas: University Press of Kansas, 1998, p.VIII.
3 See, among many others, Gerry Stoner, "Public Service Needs Good Dose of the Vision Thing," *The Citizen*, Ottawa, April 6, 1992, p.A8;

Charles H. Levine with the assistance of Rosslyn S. Kleeman, *The Quiet Crisis of the Civil Service: The Federal Personnel System at the Crossroads,* Washington: National Academy of Public Administration, 1986; Walter Williams, *Washington, Westminster and Whitehall,* Cambridge: Cambridge University Press, 1988; and David Zussman and Jak Jabes, *The Vertical Solitude: Managing in the Public Sector,* Halifax: Institute for Research on Public Policy, 1989.

4 See Canada, *Fourth Annual Report to the Prime Minister on the Public Service of Canada.* Ottawa: Privy Council Office, 1997, p.39.

5 Quoted in John Halligan et al., *The Australian Public Service: The View From the Top.* Canberra: University of Canberra-Coopers & Lybrand, 1996, p.93.

6 See David Taras, *The Newsmakers: The Media's Influence on Canadian Politics.* Scarborough: Nelson Canada, 1990; and Joshua Meyrowitz, *No Sense of Place.* New York: Oxford University Press, 1985.

7 See, among others, Doug Williams, *Problems of Governance: Political Participation and Administration of Justice in an Information Society.* Ottawa: Department of Justice, 1991, pp.10-19, and Max Kaase, "The Challenge of the Participatory Revolution in Pluralist Democracies," *International Political Science Review,* vol. 5, no. 3, pp.243-59.

8 See also Mitchell Lee Marks, "The Disappearing Company Man," *Psychology Today,* September 1998, pp.34-39.

9 See, for example, *Canada, Strengthening Our Policy Capacity,* report of the Task Force on Strengthening the Policy Capacity submitted to the Coordinating Committee of Deputy Ministers (Policy), Ottawa, April 3, 1995, p.2.

BIBLIOGRAPHY

Bourgon, Jocelyne. 1993. Management in the new public sector cultures. Presentation to the Public Policy Forum, Ottawa, October 28, 3-4.

Nye, Joseph S., Jr. 1997. Introduction: the decline of confidence in government. In *Why People Don't Trust Government,* eds. Joseph S. Nye, Jr. et al. Cambridge, MA: Harvard University Press, 1-2.

OECD. 1995. *Governance in Transition: Public Management Reforms in OECD Countries.* Paris: OECD, 15.

Peters, B. Guy, and Donald J. Savoie, eds. 1995. *Governance in a Changing Environment.* Montreal & Kingston: McGill-Queen's University Press, vii-viii.

Pocklington, Tom. 1982. Against inflating human rights. In *The Windsor Yearbook of Access to Justice.* Windsor, Ont.: University of Windsor, 85.

Savoie, Donald J. 1994. *Thatcher, Reagan, Mulroney: In Search of a New Bureaucracy.* Pittsburgh: University of Pittsburg Press.

Self, Peter. 1993. *Government by the Market? The Politics of Public Choice.* Boulder: Westview Press, 24.

PART TWO

ROLE OF NATIONAL

GOVERNMENTS

Globalization, Institutions, and Governance

GUY PETERS

The title of this chapter was given to me by the organizers of this conference, perhaps in an attempt to set a record for the most fashionable terms included in a single title.[1] Attempting to put these three together in a single paper is not a simple task, and it could go in several directions. We could talk about the role of global institutions in governance, or the governance of those global institutions, or a variety of other things. What I *will* attempt to do is to look at governance as the dependent variable, with globalization being the independent variable. In this context institutions should be conceptualized as an intervening variable. The social scientific talk here should not be taken to imply any quantitative analysis of the questions involved, but is only used to organize thinking and presentation (King, Keohane, and Verba, 1994).

INTRODUCTION

During the 1950s and through to the present, American political science theory tended to assign little or no importance to the State or its institutions, but rather emphasized the role of individual political actors (Almond, 1988). First it was behaviouralism (Eulau, 1996) and the emphasis on the behaviours of individuals, with the determinants of those behaviours being social or psychological and only rarely political in the usual sense of the term. Later rational choice theory and the methodological individualism inherent in that approach (Green and Shapiro, 1994) has tended to limit discussion of the state as an entity. In this view the motivations for action are broadly economic rather than social or psychological, but the individual still remains the principal actor. Rational choice theory does have its institutional manifestations (see Peters, 1998, chapter 3).

In the 1980s, European political science began to reassert the importance of state institutions (March and Olsen, 1984; 1989) and to some extent the nation state itself (at the extreme see Milward, 1992). In the 1990s, however, European political science theory has also tended to assign a diminished role to the state, although this time with multiple competitors for the role of providing governance to societies. These alternatives now include the global marketplace, supranational organizations and regimes, subnational organizations and governments, and networks of organizations (both public and private). The basic message of this emerging body of literature is that governance may be provided for a society, but it will probably not be the product of the conventional institutions of the nation state.

This chapter will examine governance from a rather state-centric perspective. Such a view is not conventional, and it is certainly not fashionable in contemporary political science (see Rhodes, 1997; Weller, Bakvis, and Rhodes, 1997), but it strikes me as still the best perspective from which to consider governance. Adopting this apparently quaint perspective is not done to deny that some aspects of governance have indeed changed, or that the elements in the above-mentioned collection of alternative influences over policy outcomes are not now of some consequence for the process of governing. The arguments being made, however, are first that nation-states and their governments continue to play a major, and perhaps still dominant, role in governance, and second that there has been a substantial influence of networks, subnational governments, and the global environment for some time – the changes are not as great as assumed. Third, I am arguing that analytically it remains more reasonable to begin any investigation of governance capacity from the state-centric perspective rather than from a more amorphous perspective such as global systems, networks, or the market.

If nothing else, adopting the state-centric perspective permits the analyst to determine if there has been as complete an erosion of the governance capacity of the nation-state as is often claimed. There may be some erosion, but we can not know unless we address the question directly, rather than simply assuming that there has been the change simply because we can point to interesting developments in the socio-political world. Thus, this view of governance is analogous to the argument that a researcher cannot assess implementation without beginning from the perspective of the "formators" of policy (Lane, 1983; Hogwood and Gunn, 1984, 207-8). Similarly, we can only assess whether governance efforts are successful or not by beginning with the goals determined through some more centralized process. This is all the more true given that the contenders for power in this intellectual contest appear to be even more amorphous and polycentric actors than is the traditional state, so that ascertaining what the intended direction of governance may be is that much more difficult.

GOVERNANCE

In order to make any progress in understanding what has happened with governance in contemporary societies we need to be certain that there is a clear understanding of what is meant by the term. The term "governance" is actually a very old one, but has been revived more recently, and has taken on a number of meanings (Rhodes, 1997, 46-52), and in particular has come to imply changes in the public sector that minimize the role of formal governmental actors. To some extent the role of the state can be defined away by adopting a definition that assumes that governance occurs anywhere else but within the nation state. For example, Rhodes (1997, 15) adopts a definition of governance that assumes that government has lost its capacity to govern, and that governance is now the product of self-organizing, interorganizational networks. Similarly, Kooiman (1993a, 6; see also 1998) also argues that governance in the contemporary era has become an interorganizational phenomenon, and that it is best understood through terms such as "co-managing, co-steering and co-guidance," all implying more cooperative formats for creating order in complex, diverse, and often divided political systems than might be associated with traditional governance methods. Elsewhere Kooiman (1993b, 258) defines governance as:

The pattern or structure that emerges in a socio-political system as a "common" result or outcome of the interacting intervention efforts of all involved actors. This pattern cannot be reduced to one actor or group of actors in particular.

In this chapter I will be adopting a perspective on governance that is grounded on the etymological root of the word. In this view governance implies "steering," or employing some mechanism(s) of providing coherent direction to society. This conception of governance assumes that there is a need for at least some central direction if a society is to be successful in coping with all the challenges that face it. Again, this is not to deny the importance of attempts to decentralize (Crozier and Trosa, 1992) some aspects of the public sector, or to deconcentrate still other aspects of governing within the public sector (Greer, 1994; Hogwood, 1994). Rather, the argument is that those efforts may not obviate totally the capacity of the government of the nation state to "steer." Some of the emerging Dutch literature on governance (Kickert, 1997; Bovens, 1990) argues that governance is becoming steering "at a distance." Even if performed at a distance this "steering" may still create governance through government if some capacity to guide, to direct, to influence, if not necessarily to control completely, actions in the economy and society remains in place for those governments (see also Lundquist, 1987).

   This state-centric perspective on governance has long roots in political science. Certainly the traditional "state" literature adopts this perspective as the fundamental nature of government and governing. Further, when the state was "brought back in" for the first time (Evans, Rueschmeyer, and Skocpol, 1985;

Nordlinger, 1981; Peters, 1997) there was a definite judgment that the role of government was to provide central direction to society, and if anything there was too much of a unitary actor conception of the state for some preferences. Further, there was the argument that effective states were autonomous from social forces, including perhaps "networks," that might attempt to control them. More recently, operating from the perspective of policy making under risk and adversity Dror (1986) has discussed the role of the "central mind of government," and the need for a successful government to generate guidance from the centre. Also, Richard Rose (1978) has focused attention on the role of steering as a way of understanding governance and role of the public sector in providing direction to society.[2] All of these approaches to governance assume that some degree of central goal setting is essential to governance, if governance is to mean anything more than a description of what has happened.

This "steering" conception of governance may have been useful in the past, and even the near past, but is it still relevant for the nature of governing in the contemporary period? Several critics of the traditional literature on governance also use the terminology of steering, but the concept of steering involved is substantially different (Kickert, 1997; Reichard, 1997). In that critical view steering becomes a generic concept, rather than a view of government occupying the central position in the provision of governance. Maintaining any one view of steering or another raises empirical questions. However, those questions can only be determined by searching for that steering capacity directly, rather than by assuming it away as a vestige of the past. If there has been as fundamental a shift in the role of the state as has been assumed, then any or all of the alternative conceptions of the sources of governance will be able to predict policy outcomes better than would be possible with the state-centric perspective. As Rhodes, one of the principal advocates of the "new governance" approach, has himself argued (at least in reference to the implementation aspect of governing), this loss of control is better viewed as a question or a hypothesis rather than as a certainty (see also Saward, 1997).

Prescriptively, it is the case that policy coherence and central direction are, if anything, more important in governing than in the recent past (Peters, 1997). This increased importance appears to have arisen for several reasons. First, the scarcity of resources for the public sector means that priority setting has become a crucial activity for any contemporary government (Peters and Savoie, 1996). That scarcity of public resources is, at least in part, a function of public skepticism about government and their unwillingness to pay more taxes (Nye, Zelikow, and King, 1997). The incoherent style of governing implied by some operational definitions of governance can only enhance that public skepticism.[3] Finally, the very importance of the international market makes coherence within the public sector more important. International competitiveness requires portions of government that might have dealt with each other occasionally to develop coordinated programs. And, if international fora are so important for the success of a country the government of that country might do well to present a coherent set of proposals in those arenas.

As noted above, analytically it appears that the best way of approaching the question of governance is to posit that the state is still a relevant actor, and indeed the dominant actor in goal setting. I would argue this simply because this may be a more coherent set of predictions than is possible with the alternative conceptions of governing. There is some possibility for a coherent prediction arising from the level of supranational government, but the other alternatives appear to lack any centralized direction that could offer a set of alternatives. Of course, the capacity of states to behave as a unitary actor is sometimes greatly overstated in the "state" literature, but it still appears easier to begin with that more centralized conception and find the exceptions than to begin with a null hypothesis of no order and find any pattern. An assumption of "distributed governance" (Pacquet, 1993) appears to provide little clear space at which to begin any assessment of how governance is being supplied, and the success with which it is being produced.

The reliance on conventional governance notions as a point of departure for the analysis appears especially important given the absence of clear predictions emanating from most of the competing conceptualizations of policy making. The globalization literature, for example, appears to argue for policy convergence (Schmidt, 1998; Berger and Dore, 1996), given that global forces are presumed to be so crucial for restricting the latitude of action available to government, and there must be some institutional, as well as policy, isomorphism to cope with those powerful external pressures.[4] Other versions of the impacts of globalization, however, conceptualize it as a spur to national innovation rather than an end to the nation state, and therefore argue that divergence in policy is probable (Ostry, 1997; Schmidt, 1998). The available evidence, however, does not substantiate much the convergence argument, especially in areas such as taxation that might have been thought to be most sensitive to global economic pressures (Hallerberg and Basinger, 1998).[5]

On the other hand, the network conceptualizations do not provide any means of determining reliably which of several alternatives existing within any collection of opinions will dominate the policy outcomes of the process (Peters, 1998; but see also Daugbjerg and Marsh, 1998). There is some evidence pointing out the extent to which networks process relatively similar problems in different ways and produce different outcomes (Daugbjerg, 1998). Without a stable pattern of decisions coming from similar networks determining if governance is actually being successful is difficult, if not impossible. The real danger is that governance becomes meaningless and a tautology; something happened, and therefore governance occurred. Again, the analogy with "bottom-up" and evolutionist schools of implementation research is very clear (Linder and Peters, 1998).

Propositions About Governance

The remainder of this chapter will be a series of propositions and hypotheses about governance. In some of these propositions I will be arguing that for governance to be effective certain conditions must be fulfilled. For each of these I will look at the capacity of five different actors or sets of actors to fulfill the requirements.

Those actors are the international market, supranational and international organizations, subnational governments, networks, and (of course) the state. In others of the propositions I will be arguing that the current discussion of the decline of "traditional governance" makes a number of assumptions that are perhaps false and hence the debate is somewhat ill-formed.

It might be argued that this contest is an artificial and unfair one, at least for some of the contestants being involved. In particular, the market is not necessarily conceptualized as an alternative form of governance by scholars who argue that the nation state has lost its capacity to govern (Strange, 1996; Carnoy, 1993; Rosenau and Czempiel, 1992). Most adherents of this position merely argue that traditional governance has become impossible, or that nation states can no longer govern; requiring something so amorphous as the market to govern may be an unsporting assignment of responsibilities. Interestingly, however, some of this literature does appear to assign an effective governing role to subnational governments, especially as they attract foreign investment into their regions or even their cities, but argues that national government cannot do the same thing. Whether because of size, complexity, legitimacy or degree of policy coherence one level of government is presumed to be capable of governing vis-à-vis the market while another is not.

I am not inclined to let off these doubters of traditional governance so easily. The implicit argument appears to be that the international market is indeed capable of allocating values – the familiar Eastonian definition of politics and government – and that there may be some more coordinated policy emerging from the market than might be expected (Ohmae, 1995; Rosecrance, 1997). This is true especially given that in their arguments against conventional governance they often elide into a discussion of international regimes in a variety of policy areas outside economics, and use those arguments to further deny the capacity of the state to govern in a globalized world (Crane, 1993; Rittberger, 1993). Thus, there does appear to be a stronger claim than just that the conventional notions about governance do not work; the argument is also that there are alternatives that have taken their place. If that is indeed the argument then the same criteria of coherence and control that are used to question state capacity must also be applied to markets and to international regimes.

The Governance Debate Is Ahistorical

One problem in the contemporary debate over governance is that it assumes a golden age of the state in the not too distance past. In that period the state was presumed to be pre-eminent and virtually unchallenged in its exercise of control over the economy and society. This assumption appears to be at best an exaggeration of the power of the state in the past, and at worst a failure to understand adequately some important aspects of governing in the past. For example, while there may have been a growth in the visibility of networks and other manifestations of the influence of interest groups in the public sector, these groups certainly have had a significant role in policy making in most democracies for decades. Indeed, it could be argued that contemporary networks, given their involvement of a number of competing interests and the difficulties of presenting coordinated policy recommendations, may actually represent a reduction in the real power of interest groups over the state, rather than increase that power.[6] It seems that the closer one-to-one relationships that existed as "iron triangles" in the United States or in similar manifestations in other settings accorded society greater power than the "big sloppy hexagons" now more characteristic of state–society relations.

Similarly, the contemporary influence that global forces are presumed to exercise over the public sector are assumed to be unique. In the first place, the level of international trade as a percentage of GNP is only now reaching the level found prior to the First World War (Hirst and Thompson, 1996). There certainly have been large increases in the levels of capital flows in the international economy (Turner, 1991; Strange, 1996), but it is not the case that the previous world was so autarkic. If anything, that market was less controlled than the contemporary market, given the absence of international regulatory institutions such as the International Monetary Fund, World Trade Organization and the

GATT. Further, there is substantial evidence that firms still behave as nationally based firms (Hirst and Thompson, 1996; Soskice, 1998) rather than as truly international actors, so that their ability (or even desire) to evade national controls appears overstated.

Further, if we go back a bit further in time there were organizations such as the Dutch East India Company, the British East India Company, and the Hudson's Bay Company all of which operated with even less control from government than a contemporary multinational may have to endure (Sen, 1998). Indeed, given the dearth of communication capacity at the time, the governments of the day might hardly know what those organizations were doing, much less be able to control them. Even later, firms in extractive industries often operated as governments unto themselves, especially when operating outside their own home country. In short, some level of independence of large firms is hardly anything new, nor is their assuming some role in the "management" of affairs outside their own borders.

On the other hand, the contemporary power of supranational organizations – especially the European Union – is probably unprecedented (Sbragia, 1997; Kohler-Koch, 1996).[7] Also, there is now a range of international organizations and less institutionalized international regimes[8] that may constrain the autonomy of nation states and limit their capability for exercising governance in a number of policy areas that may have once been almost purely domestic considerations. However, as we will point out below, these are largely governmental organizations that may actually enhance the capacity of the member governments to steer their own societies and economies, rather than condemn them to a life of impotence. Indeed, one version of integration theory (Moravcsik, 1991; but see Garrett and Tsebelis, 1996) with respect to the EU emphasizes the intergovernmental aspects of the arrangements, rather than the construction of a new form of polity.[9]

Governance Is About Setting Goals

One of the most important elements of governing is goal setting, or the determination of priorities. The old adage that "to govern is to choose" remains true, and it indicates that priority setting is a central feature of governing. The basic argument here is that one organization, or a single government, is the most probable source of governance in the sense of priority setting and coordination of policies. This argument has been made within national governments, as the need for increased levels of priority setting through the budget process, for example, tends to drive decisions upward to central agencies or perhaps even to chief executives, even in spite of, or perhaps because of, continuing pressures to deconcentrate and decentralize as many aspects of government as possible.[10]

Of the putative competitors as sources of governance it appears clear that the market, networks, and subnational governments are not good candidates to supply that sort of coherent direction. These institutions can perhaps manage the implementation of policy and may be able to set a direction for their own actions, but not be able to provide any broader direction. Governments also encounter major difficulties in providing coherence, given the multiple political pressures operating within each and the tendency to contain each policy within its particular "stovepipe." They are, however, perhaps the only set of institutions capable of providing the coherence that is desirable in public policy. As Hirst and Thompson (1996, 184-5) argue, it is the task of national governments to "suture" together the strands of governance and to integrate what is being done in all the policy domains.

It may well be that a state cannot itself implement any priorities that it makes. That inability may well be a function of the power of networks or subnational actors, or even of the market. This observation is a familiar finding in the implementation literature, going back at least to the original Pressman and Wildavsky (1974) analysis. More recently, the Hjern and Porter (1980) discussion of "implementation structures" and the Hanf and Toonen (1985) discussion of implementation within the framework of network theory (see also Marsh and Rhodes, 1992) also point to the difficulties of putting government priorities into effect. Again, we would only realize that these difficulties existed by beginning with a state-centric conception of priority setting that posits that what government decides at the centre should be implemented. It may appear rather rigid to adopt this top-down conceptualization, and coordination may be possible through more bottom-up mechanisms, but if so the coordination tends to be in terms of services rendered to a particular client rather than in terms of the overall patterns of policy adopted and delivered.

Governance Is About Conflict Resolution

Following from the above discussion of priority setting, I will also be arguing that governance additionally involves the capacity of the governing system to resolve conflicts successfully. Most important policy issues are characterized by differing, and often diametrically opposed, goals of the actors involved. There is a consequent requirement for some mechanisms for making authoritative determination of who wins and who loses, or a mechanism for negotiating a "win-win" solution for all actors interested in the policy question. It appears, however, that most of the alternative sources of governance are ill-suited to resolve those conflicts, and where they are well suited they often depend upon the power of the state to endorse the solution.. The mechanisms involved in making those decisions within the state may not be as consensual or as congenial as those seemingly implied by networks, but they generally can produce a decision.

This apparent inability to resolve conflicts is most evident in networks and other similar conceptualizations of governing and politics (Dowding, 1995). These models appear heavily dependent upon consensus and assume that all the actors involved in the network are in basic agreement about the issues, as well as the appropriate policies, for the area in which they are involved. At the most basic level the models assume that the participants share a common conception of the issues involved in the policy area. Indeed, some conceptualizations of network dynamics tend to exclude conflicting ideas by permitting the members of the network to define who is in and who is out of the system. This tendency to exclude uncomfortable alternatives is also evident if we take policy regimes, or "epistemic communities"

(Haas, 1992; Adler and Haas, 1992) at the international level to be the rough analogues of networks at the domestic level. In these structures as well as being some fundamental policy disagreements there still may be differences in national styles of policy, not to mention national interest, that will render policy making less than consensual.

The basic agreement on the definition of the issues appears to be extrapolated in these models to imply that there should be no conflicts over goals or priorities within the area. That happy consensus is generally not the case, however, and even if the actors may agree on the "frame" of the policy, they may well not agree, and more often disagree, on what needs to be done in the area. This conflict over ends and means may be evident for groups of subnational governments as well. It may well be that theorizing in this area has been based too much on more centralized systems, such as the United Kingdom, in which the dependence of subnational governments on the centre tends to mitigate conflict (Rhodes, 1988). In many policy areas the interest of different types of local communities may well be in opposition rather than in harmony, and a good deal of political bargaining will be about resolving those conflicts.

One conceptualization of networks that does permit conflict and indeed appears to revel in conflict is the "advocacy coalition" model developed by Sabatier and Jenkins-Smith (1995). The argument they develop represents a more realistic conception of differences over policy among the participants in a network, along with a mechanism (learning) for resolving those conflicts. If networks, or collections of subnational governments, are to be the alternatives to governance through nation states that their advocates believe them to be, then they must be conceptualized as capable of coping with the levels of conflict that are inherent in the policy-making process.

Again, the use of supranational or international organizations as an alternative source of governance may meet more of the demands for conflict resolution than do the more loosely structured models such as networks or policy communities. At one extreme, organizations such as the European Union can be conceptualized as proto-states developing many, if not most, of the characteristics of a nation state (Sbragia, 1997). They have voting rules that permit the resolution of conflicts, or at least the identification of the source of the conflict and the deferral of difficult situations until a time (or an institutional setting) at which they can be resolved with less overt conflict. These supranational organizations also have several alternative structures and arenas for sorting out conflicts through the interaction of member nations. In short, they function something more like a government than like the loose aggregation of members contained in a network.

Governance Is Not a Zero-Sum Game

There is a tendency in much of the "new governance" literature to assume that if national governments do not control the economy and society in ways in which they had in the past then they must be failing and were therefore being replaced by other forces. While this conception does recognize the general need for steering, it also appears to be a zero-sum conceptualization in which the gain of any powers or control by one actor is inevitably at the expense of some other actor. A superior conceptualization is to envisage the governance process as more cooperative, so that an increase in influence by one set of actors or one level of government in the process may actually contribute to the governance capacity of another actor.

I would argue that this indirect, and perhaps unwitting, contribution to governance capacity is the case with the growth of networks in a number of policy areas and their utilization by governments. While the traditional command and control, top-down conceptions of governing may not be in operation if there are strong networks in place, there is still governance, and it is still governance through the nation state. Many policy networks operate within a grant of power from the state, so that even if they are making decisions, those decisions must remain within certain parameters or it is likely that the state may withdraw that latitude for action. These governance structures have not grown up by their own volition like so many mushrooms, rather they represent the crafting of governance solutions for a more skeptical and impoverished era for the public sector. Anytime that a public organization can leverage the cooperation and legitimacy of private sector organizations, it certainly has an incentive to do so, but in the process may actually extend its own influence and legitimacy.

It is important to think of the opportunities that the alternatives to conventional governance present for national governments, at the same time that they are potential competitors for control. For example, several European governments have been able to use the external standards and controls generated by the Maastricht Treaty to achieve economic and social goals – especially a reduced public sector deficit – that might never have been possible with domestic politics (perhaps especially those of networks). Likewise, international organizations provide mechanisms for constraining potential economic competitors; most of these agreements are really international regulatory programs rather than agreements over free trade.[11] This "soft" geo-politics (Mann, 1997) should be conceptualized as a force strengthening the nation state rather than limiting its capacities for control, given that these arrangements are almost entirely agreements among nation states rather than truly autonomous structures. Other arrangements permit utilizing external forces to enforce national law, e.g., TREVI for policing within the European Union (Funk, 1997).

Governance Is an Adaptive Process

I will also argue that much of the denigration of the governing capacity of the traditional national state is a function of adopting a static view of governments and their abilities to make policies that meet posited goals. The autopoeitic[12] school of public administration (in 't Veld and Schaap, 1991; Bekke, Kickert, and Kooiman, 1995) argues that the capacity of society to reorganize itself enables private actors to evade attempts of government to regulate their behaviour. Their argument appears to stop there, but looking further we can also see governments attempting to adjust, both formally and informally, to changes in their environment in order to be able to continue to perform successfully their designated functions. Governments may require somewhat greater time to adjust to the environment, at least in the first instance, but there is a good deal of evidence that would argue that they are capable of learning and adapting just as do any other institutions.

As noted, adaptation of government organizations may be formal. The current round of reforms in most industrial democracies (Peters and Savoie, 1996; Peters, 1996) can be conceptualized as a set of attempts to meet the requirements of changing societies and economies. Indeed, some of the evidence presumed to indicate that governments are finished may simply be evidence of attempts at adaptation for continued effectiveness and continued governance. The increasing use of non-profit and for profit organizations to implement policy need not mean that government is abdicating responsibility but only that it has uncovered lower-cost and higher-efficiency means of achieving its collective ends. Given that these organizations may have greater legitimacy with public service clients than more "bureaucratic" public sector organizations, the governance capacity may actually be increased rather than decreased. Further, as Wilson (1997) points out, the adaptations of some states away from neo-corporatist models may strengthen their capacity for autonomous action.

The development of tax policy offers a good example of the adaptive capacity of governments. One part of the argument of the "globalization" school of critics of traditional governance is that the development of global capital markets and global currency markets make it impossible, or at least improbable, for governments to continue to raise revenue as they have in the past. That may well be true, but it also appears that those governments have learned how to raise money in other ways. So, over the past decade, the level of revenue raised from corporate taxation has been declining, given that corporations are now more mobile internationally, and pinning down their revenues to a particular location is more difficult.[13] Other forms of government revenue, however, have been increased to compensate for the losses. Personal income taxation has increased slightly, and in particular government revenue from consumption taxes and social insurance taxation (especially the employer's share as a form of corporate tax) has been increasing (OECD, 1996).

The regulatory literature also provides evidence of government organizations that adapt their modes of behaviour to cope with the changing nature of the industries being regulated, as well as to rapidly changing political values (Wood and Waterman, 1994). Firms typically will attempt to evade the controls placed upon them, but once again that evasion usually is not the end of the game and regulatory organizations have been shown to be very adept at developing new instruments for pursuing their goals. Some of those instruments may involve the self-enforcement of regulations, albeit always with the capacity of the regulator to withdraw that privilege if abused. Again, it is clear that governments can learn just as do members of networks or private firms in the international market.

Governance Is a Differentiated Activity

We have to this point been treating governance as if it were a seamless web. If, however, we think about the now standard conceptualization of the policy process as a series of stages (Jones, 1984; Ham and Hill, 1993) then successful governance necessarily involves passing through all those stages. Much of the literature that attacks conventional conceptions of governance focuses on the implementation of policies, and somewhat on the agenda-setting process. For example, the globalization challenge to governance appears to operate primarily at the implementation stage; governments may make economic policy but they can not make it effective because of the capacity of market actors to evade the actual implementation of those laws. This is, however, not all that different from the failure to implement normal domestic policies, so that there is perhaps little that distinguishes globalization from failures in normal domestic policy (see Gray, 1998).

Further, even within the general area of economic policy there appears to be differential capacity of government to influence outcomes within their own borders. For example, the growth of massive currency markets means that it is more difficult for governments to use monetary policy for economic management, but even then a quick reading of the *Financial Times* or any similar paper reveals that there continues to be some impact of policy.[14] For example, after initial action by international economic actors, the recent crisis in the Japanese economy has been deemed to be solvable primarily through national action, not the actions of the international marketplace. Government economic policy remains effective in other areas of regulation, although even here the adherents of the power of globalization would argue that the international market will limit just how active a government can be; excessive regulations will drive international capital elsewhere.

At the other end (temporally) of the policy process networks appear to be most effective at the agenda-setting stage, given that they operate by attempting to restrict the scope of conflict over an issue. Given this characteristic, networks can "pre-cook" the policy agenda of governments, or at least attempt to predetermine the range of issues and the definition of those issues to be considered. Even in this instance, however, there may be difficulties in sorting out conflicts within the policy domain and producing an integrated set of demands on the public sector. The network formulation appears to assume those problems away, but in most political settings they can be very real.

Governance also should be differentiated by policy area. As intimated above, much of the globalization debate is structured by issues arising in economic policy (Strange, 1996; Savoie, 1996). While that is certainly an important issue, especially for the survival of sitting governments (Fiorina, 1991), the economy is not a government's sole activity, and there is still a good deal of latitude for governance by very conventional mechanisms in other policy areas (and perhaps even in the economy). While no policy area is totally shielded from the effects of the international environment, some remain more fully within the capacity of governments, as usually conceptualized, to control. For example, even though social policy and the non-wage income offered to members of society is presumably influenced by the international market place, there is some evidence of divergence, or at least the persistence of differences (see Esping-Andersen, 1996; Adema, 1997). Further, it may only be through either national governments being committed to a policy or through stronger supranational and international organizations that some of the more important policy problems in the current global arena can be addressed; these are problems of the commons[15] that appear to require enforceable rules rather than just the existence of like-minded individuals (Ostrom, Gardner, and Walker, 1994).

Likewise, there may be some differentiation of governance capacity in policy areas when the potential role of networks is considered. Again, some areas (often the regulation of industrial sectors) may be heavily influenced by network structures (Wilks and Wright, 1987). Other policy areas may remain relatively autonomous from network influence. Again we would not want to attempt to deny the existence of networks of actors concerned with policy in an area that surrounds such policy. The question remains simply how much real control do these relatively amorphous structures have over national policy choices within the area. Further, some of the more extreme formulations of network theory imply that governments are largely inert, and will (or must) accept the actions of these networks even when they may not correspond to the wishes of the government of the day. We know from the implementation literature that governments cannot always control actions when they want to, but neither are they as passive as appears to be required for network formulations to hold the sway over policy that is implied. When implementation fails there is no need to concede defeat, but rather most governments go on to create new structures for implementation, or to devise new programs that can be implemented more readily.[16]

Finally, the discussion of the (presumed) decline of traditional forms of governance appears to be more problematic for Westminster systems of governing than for other types of political systems. This somewhat greater concern is a function, I would argue, of a political and administrative history of centralized control and of a political system that stresses vertical accountability and a "top-down" style. The work of Richard Rose (1974) and others on party government, for example, stressed the

capacity of a party elected to hold office to enforce its policies
throughout the entire political system. In other political systems,
even Westminster systems with federalism and/or multi-party
systems, the illusion of control by central government has not
been so great and hence the alleged fall from grace in governance
has perhaps not been so threatening (Ware, 1996). Likewise, participants in other political systems characterized by coalition
governments, corporatist politics, and/or federalism have been
accustomed to internal bargaining over policies for some time;
they may not consider that the newer governance approaches
really say very much new about the way that governments cope
with their external environments (Laver and Schofield, 1990).

Governance Requires Public Accountability

A final point about governance is that it requires some mechanism for public accountability (Jorgensen, 1997) if the decisions
made through the process are to be legitimate. This fundamental
requirement for any political process appears to give pause for
thought to the advocates of "governance without government,"
as well it should (see Rhodes, 1997, 55–9). The removal of government from the process in quite the manner that is implied in
some of this writing appears to remove any real possibility for
public accountability. The resultant processes for governing may
be more efficient, or the outcomes may satisfy some elements of
the public, but they do not appear capable of meeting reasonable
accountability standards. Thus, even within the analyses arguing
that the world of policy making and governance have changed
dramatically, there is still the nagging concern that if such an
arrangement of policy making forces were really descriptive of
the reality it might still be highly undesirable of substantial normative grounds.

The basic requirement of accountability may mean that governance without government being a central, if not the central,
actor involved may be at best an unaccountable manner of managing the business of the public sector. At worst such an arrangement can represent a departure from the path of increasing

accountability for public programs that is one element of contemporary reforms of the state. This departure from the norms of accountability and transparency is a critical question for this style of governance. Reading the literature concerning contemporary changes within the public sector indicates that one of the many evils of old style governance being addressed is the inability of citizens to influence, or even comprehend, decision processes within the public sector (Pierre and Peters, 1997); this is often phrased as a lack of transparency in the public sector. The new governance model of the public sector appears to make the process even more opaque and even more subject to buckpassing than conventional bureaucratic governance processes.

One way out of this apparent conundrum over accountability is to design governance structures that substitute other forms of public accountability for those usually provided through direct governmental involvement in processes. For example, political party connections through appointments are often denigrated as patronage or clientelism but they may be one substitute for other, more generally acceptable, forms of political accountability. If indeed there is to be an increasing use of unconventional forms of service delivery and the use of networks to manage many aspects of public policy, then we may need to develop alternative notions of accountability that are acceptable within the context of democracy. Or, and this is more likely, we may discover that there were numerous virtues in old-fashioned administrative accountability that may need to be revived.

SUMMARY

The fundamental argument put forward here is that the state is not dead but rather remains a useful analytic concept, as well as a viable actor in the governance of society. Again, this is not to deny that there have been significant changes in our understanding of the role of the state, along with some real changes in the way in which governance functions. Those points having been conceded, however, it still appears that any analysis of governance is well-advised to begin by examining what the state is attempting to do, and then determining what went wrong if and when there are deviations from those intentions. The implementation literature warns us that there will be numerous deviations, but that does not mean that the state is not a powerful actor, only that it is not a perfect actor.

The danger in all this debate over the role of the state is that it becomes merely an either/or debate. The more constructive alternative would be to attempt to construct a more contingent and nuanced understanding of the relative contributions which all these types of actors now make to the governance of society. Networks are important, the global market is playing a significant role in the management of economic affairs, and both subnational and supranational governments play significant roles. While this study has defended the capacity of nation states to exercise governance, in no way is it intended to say that this is the only relevant actor. There is a need to build all these factors into a broader and more inclusive conception of governance and the development of synthetic conceptions of the processes of managing contemporary societies and economies.

NOTES

1 I might have added rational choice but wanted to keep this intellectually respectable.

2 In another article Rose (1980) discussed governance in the United States as occurring by "two sets of hands on the tiller."

3 In fairness some conservatives may well like the bumbling style, given that it reinforces their prejudices about the public sector and further prevents government from doing anything that might impinge on their own economic freedoms.

4 In Dimaggio and Powell's (1991) terms this isomorphism would arise from coercive and mimetic processes. That is, the international environment may be sufficiently powerful to produce coercion or states may voluntarily emulate other, successful policies.

5 In this case the more familiar politics of domestic veto players and path dependency appear to prevail over economic pressures.

6 It is not clear whether networks are such a new phenomenon or the recognition of a phenomenon that was in place for some time but

lacked a name or an adequate conceptualization. I am inclined to suspect that they are something of both.

7 The "multi-level governance" (Hooghe, 1996) framework has been developed to take into account the roles of all three levels of government in European governments, retaining all the while a significant role for national governments.

8 These regimes do have many of the features of institutions (see Peters, 1998).

9 Wearing my EU hat I tend to find fault with the intergovernmental perspective. That having been said, its strength in the field indicates that one can still look at this structure as merely another aggregation of national actors.

10 This was the critique that Wildavsky (1966) made of a number of attempts to impose greater rationality on the budgetary process in the United States, and it appears to be true (paradoxically) about more recent attempts to decentralize.

11 The economist William Niskanen quipped that a true free trade agreement would need to be only one paragraph long. NAFTA, the GNP, and the WTO produce documents that are considerably longer than that.

The rational choice literature on institutions points out that one of the advantages of institutions such as the GNP and WTO is constraining competitors, while accepting the same constraints oneself (Calvert, 1995).

12 "Autopoesis": the self-referential and self-organizing character of the private sector that inhibits the capacity of the public sector to regulate.

13 The difficulty appears to be the technical one of the proper attribution of earnings in particular locales rather than the inability to collect the tax once it is levied.

14 One must assume that governments are not totally disillusioned, so that the effort at manipulating money supply is producing some benefits.

15 The problem of the commons is that individual rationality and collective rationality diverge. There is an incentive for every individual to use as much of the common resources – oil, fish, etc. – as possible but that exhausts the collective stock of those resources and everyone is worse off in the end.

16 While the "bottom-up" literature on implementation (Elmore, 1980; Barrett and Fudge, 1980) argues that formulation should be developed based on the possibilities existing within networks, governments can still attempt to develop more effective implementation systems operating from the "top-down."

BIBLIOGRAPHY

Adema, W. 1997. What do countries really spend on social policies: a comparative note. *OECD Economic Studies* 28:153-67.

Adler, E., and P. M. Haas. 1992. Conclusion: epistemic communities, world order and the creation of a reflective research program. *International Organization* 46:367-90.

Almond, G. A. 1988. The return of the state. *American Political Science Review* 8: 853-74.

Bekke, H. A. G. M., W. J. M. Kickert, and J. Kooiman. 1995. Public management and governance. In *Public Policy and Administration Sciences in the Netherlands,* eds. Kickert and F. A. van Vught. London: Harvester/Wheatsheaf.

Berger, S., and R. Dore. 1996. *National Diversity and Global Capitalism.* Ithaca, NY: Cornell University Press.

Bovens, M. A. P. 1990. Review article: The social steering of complex organizations. *British Journal of Political Science* 20:91-118.

Calvert, R. L. 1995. The rational choice theory of institutions: implications for design. In *Institutional Design,* ed. D. Weimer. Institutional Design. Dordrecht: Kluwer.

Carnoy, M. 1993 Whither the nation state. In *The New Global Economy in the Information Age,* ed. Carnoy. College Park: Pennsylvania State University Press.

Crane, B. B. 1993. International population institutions: adaptations to a changing world. In *Institutions for the Earth,* eds. P. M. Haas, R. O. Keohane, and M. Levy. Cambridge, MA: Harvard University Press.

Crozier, M., and S. Trosa. 1992. *La décentralisation: Réforme de l'État.* Boulogne: Pouvoirs Locaux.

Daugbjerg, C. 1998. Similar problems, different policies. In *Comparing Policy Networks,* ed. D. Marsh. Buckingham: Open University Press.

Daugbjerg, C., and D. Marsh. 1998. Explaining policy outcomes: integrating the policy network approach with macro-level and micro-level analysis. In *Comparing Policy Networks,* ed. Marsh. Buckingham: Open University Press.

Dimaggio, P. J., and W. W. Powell. 1983. The iron cage revisited: institutional isomorphism and collective rationality in organizational fields. *American Sociological Review* 48:147-60.

Dowding, K. 1995. Model or metaphor?: A critical review of the policy network approach. *Political Studies* 43:136-58.

Dror, Y. 1986. *Policymaking Under Adversity.* New Brunswick, NJ: Transaction.

Esping-Andersen, G. 1996. *Welfare States in Transition.* London: Sage.

Eulau, H. 1996. *Micro-macro Dilemmas in Political Science.* Norman: University of Oklahoma Press.

Evans, P. B., D. Rusechmeyer, and T. Skocpol. 1985. *Bringing the State Back In.* Cambridge: Cambridge University Press.

Fiorina, M. P. 1991. Elections and the economy in the 1980s. In *Politics and the Economy in the 1980s,* eds. A. Alesina and G. Carliner. Chicago: University of Chicago Press.

Funk, A. 1997. Forced cooperation and the reliance of the member states on the institutional framework of the EU: the case of the third pillar. Paper presented to DAAD Conference on Europeanization in International Perspective, University of Pittsburgh, Pittsburgh, PA, September.

Garrett, G., and G. Tsebelis. 1996. An institutionalist critique of intergovernmentalism. *International Organization* 50, 269-99.

Gray, P. 1998. *Public Policy Disasters in Western Europe.* London: Routledge.

Green, D. P., and I. Shapiro. 1994. *Pathologies of Rational Choice Theory.* New Haven: Yale University Press.

Greer, P. 1994. *Transforming Central Government: The Next Steps Initiative.* Buckingham: Open University Press.

Haas, P. 1992. Introduction: epistemic communities and international policy coordination. *International Organization* 46:1-35.

Hallerberg, M., and S. Basinger. 1998. Internationalization and changes in tax policy in OECD countries: the importance of domestic veto players. *Comparative Political Studies* 31:321-52.

Ham, C., and M. Hill. 1993. *The Policy Process in the Modern Capitalist State,* 2nd. ed. New York: Wheatsheaf.

Hanf, K., and T. A. J. Toonen. 1985. *Policy Implementation in Federal and Unitary States.* Dordrecht: Kluwer.

Hirst, P., and G. Thompson. 1996. *Globalization in Question.* Oxford Polity.

Hjern, B., and D. O. Porter. 1980. Implementation structures: a new unit of administrative analysis. *Organisation Studies,* 1:119-36.

Hogwood, B. W. 1994. A reform without compare?: the next steps restructuring of British central government. *Journal of European Public Policy* 1:71-94.

Hogwood, B. W., and L. A. Gunn. 1984. *Policy Analysis for the Real World.* Oxford: Oxford University Press.

Hooghe, L. 1996. *Cohesion Policy and European Integration: Building Multi-level Governance.* Oxford: Clarendon Press.

in 't Veld, R. J., and L. Schaap. 1991. *Autopoesis and Configuration Theory.* Dordrecht: Kluwer.

Jones, C. O. (1984) *An Introduction to the Study of Public Policy.* Monterey, CA: Brooks/Cole.

Jorgensen, T. B. 1997. Public in and in-between time. Paper presented at annual meeting of the European Group on Public Administration, Leuven, Belgium, September.

Kickert, W. J. M. Public management in the United States and Europe. In *Public Management and Administrative Reform in Western Europe,* ed. Kickert. Cheltenham: Edward Elgar.

King, G., R. O. Keohane, and S. Verba. 1994. *Designing Social Inquiry.* Princeton: Princeton University Press.

Kohler-Koch, B. 1996. Catching up with change: the transformation of governance in the European Union. *Journal of European Public Policy* 3.

Kooiman, J. 1993a. Socio-political governance. In *Modern Governance,* ed. Kooiman. London Sage.

_____ 1993b. Findings, speculations and recommendations. In ibid.

Lane, J.-E. 1983. The concept of implementation. *Statsvetenskapliga Tidskrift* 86:17-40.

Laver, M., and N. Schofield. 1990. *Multiparty Government: The Politics of Coalition in Europe.* Oxford: Oxford University Press.

Linder, S. H., and B. G. Peters. 1998. Excavating the normative features of process claims: a reconstruction of the 1980s debate on implementation. Unpublished paper, School of Public Health, University of Texas Health Science Center, Houston, TX.

Lundquist, L. 1987. *Implementation Steering: An Actor-Structure Approach.* Lund: Studentlitteratur.

Mann, M. 1997. Has globalization ended the rise and rise of the nation state? *Review of International Political Economy* 4:477-96.

March, J. G., and J. P. Olsen. 1984. The new institutionalism: organizational factors in political life. *American Political Science Review* 78:734-49.

_____ 1989. Rediscovering Institutions: *The Organizational Basis of Political Life.* New York: Free Press.

Milward, A. 1992. *The European Rescue of the Nation State.* London: Routledge.

Nordlinger, E. 1981. *On the Autonomy of the Democratic State.* Cambridge, MA: Harvard University Press.

Nye, J. S., P. D. Zelikow, and D. C. King. 1997. *Why People Don't Trust Government.* Cambridge, MA: Harvard University Press.

Ohmae, K. 1995. *The End of the Nation State: The Rise of Regional Economies.* New York: Free Press.

Ostrom, E., R. Gardner, and J. Walker. 1994. *Rules, Games and Common-Pool Resources.* Ann Arbor: University of Michigan Press.

Ostry, S. 1997. Globalization and the nation state. In *The Nation State in a Global/Information Era: Policy Challenges,* ed. T. Courchene. Kingston, Ont.: John Deutsch Centre.

Pacquet, G. 1993. Governance distribuée et habitus centralisier. *Transactions of the Royal Society of Canada,* Sixth Series, VI:97-111.

Peters, B. G., and D. J. Savoie. 1996. Governance in a Changing Environment. Montreal & Kingston: McGill-Queen's University Press.

Peters, B. G. 1996. *The Future of Governing.* Lawrence: University Press of Kansas.

_____ 1997. *The Politics of Policy Coordination.* Ottawa: Canadian Centre for Management Development.

_____ 1998. *The New Institutionalism in Political Science.* London: Cassell.

Pierre, J., and B. G. Peters. 1997. Citizens vs. the new public manager: The problems of mutual empowerment. Unpublished paper, Department of Political Science, University of Pittsburgh.

Pressman, J. L., and A. Wildavsky. 1974. *Implementation.* Berkeley: University of California Press.

Reichard, C. 1997. "Neues Steuerungsmodell": Local reform in Germany. In *Public Management and Administrative Reform in Western Europe,* ed. W. J. M. Kickert. Cheltenham: Edward Elgar.

Rhodes, R. A. W. 1988. *Beyond Westminster and Whitehall.* London: Unwin Hyman.

_____ 1997. *Understanding Governance: Policy Networks, Governance, Reflexivity and Accountability.* Buckingham: Open University Press.

Rittberger, V. 1993. *Regime Theory and International Relations.* Oxford: Clarendon Press.

Rose, R. 1974. *The Problem of Party Government.* London: Macmillan.

_____ 1978. *What is Governing: Purpose and Policy in Washington.* Englewood Cliffs, NJ: Prentice-Hall.

_____ 1980. Steering with two sets of hands on the tiller. In *Presidents and Prime Ministers,* eds. R. Rose and E. Suleiman. New York: Holmes and Meier.

Rosenau, J. N, and E.-O. Czempiel. 1992. *Governance Without Government.* Cambridge: Cambridge University Press.

Sabatier, P. A., and H. Jenkins-Smith. 1993. *Policy Change and Learning: An Advocacy-Coalition Approach.* Boulder, CO: Westview.

Savoie, D. J. 1996. Globalization and Governance. In *Governance in a Changing Environment,* ed. B. G. Peters. Montreal & Kingston: McGill-Queen's University Press.

Saward, P. 1997. In Search of the Hollow Crown. In *The Hollow Crown,* eds. P. Weller, H. Bakvis, and R.A.W. Rhodes. London: Macmillan.

Sbragia, A. M. 1997. Governance in the European Union. Paper for Conference on Governance Theory, Ross Priory, Dumbarton, Scotland.

Schmidt, V. A. 1998. Convergent pressures, divergent responses. In *The State Still Matters,* ed. D. Solinger. London: Routledge.

Schon, D. A., and M. Rein. 1994. *Frame Reflection: Toward the Resolution of Intractable Policy Controversies.* New York: Basic Books.

Sen, S. 1998. *Empire of Free Trade: The East India Company and the Making of the Colonial Marketplace.* Philadelphia: University of Pennsylvania Press.

Soskice, D. 1998. Convergence of economic action? German and British cases. Lecture, Nuffield College, Oxford, June 1.

Strange, S. 1996. *The Retreat of the State: The Diffusion of Power in the World Economy.* Cambridge: Cambridge University Press.

Ware, A. 1996. *Democracy and North America.* London: Frank Cass.

Weller, P., H. Bakvis, and R. A. W. Rhodes. 1997. *The Hollow Crown.* London: Macmillan.

Wildavsky, A. 1966. The political economy of efficiency: cost-benefit analysis, systems analysis and program budgeting. *Public Administration Review* 26:292-310.

Wilks, S., and M. Wright. 1987. *Comparative Government Industry Relationships: Western Europe, the United States and Japan.* Oxford: Clarendon Press.

Wilson, G. K. 1997. The state of the state in advanced industrial countries. Paper presented at Triennial Conference of the International Political Science Association, Seoul, Korea.

Wood, B. D., and R. W. Waterman. 1994. *Bureaucratic Dynamics.* Boulder, CO: Westview.

Intergovernmental Relations
and Democratic Citizenship

DAVID CAMERON
RICHARD SIMEON

As in many other countries, Canada's governance patterns are being affected by international and domestic forces of change, including globalization, new expectations of citizens, the war against deficits and – specific to Canada – the continuing preoccupation with Quebec and national unity. It is in this context that a new style of federalism – collaborative federalism – has emerged, characterized more by the principle of co-determination of broad national policies, rather than by the more traditional, federal-leadership style. This shift makes it more pressing to find ways to reconcile evolving governance patterns with democratic values and citizenship principles. Couched in the vocabulary of "multi-governance," this study finds many parallels with what other countries and organizations, especially federal countries, are experiencing and reflects on the way in which the nexus between multi-governance and democracy may evolve in the future.

INTRODUCTION

We have four sets of objectives in this chapter.

The first is to describe and explain recent changes in intergovernmental relations in Canada. "Executive federalism" or "federal-provincial diplomacy" has long been considered the defining characteristic of Canadian federalism, a combination of federalism and Westminster-style cabinet government. But these processes have come under increasing stress in recent years, as a result of larger trends in the Canadian political economy, including globalization, new expectations from citizens, the war against deficits, and the continuing preoccupation with Quebec and national unity. All these developments have led to some important changes in the nature and conduct of intergovernmental relations. These changes have not displaced executive federalism. Rather, executive federalism has been extended into a pattern that we call "collaborative federalism." We explore its characteristics and dynamics.

Second, we assess and critique this emergent model from the perspective of democratic citizenship. What are the implications of this model for democratic values such as transparency, accountability, representativeness, and citizen participation? If it is failing the citizenship test, how might the tensions between democratic values and federal practices be resolved? Such issues arise in any model of intergovernmental relations, and are certainly not new in Canada.[1] They are, however, rendered more pressing by the collaborative model.

Third, we cast the net more broadly. The challenges faced by Canadian federalism are, of course, in many ways unique to Canada, with its particular institutional and policy legacies, its regional divisions, and its linguistic duality. But at the same time, many other federal countries face the same changes in their environment and the same complexities in managing their systems. The worry about "democratic deficits" and "joint decision traps" is by no means unique to Canada. Hence we believe that Canadian reformers can learn from others; and that others might learn from the Canadian experience.

Federalism is just one example of "multilevel governance," in which power and authority are distributed among a wide range of institutions and locations. These are not simply federal and provincial. Increasingly, they involve local and regional governments "below," and a vast array of international and supranational institutions "above." Extending outward, they also include new quasi-governmental players, such as international tribunals, NGOs, and privatized institutions executing what were formerly state functions, as well as new government players in the form of emergent Aboriginal governing structures. Graphically, one might think of this phenomenon as the dispersion of power to centres or points distributed along both vertical and horizontal axes. The world of multi-level governance, as the term suggests, is multiple; it is characterized by complexity, uncertainty, fluidity, and blurred boundaries. Bodin-esque theories of sovereignty seem ill-equipped to capture this protean reality.

This poses enormous challenges to democratic citizenship. It also opens intriguing possibilities. Indeed, no longer can citizenship be adequately assessed within single national frameworks; it is "pluralized" as the governments representing and acting upon citizens are multiplied. Neither citizenship nor governance is contained any longer within the boundaries of the state, nor are states the only loci of political decision making (Wallace, 1996). Federal–provincial relations and democratization must be seen in this wider context.

Our fourth set of objectives relates to the future. What does the picture we describe suggest about the likely future evolution of intergovernmental relations? What hints does it offer about the future course of citizenship in democratic states? What roles will the public service need to be prepared to perform in the years to come, if our understanding of the world of multi-governance has merit? We intend to offer some reflections on such matters as these.

The chapter proceeds as follows. In the next section, we begin with some of the broad changes in economy and society, which frame the context for the evolution of intergovernmental relations in Canada. In the following section, we describe the specific developments within Canadian federalism, and chart the outlines of the collaborative federalism model. Next, we assess contemporary intergovernmental relations, and particularly the new model, against a range of democratic criteria, and suggest some lines of reform. We then attempt to situate the Canadian experience in a broader international and comparative context. Finally, we look ahead with some general reflections on multi-level governance and democratic citizenship.

THE CHANGING CONTEXT FOR
INTERGOVERNMENTAL RELATIONS

The institutions and practices of federalism are embedded in a broad institutional, economic, and political environment. Changes in that environment will have a major effect on the agenda for intergovernmental relations, the conflicts the process must manage, the attitudes and aspirations of those who operate them, and the dynamics of the intergovernmental relationship. The institutions and practices of federalism in turn will greatly affect how, and with what effects, the larger environment is translated into public policy. Thus, the construction of the post-war welfare state and the growth of government had profound effects on federalism; federalism in turn helped to distinguish the design of the Canadian welfare state from that in other countries (Banting, 1982; Cameron, Autumn 1996).

We note here four sets of change in the broader context for intergovernmental relations. Three of them – globalization, the preoccupation with debts and deficits, and changing citizen attitudes – face virtually all modern industrial countries. One – the salience of regional and linguistic divisions and the consequent concern with national unity – is distinctly Canadian, and is a longstanding, rather than a new, conditioning factor.

Globalization

First, many writers suggest that globalization with its flow of power and influence from national governments to supranational institutions, public and private, is also associated with a flow of power downwards to smaller sub-national states, provinces, and regions. Tom Courchene calls this phenomenon "glocalization." He and others suggest it is national governments, and the typical policy instruments that they wield, such as tariff and monetary policy, that are most constrained by globalizing forces. Central governments are therefore less able to act effectively or command loyalty at home. Conversely, it is said that the traditional areas of authority of provincial and local governments – from education to land use policy – are now more powerful instruments to enhance economic adaptation and the quality of life. It is also argued that the combination of national governments that can no longer guarantee security and the disorientation arising from global change lead citizens to look to smaller communities as sources of identity and stability, thus revitalizing local community politics. This is a controversial argument, and it can sometimes involve a grossly exaggerated view of the weakening of the nation-state. Yet there seems little doubt that globalization has been associated with some weakening of the Canadian federal government, and a broad trend to increased provincial power. Globalization and decentralization do seem to go together.

Second, globalization may have the effect of undermining national unity within a federal country. Most important here is the long-term effect of the reorientation of the Canadian economy from east–west to north–south, leading to greater economic integration with the United States, and a situation in which each of Canada's regions is integrated differently into the global economy. This means that it is even more difficult today than it was in the past to imagine a single "national" economic policy that serves all regions equally. It also suggests that the mutual dependence that arises from close economic integration in a single economy is likely to erode, leaving each region to fend for itself, increasing competition among regions, and potentially weakening support for regionally redistributive policies that have traditionally been at the centre of the Canadian "federal bargain."

Globalization, as well, is no longer a matter solely of relationships among states. Within the state, the forces associated with globalization reach deep into each domestic society and economy, forcing all levels of government to respond to the resulting challenges. But the reverse is also true; globalization means that federalism no longer stops at the border. It is projected into the international arena as provinces and cities seek to enhance their presence in global markets and the minds of investors. While budget constraints have led to the closing of several provincial offices abroad, provinces (and cities such as Toronto) are active in a wide variety of international activities. So are American

states and localities – and for similar reasons.[2] States and localities make many agreements with other subnational governments. In North America, there are more than 400 agreements
between Canadian provinces and American states, involving
all provinces and 46 states, with the respective federal governments as partners in about half of them (Fry, 1993, 19–20).

Moreover, federal countries need to coordinate their domestic
relationships in order to be able to speak with one voice in the
international arena. In Canada, the limited federal treaty-making
power makes this especially important, and many of the most
critical recent issues in international trade politics (negotiation of
the North American Free Trade Agreement, the trade in soft-
wood lumber between Canada and the United States, and the
regulation of salmon fishing on the West Coast) have all been
greatly affected by the politics of federalism within Canada. The
need for closer collaboration in such areas has its parallel in the
u.s., where "vastly improved intergovernmental cooperation
will be needed in the future in order to maximize u.s. economic
interests in the international arena." (Fry, 1993, 19–20). The role
of subnational entities in the decision-making processes of the EU
is a major issue in countries such as Germany and Spain, and the
emergence of a "Europe of the regions" is a live political and policy issue throughout the European community. In fact, even a
state like China – no friend to federalism and a jealous guardian
of its own sovereign prerogatives – has found itself tolerating the
expression of a remarkable degree of international personality on
the part of at least two of its subnational units. Both Hong Kong
and Macau have their own currencies. Both Hong Kong and
Macau have independent seats in the World Trade Organization
(wTO) and the former is a member of the Asia Pacific Economic
Cooperation Forum (APEC) as well.

Changing Citizen Attitudes

Intergovernmental relations in Canada have traditionally exhib-
ited the characteristics of what Arend Lijphart calls elite accommodation:[3] bargains made by autonomous elites free to negotiate

on behalf of their populations, and sure of their ability to implement whatever agreements are reached. Such a model requires a high degree of citizen deference to governments. This essential condition has been greatly undermined both in Canada and other Western countries. On the one hand, there has been a sharp decline in levels of trust in the wisdom, probity, and competence of governments of all kinds; on the other, there is a growing demand that citizens have a greater say in decisions which affect their lives. Significantly, in Canada these developments have, as we shall see, been focused heavily on intergovernmental relations. Citizen mobilization effectively killed intergovernmental agreements on the constitution at two critical moments, in 1990 and 1992. A major challenge for Canadian intergovernmental relations, then, has been to adapt the process to accommodate heightened citizen demands. In addition, while regional and linguistic divisions remain high on the Canadian agenda, recent social change has brought to the fore a variety of other interests and identities – of women, multicultural groups, aboriginal peoples – that are not defined in terms of the traditional territorial divisions institutionalized in federalism. This too challenges intergovernmental relations: how can these new forces be incorporated into an institutional framework that grants privileges and institutionalizes the territorial dimension of political life?

Debts and Deficits

In the 1960s and 1970s, some of the most intense federal–provincial conflict resulted from the growth of government. Both levels, with increased revenues in hand, sought to respond to the developing public agenda. They collided at many points, each level blaming the other for invading its jurisdiction. This was the "federalism of growth," or "competitive state-building."

In the 1980s the focus shifted: now the size of government, and the resulting deficits dominated the public agenda. In intergovernmental relations, this meant not so much competitive expansion, but rather competitive retreat, as each level sought to shift financial burdens to the other. The "federalism of restraint" meant a heightened concern with the costs of duplication and overlapping, a desire to "disentangle" responsibilities rather than expand de facto concurrency, and an explosion of off-loading and downloading, as burdens were shifted from Ottawa, to provinces, to local authorities, and, ultimately, to citizens.

With deficits in all Canadian jurisdictions except British Columbia now being brought under control, it remains to be seen what impact this will have on government behaviour and intergovernmental relations. Now that the deficit dragon has been slain, a debate has begun in Ottawa and the provincial capitals about the proper mix of tax reduction, debt reduction, and public expenditure which should shape future public policy. The 1999 and 2000 federal budgets bear the marks of this struggle. They demonstrate that renewed fiscal health in Ottawa has produced strong pressures within the governing party to increase visible federal initiatives and to resist decentralist pressures.[4]

National Unity

Since the 1960s, the overwhelming priority for intergovernmental relations has been to find ways to manage the country's linguistic and regional divisions. The constitution has dominated the agenda in a largely failed series of attempts at "mega-constitutional change" in 1968–71, 1980–82, 1987–90, and 1992 (Russell, 1993). Each of these episodes was carried out largely in the intergovernmental arena. Those that failed did much to corrode the legitimacy of that process; the one that succeeded, or partially succeeded – namely, the patriation of the Constitution in 1982 – has also been challenged on grounds of legitimacy, especially in Quebec.

In addition, this constitutional preoccupation meant that all other substantive issues – from health to the environment – were viewed through the lens of "how does this affect the constitution?" "What will be the effect in Quebec?" "Can we get intergovernmental agreement?" Not: "What is the best policy for agriculture, youth, or the environment?" The participants were largely political strategists engaged in these questions, rather than officials and groups with commitments to and expertise in the various functional areas. This tendency has had a profound effect on intergovernmental relations in Canada.

The focus on region and language has also strongly reinforced decentralist trends. Quebec governments, federalist and separatist, have always strongly resisted any expansion of federal power. Other provinces, with their own sense of alienation and lack of power within the national government, have increasingly responded in kind. The doctrine of "the equality of the provinces," which was implicit in former Prime Minister Pierre Trudeau's hostility to special status for Quebec and which was popularized by former Newfoundland Premier Clyde Wells, has turned out to be a powerful agent of decentralization, since any power offered to Quebec must equally be available to other provinces.

These background factors do not all push in the same direction, or raise similar issues. They do suggest the environment for intergovernmental relations is increasingly complex. Management of the federation must take into account multiple and often conflicting pressures. We turn now to look at how the provinces and federal government are doing it.

RECENT TRENDS IN INTERGOVERNMENTAL RELATIONS: THE EMERGENCE OF COLLABORATIVE FEDERALISM

The outlines of a discernibly different pattern of Canadian intergovernmental relations have begun to emerge in the 1990s, the result – at least in part – of the forces identified in the previous section of this chapter. For the purposes of this discussion, we will designate this emergent pattern "collaborative federalism," a pattern in which the governance of Canada is seen as a partnership between two equal, autonomous, and interdependent orders of government that decide national policy collectively.

We should make several points clear at the outset.

- The distinctive pattern of intergovernmental relations which we describe has its roots in what preceded it; the seeds of the new are embedded in the old.

- In consequence, we are not positing a dramatic break with the past; there is real continuity in the evolving patterns of intergovernmental relations. The subject does not lend itself to analytically distinct, ideal types.
- Our focus in this chapter is primarily on what might be termed "summit federalism," the high politics of the federation which typically engages the country's top federal and provincial leaders and involves either a complex, interrelated set of issues, or a specific issue of high importance.
- There is no single pattern of intergovernmental relations in Canada. Its nature varies according to level (with First Ministers' relationships most dominated by strategic and status concerns), and according to the issue area being considered. In some areas a tradition of cooperation has developed among officials at both levels, in other areas mistrust dominates the relationship.
- What we say here about the relations among federal and provincial governments in Canada parallels in many important ways what other students of federalism are saying about other federations. In addition, there are a number of striking similarities between intergovernmental relations within Canada, on the one hand, and international relations in a globalizing world, on the other. We plan to return to this last point towards the end of the chapter.

Observations on the Evolution of Intergovernmental Relations Since the Second World War

As the country has evolved, so, too, have intergovernmental relations (Smiley, 1979; Simeon, 1997a.).

The era of "cooperative federalism" of the 1950s and 1960s was characterized by sector-specific relations among relatively decentralized governments and bureaucracies, both in Ottawa and the provinces. Ottawa had the resources and status necessary to exercise a vigorous post-war leadership role. Governments, represented in line departments by officials with long experience in a given program or policy area, were able to work out practical arrangements with one another, and the level of tension in the federation, by and large, was low, with the important exception of Quebec which fought a long rear-guard action against the expansion of the welfare state under federal leadership.

The construction of the Canadian welfare state began to fray this system somewhat. It deeply engaged federal institutions, because, while Ottawa had the money, most of the major elements of the welfare state lay within provincial jurisdiction. Nevertheless, the system successfully adapted to these new roles for government, with minimal changes in the formal distribution of power. The key policy instrument was the federal spending power, exemplified by the proliferation of shared-cost programs. This pattern was made possible by the broad national consensus on what Smiley called the "Second National Policy" of the welfare state, by rapid economic growth, and by the fact that the central issues of the welfare state did not divide the country on regional lines.

In the course of the 1960s the country moved into a different phase. Quebec's Quiet Revolution unleashed a progressive nationalism that transformed the province and challenged traditional assumptions about the nature of the country and the character of Canadian federalism. This profoundly altered the intergovernmental agenda, placing the constitution at its heart. The general growth of the public sector meant that governments were increasingly likely to bump into one another in the execution of their mandates and the pursuit of their political ambitions. Moreover, by the 1970s, a growing regionalism, particularly in the west, and an increasing assertiveness in the English-speaking provinces added to the pressure. Trudeau's assumption of the prime ministership in 1968 sharpened the ideological conflict between Quebec City and Ottawa, and, in due course, between Ottawa and several western capitals; very different views of the country began to emerge. Provinces were no longer willing to defer to federal financial and policy leadership.

The result was that, in the latter part of the 1960s and throughout the 1970s, Canada experienced a higher level of intergovernmental tension. "Cooperative federalism" became "competitive federalism." Governments began to concentrate power in new central agencies, including stronger cabinet offices, finance departments, and in many cases, ministries or agencies dedicated to managing the intergovernmental relationship. They began to link strategically and for negotiating purposes that which had been separate before. Negotiating agendas became more complex and involved first ministers directly more often than used to be the case. There were more frequent meetings of first ministers and they began to be televised, thus creating a public audience for intergovernmental conflict, and a public stake in the outcomes.

The re-election of the Trudeau-led Liberals in the 1980 election marked the beginning of the period of the most intense conflict the country had known since the Second World War. While in part the result of the objective conditions in which the country found itself, it was provoked by the willingness of the Trudeau government to bring matters to a head in two key areas – the constitution and energy policy. The federal government's National Energy Program (NEP) and its determination to patriate the constitution with or without provincial consent had an explosive effect on intergovernmental relations.

These two initiatives expressed an aggressive, Canadian nation-building point of view. It confronted a fundamentally different vision of the country, grounded in province-building in several of the English-speaking provinces and francophone nationalism in the province of Quebec. Fundamentally different visions of the country were forced into painful public debate; they divided the country regionally and raised difficult questions about the role of the federal government in defining and defending a national community; they directly challenged the status and self-image of governments and political leaders, framing the issues in zero-sum terms in circumstances in which none of the participants could afford to lose. The public was drawn into these battles, at the beginning as a resource for the battling government actors, later as a participant in its own right.

By the mid-eighties, new political leadership was coming on the scene and the intergovernmental agenda had changed. The Canadian Constitution had been patriated, albeit without the consent of Quebec. Energy policy had receded as a pressing public issue, although the scars of the conflict were to last a long time. The large economic policy matter that engaged both orders of government was North American free trade. This development could have major implications for provincial powers, and so provinces were anxious to be fully consulted. Towards the end of this period, a series of decisions by the Progressive Conservative government led by Brian Mulroney, which appeared to fly in the face of basic considerations of regional equity and his own strongly stated commitment to intergovernmental collaboration, undermined federal–provincial harmony and accentuated interregional rivalries. Among the many examples we note just a few: a decision to award the maintenance contract for the Canada CF-18 military fighter to Montreal instead of Winnipeg; a cap placed on the growth of federal payments to the wealthier provinces under the Canada Assistance Plan, which entailed sharing of the costs of welfare; immigration, where Quebec reached an advantageous agreement with Ottawa, and where provinces and municipalities were left to deal with the economic and social challenges of integrating new immigrants. The sense of "fairness" essential to harmonious intergovernmental relations was undermined.[5] Fiscally, it was during the 1980s that the attitudinal ground was prepared for the assault on federal and provincial deficits, which was to be launched in the following decade.

On the constitutional front, the negotiation of the 1987 Meech Lake Constitutional Accord, designed to permit Quebec to sign onto the 1982 Constitution, perfectly exemplified executive federalism – in secret, among heads of government, with the public deliberately excluded from the process. Among the provinces, only Robert Bourassa's federalist Quebec government referred the draft agreement to the legislature before it was signed in final form. Nevertheless, despite the almost unanimous support for the agreement among virtually all Canadian elites, a groundswell of citizen opposition paved the way for its defeat. Meech's failure reinvigorated the sovereignist forces. It also led to the more inclusive and more participatory, but ultimately abortive

Charlottetown effort, a comprehensive package of constitutional amendments aimed at addressing Quebec's concerns and the priorities of the other provinces simultaneously. This was brought to an end with its rejection in the national referendum of 1992. The drive to "cut a deal" pre-empted the kind of public deliberation essential to securing consensus on constitutional change.

This period was marked by a continuation of active summit federalism, with a series of high-profile televised first ministers' conferences, and the maintenance of a fairly high level of conflict – but with a new twist. Where the 1980–82 patriation process involved bitter conflict among governments, the Meech Lake and Charlottetown experiences revealed conflict *between* governments and citizens – between political elites, on the one hand, and organized interests and the population at large, on the other. At the beginning, all governments agreed to Meech Lake; dissenting voices in English-speaking Canada swelled to a tidal wave outside the government circle – from legislatures, from Aboriginal peoples, from activists empowered by the Charter of Rights and Freedoms enacted in 1982, from many Canadians concerned about or opposed to the policy implications of the proposed amendments. Significantly, too, the process of executive federalism used to negotiate the deal was subjected to withering criticism. What right did these "men in suits" have to play with "our" constitution? The Charlottetown round of constitutional discussion made ample provision in many ways for public involvement, but the Accord suffered the same fate as Meech; supported by all governments and most opposition parties, and by Aboriginal leaders, it was decisively rejected by the Canadian population in the 1992 referendum. Looking back, it is apparent that Charlottetown marked the end of an era in intergovernmental relations. Elite accommodation no longer worked.

Some Lessons

This review suggests some lessons about the nature of conflict in federal-provincial relations. There will be greater tension:

- When differing ideologies exist. If there is tacit agreement among governments and citizens about the nature of politics, the role of government, the central problem confronting the public sector, the extent to which radical change is necessary, and so forth, this will reduce the likelihood that intergovernmental relations will be poisonous.
- When the status, recognition and identity of regions, communities, and governments are seen to be at stake in intergovernmental negotiations. Using shared perspectives and expertise to solve practical problems encourages compromise; challenging a player's status or identity is almost certain to create conflict. Symbolic issues are much more difficult to resolve than practical problems. Increasingly from the 1960s, intergovernmental relations came to embody "identity politics."
- When issues play out differentially along regional or linguistic lines. The National Energy Program set the West, particularly Alberta, against central Canada. "Let the Eastern bastards freeze in the dark" versus the "blue-eyed sheiks of Alberta" is a coarse reminder of the interregional animosity that existed at that time. The CF-18 incident, which involved allocating a lucrative aircraft maintenance contract to Montreal rather than Winnipeg, envenomed French–English relations and was one of the chief regional grievances behind the formation of the western-based Reform Party. The federal cap on the Canada Assistance Plan drove a wedge between the wealthy provinces (Alberta, British Columbia, and Ontario) and all the rest; it was the impulse behind the push for constitutionally binding intergovernmental agreements during the Charlottetown negotiations.
- When neither government is prepared to defer to the other. In the immediate post-war period, there was considerable agreement among both citizens and governments that Ottawa was the "senior" partner – equipped with political and financial strength and a self-confident bureaucracy. By the 1970s, Quebec had come to see itself as the primary political expression of the Quebec people, and western provinces had come to see

themselves as defenders of a regional interest that was not
represented in Ottawa, with its weak Senate and governing
parties which had to pay attention to the more populous central Canada. Neither their politicians, nor their increasingly
professional bureaucracies were prepared to defer to Ottawa.

- When the primary concerns of governments become blame
  avoidance, the winning of credit, and the enhancement of
  their own political status relative to other governments. While
  these are obviously virtually universal phenomena, many factors will affect whether such concerns are in the foreground
  or background during intergovernmental negotiations.

Other developments during this period also shaped the way
in which citizens viewed intergovernmental relations, and
increased demands for greater democratic accountability in the
conduct of intergovernmental affairs.

The public's faith in government declined dramatically and
the public's demand for a voice in government decision making
increased. Canada mirrored developments in other advanced
countries as described by Ronald Inglehart and Neil Nevitte. The
former charts the outlines of a "post-materialist" society, (Inglehart, 1990) while the latter speaks of the decline of deference
(Nevitte, 1996; Inglehart, Nevitte, and Basanez, 1996).

In Canada, citizen disaffection from government and demands
for increased participation focused chiefly on the constitutional
domain. Since 1982, the assent of the country's legislatures has
been required to effect constitutional amendment. This opens the
door to fuller legislative participation at various stages of the
process; white and green papers, legislative committees, public
hearings and the like, now characterize the approach most jurisdictions take to constitutional reform. Much of this legislative
activity involves the public as well, and there is widespread
recognition, on the part of all governments, that Canadians must
be given a voice in proposals to alter the Canadian Constitution.
In addition, several provincial jurisdictions now require that referendums be held before a constitutional resolution can be
passed through a provincial assembly. It is clear that informed

popular consent is now recognized to be essential in constitutional politics, but it would be false to assert that we know how
to make this newly democratized system work. Indeed, so complex and fraught with difficulty is the process of comprehensive
constitutional change, that governments now fight shy of touching the Constitution at all.

Oddly enough, the rising demand for public access and popular participation has had relatively little impact on intergovernmental relations outside constitutional politics in the period in
question. The popular mobilization against executive federalism
was thus limited.

Intergovernmental Relations After the 1992 Demise of the Charlottetown Constitutional Accord

The nature of intergovernmental relations shifted discernibly
after the demise of the Charlottetown Accord. The shift owed
something to our experience in that constitutional round. With
the fatigue and frustration that followed the failure of yet another major exercise in constitutional renewal, both political leaders
and citizens at large turned away from such inherently divisive
exercises. Now attention would turn to "making the federation
work," and finding solutions through informal adaptation of
what had already proved a highly flexible regime, rather than
through constitutional change (Lazar, 1998).

Other factors also contributed to the shift. The first was a
change in governments and political leadership. For example, in
1993, Jean Chrétien and the Liberals took office in Ottawa, putting into office a pragmatic politician who had been burned by
the constitution in the past and whose every instinct was to govern in a low-key, practical, step-by-step fashion, eschewing ideology or dramatic gestures. With respect to federalism, he was
Trudeau's pupil, with little interest in deferring to the provinces.
(Ottawa, Trudeau once famously said, was not about to "become
the head waiter to the provinces.")

In 1994, the Parti Québécois under Jacques Parizeau took
power in Quebec City, displacing the Liberals after their second

term of office. While this set the stage for the drama and travail of the 1995 referendum on sovereignty, it had an unfortunate simplifying effect on intergovernmental relations. The PQ government had no interest in working with other governments in the management of the affairs of the federation. It would grab whatever was available, and it would, predictably, complain about the alleged injustices systematically visited upon Quebec, but it would decline to participate with other governments in carrying on the business of the country. A posture of minimal participation has been sustained under Premier Lucien Bouchard, Parizeau's successor, down to the present.

Change was also going on in the other provinces. Alberta Premier Ralph Klein, elected in 1992, initiated the war against big government and the public sector. In 1995, the "common sense revolutionaries" were elected in Ontario. Mike Harris and his colleagues believed that the previous Liberal and NDP governments had left the province in a mess and that the solution was to "cut fast and cut deep." As with Klein, Harris' focus in the first years of the mandate was exclusively domestic, internal, and inward looking. The Tories had little interest in what was happening elsewhere in Canada. Both premiers, however, soon discovered that no First Minister can avoid a concern with national unity, and that citizens angered by policy change within the province could and would turn to Ottawa to protect their interests.[6] Hence success on their domestic agendas demanded some basic changes in how the federal system operated.

By the 1990s the politics of deficits was also driving the shift to a new model of intergovernmental relations. There was now a broad public and governmental consensus that public sector debt was far too high, that deficits had to be eliminated, and that the pain associated with bringing federal and provincial finances under control would have to be borne. All governments began programs of action to address these fiscal concerns, which involved some mix of cost-cutting, revenue generation, privatization, efficiency measures, and downloading (Canada West Foundation, 1998).

Central to Ottawa's deficit reduction strategy was what might be called the exercise of the federal spending power in reverse.

Utilizing this "dis-spending power," the federal government enacted substantial reductions in the transfers to the provinces for social programs (a reduction from $18 billion to a floor of $11 billion, later adjusted to $12.5 billion, in federal support for health care, social assistance, and higher education). Federal transfers under these programs were rolled into the new Canada Health and Social Transfer (CHST), which promised provinces greater freedom from federal conditions (though the conditions under the Canada Health Act remained, as did the prohibition against restricting social assistance on the basis of residency).

Several points are worth making here. First, because of the broad consensus, these actions did not occasion the intense conflict that might have been expected in other circumstances. The criticism was muted relative to the magnitude of the damage being inflicted on provincial budgets, though as deficit pressures eased in the late 1990s, demands for a restoration of the money that had been cut intensified. Second, Ottawa's power over the provinces, and certainly its legitimacy, were reduced along with the reduction in fiscal transfers. If Ottawa was no longer paying the piper, what right did it have to call the tune? Third, the federal cuts fostered a wave of what we would call "secondary downloading," that is, reductions in the transfers provinces were able or willing to make to their transfer agencies (hospitals, municipalities, universities, colleges, social agencies, schools, and the like). The effects of federal–provincial relations thus reverberate throughout Canadian society. Finally, the net effect of this experience (federal cuts, downsizing the country's social, health, and educational systems, coping with the full brunt of the public anxiety and opposition that this entailed) is to invest the provincial governments with a stronger sense of their autonomy, their responsibility and their right to judge, within their spheres of jurisdiction, what the national, as well as the provincial interest requires.

The Emergence of Collaborative Federalism

These developments set the stage for the strengthening of what we call "collaborative federalism." By this we mean an intergovernmental process by which national goals are achieved, not by the federal government acting alone, or by the federal government moulding provincial behaviour through the exercise of its spending power, but by some or all of the eleven governments and the territories acting collectively.

It can take two forms. First is collaboration among federal, provincial, and territorial governments (FTP in the current intergovernmental jargon), seeking an appropriate balance between federal, provincial, and territorial roles and responsibilities. It is based on the premise that both levels possess strong fiscal and jurisdictional tools, and that as a result effective policy depends on coordination among them. Second, however, is collaboration among provincial and territorial governments (PT), with Ottawa on the sidelines. This is based on the view that under the constitution, health, welfare, and education are provincial jurisdictions. "National" policies and standards in these areas, therefore, are matters for provinces together to decide. "National policy" does not necessarily mean the national government must do it. This introduces a strong element of "confederalism" into the Canadian model.

The collaborative model is also an alternative to constitutional change. Many of the issues unsuccessfully dealt with in the failures of Meech Lake and Charlottetown have re-emerged in the intergovernmental arena – the Economic Union, the Social Union, "who does what" in terms of jurisdiction, and the spending power. But now, rather than being expressed in the uncompromising language of constitutional clauses, and enforced by the courts, they are to be expressed as intergovernmental "Accords," "Declarations," and "Framework Agreements."

The first concrete example of this was the Agreement on Internal Trade (AIT).[7] When Charlottetown was defeated, Ottawa's objectives with respect to the economic union went down with it. The federal government therefore initiated multilateral negotiations with the provincial governments designed to reduce internal barriers to the mobility of goods, capital, and services in Canada. First ministers signed the Agreement on Internal Trade in 1994, and it was implemented in July 1995. Although it tracks the approach of international trade agreements such as the NAFTA closely, it is a non-binding political arrangement; it contains, for example, a formal dispute settlement mechanism, but its rulings do not have legal effect. There is an Internal Trade Secretariat, but it is not as yet clothed with significant authority. Considering the historical difficulty the country has had in achieving a more fully integrated economic union, and provincial resistance during Charlottetown, the negotiation of the AIT must be regarded as a major intergovernmental accomplishment, but understood principally as a significant first step.[8] It is an accomplishment, however, that is effectively unknown to the vast majority of Canadians. Few realized the agreement was being negotiated; few realize it is now in operation.

The Agreement reflects some important dimensions of collaborative federalism. It demonstrates that despite its constitutional responsibility for interprovincial and international trade, Ottawa has neither the power nor the legitimacy to define and enforce the Canadian economic union. An alternative approach – to define the rules in the constitution and make them judicially enforceable – is also impossible. Hence negotiated intergovernmental collaboration becomes the only way to make progress.

Identical forces are at work with respect to the "social union" and national unity. With respect to national unity, the Premiers developed the Calgary Declaration in the aftermath of the 1995 Quebec referendum; it was an attempt to square the circle of citizens' rights, equality of the provinces, and recognition of Quebec's distinctiveness. This was an initiative undertaken by the provinces and pushed successfully to a conclusion by them, with Ottawa largely in the role of bystander. It has been approved by every provincial legislature outside of Quebec.

The social union, like the economic union, is predicated on the idea that a defining characteristic of a unified country is a shared and common set of aspirations, standards, and norms with respect to the basic elements of social citizenship. As with the economic union, two questions arise: how will common national standards be balanced against the variations that federalism encourages; and who is going to define and police the standards? In the case of the social union, a third question arises: How is the federal spending power, which lies at the base of Ottawa's fiscal transfers to the provinces and which was a crucial instrument in constructing the Canadian welfare state, to be exercised and how is it to be controlled?

Faced with severe financial cuts and federal retreat, the provincial governments and territories took the initiative. This involved not only occupying the space vacated by the federal government but also working to devise national policies. As they came to terms with the new fiscal and policy realities, provinces began to work collaboratively to fashion common policy approaches, to undertake joint initiatives and to present coherent proposals to the federal government. Throughout most of this process, Quebec declined to participate, but the other provinces and territories proceeded regardless. Their evolving consensus, even when confronted with the indifference or opposition of the federal government, has proven to be remarkably strong, considering the diversity of interests and circumstances represented around the table.

The process of intergovernmental discussion culminated on February 4, 1999, when Ottawa and all the provinces except Quebec signed the *Framework to Improve the Social Union For Canadians*. It explicitly endorses the power of Ottawa to spend in areas of provincial jurisdiction, while at the same time ensuring that new programs will not be introduced or existing ones changed without due notice and substantial provincial consent, and making it clear that provinces remain responsible for program design and delivery. It contains the following elements: a statement of general principles; a mobility provision applying to the social-policy field; commitments respecting public accountability and transparency; notice provisions; rules governing the exercise of the federal government's spending power; and procedures for dispute avoidance and dispute resolution. The agreement is to be reviewed by the signatories before the end of its three-year term. While this framework agreement is a considerable achievement of collaborative federalism, it should be noted that the document remains loose and fairly general in character, and that the proof of the agreement will be found in the commitment and follow-through the participating governments bring to its implementation.

The sovereignist Government of Quebec joined the social-union negotiations in the summer of 1998, recognizing that, in the pending election campaign, it would have some political difficulty in justifying not participating in this intergovernmental process. It declined, however, to sign the February 1999 agreement on the grounds that the final, negotiated compromise – particularly with respect to the federal spending power – watered down excessively the earlier draft provisions which had been acceptable to Quebec. Its absence means that Quebec continues to march to a different drummer, de facto if not constitutionally.

The social-union process and the Calgary Declaration display certain shared characteristics. Both are the products of provincial initiative and interprovincial negotiation. Both tackle, in their own way, the national-unity question, and have been carried out largely in the absence of Quebec, but in full consciousness of the impact they will have on Quebec opinion. Both have also been pursued with the goal of improving how the federation functions; the reformist impulse in each case is clear, and the two are consistent with each other in their general approach. Both are grounded in a collaborative model of intergovernmental relations which assumes autonomous actors, coming together on the basis of equality, achieving a common position through a process of open negotiation and bargaining, where the penalties of non-agreement are either weakly specified or unclear. Both enhance the role of the provinces relative to that of the federal government.[9]

There is one area where the two measures differ markedly, and that is in the position they accord to the public and to the respective legislatures. From the beginning the participants in the Calgary process were committed to a process of public consultation (albeit carefully managed to minimize dissension). The Calgary document was put forward as a discussion document, and hearings, surveys, and focus groups were held before legislatures were asked to vote on it. The *Social Union Framework*

Agreement, on the other hand, was purely the product of participating governments; it was negotiated at meetings held behind
closed doors; and the process had a very low public profile. Not
only was the public absent from the discussion, it was not really
until the February 1999 meeting of First Ministers, which concluded the agreement, that the matter was brought seriously to
the attention of Canadians. The Agreement is a classic example
of elite accommodation. In this case, however, the massive public mobilization, so evident in Meech and Charlottetown, was not
repeated. This may suggest that the stakes are lower, and public
engagement less, when governments seek accommodation outside the constitutional arena. In addition, the fact that Jean
Charest and the federalist Quebec Liberal Party supported the
Parti-Québécois Government in its refusal to sign the Accord
meant that there were no grounds for it to develop into a big
public issue in Quebec.

The Institutions of Collaborative Federalism

The emergence of the collaborative model has had an important impact on the institutions of intergovernmental relations.
Perhaps the most obvious change is in the role and position of
the Annual Premiers Conference (APC). Initiated at the instiga-
tion of Quebec in the 1960s as little more than a regular summer retreat for premiers and their families, the APC has evolved
into a significant intergovernmental institution. Long lurking
in the shadows cast by the federal–provincial First Ministers
Conference (FMC), it has moved into prominence as the frequency and significance of the FMCs has declined. Held every
August under a rotating chairmanship, this association of
provinces has become a full-fledged intergovernmental meeting, professionally supported by provincial civil servants,
preparing and receiving position papers, issuing commu-
niqués, launching projects to be undertaken by the relevant
ministers, and so forth. The Chair has recently assumed a substantive role as the spokesperson for the premiers between
meetings. It was at one of these meetings that both the Calgary

Framework and the social-union initiative were begun, and their progress has been reviewed and guided in successive meetings of premiers.

Another institutional forum that is assuming much greater importance in the present era is the ministerial council, sometimes federal–provincial, sometimes purely provincial. Such councils have existed for many years. But recently, they have greatly increased in number, have become more institutionalized, and have played a more formal role in carrying out mandates assigned by First Ministers. They have become the workhorses of the system and are gradually assuming a solidity and continuity that they have not typically had before. Councils now exist for ministries concerned with social policy renewal, forestry, transportation, education, and the environment. Other groupings of ministers go by names such as Forums, Committees and meetings of "Ministers Responsible." Some meet regularly, others on an ad hoc basis.

The pace and intensity of intergovernmental meetings at the senior levels of Deputy Ministers, Ministers, and First Ministers have varied considerably over time with the changing policy agenda, and the political interest of governments. Between 1973 and 1984, there was a slow increase from about 40 to 60 meetings a year, with a peak of 103 in 1979. During the tenure of Prime Minister Mulroney, who had a strongly stated commitment to cooperative federalism, the number never dropped below 82 per year, with peaks of 130 in 1985–86 and 127 in 1992–93. The frequency dropped slightly after the Liberals were re-elected (and slumped to 47 in the freeze following the 1995 Quebec referendum). Since then, the frequency of meetings has increased to 70 in 1997–98, and to 98 in the calendar year 1998. In 1997–98, 60 per cent of meetings involved federal, provincial and territorial governments, and 40 per cent involved provinces and territories meeting separately. The most common subjects for negotiation are those at the top of the country's political agenda: social policy, the environment, health, economic policy, and education (Canadian Intergovernmental Conference Secretariat, 1998).

The Provincial/Territorial Council on Social Policy Renewal has been particularly active. Acting under the instructions of the premiers, sectoral ministers and officials have developed position papers and fashioned strategies for the consideration of the premiers and to prepare for federal–provincial discussion. The Council's efforts prepared the way for the recent agreement on the social union, and it will play an important role in helping to make it work.

An institution which, in a sense, awaits full development and implementation, is the binding intergovernmental agreement. Intergovernmental agreements are not legislation – at least until they have been enacted by every legislature. This means they are not legally enforceable through the courts. The AIT provides a model, drawing from experience with the dispute-settlement mechanisms found in international trade treaties, but, as we noted, it is not binding on the government signatories. The full-scale implementation of the collaborative approach to intergovernmental affairs will surely require the development of a binding version of this regulatory mechanism. This will be a difficult challenge in the Canadian constitutional system, where each government is responsible to its own legislature, and governments cannot bind future legislatures. Thus, there is a deep tension between the logic of collaborative intergovernmentalism, and the logic of parliamentary government.

Assessing the Pattern of Collaborative Federalism

While the content and specificity of intergovernmental processes and agreements vary widely, a review of several recent examples displays some common threads:

- The equality between provinces and Ottawa is underlined by the fact that most Councils and meetings are co-chaired by a federal and a provincial minister.
- The northern territories of Canada – Yukon, NWT and, one assumes, the newly established Nunavut – are now fully

integrated with the provinces. Meetings are "Federal/Provincial/
Territorial" or "Provincial/Territorial" despite the fact that
the territories remain constitutional offspring of the federal
government. This evolution towards provincial status has
been scarcely remarked.

- The absence of Quebec. Usually Quebec's representatives participate in meetings, but it disassociates itself from the agreement.
  Quebec's position is that fields like education, welfare, and
  health are exclusive areas of provincial jurisdiction. Hence federal–provincial partnerships enunciating national standards and
  norms are little better in principle than federal unilateralism.
- Most agreements stress that the formal constitutional powers
  assigned to governments remain intact; the goal is to exercise
  these powers "in a coordinated manner."
- There is a consistent attempt to minimize duplication and
  overlapping, in order to achieve greater efficiency and cost
  saving.
- Consistent with the doctrine of the "New Public Management,"
  agreements emphasize the need to share "best practices," to
  develop performance indicators, and to monitor results.
- A common pattern is for a framework agreement to be
  reached among all governments, which is then followed by
  individually negotiated bilateral agreements.
- All agreements pay at least lip service to the need for
  greater transparency and for clearer lines of accountability
  in intergovernmental relations.
- An increasing number of agreements explicitly acknowledge
  the need to "engage stake holders" and to "build linkages to
  other structures in the broad social and economic environment."
- While these developments reflect a greater degree of institutionalization in Canadian intergovernmental relations (IGR), it
  is important not to exaggerate the change. Compared to the
  German federation or the European Union, Canadian IGR
  remains highly fluid and ad hoc. The process has no constitutional or legislative base, no established schedule of meetings,
  little backup by bureaucrats linked to the success of the

process rather than to individual governments, no formal decision rules, and no capacity for authoritative decision making.

• This means that the scope or extent of intergovernmental relations remains heavily dependent on whether the First Ministers, especially the Prime Minister, find it advantageous or not. The system in this sense is quite fragile.[10]

Two leading students of Canadian federalism have recently provided strong intellectual support for this collaborative or partnership model. André Burelle, in *Le mal canadien* (1995), proposes a partnership based on interdependence and "non-subordination." Canadian governments would develop a comprehensive "Pact on the Canadian Social and Economic Union," setting out basic rules including those governing budget policies. A permanent council of first ministers would establish common standards, and would make binding decisions, either by unanimity or qualified majority, much along the lines of the Council of Ministers of the EU. Such institutions would "become the instrument that permits, on the one hand, the accommodation of the right to difference of the federated communities without balkanizing the country and, on the other, the reinforcement of the Canadian union while respecting the share of sovereignty recognized by the constitution to the partner-states in the federation." (Burelle, 1995, 162).

Tom Courchene, for his part, starts with the premise that Canadians are deeply committed to preserving and promoting their social union, with its national standards, even as "social policy is undergoing substantial, indeed unprecedented, decentralization." (Courchene, 1997). The only way to square this circle is to bring the provinces "more fully and formally into the key societal goal of preserving and promoting social Canada." In his model, provinces would retain full responsibility for health, education, and welfare, but there would be an enforceable interprovincial or federal–provincial accord setting out a framework of principles and standards that provinces must meet. Thus Burelle and Courchene take us a long way towards a confederal intergovernmental model for Canadian intergovernmental relations.

It is far too early to judge the success of this new model. Indeed, the different actors may define "success" very differently.

- For some the process itself might constitute success, if it leads to more cooperation, less intergovernmental conflict, and the like.
- For provinces, especially the more assertive ones such as Ontario and B.C., success is found in their ability to wrestle the initiative from Ottawa, limit its ability to "intrude" on their programs and priorities, and increase their autonomy in shared jurisdictions.
- For smaller, poorer provinces, autonomy is less important than ensuring the continued flow of federal dollars.
- Quebec, on the evidence, will approach this emerging pattern with deep reservations, seeing advantages in it to the extent that it offers them allies in their bid to confine the freedom of action of the Government of Canada, but fearful that the effective extension of collaborative federalism may simply replace Ottawa's oversight and direction with the collective oversight and direction of the English-speaking provinces.
- Success for Ottawa is presumably being able to retain its influence and visibility, particularly in an era of budget surpluses. It will wish, so far as possible, to retain the capacity to contribute through a wide array of policy instruments to the satisfaction of the social needs and aspirations of Canadians. In particular, it will seek to maintain direct links to citizens by providing benefits directly to them rather than indirectly through the provinces.

Thus most governments in the interdependent world of Canadian federalism will seek to maximize their freedom of action, and minimize external constraints, fiscal or regulatory, while some – especially the fiscally weaker jurisdictions – will be prepared to trade off some autonomy in return for adequate and stable financial assistance.

"Success" will be defined very differently by those groups not concerned with federalism or the relative status of governments, but rather with substantive policy and outcomes. They will ask:

does this process enhance or impede achievement of the policy objectives we are interested in? Answers will of course vary depending on the group in question. To the extent that collectively governments can achieve together what none could do separately, or to the extent that they are able to coordinate into a single whole policies and programs at all levels, and to the extent that the costs and frustrations of overlap and duplication can be reduced, then collaborative federalism serves all Canadians. Moreover, it suggests a reasonable way to balance sensitively the inevitable tension between national norms and standards on the one hand, and the desire to respond to the specific needs, circumstances, and preferences of different provincial communities on the other.

However, there are many potential costs to this collaborative model – which have been well described in the literature on the European Union. The "joint decision trap" emerges when autonomous, interdependent actors committed to consensus decision making seek to make decisions. The time and cost of coordination can escalate; solutions may be avoided or simply express the lowest common denominator. The institutional concerns of the actors – for status and recognition, to win credit and avoid blame – can dominate the substantive issues themselves. None of these dilemmas is easily resolved.

Our concern, however, is with the implications of this process for democracy. To that we now turn.

DEMOCRATIC DEFICITS AND AGENDAS FOR REFORM

In 1979 Donald Smiley, the dean of Canadian students of federalism, opened his critique of executive federalism this way:

My charges against executive federalism are these:

First, it contributes to undue secrecy in the conduct of the public's business.

Second, it contributes to an unduly low level of citizen participation in public affairs.

Third, it weakens and dilutes the accountability of government to their legislatures and to the wider public (Smiley, 1979).

Two decades later, with intergovernmental relations even more central to Canadian policy making, many observers echo these words.[11] They suggest that, despite the fact that we live in a very different intergovernmental environment, we have in a democratic sense progressed little. Many of the classic features of intergovernmental relations persist. Governments often filter the aspirations of citizens through their own institutional interests. Meetings are usually held behind closed doors. The discourse of fiscal federalism remains arcane and obscure. Lines of responsibility are blurred and indirect. Citizens typically have scant timely or effective access to the intergovernmental process.

To take just a few examples:

- The fiscal transfer mechanisms, which constitute the financial backbone of our country, draw a veil between cause and effect. How is a citizen to know if a closed clinic in Moose Jaw or a large increase in college fees in Ontario is the result of a budget decision taken in Ottawa the year before? (Simeon, 1997).
- The Agreement on Internal Trade was developed with little public involvement, is replete with "grandfathering" of existing practices, and makes it difficult for citizens to gain access to its enforcement mechanisms (Howse and Monahan, in Trebilcock and Schwanen, eds., 1995).
- There has been scarcely any public or parliamentary discussion of proposals for the social union or of shared responsibilities in the environmental field, both of which have engendered deep suspicion in the relevant policy communities.

More generally, Keith Banting notes that federalist values and democratic values are often in tension. He describes the social policy discussion as "the strongest form of intergovernmentalism – the co-determination model." And he warns that it is "worth remembering the democratic critique of such potent intergovernmentalism" (Banting, 1998). Another astute observer, Roger Gibbins, argues that such collaborative models would, "at least at the margins, reduce the role and effectiveness of legislatures, of political parties, elections, interest groups and the public. They would promote government that is less accountable, and in that sense, less democratic." The combination of decentralization and intergovernmentalism "moves decisions out of legislatures and into fora relatively insulated from public pressure, partisan debate and electoral combat" (Gibbins, 1997; Phillips, 1995; Biggs, 1996). Many others express similar views.

Whether it is dealing with the environment, social policy, or the tragedy of tainted blood, intergovernmental decision making often appears opaque, inaccessible to citizens and more concerned with protecting the institutional interests of the governmental actors than with responding to citizen concerns.

These are powerful criticisms, and we agree with most of them, subject to three important qualifications.

First, to a certain extent they may be misplaced. The pattern of intergovernmental relations is mainly a product, and reflection, of the larger institutional structure in which it is embedded. That, of course, is the Westminster system of cabinet – we prefer "First Minister" – government, with its extreme concentration of power in the executive. As Fletcher and Wallace point out, "executive federalism is more a consequence than a cause of executive dominance in the modern parliamentary system."[12]

Second, these critiques ignore some developments that have enhanced transparency and accountability.

- This is most evident in the constitutional arena. Following the demise of the Meech Lake Accord in 1990, the subsequent round of constitutional discussions paid much more attention to citizen views – proposals were put forward for public discussion and legislative scrutiny before governments went behind closed doors. The federal government sponsored five major public conferences. When the intergovernmental bargaining began, representatives of Canada's major aboriginal groups were at the table. And when governments had completed their work, it was submitted to the people in a national referendum – which was defeated. Prior to the 1980–82 round, constitutional amendment was a purely executive act; in the amending formula of 1982, legislative ratification became required; today, it appears to be an established convention that no significant constitutional change will be passed without popular consent.

- In the 1997 Calgary Declaration, a non-constitutional national-unity initiative, the nine provincial governments, excluding Quebec, committed themselves to a process of public information and consultation, culminating in legislative resolutions. The Declaration has now been passed in all nine provinces.
- In more "normal" policy areas, such as agriculture, the environment and fisheries, various intergovernmental forums have experimented with round tables and other devices to bring members of the substantive policy community together with ministers or officials of the federal and provincial governments.
- On the legislative front, the presence of two largely regional parties in the federal parliament has led to a somewhat wider debate on federalism issues there. The Reform Party has drafted a proposed "New Canada Act" that calls for "a new partnership agreement between Canada and the provinces," limits on the federal spending power, recognition of municipal governments as the "first level of government in Canada," election of the Senate, and a Constituent Assembly for any future round of constitutional revision (Reform Party of Canada, 1998). However, the dominance of the government party and the tyranny of party discipline place sharp limits on Parliament's potential as an arena for intergovernmental accommodation.

Third and finally, it is important to recognize that much of the democratic deficit does not lie in federalism itself, but in the pervasive role of intergovernmentalism in general, which in turn arises out of interdependence and overlap. These are features of modern societies and modern governments in themselves, witness the rampant and largely unaccountable intergovernmentalism of the European Union. So to the extent that current discussions of disentanglement and rebalancing lead to clearer definitions of roles and responsibilities, lines of accountability will be sharpened, and the classic democratic virtues of federalism – governments closer to the people, the ability to tailor policy to local preferences, and intergovernmental competition to attract citizen support – will become more prominent.

For all these reasons we perhaps need to temper the democratic critique of executive federalism somewhat. In a sense, the problem may be that the democratic expectations of citizens continue to outpace the very limited advances that have been made to democratize the process. So the democracy agenda remains very much alive.

A Democratic Agenda

There are many conceptions of democracy and hence many different criteria or standards that can be brought to bear in assessing any set of institutions and processes. We suggest three critical dimensions.

- The first flows from the idea of representative government. The key here is accountability. Citizens should know who is responsible for making the decisions that affect them, and have the means to punish them at the ballot box.
- The second flows from the idea of deliberative democracy. The keys here are deliberation and dialogue, in which governments engage with citizens to shape broad policy choices. This requires that processes be accessible to interested parties, that key decisions are not pre-cooked by a "cartel of elites," (Breton, 1985) and that discussions are open, transparent, and conducted in a public language that is understandable.
- The third flows from the idea of direct or populist democracy in which citizens and groups participate directly in making the decisions that affect them. Hence referenda, constituent assemblies, recall, and other such devices.

Each of these elements has a role in a reformed system of intergovernmental relations.

The first level suggests that what citizens want most is governments that are capable of performing effectively – making and implementing decisions that respond to their needs. Referring to the EU, Marcus Horeth calls this "output legitimacy." The success of the European enterprise, and therefore its justification, depends on its utility in providing substantive results for the participating countries [provinces] and their populations." (Horeth, 1998, 6–7) And, indeed, the vast bulk of intergovernmental relations, especially below the level of ministers and First Ministers, involves the technical, administrative, and procedural requirements to make a highly complex system work. The requirement here is not for greater citizen participation, but for enough clarity and accountability for citizens to judge results.

Higher standards of public participation in deliberative processes need to be applied when intergovernmental fora are discussing broad policy directions, enunciating fundamental values, and establishing standards – in short where intergovernmental bodies approach the status of legislatures. In such areas, we need to strengthen the role of legislatures in public deliberation of policy and ensure that the major social and economic groups whose interests are most deeply engaged are present and can make their voices heard.

The bar needs to be set highest when intergovernmental relations deal with issues that are "constitutional" in the broad sense of the term – issues that relate to core values, identities and national purposes, and basic institutional reform. This is where broad public debate and discussion is necessary before governments get together, and where democracy would normally require consent through referenda. Citizens must be engaged at every stage; these are not matters that can be left to the intergovernmental decision makers themselves.

With these broad considerations in mind, we suggest a number of possible reforms to enhance the democratic legitimacy of collaborative federalism. They rest on two accountability strategies: the accountability of individual governments to their own legislatures and citizens for their conduct in the intergovernmental arena, and the accountability of the intergovernmental institutions and mechanisms themselves (Horeth, 1998, 8). There is a potential tension between these two broad strategies. Strengthening the policy role of intergovernmental institutions, even if those institutions themselves become more transparent and accessible, weakens the authority of the constituent legislatures. But subjecting executives of federal and provincial governments to great democratic control over their intergovernmental activity may reduce the decision-making capacity of the intergovernmental institutions (Horeth, 1998, 18).

Clarifying "Who Does What"

First, democracy will be served if the role that executive federalism plays is as limited as possible. We recognize, though, that the whole trend of modern government and modern life makes the notion of "watertight compartments" less and less tenable. Executive federalism is born of the necessary implications of interdependence. In an ideal world, however, each jurisdiction would be fully responsible and accountable for a specified set of activities. There would be little need for elaborate intergovernmental mechanisms. Minimizing the scope of collaboration and intergovernmentalism reduces the democratic deficit and avoids the "collective action" or "joint decision trap" problems inherent in consensual decision making among autonomous but interdependent actors (Scharpf, 1988; Breton, 1985; Kennett, 1998). Hence we endorse efforts to clarify roles and responsibilities, either constitutionally, or non-constitutionally, to the extent that that is feasible, while recognizing that the potential for progress in this area is modest.

As John Richards puts it: "Accountability matters. One – and only one – level of government should in general be responsible for any particular domain of social policy, and we should require the responsible government to raise necessary revenues via own-source taxation." (Richards, 1998, 83) Or, as an American scholar has written, "It is impossible to hold someone accountable if one cannot tell whether the person was responsible for the act." (Zuckert, 1992, 132).

Opening Up the Intergovernmental Process

But, as we have suggested above, we know that interdependence and shared responsibilities are inevitable in all complex systems. Hence, the need to open up intergovernmental processes themselves.

First is the need for increased transparency. Citizens must know what is being discussed, what positions their representatives are taking, what decisions have been made. Not all meetings need be open to the public, but schedules of meetings and agendas should be widely published. The current exemption of federal–provincial matters from the provisions of federal and provincial Freedom of Information Acts (FOI) should be abolished.

Second, consultation with affected groups needs to be built more fully into the process. There are two possible ways to approach this. It can be indirect – in the sense that governments would consult widely among their own constituencies before engaging in intergovernmental discussions. The problem is that many of the affected interests cross provincial boundaries, and are not defined by territory. The alternative is to engage citizens and groups directly in the intergovernmental machinery itself, with Councils of Ministers holding their own hearings and consultations.[13] Public impact directly on the intergovernmental table has the additional advantage of helping to ensure that the partisan or institutional interests of governmental actors will not trump substantive concerns. It has the disadvantage of complicating lines of accountability back to the respective legislatures.

Monitoring Collaborative Federalism

The more federal–provincial collaboration extends to intergovernmental agreements on policies, standards, regulations, and dispute settlement mechanisms, the greater the role for citizens in monitoring them. Citizens should be represented in procedures to monitor and enforce implementation, and should have direct access to dispute-settlement mechanisms.

The more general point is that the more relations among governments in Canada come to supplant the normal legislative process within each of them, and the more the First Ministers Conference or the Annual Premiers Conference comes to be a "super-legislature," then the more we should subject the processes to the same standards of democratic debate and accountability that we now apply to legislatures.

Enhancing Legislative Federalism

Democratic federalism would be much enhanced by bringing parliament and legislatures much more fully into the process. As Horeth points out, in the EU, "democratic legitimation necessarily comes through the feedback of the actions of the European institutions into the parliaments of the member-states." (Horeth, 1998, 7) Powerful institutional forces – notably the tyranny of party discipline and the failure of the Canadian Senate effectively to represent regional and provincial views in the federal parliament – make this difficult. Legislatures play little role in monitoring intergovernmental relations or as arenas for public debate about federalism issues.

Even in this context, much could be done by such measures as:

- the establishment of standing committees on intergovernmental relations
- the holding of debates or committee hearings on intergovernmental issues before First Ministers Conferences
- legislative ratification of all major intergovernmental agreements
- the participation of Opposition members on governmental negotiating teams

Direct Democracy

The most powerful way to ensure collaborative federalism responds to citizen views is, of course, to give citizens a direct role. The potentially decisive impact of direct democracy has already been seen in the referendum which defeated the Charlottetown Accord in 1992. It now appears to be an established, if brand new, convention that major constitutional amendments require ratification by referendum. This is likely to change the dynamics of future constitutional debates. It would be interesting to know, for example, how both the process and the results of the Charlottetown Accord might have been different had the governmental negotiators known *at the outset of the talks* that their work would be judged by citizens.

Direct democracy at the provincial level may also have important implications for the larger intergovernmental dynamic. The impact of two, and perhaps more, referendums in Quebec is sufficient proof of that. But other provincial direct-democracy initiatives could also have an impact on intergovernmental relations. The election of a Senate candidate in Alberta may be just a straw in the wind here. To the extent that provinces move in the direction of many u.s. states, permitting citizen groups to take the initiative by placing policy issues on the ballot, a new source of innovation and destabilization is introduced. In the u.s., state level initiatives, such as California's proposition 13, have significantly influenced the national policy agenda (Agranoff, 1993).

More fundamental reforms of the Canadian system, such as relaxing party discipline, reforming the Senate to ensure more legitimacy and a more effective representation of regional voices in the central parliament, and reforms to the electoral system, would be required to replace executive with legislative federalism. But even within the present institutional constraints, much can be done to enhance the role of legislators, and, by extension, their constituents, in the process.

CANADA IN COMPARATIVE PERSPECTIVE

Most of the developments in Canadian federalism we have described have important parallels in other federal countries; they are driven by many of the same forces – globalization, fiscal pressure, new citizen attitudes, and the need to accommodate territorially based subnational identities – and raise many of the same questions about democracy and effective governance.

Devolution and decentralization, whether formal or informal, are common trends. At the broadest level, Spain (Agranoff, 1993), Belgium (Hooghe, 1993; Witte, 1992), and now Britain (Bradbury, Autumn 1997; *The Economist*, March 1999), have all in recent decades moved from unitary to federal or quasi-federal status.

Among existing federations, the tendencies are somewhat more mixed. In the United States, the federal retreat began with Reagan's new federalism in the 1980s, and has continued with the massive shift to the states of responsibility in social and welfare policies in the 1990s – the "devolution revolution." (Cole and Stenberg, 1996). This has led to a high level of innovation in state and local governments, though many observers worry that this fosters a "rush to the bottom." However many elements of "coercive federalism" imposed by Washington on the states remain, for example, in the form of "unfunded mandates,"[14] and it is clear that the degree of federal direction of the states in areas of shared jurisdiction remains far greater than is the case in Canada (Kincaid, 1990) As one observer put it, "devolution was more talk than action in the Congress and the White House as state–local concerns were conveniently put aside whenever political expediency or national-credit-seeking came to the fore." (Weissert, 1998, 4). In addition, while the number of states and the institutional structure of divided government in the u.s. make collaborative federalism on the Canadian model virtually impossible there, some elements of it can be seen. For example, state attorneys-general took the initiative in mounting a national strategy to deal with cigarette makers, and in launching antitrust campaigns against major airlines and computer companies (Weissert, 1998, 4). In November 1997, the four major state organizations, the national Governor's Association, Council of State Governments, National Conference of State Legislatures, and American Legislative Exchange Council held a "summit on federalism." They developed an eleven-point plan to bring better balance to the "federal state partnership" including requirements that Congress state its constitutional authority for any bill affecting the states, limits on federal pre-emption of state laws, streamlined block funding, and clarification of rules about unfunded mandates. The response was a presidential Executive Order on federalism that gave little weight to these concerns and was withdrawn after state opposition (Weissert, 1998, 24).

In Germany, observers are divided in their assessments. Some argue that German participation in the EU has "resulted in a significant shift of power from the Federation to the Länder," (Goetz, 1995, 105) and that economic globalization has "undermined the economic policy-making autonomy of the German federal government," while prompting "decentralization of other kinds of policy-making authority within the federal system." (Deeg, 1996, 27) Others argue that "the Länder have become increasingly marginalized as a direct consequence of German membership in the EU," and that the balance of power has been "significantly tilted in favor of the federal government."(Burgess and Gress, 1991, 245).

Downloading, off-loading, and reduced roles for national governments are common phenomena across federations. This in turn has led states and provinces elsewhere to occupy vacated policy space, and to engage in greater political dynamism and policy innovation.

In some cases, such as Australia, contemporary pressures have led to an increased emphasis on collaboration to manage interdependence, reduce the costs of overlap and duplication, and the like. The Council of Australian Governments (COAG), established in 1992, institutionalized this process, generating a framework of collaboration perhaps more developed than the Canadian (Watts, 1996, 52). At the same time, competition for scarce resources and investment has led to increased competition, and increased disparities among units in the federal system.

In many federations, especially those in member countries of the European Union, intergovernmental relations are increasingly interwoven with international relations.

These commonalities and differences suggest that there is a rich comparative research agenda for the comparative study of how different federal systems are affected by, and respond to, globalization, increased domestic diversity, and changes in the role of the state (Boeckelman, 1996).

But these parallel developments also raise similar questions about citizenship and democracy. The terms "democratic deficit" and "joint decision trap" which we now debate in Canada arose first within the context of the European Union. In many countries there is worry that the inherent complexity of intergovernmental relations strengthens the hands of technocrats and executives at the expense of legislators and citizens (Goetz, 1995, 99; Keating, 1997).

There are also commonalities in the remedies under discussion in other federal countries. The debate on "subsidiarity" in the European context focuses on minimizing the democratic deficit by ensuring that only those matters for which the need for collective action is fully demonstrated are elevated to the supranational level. Parallel attempts to develop a principled approach to who does what have been going on in the United States (Rivlin, 1992). Similarly, the Canadian debate about how the combination of devolution and decentralization will affect the ability to develop and sustain national standards, common levels of service across the country, and avoid a "rush to the bottom" in which competitive pressures lead to progressive erosion of redistribution, is echoed elsewhere, especially in the United States (Peterson and Kelly, 1996; Cook, 1995). Here again is a rich field for comparative research. As Alain Noel suggests, decentralization is such a multi-faceted concept that no simple generalizations can be made about its consequences for policy or democracy (Noel, 1997; *National Tax Journal*, June 1996).

These brief references reinforce our view that Canadians have much to learn from comparative experience, and vice versa.

They also convince us that a full exploration of the pitfalls and potentials for democratic citizenship must go beyond the traditional federalist concerns with the relationships between central and provincial or state governments. Federal arrangements are just one facet of a much larger phenomenon: that of "multi-level governance," defined by Gary Marks as systems "characterized by co-decision making across several nested tiers of government, ill-defined and shifting spheres of competence, ... and an on-going search for principles of decisional distribution that might be applied to this emerging polity" (Marks, 1996; Hooghe, 1996).

The world of multi-level governance is one of multiple identities and centres of power, from local neighbourhoods to the entire globe; a world of interdependence and connectedness, in which authority is blurred, fluid, and shifting; a world in which the interests and concerns of both the economy and civil society spill over and cut across lines drawn on maps and powers set out in national constitutions. The phenomenon of "glocalization" requires that we move both downwards, to encompass within intergovernmental relations the roles of local and regional governments, and of emerging centres of power such as Aboriginal governments. It requires that we move "upwards" to encompass the ever-increasing range of international and supranational institutions. And it requires us to understand that the flow of information, ideas, and power moves freely across all these political divisions, and that responsibility for discrete policy issues is seldom neatly packaged at one or another level. The reality is interdependence: the problems are simultaneously local, regional, national, and international; so too are the solutions. The very ideas of community and citizenship have become multi-faceted and multi-dimensional.

Clearly, this is not easy to deal with, either conceptually or practically. As David Held points out:

If the agent at the heart of modern political discourse, be it a person, a group, or a collectivity is locked into a variety of overlapping political communities – domestic and international – then the proper "home" of politics and democracy becomes a puzzling matter (Held, 1996, 225).

Where, he asks, is the "appropriate locus for the articulation of the democratic political good?"

Certainly multi-level governance poses immense challenges for democratic citizenship. If accountability and knowing who is responsible is difficult in a two-level federal system, it is even more so when there are many levels, and no definitive guide-book. If citizens feel powerless in their domestic politics – the arena within which traditionally they have held their rights and responsibilities – what of their efficacy in the larger global arena? As Mark Zacher points out there has been a veritable explosion of international agreements, treaties and tribunals in recent years, and most remain heavily executive and bureaucratic, thickly insulated from popular pressures (Zacher, 1999).

Our belief, however, is that this world of multi-level governance is Janus-faced; it offers both threat and opportunity (Simeon, 1997b). Decentralization to local units multiplies the opportunities for citizen participation; globalization multiplies the available political arenas and opens the pathway to a global civil society, able to address global problems beyond the reach of national or local governments.

The challenge to democracy and citizenship operates at each level of the multi-level chain. We have focused on democratizing Canadian intergovernmental relations. But this agenda extends equally to other levels. Democracy can no longer stop at national borders.

Moreover, the insights of scholars seeking a more democratic international order can be brought to bear on Canada's domestic affairs. David Held, among others, argues that the traditional Westphalian model of international relations constructed out of the executive-centred interactions among sovereign states no longer describes modern realities. Such a model lies "at some considerable distance from what might be called a 'thicker' ordering of global affairs" (Held, 1995, 270). He seeks to define a model of cosmopolitan governance that creates an overarching set of rights, obligations, and standards to govern the behaviour of all institutions – local, national, and international. Under that umbrella would be a variety of procedures and practices to render international institutions open, responsive, and accountable. Such a world is still embryonic, but it is being driven increasingly by the global mobilization of citizen groups.

How is this relevant to Canada? Well, intergovernmental relations in Canada look a lot like the Westphalian model of international relations (Simeon, 1972; Smiley, 1979). It is just as obsolete here. So the recommendations of scholars like Held – for overarching democratic norms, processes open to multiple identities and diverse views, transparency, and a greater role for citizens – all have powerful relevance for Canadian reformers as they seek a collaborative approach to securing the economic and social union in their highly decentralized federation.

CONCLUDING THOUGHTS ABOUT THE FUTURE

How might the nexus between intergovernmental relations and citizenship evolve as we move into the twenty-first century? Speculating about the future is a risky business, given that modern life appears to be characterized as much by discontinuities and surprises as by patterns and stable evolution. We will, however, by way of conclusion, hazard a few thoughts about what may occur.

Multi-level Governance

At the most general level, that of multi-level governance broadly defined, one might anticipate several things.

States will continue to be, as they have been in the past, the venue where the combined exercise of power together with accountability for its use has been best worked out. Although by no means ideal, democratic states have achieved a higher level of development in this respect than have other "competing" organizations and institutions. The equation between the accumulation of power sufficient to address the central public purposes of modern life, on the one hand, and the existence of democratic processes adequate to impose a degree of popular control, on the other, has been better struck by the modern democratic state than by any other competitor. Certainly, international political organizations, global private-sector corporations, military alliances, and international trade agreements do not measure up to the challenge. Nor, domestically, do cities, self-regulating industrial sectors, churches, Aboriginal governments or cooperative associations – at least, not yet. There are few indications so far that this signal advantage, which rests with the modern democratic state, is about to disappear or be displaced by another, better alternative.

Nevertheless, it seems clear as well that severe challenges to the democratic state are likely to continue for the foreseeable future. We appear to be living through a period which Daniel Yankelovich has characterized as "the exhaustion of the paradigm of the nation-state."[15] It is clearly under assault, but what will arise to replace it is obscure indeed. Thus, during the next while, we think the dispersion of power away from the modern state is likely to continue. Power, not always clothed with authority or legitimacy, will migrate upwards, downwards, and outwards, in favour of public and private international organizations, municipal, local, and regional governments, and non-state and quasi-state actors within national communities which will continue to assume functions previously performed by the state.

We would anticipate that a growing demand for public accountability and popular control will track the continuing dispersion of power we have described in the previous point. An ad hoc, international, internet-based popular resistance successfully stopped the Multilateral Agreement on Investment (MAI) in its tracks. The World Trade Organization meetings in Seattle in the autumn of 1999 were disrupted by militant public opposition. These may be harbingers of things to come, and a sign that "executive federalism," disconnected from the publics it is allegedly serving, is as problematic at the global level as it is, say, in the European Union, or in the Canadian federation. There are signs of restiveness within the global economy as well. George Soros, the international financier, is just one of many voices arguing for some public control over the untrammelled international movement of capital.

It used to be the case that a company's return to profitability meant its workers' return to employment; today, profits soar while jobs are shed and inconvenient plants in uncompetitive countries are closed. The old moral contract which bound workers and owners together seems to have been turned on its head. And, too often, governments are the handmaidens of this destructive cycle. Citizens in the industrial democracies are less

and less willing to absorb the social and economic costs of globalization, and a mounting backlash is setting in. Klaus Schwab
and Claude Smadja, respectively the founder and managing
director of the World Economic Forum, global capitalism's annual convention, underlined these concerns at the start of the 1996
Forum meetings. Noting that the backlash is "threatening to dis-
rupt economic activity and social stability in many countries,"
they argued that "public opinion in the industrial democracies
will no longer be satisfied with articles of faith about the virtues
and benefits of the global economy. It is pressing for action."
They declared that today's key issue is "to make apparent the
social returns of global capitalism.... Moral considerations aside,
there can be no sustainable growth without the public at large
seeing itself as the major stakeholder in the successful functioning of the economy" (Schwab and Smadja, 1996).

This rising popular concern is likely to take two forms. The first
is to seek to subject to democratic control those international
forces and agencies currently operating beyond the public's
grasp. This is an effort at democratizing globalization by globalizing democracy, and it is a daunting task. The second form this
concern is likely to take is domestic; it is to seek to reinvigorate
the nation-state and to clothe it once again with the capacity to
control on behalf of its citizens the powerful social and economic
forces shaping the national community. This, also, is a challenging assignment. Given the difficulties plaguing each of these
exercises, it is to be expected that progress will be slow and significant reforms will not be easily won. Yet a prominent feature of
the times ahead, we would argue, will be the effort, in many different countries, situations and organizations, to achieve democratic reforms to match the new world which is disclosing itself.

Intergovernmental Relations and Democracy in Canada

With respect to intergovernmentalism and democracy within
Canada, it is possible to be more concrete.

We have described in this chapter the emergence of a discernibly different form of intergovernmental relations which we

have characterized as collaborative federalism. Is this emergent phenomenon likely to be a durable feature of our federation over the next several years? Some would argue that this form of intergovernmental relations was at bottom a response to the growing fiscal incapacity of the federal government, and that, with Ottawa's return to financial health, it will rapidly disappear from the scene. Certainly, the Government of Canada's last budget in February 1999 – its first of the new era – substantially altered the situation and the federal–provincial dynamic. It made clear that federal cash greases the skids of federal–provincial cooperation and increases the traditional kind of leverage Ottawa has had over the provinces through the exercise of its spending power.

Yet, having said that, we would suggest that there are reasons to believe that collaborative federalism will remain a feature of the scene in the future.

- One reason is that Canadians consistently rate cooperation among their governments as an important objective, and collaborative federalism is an approach that responds to that demand.
- Another reason is that earlier approaches, based on clear federal leadership and the relatively autonomous use of the federal spending power, are no longer nearly as feasible as they once were. Indeed, Ottawa, recognizing that the game has changed, has made commitments sharply limiting its freedom to act in the old ways.
- A third reason is that the achievements of collaborative federalism – the AIT, the Calgary Accord and the Social-Union Framework Agreement chief among them – make it more likely that the procedure will be followed in the future. The social-union agreement, for example, has a three-year review commitment built into it. There is now at least a degree of momentum behind the utilization of this approach.
- A fourth reason is that the provinces and territories have learned that they can make significant progress, setting their own agenda, and working among themselves. The interprovincial dynamic is a counterpoint to the federal–provincial

relationship which classically defined intergovernmentalism in Canada. Indeed, the institutionalization of this approach via the Annual Premiers Conference and ministerial councils adds some administrative muscle to what otherwise might be a more insubstantial impulse.

- A fifth reason is that governments have found that they can achieve accommodations through collaboration on substantive policy which are impossible to achieve in the constitutional forum.

At the most general level, if one looks at the evolution of the Canadian federation over the last four decades, federal dominance has been substantially defined by two powerful forces: nation-building in Quebec and province-building elsewhere. These forces have had a major impact on the Government of Canada and its capacity to call the intergovernmental shots. While it has by no means been a zero-sum game, the maturing of provincial governments has altered the balance of power within Confederation and has redefined the manner in which Ottawa can seek to achieve its objectives. Collaborative federalism, in our view, fits logically into the broad development of Confederation during the last four decades.

To say that collaborative federalism is likely to be a feature of intergovernmental relations in the future is not to say that it will be the only game in town. Many of the things that matter most to Canadians – and therefore to the federal government – fall broadly within provincial jurisdiction. To the extent that Ottawa's freedom of action is constrained in the undertaking of shared-cost and block-funded programs with provinces, it will quite naturally seek other approaches where its ability to act will be unimpeded. For example, in the future we may expect to see Ottawa, where possible, taking initiatives in the social policy field via the tax system or by means of direct grants to individuals and organizations. An example of the first, using the taxation system to achieve social goals, is the Child Tax Credit, although in the event this initiative was the product of federal–provincial cooperation; an example of the second, the direct grant approach, is Ottawa's Millennium Scholarship Fund, a controversial undertaking, particularly in Quebec. While the use of these alternatives will not, of course, permit Ottawa to avoid political controversy, it will put it in a freer position in which its capacity to act will not be subject to the will of the provinces.

Our thinking about collaborative federalism needs to be set in the larger context of multi-governance in Canada. It will become increasingly necessary to look to the role of local, territorial, and Aboriginal governments and their interface with provincial, national, and international institutions. This study has followed a standard Canadian pattern: municipalities have not figured greatly in our analysis. This is so not only because municipalities have no independent constitutional status on their own, but also because provinces tend to control tightly the structure and powers of local governments. If Canada is one of the most decentralized federations in terms of federal–provincial relations, it is one of the most centralized in terms of provincial–municipal relations. This has robbed the very governments that are closest to the citizen and the most involved with the quality of their daily lives of much of their potential dynamism and vitality. This at a time when cities and city regions are the centres of economic and cultural innovation, are increasingly multicultural, and, in many cases, are increasingly linked to national and international networks rather than to their provincial hinterlands. Enriching democratic multi-governance must involve them.

In addition, Canada is experimenting with yet other institutional forms outside the traditional federal–provincial–municipal framework. Canada's northern territories are acting more and more like provinces rather than federal protectorates. The creation of the new territory of Nunavut, with a population made up largely of Inuit people, is Canada's first full experiment with Aboriginal self-government. Aboriginal peoples elsewhere in Canada are also seeking to define their own models of self-government. They too will become players in a multi-governance world.

What of the nexus between democratic citizenship and intergovernmental relations? We would expect the situation to vary according to the specific circumstances of the case.

- First, at the operational and administrative level of intergovernmental relations, where the policy and political content is low, the technical content is high, and goals and professional values are widely shared among federal and provincial officials, we would expect the work of the federation to be carried on in much the same way it has been conducted for generations – in a low-key, business-like fashion, out of the public eye, involving almost exclusively federal and provincial officials. This sphere, where the features of classical cooperative federalism live on, will not attract more public interest in the future than it has in the past. Here the operative assumptions of representative democracy will continue to prevail; citizens – if aware of the work at all – will want this work done and done well, but they will have scant interest in being consulted about it or involved in the process.
- Second, at what might be called the sectoral level – the level at which significant program, policy and political issues, and influential constituencies and organized interests are in play – we anticipate that the pressure for meaningful public involvement will continue to grow, as it has in recent years. Fisheries policy on one of our three coasts, Aboriginal treaty and land claims negotiations, industrial and academic R and D programs, immigration policy, training programs – these matters do not normally engage the political community as a whole, but they affect and will attract the attention of significant sectors of Canadian civil society. In such areas as these, we believe that the demand from the relevant publics to be directly involved in the elaboration of the arrangements federal and provincial governments are making on their behalf will be unrelenting, and will involve an insistence that non-governmental voices be heard at an early stage of the policy process, when governments are still defining the issue, refining the options, considering the resource allocations and implications.
- Third, at the system level, we find issues which go to the heart of the conceptualization and functioning of the federation; these are, in this sense, constitutional in character. The Agreement on Internal Trade, the Calgary Accord, the Social

Union Framework – these would all qualify as system-level issues. Ironically, we think a case could be made that the demand for public participation in system-level intergovernmental negotiations is likely to be less than the demand for participation in sectoral matters involving the two orders of government, even though the issues dealt with are as big or bigger. With the latter, there is, in a sense, an already organized, engaged public which can become activated fairly rapidly if intergovernmental negotiations directly touching their concerns occurs. With the former, the matters are likely to be perceived as abstract, at one remove from daily life. They commonly deal with what might be called the architecture and processes within which concrete matters are addressed, rather than with the concrete matters themselves. Because of their systemic character, the issues do not normally relate directly to an organized constituency, but to a broad public interest which is often hard to define and hard to grasp. Thus it takes time for system concerns to ripen and be explained to the public, and time for intergovernmental negotiations to stimulate broad citizen reaction. Once that occurs, as we have seen with Meech Lake and Charlottetown, the voice of citizens can be powerful and, in fact, decisive, but momentum is slow to build. Therefore, the popular pressure to open up these intergovernmental processes may not be all that great, even if the need for transparency is acute. This places a heavy procedural burden on the government actors themselves.

Citizens and Public Servants

This brings us to our final remarks. In this chapter we have tended to look at intergovernmental relations primarily from the perspective of the citizen. But how does the picture we have sketched look to the public officials who have the responsibility for making the system work? If our hunches about the future have merit, what does this imply for the way in which the public's servants carry on the public's business?

Clearly, it suggests that the conventional model of public administration, already under severe stress, will be tested further in the years to come. The simplistic model of ministers deciding and civil servants implementing implies that the bulk of the citizen–government interface should be handled by the politicians. Yet everything we have learned about multi-governance and the new face of intergovernmental relations suggests that this implication, if it ever was valid, is woefully inadequate for understanding and shaping the current reality. Increasingly, public servants need to be capable of interacting comfortably with the public in many different situations and forums. The democratic requirements of the situation call for nothing less. Yet this public, "political" role is something with which few civil servants are comfortable.

This is, in part, for a very good reason, given that it implies the need to seriously adapt the system of parliamentary government and the principles of ministerial responsibility that lie at its heart. Any public servant who has been encouraged generally to speak with the public and then has suffered for what he or she has specifically said will know that we lack a theory and a specification of roles adequate to cope with the new reality.

Beyond that, there is another challenge to our conventional understandings of parliamentary government which we mentioned earlier in the chapter. To the extent that some of the most important business of the country is conducted via intergovernmental processes and embedded in emergent intergovernmental institutions, questions of transparency, accountability, and democracy arise anew. In these circumstances, it seems manifestly inadequate to rely solely on the distinctive accountability lines that run back from each government to its own cabinet and legislature. What about the responsibility of the intergovernmental participants themselves, taken collectively? What relationship does or should the citizen have to these powerful intergovernmental forums where significant decisions are being made?

Here we have little in the way of theory or practice to guide us; yet, on the evidence so far, we are a very long way from repairing this breach in our democratic theory. Ways of filling the gap will not be easily found. However, any progress that can be made in tackling this growing intergovernmental problem will be of benefit to the much broader field of multi-governance as well.

CONCLUSION

The intergovernmental experience of existing federations displays a rich array of structures, processes, institutions, and mechanisms for coping with the inevitable overlap and interdependence that are features of modern life. While each federation has followed a distinctive path, based on its own particular circumstances and conditions, all are responding to the same functional requirement, namely, to find effective ways of managing the interface among governments. The capacity to manage the interface will be of increasing importance in the future as new federal systems are created and as multi-tiered governing structures proliferate in the modern world.

It is easy to get lost in the technicalities of these processes, and to concentrate analysis on the structures and mechanisms by which intergovernmental competition is regulated or intergovernmental cooperation is fostered. There is, however, as we have argued above, another – and ultimately more important – context within which to set intergovernmental relations, namely, the framework of democratic norms and values. There are deep democratic challenges facing modern governments of every stripe. These challenges are doubly difficult when one considers governments in their relations with one another.

After all, it can be said that there is a theory and there are fairly muscular institutions which together, justify the adjective "democratic" in the phrase, "the modern democratic state." So far, however, there is neither an equivalent theory nor are there equivalent institutions which would permit us to speak comfortably about "democratic intergovernmental relations." Yet intergovernmental relations are a central feature of modern political life – not just in federations – and they are likely to become more so in the years ahead. Democratizing intergovernmental relations is one of the central challenges confronting governance at the beginning of the new century.

NOTES

1 As early as the mid-sixties, parliamentarians worried about the emergence of a new level of government that would undermine parliamentary sovereignty. See Richard Simeon, *Federal–Provincial Diplomacy*. Toronto: University of Toronto Press, 1972.

2 For a detailed description and analysis, see Earl H. Fry, "The Expanding Role of State and Local Governments in u.s. Foreign Affairs." Paper presented to the American Political Science Association, Boston, September 3, 1993. For example, at the time of writing, California maintained an Export Finance Office, a State World Trade Commission, an Office of Foreign Investment, another for Export development, and eight, soon to be 11, offices abroad, p.14.

3 Hudson Meadwell labels the Canadian model "consociational federalism." See "Nations, States and Unions: Institutional Design and State-Breaking in the Developed West." Paper presented to the American Political Science Association, Boston, September, 1998.

4 The Canada Millennium Scholarship Fund was an earlier harbinger of this tendency. It will channel federal aid to post-secondary education directly to students, rather than through provincial governments, and has attracted the ire of several provinces, most notably Quebec.

5 Indeed, the Ontario government labelled its attack on the federal policies, the "Fair Shares" campaign. Queen's Park commissioned a series of ten analytical studies by the consulting firm, Informetrica, which offered Ontario's first cost-benefit analysis of Canadian federalism.

6 This, despite Ottawa's own aggressive deficit cutting which severely affected the provinces. It was most evident in the health care field.

7 The plans to implement a functional consolidation of Canadian stock exchanges, announced by the exchanges in the Spring of 1999, offer an example of the extent to which transnational economic integration is imposing a discipline on domestic, non-governmental regulators, whether the governments will it or no. The consolidation planning was undertaken by the exchanges themselves, in recognition of the imperatives of world financial markets, and in several cases against the first preferences of the relevant Canadian governments themselves.

8 Such critics as Daniel Schwanen and Robert Howse, while applaud- ing the AIT as a very useful first step, argue that it needs to be strengthened (Daniel Schwanen, *Drawing on Our Inner Strength,* C.D. Howe Institute Commentary, June 1996; Robert Howse, *Securing the Canadian Economic Union,* C.D. Howe Commentary, June 1996.) They recommend, for example, that the Secretariat should be empowered to analyze obstacles to implementation and to recommend solutions, that the member governments should vote by qualified majority rather than by the consensus system currently in place, that access to the dispute settlement mechanism should be extended to private parties, and that public education on the existence and purposes of the AIT should be undertaken.

9 There is no question but that the social-union *process* was a provin- cially driven initiative. There is debate, however, about whether the social union *agreement* works more to the advantage of Ottawa or the provinces. The variety of ways in which it has been interpreted is one of the more striking features of this latest accomplishment of col- laborative federalism.

10 This is also the case in another parliamentary federation, Australia. There a highly promising exercise in intergovernmental collabora- tion, the COAG process, effectively came to a halt when the national government was changed in 1996.

11 It is important to note that the question we address is not whether *federalism* is democratic; our focus is on intergovernmental rela- tions within federalism. For a recent summary of the pros and cons of federalism in terms of democratic accountability, see William Downs, "Accountability in Systems of Multilevel Governance: American Federalism in Comparative Perspective." Paper present- ed to the American Political Science Association, Boston, Septem- ber 3-6, 1998. To the federalist "virtues" as a check on the abuse of power, multiplying points of access, assuring attention is paid to local concerns, and socializing potential leaders, he contrasts the "vices" of excessive complexity and hence blurred lines of respon- sibility, the likelihood of "voter fatigue," and the diminished role of *local* government.

12 Quoted in Kenneth Norrie, Richard Simeon and Mark Krasnick, *Fed- eralism and the Economic Union.* Research Studies for the Royal Com-

mission on the Economic Union and Canada's development Prospects. 59. Toronto: University of Toronto Press, 1986, p. 157.

13 As interest groups have come to play a greater role in affairs of the European Union, there has been a similar debate about the relative merits of direct and indirect modes of representation.

14 In 1997, for example, new or unfunded mandates were proposed to direct states' action with respect to drunk driving, Food Stamp administration, welfare and Medicaid (including a requirement that state Medicaid programs must pay for Viagra!).

15 A remark he uttered at a "Scenarios for the Future" retreat, La Sapinière, Quebec, November 1997.

BIBLIOGRAPHY

Agranoff, Robert. 1993. Intergovernmental politics and policy: building federal arrangements in Spain. *Regional Politics and Policy* 3 (Summer):1-28.

Banting, Keith. 1986. *The Welfare State and Canadian Federalism*. Montreal & Kingston: McGill-Queen's University Press.

_____ 1998. The past speaks to the future: lessons from the postwar social union. In *Canada: The State of the Federation, 1997*, ed. Harvey Lazar. Kingston: Institute of Intergovernmental Relations, 39-69, 64.

Biggs, Margaret. 1996. *Building Blocks for the New Social Union*. Ottawa: Canadian Policy Research Network.

Boeckelman, Keith. 1996. Federal systems in the global economy. *Publius* 26 (Winter):1-10.

Bradbury, Jonathan. 1997. The Blair government's white papers on British devolution. *Regional and Federal Studies* 7 (Autumn):115-133.

Breton, Albert. 1985. Supplementary Statement. In Royal Commission on the Economic Union and Canada's Development Prospects, *Report*, Vol. III. Ottawa: Supply and Services.

Burelle, André. 1995. *Le mal canadien*. Montreal: Fides.

Burgess, Michael, and Franz Gress. 1991. German unity and the European Union. *Regional Politics and Policy*, Vol. 1:242-259, 245.

Cameron, David R. 1994. Half-eaten carrot, bent stick: decentralization in an era of fiscal restraint. *Canadian Public Administration*, vol. 37, no. 3 (Autumn).

Canada West Foundation. 1998. *Red Ink IV: Back From the Brink?* Calgary.

Canadian Intergovernmental Conference Secretariat. *Report to Governments, 1997-98.* Ottawa: CICS.

Cole, Richard L., and Carl W. Stenberg, 1996. Reversing directions: a ranking and comparison of key intergovernmental events, 1960-1980 and 1980-1945. *Riblins* 26 (Spring):25-41.

Cook, Gareth. 1995. Devolution chic: why sending power to the states could make monkey out of Uncle Sam. *The Washington Monthly* 27 (April):9-17.

Courchene, Thomas. 1997. ACCESS: a convention on the Canadian economic and social systems, August 1996. A paper prepared for the Ontario Ministry of Intergovernmental Affairs, p. 2. Reprinted in the Institute of Intergovernmental Relations, *Assessing ACCESS* Kingston: Institute of Intergovernmental Relations.

Deeg, Richard. 1996. Economic globalization and the shifting boundaries of German dederalism. *Publius* 26 (Winter):27-53, 27.

Economist. 1999. Towards a federal Britain: an England of regions. March 27:23-5.

Fry, Earl H. 1993. The expanding role of state and local governments in U.S. foreign affairs. Paper presented to the American Political Science Association, Boston, September.

Gibbins, Roger. 1995. Democratic reservations about the ACCESS models. In Institute of Intergovernmental relations, *Assessing ACCESS: Towards a New Social Union.* Kingston: Institute of Intergovernmental Relations, 41-44.

Goetz, Klaus. 1995. National governance and European integration: intergovernmental relations in Germany. *Journal of Common Market Studies* 33 (March):91-116, 105.

Held, David. 1995. *Democracy and the Global Order: From the Modern State to Cosmopolitan Governance.* Stanford: Stanford University Press.

Hooghe, Liesbet, ed. 1996. *Cohesion Policy and European Integration: Building Multilevel Governance.* Oxford: Oxford University Press.

_____ 1993. Belgium: from regionalism to federalism. *Regional Politics and Society* 3 (Summer):44-67.

Horeth, Marcus. 1998. "The trilemma of legitimacy – multilevel governance in the EU and the problem of legitimacy. Discussion paper C11, Center for European Integration Studies, Rheinische Friedrich-Wilhelms-Universitat Bonn. 6-7.

Howse, Robert. 1995. Between anarchy and the rule of law: dispute settlement and related mechanisms in the agreement on internal trade. And Patrick J. Monahan, To the extent possible: a comment on dispute settlement in the agreement on internal trade. In *Getting There: An Assessment of the Agreement on Internal Trade*, eds. Michael J. Trebilcock and Daniel Schwanen. Toronto: C. D. Howe Institute. 170-195 and 211-218.

Inglehart, Ronald. 1990. *Culture Shift in Advanced Industrial Society*. Princeton: Princeton University Press.

Inglehart, Ronald., Neil Nevitte, and Miguel Basanez. 1996. *The North American Trajectory: Social Institutions and Social Change*. New York/Berlin: Aldine de Gruyter.

Decentralization Conference. 1997. Is decentralization conservative? Federalism and the contemporary debate on the Canadian welfare state. Paper prepared for Conference on Decentralization: Dimensions and Prospects in Canada. University of Western Ontario.

Keating, Michael. 1997. Challenges to federalism: territory, function and power in a globalizing world. Paper presented at Conference on Federalism, University of Western Ontario, October.

Kennett, Steven. 1998. *Securing the Social Union: A Commentary on the Decentralized Approach*. Kingston: Institute of Intergovernmental Relations.

Kincaid, John. 1990. From cooperative to coercive federalism. *The Annals of the American Academy of Political and Social Science* 509 (May):139-152.

Lazar, Harvey, ed. 1998. *Canada: The State of the Federation, 1997*. Montreal & Kingston: McGill Queen's University Press.

Marks, Gary. 1996. Structural policy and multilevel governance in the EC. In *Processes of European Integration, 1880-1995: States, Markets and Citizenship*, eds. J. Klausen and L. Tilley. *National Tax Journal* 49 (June).

Nevitte, Neil. 1996. *The Decline of Deference*. Peterborough: Broadview Press.

Noel, Alain. 1999. Is decentralization conservative? federalism and the contemporary debate on the welfare state. In *Stretching the Federation: The Art of the State in Canada*, ed. Robert Young. Kingston: Institute of Intergovernmental Relations, Queen's University, 195-219.

Peterson, Paul, and Kevin Kelly. 1996. Leave it to the states and it won't get done. *Commonweal* 123 (February 9):11-14.

Phillips, Susan. 1995. The Canada health and social transfer. In *Canada: The State of the Federation, 1995*, eds. Douglas Brown and Jonathan Rose. Kingston: Institute of Intergovernmental Relations, 65-96.

Quoted in Norrie, Kenneth, Richard Simeon, and Mark Krasnick. 1986. *Federalism and the Economic Union.* Research Studies for the Royal Commission on the Economic Union and Canada's Development Prospects.

Reform Party of Canada. 1998. *New Canada Act: An Act to Modernize Our Government for the 21st Century.* Ottawa.

Richards, John. 1998. Reducing the muddle in the middle: three propositions for running the welfare state. In *Canada: The State of the Federation, 1997. Non-Constitutional Renewal,* ed. Harvey Lazar. Kingston: Institute of Intergovernmental relations, 71-104, 83.

Rivlin, Alice. 1992. *Reviving the American Dream,* Washington: The Brookings Institution.

Russell, Peter. 1993. *Constitutional Odyssey,* 2nd. ed. Toronto: University of Toronto Press.

Scharpf, Fritz. 1988. The joint decision trap: lessons from German federalism and European integration. *Public Administration* 66 (Summer):236-278.

Schwab, Klaus, and Claude Smadja. 1996. *Globe and Mail,* February 16, 1996.

Simeon, Richard. 1972. *Federal-Provincial Diplomacy.* Toronto: University of Toronto Press.

_____ 1997a. The politics of fiscal federalism. In *The Future of Fiscal Federalism,* eds. T. J. Courchene and Keith Banting. Kingston: School of Policy Studies.

_____ 1997b. Citizens in the emerging global order. In *The Nation-State in a Global/Information Order: Policy Challenges,* ed. T. J. Courchene Kingston: John Deutsch Institute for Economic Research, 299-314.

Smiley, D.V. 1979. An outsider's observations of intergovernmental relations among consenting adults. In *Confrontation or Collaboration: Intergovernmental Relations in Canada Today,* ed. Richard Simeon. Toronto: Institute of Public Administration of Canada.

Wallace, William. 1996. Governance without statehood: the unstable equilibrium. In *Policy-Making in the European Union,* 3rd. ed.,

439-60, eds. Hellen and William Wallace. Oxford: Oxford University Press.

Watts, Ronald. 1996. *Comparing Federal Systems in the 1990s.* Kingston: Institute of Intergovernmental Relations, 52.

Weissert, Carol S. 1998. The state of American federalism, 1997-1998. Paper presented to the American Political Science Association, Boston, September 3-6.

Witte, Els. 1992. Belgian federalism: towards complexity and asymmetry. *West European Politics,* 15 (October):95-117.

Zacher, Mark. 1997. The global economy and the international political order. In *The Nation State in a Global Information Order: Policy Challenges,* ed. T. J. Courchene. Kingston: John Deutsch Institute for Economic Research, 67-95.

Zuckert, Michael P. 1992. The virtuous polity, the accountable polity: liberty and responsibility in "The Federalist." *Publius* 22 (Winter).

How Do We Know How Good Public Services Are?

CHRISTOPHER POLLITT

PREAMBLE

If the question is: "How can we tell how good the public service is?" then the basic answer which has been given by many OECD countries over the last decade or more is "by measurement." The most intense and obvious manifestations of this trend have been legible in Australia, New Zealand, and the United Kingdom, but overt measurement also appears to have increased significantly in Canada, the United States, the Nordic countries, and the Netherlands (e.g., Boston et al., 1996; OECD, 1997; Sandberg, 1996; Sorber, 1996; Summa, 1995; Wholey, 1997). Of the U.K. it has been observed that:

No public sector employee has escaped the ever-extending reach of performance evaluation schemes. The pressure to meet targets or performance standards – whether hospital waiting lists, school exam results, crime clear-up rates or university research ratings – has introduced profound changes in public organisations. As PIS (Performance Indicators) have become increasingly linked to resource allocation and individual financial rewards, so organizational cultures and individual behaviours have been transformed (Carter, 1998, 177).

Writing more generally, of European developments as a whole, Bouckaert perceived that:

there are some major common evolutions in implementing performance measurement in all European countries.

Measurement is becoming more extensive. More levels... and more
fields... are included.

Performance measurement is becoming more intensive because more
management functions are included (not just monitoring but also decision-making, controlling and even providing accountability).

Finally, performance measurement becomes more external. Its use is
not just internal, but also for the members of legislative bodies, and
even for the public (Bouckaert, 1996, 234 – the two "even"s in this quo-
tation are eloquent).

In the New World, too, the measurement of public sector performances has been a growth industry. In the u.s. the National
Performance Review and the 1993 Government Performance and
Results Act (GPRA) together precipitated a virtual orgy of measurement. GPRA is particularly significant, in that its measurement
demands reach across the whole federal government. It "requires
agencies to plan and measure performance using the 'program
activities' listed in their budget submissions" (General Accounting Office, 1997a).
    Another aspect of the spread of measurement is the relatively
rapid development, in many countries, of performance audit and
of quality improvement schemes. Performance audit comple-
ments rather than replaces the more traditional forms of financial
audit (Pollitt et al., 1999). Power (1997), for example, documents
and analyses a u.k. "audit explosion" during the 1980s and 1990s.
Hood et al. (1998, 66) conclude that "regulation inside government has grown substantially in the u.k. public sector in direct
staffing and spending over the last 20 years," where regulation is
defined as "audit, grievance-chasing, standard-setting, inspection
and evaluation" – mostly activities which frequently involve
measurement (ibid., 61). On the quality front the proliferation of
"citizens' charters" (at national levels Belgium, Finland, France,

Italy, Portugal, U.K.) and applications of various forms of TQM lead directly to the formulation of standards, many of them quantitative, and then the monitoring of those standards by a wide range of bodies and groups (see, for example, Gaster, 1995; Joss and Kogan, 1995; Pollitt and Bouckaert, 1995; Prime Minister, 1991).

The move towards quantified measures, targets, and standards is not an adjunct of any one political party or ideology. It was manifest under the Conservatives in the U.K. from the early 1980s until their defeat in 1997, and their Labour successors promised more of the same "new quality standards," "new efficiency targets," and so on (see Chancellor of the Exchequer, 1998, 13 et seq. and Prime Minister and Minister for the Cabinet Office, 1999). It was visible under the New Zealand Labour governments of 1984 to 1990 and the more conservative National Party government which followed. In Finland it was as much practised by the conservative-led Holkeri coalition of 1987–1991 as by the centre-right coalition of Aho (1991–1996) or Lipponen's "rainbow coalition" since 1996.

Measurement, it is believed by some, will reveal how good or bad public services really are, and whether they are changing for better or worse. Once we have an activity firmly pinned under the measurement microscope, then politicians and managers will know what to do about it. "What gets measured, gets managed" is a catchphrase which has rung around many public sector management conferences and workshops. The most ambitious – or most naive – version of this vision envisages the state of grace as one in which programme decisions become almost automatic. In this managerial utopia the performance measures will show what is working and what is not, and budgetary allocations, divisional targets, personal objectives (articulated through the appraisal system) and performance pay are then all lined up behind the most effective and efficient activities. The best available choices can be virtually read off from the performance information routinely furnished to top decision makers and line managers alike. Everyone knows the score.

There are several difficulties with this form of belief in measurement – and even in much less extreme credos than "automaticity."

The aim of this chapter is to explore these difficulties, identifying the limitations of measurement as a way of judging public services. The "message," however, is not that the measurement approach should be abandoned (a pointless message anyway, since too many governments are too far down the measurement road). Rather the argument will be that measurement activities need to be rethought so as to integrate them more carefully with traditional concerns about the structuring of democratic institutions and the quality of public debate. Performance measurement can be immensely useful and illuminating, but measurements will always be only one component in the process of taking public decisions, and frequently quite a limited and fragile one at that. It is from the interactions between data, institutional structures, and the play of political ideas and doctrines, that policies and programs emerge and evolve.

THREE SPECIES OF MEASUREMENT PROBLEM

Returning to "what gets measured gets managed," a first observation would be that the catchphrase would be more accurate if it were re-worded as "What gets measured, gets attention" – which is a far cry from getting managed. But the difficulties go deeper than this. One may distinguish at least three, interacting types of problem:

- Conceptual problems (how far are the measures meaningful and understandable to the various social, political, and public service groups which are affected by them?)
- Motivational problems (mainly – though not entirely – small "p" problems of bureaucratic politics: who measures who, for what purposes and with what safeguards against distortion and misuse?)
- Technical problems (can everything important be measured, and measured reliably, at reasonable cost and without too much delay?)

The thrusting public sector managers and political reformers of the late 20th and early 21st centuries are hardly the first would-be improvers to face these difficulties. It should not be forgotten that, for example, President Brezhnev and the Soviet central planners collided with them thirty years ago. Thus, at the 1976 Communist Party Congress, Mr. Brezhnev found there was a need to warn against the temptation for enterprise managers to succumb to the "chase after intermediate results" (Pollitt, 1990, 170–171). Even further back, the u.s. federal government attempted to introduce performance budgeting in the late 1940s and 1950s. It then launched PPBS during the 1960s, and Management by Objectives and ZBO during the 1970s – all systems founded upon the development of new areas of measurement and calculation. Yet each of these fell well short of its original aspirations – despite leaving useful residues of practice and perspective, each is now famous mainly as an acronym for failure (General Accounting Office, 1997a; Jones and McCaffrey, 1997, 48). History furnishes many other examples of obstacles in the way of realising the appealing vision of measured governance.

In this chapter I will discuss each of the three categories of problem, in the order indicated above. Having identified some of the most general difficulties, the final section ("Down the measurement road") will take a more positive – and a more normative – turn. It will briefly examine some possible elements for a system that would provide better answers than we yet have to the question: "How good is the public service?"

CONCEPTUAL PROBLEMS: MEASURING AND VALUING

"A man who knows the price of everything and the value of nothing" (Lord Darlington, in Oscar Wilde's *Lady Windermere's Fan*, 1896).

Wilde's memorable quip should alert us to the danger that governments may end up knowing how much everything costs, how long everything takes, what percentage of errors are committed in processing various kinds of claim, how many output targets have been met and many other things, yet will remain ignorant of the values which different groups of citizens place upon different public services, and of the reasons why those values are held.

In the play, Lord Darlington delivers his now-famous line when he is asked by another character to define a cynic. However, the definition might also be thought to fit some other contemporary characters – a certain type of accountant, for example, or managers who are a little short on imagination.

The basic conceptual problems are simply stated. Let us assume for a moment that we could measure the costs and the results of some public service with great accuracy. Let us further assume that these measurements showed the service to benchmark among the best in the world. Perhaps it is a state school system and it shows low costs per pupil combined with high standardized test scores on most subjects in the curriculum. Does this make it a "good" service? My answer is "perhaps." It depends whether citizens, students, and parents place a high value on low costs and high test scores. Most probably, many of them will. But most probably, also, there will actually be considerable diversity among the three groups (citizens, students, and parents) as to what exactly is most important in education. Some will value test achievements but others will be interested in the inculcation of self-discipline and others still will place happiness, or creativity, or the encouragement of high ethical standards, or the separation of girls from boys, above passing exams. In a modern society it is highly unlikely that there will be a complete value consensus on such issues. This opens up the possibility that what will be a "good" school for one group of students may be an unsatisfactory school for another.

The school system example is actually a less controversial one than many other public services. Take, as three more difficult cases, prisons, unemployment benefits payment offices, and the u.k. Child Support Agency. For all three there are widely divergent views as to what should count as "good." Some groups in society want to see prisons as places of punishment – harsh regimes which exact a price for the inmates' previous anti-social behaviour. Others want these same institutions to act as rehabilitation vehicles, preparing prisoners for the most rapid possible return to normal society. Quite clearly the prison regime that would be designed to fit the first objective would be different from the one that would be designed to fit the second. Equally, there is a divergence between those who see unemployment benefits principally as a means of permitting the unfortunate to continue to live a relatively normal life and those who insist that such benefits should be set at the lowest possible level so as to oblige the lazy and the "scroungers" actively to seek jobs. The performance indicators this latter group might devise for an unemployment benefits service would look rather different from those the former group would choose – and they would also be interpreted differently. As for the third example, the u.k. Child Support Agency was from the beginning surrounded by controversy, part of which was related to the existence of widely divergent views in society as to the fundamental desirability (or otherwise) of chasing separated fathers and forcing them to pay more towards the upkeep of their offspring.

These are some of the fundamental reasons why performance indicator sets for some public services can never be "complete" or "objective" or even stable over long periods of time (there are also motivational reasons, which will be dealt with in the next section). For the more socially controversial or complex programs, any feasible set of indicators will probably never be large and diverse enough to capture all the aspects which all the stakeholders deem to be important to them. Still less can they be safely aggregated to form some single index of how "good" things are (however much budget staff might delight in such a yardstick). Furthermore, values shift over time, and thus indicator sets may need to shift too. Public attitudes to – for example – long queues, opening times, unmarried mothers, the sensitivity of public services to ethnic minorities or the physically disabled, and many other things – seem to have shifted significantly within a generation. It is worth adding that shifts in fashion for dominant indicators are by no means confined to the public sector. In a seminal article, Meyer and Gupta show how measures of corporate performance in the market sector of the economy have also undergone frequent shifts over time (Meyer and Gupta, 1994).

Of course, not every public service bristles with the same level of controversy as prisons or schools or child support. One imagines that there exists a wider social consensus over, say, the appropriate measurement of the performance of an agency which issues driving licences or collects road tax. Users will presumably want it to be simple, fast, cheap, and polite. Indicators can be devised to represent each of these qualities. Yet even here there can be complexities. A government may wish to use driving licences as an instrument in an environmental campaign to discourage car ownership (by making driving licenses or car tax, or both, increasingly expensive). Or it may be concerned to identify and disqualify would-be drivers with a record of alcohol abuse (and therefore want to check the status of applicants very carefully). Nevertheless, the main point stands – some services are simpler and more likely to command social consensus than others, and it is an empirical question as to which these are.

Some commentators would see the foregoing as far too pessimistic. After all, it may be objected, opinion polling and customer satisfaction surveys have now been developed into a fine art. The current Labour government in the U.K. has made extensive use of these techniques. When Mr. Blair writes that "People want more money spent on education, health, crime prevention and transport. They will get it," he knows that his assertion is supported by extensive survey data (Chancellor of the Exchequer, 1998, forward). Similarly, the Blair administration has made much of the formation of a 5,000-strong "People's Panel" which is consulted on a range of public service issues. At $184,000 per annum this seems a bargain if it can ensure that public services measures are aligned with social values.

Unfortunately, of course, it is not – and could not be – as simple as that. There may be a high degree of consensus in favour of spending more on health care, but this consensus is likely to begin to break down as soon as one enquires which of the many kinds of health care fresh monies should first be allocated to, or, indeed, exactly how the performance of a particular health care activity should be judged. At a more detailed level, if the People's Panel works perfectly then it will reflect the kinds of value differences alluded to above – still leaving the government to decide how far to balance or choose between the different values and orders of preference which exist "out there" in the community. Cleavages of view between service users and tax-paying non-users are common, particularly so when the users may in some sense be defined as "non-contributors" (criminals, immigrants, even the long-term unemployed). The saying "to govern is to choose" is not outdated by the availability of survey data. Indeed, such data may make the choices even harder to arrive at, in so far as governments may now see all the more clearly which groups they are disappointing by their decisions, and by how much. The Blair government has already come in for considerable criticism for appearing to trim to the tune of the pollsters on a number of issues, such as policies affecting the countryside. Governing involves more than minimizing current levels of citizen dissatisfaction.

This last point is so fundamental that it deserves an illustrative example. Assume that a management reform has brought together the system for allocating a local educational budget with a system for measuring and comparing the quality of individual local schools. (In fact this would be a considerable advance since, as we shall see later, the integration of budgeting and performance measurement has generally proven very hard to achieve.) Further assume that there is a reasonable local consensus that the measures in place capture the most important features of a "good education." The results show that school X is performing well on all counts, school Y is average, and school Z has low quality scores all round. What, then, should be the consequence for budgetary resource allocation? One strategy would be to reward the successful, shifting resources away from Z (and possibly Y as well) so as to reinforce the fine achievement at X. Another possibility would be the reverse – to shift money or staff away from X and Y in an attempt to infuse the "failing" school – Z – with fresh resources for improvement. This second strategy could be further supported by arguments that, per pound spent, bigger gains could be expected at the failing school than at the already excellent school (where the frontiers of efficiency had already been reached). It could be represented as an egalitarian strategy, seeking to give every child in the locality an equal chance. On the other hand, such egalitarianism might well be received as acutely demotivating by the staff and parents of school X, whose reward for winning the performance race was to have their budget cut! Whatever strategy was chosen, the final decision would no doubt be politically very difficult. But note that the existence of a performance measurement system, and the policy of linking it with the allocation of resources, however impeccable from the point of view of rational policy making, has probably made the job of the decision makers more rather than less difficult (at least from a political point of view). Previously the budget could have been allocated according to some general principles, or by making incremental changes from the historical distribution, without the complication of having to face performance data on individual schools.

Furthermore, it is not simply a matter of differences between groups or sections of society. There is also the fact that real people, unlike some economists' models of real people, do not appear to possess transitive, coherent, stable preferences. On the contrary, they seem to want mutually contradictory things, according to the moment, the context, and the way issues are presented. Lower taxation but more spent on education and the health service. Greater protection for privacy but no censorship. A cleaner environment but no more restrictions or taxation on the motorist. And so on.

In short, what constitutes a "good" public service in the eyes of a diverse, multicultural citizenry will itself be (at any given moment) somewhat diverse and (over time) subject to change. No amount of measurement can "solve" value differences of his kind, and neither can measurement alone dictate what actions should follow when performances are assessed as good or poor. Optimists argue that, in practice, for many public services, the differences and the rates of change in values are not unmanageably great. They therefore conclude that a single set of key performance indicators can represent the consensual preferences of the majority without too much distortion. Public services can be steered in line with democratically confirmed priorities. The less optimistic suggest that both the variety of views and their volatility are much greater than is often supposed, and that this renders much performance measurement of doubtful validity. One weakness of this more critical position is that it leaves unanswered the question of how public services are to be steered and shaped, if not by measurement of some kind?

A middle position between these two extremes might be to acknowledge that performance measurement will always be imperfect but can, in certain contexts, perform at least two useful functions. First, up to a point, it can guide managers and service deliverers and – when carefully presented – can enhance the quality of democratic debate about what services should be doing. But it can do these two things much less well for some types of issue than others (see section on technical problems below) and, even where measurement works relatively smoothly, it can hardly ever achieve "automaticity." Measures almost always need to be interpreted, and combined with other, non-quantitative considerations, sensibilities and values, before the "tough choices" can be made. Knowing what is happening out there – and even knowing what the citizenry think of it – is not at all the same as knowing what to do next.

MOTIVATIONAL PROBLEMS

Our measures are not misleading, they measure the things we want them to measure; they may not measure the things you want them to measure (H.M.Treasury official, responding to questions from a Parliamentary Select Committee about PIs in the public sector expenditure white paper – House of Commons, 1988).

It has been widely recognized that the attempt to measure aspects of public service performance frequently leads to resistance, gaming, and other motivationally based distortions, both inside and outside the organizations responsible for service delivery (Hood, 1976; Pollitt, 1990; Smith, 1993). Sociologists, in particular, have documented such distortions for more than half a century. For example, imposition of the paraphenalia of target-setting and performance measurement can lead to staff reducing effort and commitment – so as to achieve the required standard and nothing more (Gouldner, 1954). It can also lead to "tunnel vision," where concentration on some measured aspect of performance leads to the neglect of some other, important but unmeasured aspect (Smith, 1993). Other perversions can arise from the temptation to manipulate data so as to give the best possible impression of the organization's performance (Hencke, 1998; National Audit Office, 1995).

Such distortions are by no means particular to the public sector. Meyer and Gupta (1994, 310) formulate a general proposition concerning the tendency for performance indicators to get "worn out" and progressively less useful as time goes by. They write of a loss of variability, defined as "a measure's capacity to capture a range of performance outcomes":

performance measures lose variability for several reasons. One is positive learning resulting in actual performance improvement. Another is perverse learning resulting in the appearance but not the fact of improvement. Running down also occurs due to selection of high performers, and suppression of measures exposing persistent differences in performance outcomes.

Clearly, while the first of these three reasons is a virtuous one, the second and third are perverse and are directly linked to motivational considerations.

It would be most unwise to assume that mere awareness of the existence of such perverse effects means that they can always be foreseen and eliminated. For example, when, in the early 1990s, a publication count was made one basis for "scoring" the quality of research in u.k. university departments, the number of journals went up, the number of publications went up, and some departments started to "buy in" high-publishing individual academics just before the deadline for the count. All this "gaming" was perfectly understandable – and to some extent foreseen – but it happened nonetheless. Its relationship to more fundamental concepts of underlying research quality was, to put it mildly, opaque.

New Zealand has become famous for the relative coherence and sophistication of its public management reforms (Boston et al., 1996; Pollitt and Summa, 1997). It is therefore particularly significant to find a New Zealand minister acknowledging that the new, intensively measurement-oriented system contains dangers:

One [danger is that] risky, unattractive but nevertheless important functions might start to fall between the cracks, or that absurd demarcation disputes might arise, of the kind that used to be endemic in the cloth-cap trade unions of old. If 'output fixation' distracts departments from outcomes and 'contract fixation' encourages them to ignore everything that isn't actually specified, aren't these things very likely to happen? (The Hon. Paul East, Minister of State Services, addressing senior New Zealand public managers, October 9, 1997 – East, 1997)

The minister's remarks draw attention to one of the limits of the measurement approach – at least when it is combined with a "contract fixation." If only what gets measured gets attention and – crucially – if trust is low (so that what is written down in the rules and contracts becomes all-important), then complex services of the type that are common in the public sector become almost impossible to manage. There are just too many aspects that have to be specified, measured, and monitored. In the mid-1990s a research student of mine found a local authority contract for cutting the grass in public spaces that ran to more than 70 pages of detail. It was certainly performance-oriented, but was it sensible? Achieving good performance frequently involves crucial variables which are very difficult to specify in the form of quantitative indicators. Current attempts to formulate a general model of effectiveness in government organizations stress the importance of these measurement-slippery factors, including supportive behaviour by key external stakeholders, optimal operating autonomy, possession of an attractive mission and certain types of leadership behaviour (Ingraham, Thompson, and Sanders, 1998; Rainey and Steinbauer, 1999). Sensitive performance measurement can work alongside these qualitative factors, but clumsy measurement may work against them.

It should be noted that contemporary trends in public service delivery can accentuate motivational measurement problems. As has been widely observed, the fashion in many countries is increasingly for service delivery through "partnerships," and for programs and projects to include some sort of competitive bidding procedure for scarce funds. Two recent empirical studies in the U.K. noted that there was:

a tendency for bids to stress quantifiable output measures over qualitative outcomes (and to 'talk these up') (Lowndes and Skelcher, 1998, 326).

The existence of possible motivational distortions to measurement (allied with the normal human propensity for error) mean that it is desirable to validate performance data. This is an area into which national audit bodies have been moving in several countries; for example, in 1998 the U.K. National Audit Office produced a handbook entitled *Validation of Performance Measures* and since 1993 the Swedish Riksrevisionsverket has audited agencies' annual performance reports. In some cases data have been found to be wildly inaccurate – Boivard and Gregory cite an example of a survey which revealed that what had previously been a 100% success rate for trainees needed to be revised downwards to 25% (Boivard and Gregory, 1996, 264; see also Hencke, 1998).

Alongside measurement of results, target-setting is another activity which merits cautious scrutiny. Who sets targets, and with what intentions – to stretch an organization by giving it a tough challenge, to have an easy life, to shift attention from one doubtful aspect to another, more favourable one? In the case of the U.K.'s Next Steps agencies it appears that one motive behind the benchmarking exercise launched in 1995 was the suspicion of the then Deputy Prime Minister that agencies were putting forward targets which were often no tougher – and sometimes easier – than in previous years (Chancellor of the Duchy of Lancaster, 1997, 8–15, and interviews).

These aspects of the "politics of performance" are by their nature difficult to map and assess, but it would be naive to assume that all was well and checking was not required – especially when (as is increasingly the case) an organization's revenues are linked to its measured performance. "Gaming" around performance measures usually takes place on a different time scale from the value shifts referred to in the section on conceptual problems. As Meyer and Gupta (1994) show, conceptual fashions shift over the medium or long term, and may represent genuine (or at least cyclical) developments in thinking about the nature of performance. Gaming, however, takes place in the short run, and has as its main purpose to maximize one's score under the existing system, and thereby "save face." When performance measures are linked to issues of status, reputation, promotion or revenue, then the design of a PI system inevitably becomes also the design of a system of incentives and penalties. For this purpose, one might argue, the knowledge of the social psychologist is just as relevant as that of the manager or the accountant.

TECHNICAL PROBLEMS

Outstanding maintenance applications over 52 weeks old: 1994/95 target = 1%, outturn = 50%. Note: older cases became increasingly complex to clear and effort focused on newer cases (extract from the entry for the Social Security Child Support Agency in the 1996 Next Steps Agency Review – Chancellor of the Duchy of Lancaster, 1997, 131).

A good individual measure is one which is valid, reliable, functional and "owned" by those who collect and use the data (Pollitt and Bouckaert, 1995, chapter 2). A good set of measures needs to have additional properties. For example, the set should cover all the aspects of the service which are of importance to the major stakeholders (comprehensiveness) yet should not be so large as to be unintelligible (transparency). In practice, President Nixon's 1973 Federal Productivity Program generated more than 3,000 performance indicators; by the late 1980s health authorities in the U.K. were using a set of well over 1,000 indicators and the review of the 1996 performance of the U.K.'s Next Steps agencies – mainly consisting of lists of indicators – ran to 314 pages (Chancellor of the Duchy of Lancaster, 1997).

An indicator set should also be reasonably stable over time – otherwise it becomes impossible for users, legislators or even the managers themselves reliably to identify trends over time (and therefore be able to say whether the service is getting better or worse). A recent study of decentralized management in u.k. schools, hospitals, and socially-rented housing organizations found that it was rare for any of these service delivery agencies to possess time series stretching back for more than a very short period. Data categories and organizational boundaries had changed repeatedly (Pollitt, Birchall, and Putman, 1998). Another study – of the "Key Performance Indicators" for ten u.k. Next Steps agencies – showed that more than two-thirds of these indicators were dropped or replaced within a six-year period (Talbot, 1997, 2). As noted earlier, there seems to be a strong tendency for individual indicators to "wear out" and be modified or replaced (Meyer and Gupta, 1994). Sometimes this cycling may be perfectly justifiable (values have shifted; a measure has ceased to discriminate; a technical improvement has been discovered), but on other occasions measures may be changed for defensive reasons – to conceal or obscure aspects of performance which do not redound to the credit of the body concerned.

Furthermore, the linkages between objectives, inputs, outputs, and indicators are often obscure or absent. In Talbot's 1996 study, almost half the agencies' aims and objectives did not seem to be covered by any indicator at all. In Canada, the 1997 Treasury Board publication *Accounting for Results* was claimed to mark a step forward in performance reporting (President of the Treasury Board, 1997). "This document and the accompanying Departmental Performance Reports set out the government's result commitments and provide information on achievements related to those commitments" (p1). However, closer inspection revealed that few of the departmental commitments were quantified, and the main measures presented were the aggregated budgetary inputs for each agency (not broken down into activities or programs). One might say that this was a case – by no means a unique one – where considerably more measurement was required before the title of the document could be fully justified. In the u.s., analyses of the first generation of departmental and agency performance plans under the 1993 Government Performance and Results Act revealed frequent gaps between goals, strategies, measures, and planned actions. The following assessment specifically concerned the Department of State, but other analyses made it clear that some of the identified weaknesses were widespread:

The Department of State's fiscal year 1999 annual performance plan generally falls short of meeting the Results Act's requirements. Specifically, State's plan does not clearly describe the agency's intended performance, the strategies and resources that will be used to achieve the performance goals, or how it will ensure credibility of the information used to assess agency performance (General Accounting Office, 1998; see also the challenges identified in General Accounting Office, 1997b).

More broadly, an overview of public management reform in ten oecd countries comes to the conclusion that reliable measures of increases in efficiency and effectiveness resulting from those reforms are rare, and that, despite much rhetoric, "disconnects" between success claims and valid evidence are commonplace (Pollitt and Bouckaert, 2000, chapter 5).

Nevertheless, much experience of designing indicator sets has been accumulated, and much sensible advice has been formulated (e.g., h.m. Treasury, 1992; Likierman, 1993). However, knowing what problems may arise is not the same as being able to solve them. Although much progress has undoubtedly been made, it is noticable that, in the u.k. at least, some of the basic imbalances identified in the mid-1980s – such as an over-emphasis on process, economy, and efficiency measures relative to measures of outcomes, quality, and user satisfaction – are still present in pi systems a decade later (Pollitt, 1986; Carter, 1998). It is just so much less difficult and less risky to measure what is going on inside the organization than to go outside and begin measuring outcomes, impacts, and the attitudes of citizens to those impacts. This seems to afflict many countries – it appears in New Zealand (East, 1997; Pollitt, 1997) and in many evaluations of EU structural fund programs (Centre for European Evaluation Expertise, 1998). [This is not to suggest that all process and output measurement should be abandoned. Such data are essential for management, and also form the basis for audit trails. It is a commonplace that good internal monitoring of processes and outputs are a crucial foundation for successful evaluations.]

Another common weakness of PI systems is that they link weakly or not at all to processes of budgeting and resource allocation. The testimony to the failures and difficulties here is very extensive (see, e.g., Bouckaert and Ulens, 1998, 4; Gianakis, 1996; Jones and McCaffrey, 1997, 47–49; Mayne, 1996, 13–14; Rubin, 1992, 13; Sandberg, 1996, 167; Sorber, 1996, 311; Summa, 1995). In many jurisdictions budget allocations – especially at the higher levels – continue to be made with little or no relation to measured performance. In a review of half a century of American attempts to establish performance budgeting the General Accounting Office concluded as follows:

Since 1950, the federal government has attempted several governmentwide initiatives designed to better align spending decisions with expected performance...Consensus exists that all of these efforts, whether launched by the legislative or executive branch, failed to shift the focus of the federal budget process from its longstanding concentration on the items of government spending to the results of its programs (General Accounting Office, 1997a, summary).

The obstacles to such attempts, both in the U.S. federal government and elsewhere, have been partly motivational – for example, politicians do not necessarily want budget trade-offs to be illuminated by performance data (as in the example of schools X, Y, and Z cited above). However, some of the problems have been more technical in character. For example, one persistent technical problem is that "performance" is usually best understood in relation to a program (to reduce crime, improve reading skills among deprived communites, etc.) rather than a particular institution.

However, most budgets – and their associated accounting and accountability requirements – are tied to specific institutions, rather than to programs. Increasingly, programs are implemented by a variety of departments and agencies, working (hopefully) in partnership. This makes it hard to link budgets to programmatic measures, and also increases the difficulty of achieving consensus on what the appropriate measures should be (not to speak of responsibility for "results").

This leads us to the more general point that the sets of measures used by different actors in the process of policy making, implementation, monitoring, auditing, evaluation, and use need to be related to each other and mutually compatible. If the annual budget-making process proceeds on a basis which pays little or no attention to the performance indicators used for reporting to the legislature, then this divergence is a potential source of tension and confusion for members of the organization concerned. What may have begun as a technical problem takes on motivational aspects. To achieve a reasonable degree of integration between these historically and usually quite separate systems is very difficult and seems to take a long time – if it is ever achieved. One current trend in a number of countries is to adopt accruals accounting systems. In theory these hold out the promise of providing a more transparent basis for measuring the financial performance of public sector organizations (Likierman, 1995; 1998). However, anyone with a sense of the history of previous attempts to integrate planning and budgeting, or performance management and financial management, will "wait and see" before accepting any claim that accruals accounting can "fix" this particular problem. The literature already contains warnings of various kinds (e.g., Heald and Georgiou, 1995; Jones, 1998; Gillibrand and Hilton, 1998).

Beyond the problem of integrating different management systems (budgeting, accounting, etc.) within a particular organization lies a yet more challenging layer of complexity. This may be summarized in the question raised above: "How may performance be assessed when a program is being delivered by an assortment of quite different types of organization, rather than by a single organization or homogenous set of organizations?"

Each constituent organization may have its own set of targets, standards, measurement systems, etc. Such complexity is, in many areas of public policy, becoming the norm rather than the exception. In U.K. community care, for example, local authorities are supposed to cooperate with health authorities, voluntary organizations, and commercial companies in order to deliver a patchwork of local services to a diverse body of users. Urban regeneration programs are equally, if not more complex. In the case of the EU's structural funds, the complexity becomes multinational as well as multi-level and public–private, with the European Commission, the national governments, regional authorities, local authorities, and local enterprises all routinely involved. Little wonder, then, that evaluation of such programs becomes problematic and reliable monitoring data are often hard to come by (Barbier and Simonin, 1997; Centre for European Evaluation Expertise, 1998; Lowndes and Skelcher, 1998; PUMA, 1999).

Finally, we come to the procrustian technical issue of "compared with what?" Against which comparative criterion is one to pronounce a particular value for an indicator as good, acceptable or inadequate? Is an 80% exam pass rate acceptable? Is a cost of $10,000 per net job created high, low, or about right? In general terms there are a number of standard responses to this type of question, each with its own mixture of advantages and limitations. The most common comparisons are as follows:

1 Against the organization's own targets (as with the Child Support Agency example quoted at the head of this section);
2 Against own past performance (e.g., by time series);
3 Against other similar organizations (e.g., "league tables" of schools or hospitals, as in the U.K. system);
4 Against some professional standard (the ambulance must arrive within x minutes of the call; the Ph.D student must receive at least y hours of personal supervision per semester);
5 Against some abstract model of a well-functioning organization (e.g., the European Foundation for Quality Management's Business Excellence Model – see Next Steps Team, 1998 and Talbot, 1997).

"Benchmarking" is a popular term denoting a process which, in its different forms ("competitive," "generic," "functional," etc.) uses different types of comparison, including 3, 4, and 5 above. The broadest comparisons may be achieved using technique 5) – which is that recently adopted by U.K. Next Steps agencies and which is also being studied by OECD/PUMA. It will permit comparisons between public agencies with widely differing missions, between public and private sector organizations, and between organizations in different countries. It is, however, an approach which is only just beginning to be used and which is also only just beginning to be subjected to a serious critique (Talbot, 1997). There are the usual arguments between particularity (favouring comparisons of types 1 and 2 and to some extent 3), and generality (favouring 4 and 5). What is clear is that the technical choice of comparator can have significant consequences. The same service may score well against one criterion and poorly against another. Focusing on a series of "big issues," Bok (1997) argues that the U.S. federal government has significantly improved its performance over recent decades but that if one changes the criterion from (in my terms) 2 to 3 one is obliged to conclude that U.S. governments have done significantly less well than the governments of Canada, France, Germany, Japan, Sweden, and the U.K.

Left to their own devices many organizations (and governments) would presumably choose the types of criteria against which they show up best. Yet a "balanced scorecard" containing most or all of the kinds of criteria listed above is likely to be too expensive and elaborate for most small- or medium-sized organizations to contemplate.

To summarize, extensive national and international experience has been accumulated on the subject of designing and implementing performance indicator systems. This indicates the frequent presence of certain technical problems. Principal among them are:

1 An undue emphasis on process measures (which are easier to collect) rather than output or outcome measures;

2 An undue emphasis on output rather than outcome measures, resulting in some loss of focus on final impacts. Data
  concerning outcomes tend to be more expensive and difficult
  to collect, as well as more difficult confidently to attribute to
  the activity or program in question;
3 The absence of clear links between an organization's stated
  aims, its internal allocation of resources, and the key indicators by which it measures its performance;
4 Too-frequent changes in indicators. These undermine the
  possibility of constructing time series and facilitate gaming
  and opportunistic behaviours;
5 Failure to integrate indicator systems from different parts of
  an organization's operations and – even more so – across sets
  of organizations which are working in partnerships or networks to deliver programs;
6 Failure to make a clear or reasoned choice of criteria for comparison.

NOTHING BUT PROBLEMS?

At this point it may be necessary to reiterate that this chapter is
intended to examine the limits and common problems of measurement as a way of knowing about the character of public services, but not to deny either its fundamental usefulness or the
scope for its further development. It should be readily acknowledged that it is usually much harder – if not impossible – to form
a reliable judgment as to the quality of public services without
measurement. It is, for example, tremendously useful to know
how many schoolchildren can read and write to a particular standard at a particular age. It is similarly vital for there to be information in the public domain about peri-operative mortality rates
for specific procedures, by hospital and by individual doctor. Had
such data been widely available in the past, certain tragedies
would more likely have been avoided, or at least detected earlier.
Even today such information is not available in many jurisdictions, despite its technical feasibility. Similarly, it is important for
managers to know whether the error rates in processing claims or

making grants are moving up or down, and how they compare between one office and another. And changes in the rate of escapes from prisons are a legitimate matter of public interest (Chancellor of the Duchy of Lancaster, 1997, 114). But this is not a study about the successes of performance measurement. It is about its limits, written in a climate where performance indicators seem to have achieved wide ascendancy, and are not infrequently used as ways of closing debate and/or of dismissing other kinds of information or insight.

DOWN THE MEASUREMENT ROAD

In this last section I turn from analysis to (mild) prescription – or, at least, suggestion. Consideration will be given to what an advanced system of performance measurement in a modern liberal democracy might look like – given the various pitfalls and limitations noted in earlier sections. Perhaps I should add that the foregoing analysis does not stand or fall by this more prescriptive part of the essay. Readers are at liberty to agree with much of what has been said so far, yet still profoundly to disagree with the recipe offered below!

In any case, the elements suggested below would not solve all the problems referred to above. Some of these "problems" are actually more properly termed "trade-offs" or "dilemmas" – awkward choices rather than solvable problems. Some are cyclical or recurrent problems which occur as performance indicator systems evolve through time. There is a sense in which there may be a curvilinear relationship between the stability of indicator systems and their usefulness as inputs to debates about policy and program success. Over-rapid change in indicators destroys the opportunity to build up interpretive sophistication and it removes the possibility of creating time series. Over-sluggish change among indicators reduces their discriminatory power and permits the growth of gaming and manipulation (Meyer and Gupta, 1994). The most that might be claimed for the suggestions developed here is that they would recognize these dilemmas and directly address some of the most persistent biases and weaknesses which have been observable in performance measurement systems in a number of countries over the past quarter of a century.

It should also be remarked, en passant, that the "much more measurement" road is not the only one. To say that all OECD members are taking an interest in measurement is not to say they are all doing the same thing (Pollitt and Bouckaert, 2000). The "measurement mentality" does not seem to have gone as far in, say, Germany or France as in North America, Australasia, and the U.K. The "New Public Management" model, which places performance measurement at the centre of things is by no means universally regarded as the best way forward (see, e.g., Derlien, 1997; Flynn and Strehl, 1996). For example, the use of market-type mechanisms (MTMS), which often require step-change increases measurement and monitoring, has been less wide-spread in France, Germany, and even the Nordic countries than in the U.K. and Australasia. In the former group of countries the distinctiveness of public service is perhaps more readily acknowledged, compliance with the law still occupies a more predominant place in the general scheme of things, and the virtues of competition are not seen as having quite such a near-universal domain. Various combinations of trust and ethical commitment are sometimes cost-effective alternatives to regimes of intensive performance monitoring. One of the weaknesses of the NPM approach, at least in its more puritanical forms, is the way in which it can undermine both trust and commitment within public service organizations (Canberra Bulletin of Public Administration, 1997; Kernaghan, 1997). Once lost, both are hard to restore. It would be misleading, however, to make too much of this point: performance indicators have been increasingly resorted to in all these countries, even if the balance sought between modernizing the state and minimizing it has varied.

At any event, the main objective of this final section is to suggest ways in which the validity and reliability of measurements of public service performance could be increased. These remarks will be organized in the form of two broad propositions. Both concern the greater integration of performance measurement systems with the wider institutions and processes of democratic governance:

- There needs to be a more determined attempt to relate measurement issues to the changed institutional patterns in reformed public sectors, and
- Performance measurement needs to continue to move "outwards"

Each will be discussed in turn.

Classic NPM thinking almost instinctively favours decentralization and organizational flexibility. Single purpose agencies are preferred to multi-purpose bureaucratic ministries, "mixed markets" of provision are preferred to exclusively public sector service production. Organizations are expected to adjust to their changing environments – and in practice they are frequently forcibly "adjusted" by restructurings from on high (Boston et al., 1996; Pollitt, Birchall, and Putman, 1998). However, the argument here will run directly counter to these NPM orthodoxies (and thereby risk the usual taunts of conservatism and backwardness). The proposition is that what good data sets require are uniformity and stability. Data need to be collected in standardised and well-understood formats right across the relevant program or policy field. The core of what is collected should not be subject to constant change.

This does *not* mean that the format of service delivery organizations must somehow be artificially frozen. What it does mean, however, is equally unfashionable: that there needs to be an adequately independent and powerful data authority that can ensure that data categories remain uniform and tolerably stable, even if the shape and identity of the organizations supplying that data are constantly changing. It makes no sense, for example, to pass a Government Performance and Review Act requiring the collection of more sophisticated data and then promptly institute other reforms which significantly inhibit the capacity of central agencies to demand information from service providers (Radin, 1998). Greater stability and uniformity would ease some of the technical problems identified earlier. Equally, when changes are envisaged (as the arguments above indicate will be far from rare) there is an obvious case for having the advantages and disadvantages of these aired by a body that does does not have the axe of its own performance to grind.

The notion of a central data authority will bear some further discussion. First, it is not necessary for such a body actually to *collect* the data itself. It can restrict itself to ensuring that the data are collected by others. Nor does it need to have any authority over additional data, which other public bodies may choose to collect for their own purposes. Second, the central data authority will need considerable independence. Whilst it should be required to take into account the compliance costs it is imposing on others, it should not be susceptable to political or managerial pressure to avoid collecting or publishing what it considers to be performance information which is in the public interest. Statutory independence is an ancient democratic device for minimizing certain kinds of motivational problem – especially with information. That is why national audit offices are usually given a high degree of autonomy. Third, the data authority's terms of reference should make it clear that it is a prime part of its mission to develop and supply key performance information to audiences "external" to executive government – the legislature, the general public and the media. The needs of such audiences are discussed further under the second main proposition, below.

There is also a need to validate the data which are supplied to the central data authority – that is, to check whether they are valid and reliable. However, a central data authority that has responsibility for designing core data sets may not be a sufficiently candid critic of its own design, so there would be some advantage in organizing validation as a separate function. Again, there is an argument for locating this function outside the executive, possibly with an existing audit institution. A number of audit offices have already started to operate in this field, including the Swedish RRV and the U.K. NAO (Pollitt et al., 1999):

The National Audit Office are at the forefront of developing the methodology by which performance measures can be validated and we would like to see greater public reporting and auditing of performance data (National Audit Office, 1997, 1).

Validation is not the only form of external investigation which is desirable in order to maintain the health of the system by which the strengths and weaknesses of our public services are measured. Validation reassures as to the validity and reliability of the data but it does not tell us why the performance of agency X or program Y is good or bad, improving or slipping. To achieve causal insights a more evaluation-like investigation is needed. Once more, in a liberal democracy, there are strong arguments for creating a capacity for such studies outside the executive. Audit offices are one possible home for an evaluation function, but they are not necessarily ideal (Pollitt et al., 1999, chapter 11). Another possibility would be free-standing evaluation units reporting to legislatures, or units situated in independent foundations on the u.s. or German models. The main point is that fully-fledged "performance governance" would include a capacity for independent, "summative" evaluations oriented primarily towards external, public accountability. In practice, however, most of the recent growth of evaluation in Europe has been of the internal, "formative" kind, aimed more at the needs of operational managers and program directors (see, e.g., Barbier and Simonin, 1997; Centre for European Evaluation Expertise, 1998; Pollitt, 1998; for more on the distinction between summative and formative, see Patton, 1997, 75–79). [The argument here is not against formative/managerial evaluations, which are necessary and useful and can make substantial contributions to the improvement of performance measurement systems, but rather for summative evaluations for public accountability as well.]

The second basic proposition was that performance measurement should continue to move "outwards." That is, encouragement should be given to those who are trying to effectuate the two crucial strategic shifts – from outputs to outcomes and from an internal, managerial audience to an external audience of legislators, media, citizens, and service users. Both shifts have begun (e.g. Chancellor of the Duchy of Lancaster, 1997; President of the Treasury Board, 1997; Prime Minister and Minister for the Cabinet Office, 1999) but both are difficult, and setbacks can easily occur.

It has to be admitted that, to date, the record of legislative interest in performance data has been less than overwhelming (e.g., Carter, Klein and Day, 1992, 182–183). On the other hand, the interests of the legislators and public have not necessarily been to the fore when indicator sets have been being designed (e.g., Boivard and Gregory, 1996, 265–268). A good example of this was the original u.k. Citizen's Charter, where central government issued a white paper containing all manner of measurable standards for public services without consulting the citizens who were supposed to be its beneficiaries (Prime Minister, 1991). Yet, despite the difficulties and limitations, in both the u.s. and the u.k. public interest in performance data about schools, universities, and hospitals has been considerable. Professionals on the "inside" sometimes decry both the validity of the data and the average level of public understanding, but these may be problems which diminish with more practice (on both sides) rather than reasons for abandoning the effort to supply the public with a type of information for which they clearly possess an appetite.

Thus one step towards encouraging greater public and political interest would be to give citizens and legislators a larger say in what is collected in the first place. This would involve the now-familiar mechanisms of focus groups, citizens' panels, and sample surveys. However, there would be significant differences from the way in which this has usually been done. It would not be a self-interested government or political party that was conducting the exercise in private, but a fully independent data authority in public. Nor would the questions asked be of the usual satisfaction type ("how satisfied are you with service X: very satisfied, fairly satisfied or not satisfied?"). Instead the data authority would seek to accumulate three crucial bodies of knowledge. The first would concern what information citizens would most like to have about the service in question. The second would focus on why this particular information was seen as being of prime significance. The third would concern the most effective channels and formats through and by which performance data could be communicated to different sections of the public. These might include leaflets, videos, television, and radio transmissions, the internet, displays in public buildings and spaces, and so on. One could see this kind of research as constituting one important strand in the currently fashionable (in the U.K.) topic of "education for citizenship."

By taking this direction, performance measurement would not be doing anything particularly new. One of the principles at the basis of the modern quality movement has long been that it is the customers, not the experts, who tell management what quality means to them (Pollitt and Bouckaert, 1995). For some jurisdictions, and some services, developments along these lines are already taking place. Yet there are also some public service organizations whose contacts with service users (and especially with the wider public) remain narrow and unimaginative. In the scenario envisaged here, citizens would be brought in at two levels. First, they would be consulted by the central data authority over the contents of the minimum data set for each main service. Second, they would also be consulted by the management of each service, who would be seeking a more detailed picture of user needs and preferences, geared to each context and locality. Both levels of activity would help ameliorate (though not remove) some of the conceptual difficulties alluded to earlier. Both would ensure that performance indicators sets changed with the times, but more in tune with public values and preferences and less because of managerial manipulation or purely technical momentum.

The above suggestions fall far short of comprehensiveness. Some of the problems identified in this paper would remain untouched, even if a central data authority, plus adequate collection, validation, and evaluation arrangements were to be put in place. Nevertheless, the establishment of a closer link between questions of institutional design and measurement issues, together with an increased emphasis on providing information for the public domain, could be important elements in a shift from performance management to democratic performance government.

BIBLIOGRAPHY

Barbier, J-C., and B. Simonin. 1997. European social programmes: can evaluation of implementation increase the appropriateness of the findings? *Evaluation* 3, 4, October:391-407.

Boivard, T., and D. Gregory. 1996. Performance indicators: the British experience, 239-273. In *Organisational Performance and Measurement in the Public Sector*, eds. A. Halachmi and G. Bouckaert. London: Quorum Books.

Bok, D. 1997. Measuring the performance of government, 55-76. In *Why People Don't Trust Government*, ed. J. Nye, P. Zelikow, and D. King. Cambridge, Mass.: Harvard University Press.

Boston, J., J. Martin, J. Pallot, and P. Walsh. 1996. *Public Management: the New Zealand Model*. Auckland: Oxford University Press.

Bouckaert, G. 1996. Measurement of public sector performance: some European perspectives, 223-237. In *Organisational Performance and Measurement in the Public Sector*, eds. A. Halachmi and G. Bouckaert. London: Quorum Books.

Bouckaert, G., and W. Ulens. 1998. *Mesure de la performance dans le service public: exemples étrangers pour les pouvoirs publics belges*. Bruxelles: Services Fédéraux des Affaires Scientifiques, Techniques et Culturelles.

Canberra Bulletin of Public Administration. 1997. *Public Service Legislation 1997* (theme issue), No.85, August:1-55.

Carter, N. 1998. On the performance of performance indicators, 177-194. In *Evaluation des politiques publiques*, eds. M-C. Kesler, P. Lascoumes, M. Setbon, and J-C. Thoenig. Paris: L'Harmattan.

Centre for European Evaluation Expertise. 1998. Development of evaluation of structural interventions in the member states. Draft synthesis, March, Lyon, C3E.

Chancellor of the Duchy of Lancaster. 1997. *Next Steps agencies in government: Review, 1996*, CM3579. London: The Stationary Office.

Chancellor of the Exchequer. 1998. Modern public services for Britain: investing in reform, Cm4011. London: The Stationary Office.

Derlien, H-U. 1997. *From administrative reform to administrative modernisation*. Verwaltungswissenschaftliche Beitrage 33, Bamberg, University of Bamberg.

East, P. 1997. From outputs to outcomes. Speech delivered by the Hon. Paul East, Minister of State Services, to the New Zealand Public Service Senior Management Conference, Wellington, October 9.

Flynn, N., and F. Strehl. 1996. *Public Sector Management in Europe*. London: Prentice Hall/Harvester Wheatsheaf.

Gaster, L. 1995. *Quality in Public Services: Managers' Choices*. Buckingham: Open University Press.

General Accounting Office. 1997a. Performance budgeting: past initiatives offer insight for GPRA implementation. GAO/AIMD-97-46. Washington DC, March 27.

_____ 1997b. Managing for results: analytic challenges in measuring performance, GAO/HEHS/GGD-97-138. Washington DC, May 30.

_____ 1998. The Results Act: observations on the Department of State's Fiscal Year 1999 annual performance plan, GAO/NSAID-98-210R. Washington DC, June 17.

Gianakis, G. 1996. Integrating performance measurement and budgeting, 127-143. In *Organisational Performance and Measurement in the Public Sector*, eds. A. Halachmi and G. Bouckaert. Westport CT: Quorum.

Gouldner, A. 1954. *Patterns of Industrial Bureaucracy*. New York: Free Press.

Gillibrand, A., and B. Hilton. 1998. Resource accounting and budgeting: principles, concepts and practice – the MoD case. *Public Money and Management* 18:2, April/June:21-28.

Heald, D., and G. Georgiou. 1995. Resource accounting: valuation, consolidation and accounting regulation. *Public Administration* 73:4, Winter:571-579.

Hencke, D. 1998. Jobcentres fiddled the figures. *Guardian*, January 8:2.

H.M.Treasury. 1992. Executive agencies: a guide to setting targets and measuring performance. London: HMSO.

Holmes, M., and D. Shand. 1995. Management reforms: some practitioner perspectives on the past ten years. *Governance* 8:4, October:551-578

Hood, C. 1976. *The Limits of Administration*. London: Wiley.

Hood, C., O. James, G. Jones, C. Scott, and T. Travers. 1998. Regulation inside government: where the new public management meets the audit explosion. *Public Money and Management* 18:2, April/June:61-68.

House of Commons. 1988. The Government's public expenditure plans 1988/89 to 1991/92, CM288, HC299, Second Report of the Treasury and Civil Service Committee, London: HMSO.

Ingraham, P., J. R. Thompson, and R. Sanders, R., eds. 1998. *Transforming Government: Lessons From the Reinvention Laboratories.* San Francisco: Jossey-Bass.

Jones, L., and J. McCaffrey. 1997. Implementing the chief financial officers act and the government performance and results act in the federal government. *Public Budgeting and Finance* 17:1, Spring:35-55.

Jones, R. 1998. The conceptual framework of resource accounting. *Public Money and Management* 18:2, April/June:11-16.

Joss, R., and M. Kogan. 1995. *Advancing quality: Total Quality Management in the National Health Service.* Buckingham: Open University Press.

Kernaghan, K. 1997. Values, ethics and public service, 101-111. In *Public Administration and Public Management: Experiences in Canada,* eds. J. Bourgault, M. Demers, and C. Williams. Quebec: Les Publications du Quebec.

Likierman, A. 1993. Performance indicators: 20 early lessons from managerial use. *Public Money and Management* 13:4, October/December:15-22.

_____ 1995. Resource accounting and budgeting: rationale and background. *Public Administration* 73:4, Winter:562-570.

_____ 1998. Resource accounting and budgeting where are we now? *Public Money and Management* 18:2, April/June:17-20.

Lowndes, V., and C. Skelcher. 1998. The dynamics of multi-organisational partnerships: an analysis of changing modes of governance. *Public Administration* 76:2, Summer:313-333.

Mayne, J. 1996. Implementing results-based management and performance-based budgeting: lessons from the literature. Discussion Paper No.73, Ottawa: Office of the Auditor General of Canada.

Meyer, M., and V. Gupta. 1994. The performance paradox. *Research in Organizational Behaviour* 16:309-369.

National Audit Office. 1995. *The Meteorological Office: Evaluation of Performance,* HC693, August 29. London: HMSO.

_____ 1997. *Annual Report, 1997.* London: National Audit Office.

Next Steps Team. 1998. *Towards Best Practice: an Evaluation of the First Two Years of the Public Sector Benchmarking Project, 1996-98.* London: Office of Public Service (Cabinet Office).

Patton, M. 1997. *Utilisation-focused Evaluation: the New Century Text,* 3rd ed. Thousand Oaks, Calif.: Sage.

Pollitt, C. 1986. Beyond the managerial model: the case for broadening performance assessment in government and the public services. *Financial Accountability and Management* 2:3, Autumn:155-170.

———. 1990. Performance indicators: root and branch, 167-178. In *Output and Performance Measurement in Government: the State of the Art,* eds. M. Cave, M. Kogan, and R. Smith. London: Jessica Kingsley.

———. 1997. Looking outcomes in the face: the limits of government action. Speech to the New Zealand Public Service Senior Management Conference, Wellington, October 9.

———. 1998. Evaluation in Europe: boom or bubble? *Evaluation* 4:2, April:214-224.

Pollitt, C., and G. Bouckaert. 1995. *Improving the Quality of European Public Services: Cases, Concepts and Commentary.* London: Sage.

———. 2000. *Reforming Public Management: a Comparative Analysis.* Oxford: Oxford University Press.

Pollitt, C., and H. Summa. 1997. Trajectories of reform: public management change in four countries. *Public Money and Management* 17:1, January/March:1-13.

Pollitt, C., J. Birchall, and K. Putman. 1998. *Decentralising Public Management: the British Experience.* Basingstoke: Macmillan.

Pollitt, C., X. Girre, J. Lonsdale, R. Mul, H. Summa, and M. Waerness. 1999. *Performance or Conformity? Public Management and Performance Audit in Five Countries.* Oxford: Oxford University Press.

Pollitt, C., and Bouckaert, G. 2000. *Public Management Reform: a Comparative Analysis.* Oxford: Oxford University Press.

Power, M. 1997. *The Audit Society: Rituals of Verification.* Oxford: Oxford University Press.

President of the Treasury Board. 1997. *Accounting for Results, 1997.* Ottawa: Treasury Board of Canada Secretariat.

Prime Minister. 1991. *The Citizen's Charter: Raising the Standard,* Cm1599. London: HMSO.

Prime Minister and Minister for the Cabinet Office. 1999. *Modernising Government,* Cm.4310. London: The Stationary Office.

PUMA. 1999. *Managing Accountability in Intergovernmental Partnerships,* PUMA/RD(99)4/Final. Paris: PUMA/OECD.

Radin, B. 1998. The government performance and review act (GPRA): hydra-headed monster or flexible management tool? *Public Administration Review* 58:4, July/August:307-316.

Rainey, H. G., and P. Steinbauer. 1999. Galloping elephants: developing elements of a theory of effective government organisation. *Journal of Public Administration Research and Theory*, J-Part 9:1:1-32.

Rubin, I. 1992. Budgeting: theory, concepts, methods, and issues, 3-22. In *Handbook of Public Budgeting*, ed. J. Rabin. New York: Marcel Dekker.

Sandberg, B. 1996. Annual performance accounting and auditing: is it possible? 167-186. In *Organisational Performance and Measurement in the Public Sector*, eds. A Halachmi and G. Bouckaert. London, Quorum Books.

Smith, P. 1993. Outcome-related performance indicators and organisational control in the public sector. *British Journal of Management* 4:135-151.

Sorber, B. 1996. Experiences with performance measurement in central government: the case of the Netherlands, 309-318. In *Organisational Performance and Measurement in the Public Sector*, eds. A. Halachmi and G. Bouckaert. London: Quorum Books.

Summa, H. 1995. Old and new techniques for productivity promotion: from cheese slicing to a quest for quality. In *Public Productivity Through Quality and Strategic Management*, eds. A. Halachmi and G. Bouckaert. Amsterdam: Ios Press.

Talbot, C. 1996. Ministers and agencies: responsibility and performance. Paper submitted to the House of Commons Public Services Committee, Pontypridd, University of Glamorgan Business School.

_____ 1997. Public performance: towards a public service excellence model. Discussion Paper No.1, Llantilio Crsenny, Monmouthshire, Public Futures.

Wholey, J. 1997. Trends in performance measurement: challenges for evaluators, 124-133. In *Evaluation for the 21st Century*, eds. E. Chelimsky and W. Shadish. Thousand Oaks, Calif.: Sage.

PART THREE

RETHINKING THE

BOUNDARIES

Blurring the Public–Private Divide

VINCENT WRIGHT

An overarching question about the revitalization of the public sector is where the dividing line between the public and the private sectors should be drawn. Over the past half century that line has moved back and forth several times. During the period from the 1950s until the 1970s the tendency was for the public sector to expand and to assume responsibilities that historically would have been private. Governments took responsibility for a variety of economic activities that as easily could have remained private, if generally publicly regulated, industries. There was also a massive expansion of social programs to include an ever widening array of social benefits that went to the middle classes as well as the less affluent.

The oil shocks of the 1970s, and particularly the election of a group of dedicated conservative leaders from the late 1970s onward, produced a major reversal of the role of government in Western democracies. Privatization and deregulation were the mechanisms for reducing the role of the state in economic affairs (Wright, 1994). Social programs were cut back, and in some cases eliminated entirely (Pierson, 1998). Retrenchment and modernization became euphemisms for a large-scale retreat of the state from the social and economic responsibilities it had assumed only a few decades previously. Further, for many politicians and for much of the public the private sector and the market have now become the exemplars of the most efficient and effective ways of achieving goals, whether public or private (Taylor-Gooby, 1998). After several decades of sustained attacks on the public sector there does appear to be a need for the revitalization, and perhaps the reconceptualization, of the public sector.

The shifts in the fortunes of public programs were mirrored in the fortunes of the public servants who administered those programs. In the immediate post-war period, and generally until the advent of the conservative governments mentioned above, public servants in most Western societies were respected, and assumed to be capable of managing the economy and society effectively. At the end of the century public servants generally are labelled as part of the problem, rather than part of the solution. The public service has been downsized along with other aspects of government, and the monopoly of career public servants over the most influential public sector positions has been lost. The idea of a set of exclusive analytic and managerial skills crucial in government in now rejected in favour of a generic approach in which management is management (see Stewart, 1998).

This chapter will examine the changing relationships between the public and private sectors, and the tension that now exists between the two. While using an historical perspective to frame the discussion, the principal issues and questions raised will be contemporary and prospective. What policies and activities are most appropriate, or essential, for government to retain as components of their distinctive role in the contemporary world? Do the activities identified as peculiarly public need to be performed by members of the public service, or are there alternative ways of delivering the services? How can government reclaim its legitimacy and justify its continued existence?

THE TRADITIONAL MODELS

The changes discussed briefly above occurred within the context of a collection of traditional models of public–private sector relationships that were at that time found to be inadequate. Although different conceptions of public–private relationships existed in different political settings, the general pattern was to emphasize the separation of the two sectors, and the consequent need for a clear dividing line between them. Likewise, conceptions of the public service then in common usage emphasized the need to maintain a distinct public service to ensure the probity and accountability of public action.

Different Traditional Models of Relationship

Although the several accepted models of public–private sector relationships did have some common features, they also had their distinctive features. They also arose in different social and political circumstances. Probably the most widely dispersed of the models was the Weberian conception of bureaucracy and of the nature of government (Weber, 1958). Even where the concept was not accepted as an operational definition of the appropriate relationships between the two sectors, this model was important for thinking about the appropriate means of organizing the public sector (see Page, 1994) and was (and is) part of the intellectual baggage of anyone interested in the nature of the public sector in industrialized democracies.

France and countries such as Spain and Italy, in which the conceptualization of the public sector has been greatly influenced by the "Napoleonic Model" (Wünder, 1995), have a somewhat different concept of the proper relationship between the public and private sectors. In the Napoleonic conception the public sector tends to exercise the dominant position in society, and the public sector has a history of taking a leading role in a number of economic and social sectors. Further, the elite prepared for service in the public sector tended, through *pantouflage*, to become powerful in the private sector as well. Thus, this model produces closer integration between the two sectors than might be expected given the intellectual foundations.

The pattern of governing that developed in the Anglo-American democracies, perhaps more than the others, stressed the separation of the two sectors, but tended to accord the dominant role to the private sector.[1] These societies implemented a more or less Lockean, contractarian conception of the relationship of the two sectors, with the people making an implicit contract with the state to perform only a limited range of functions. Likewise, the separation of the public service from the private sector has tended to be greater in Anglo systems, *pace* the American pattern of back and forth movement of a number of senior officials (although few of these formally are civil servants). The guiding assumptions of the Anglo-American approach to the public sector were very much those of separation, primarily to ensure integrity in government and, at least in the Wilsonian formulation, also to depoliticize the public service as much as possible (Doig, 1987).

THE TRADITIONAL MODELS IN PRACTICE

The traditional models of state and society relationships were interesting intellectually but in practice tended to be ignored perhaps as much as they were honoured. For all the dominant notions about the need for separation of the public and private sectors the practice was a good deal of mixing of the two and a number of ways in which each influenced the other. This blending of the sectors is perhaps to be expected, given the complex patterns of governance required in any modern society. However, it is important to understand what has happened historically in order to be able to interpret better the contemporary public sector and the changes it has undergone. The melding of the public and private sectors has taken a variety of different forms.

Personnel   The public and private sectors were assumed to be separate but in reality there has been movement among them in a number of countries. This movement is well known in the United States, and in the *pantouflage* in France. In reality there has been more movement in most systems than the conventional wisdom would admit. Further, in many traditional systems public servants have been politicized, and senior officials would almost certainly have a known partisan allegiance.

Service Delivery   Although services may have been conceptualized as being public they have for years been delivered through private sector agents. These services range from banks delivering guaranteed loans to cabin attendants in airplanes enforcing various safety regulations. Government services often have been the product of interactions of the two sectors and in a number of policy areas government has relied on self-regulating organizations – ranging from medical professions to milk marketing boards – to deliver services.

Finance   There also has been a long history of using private sector financing for public programs, as well as some use of public funding to assist private enterprise. This financing is often indirect, such as providing guarantees for loans or tax forgiveness. Still, these forms of finance may have made possible private projects that otherwise might not have been undertaken.

Policy Leverage   The public and private sectors also have tended to leverage each other. This is especially true of the capacity of the public sector to leverage private action through instruments such as tax expenditures and cost-sharing grants (Salamon, 1989) that require private financial participation if accepted. Likewise, governments may be leveraged by the private sector by the willingness of firms to cooperate in projects in exchange for tax concessions or other type of benefits from government.

Neo-corporatism and Networks   Mechanisms for managing the relationships between interest groups and government also result in a blending of the public and private sectors. These institutions essentially confer formal status on those groups and thereby also reduce the autonomy of the public sector to make its own decisions.

Regulation   Even when government did not play a significant role as a market actor, e.g., through nationalized industries, it could still exert substantial influence over markets. For example, American governments have owned relatively little but have played a major role on the economy through regulation (Peters, 1998).

Objectives Pursued   Finally, the objectives pursued by the public and private sectors often were closely correlated, even in the traditional models. This compatibility of policy goals was often a function of the close connections of interest groups to government, and the movement of personnel back and forth between the sectors. Further, over time even the most *étatiste* government could not afford to be divorced entirely from the aspirations of its own citizens.

In summary, the traditional intellectual models of interactions between the public and private sectors promoted separation of the two sectors, but in practice there has been much greater ambiguity in the definition of public and private. The reality of providing public services frequently has involved mutual influence and cooperation, rather than separation. Likewise, individuals over a personal career may have played a variety of different roles in the two sectors. In European administrative systems the movement has tended to occur once, generally with the individual leaving the public sector for a more lucrative post in the private sector.

A USEFUL FICTION?

Although the reality of the connections between the public and private sectors may be greater interaction than is usually assumed, the idea of separation remains a useful fiction for governments. The idea that the two sectors could maintain their distinctiveness was also a means of defining an inalienable role for the public sector. This fiction provided an ongoing justification for the large state policy domains that had grown up in Europe, and for a large and powerful public service to provide (or at least oversee) those services. There have been a number of ways in which the fiction of a stark separation between the sectors has been supported, and a reality to some degree has been created by the reiteration of that theory.

DEFINING A PUBLIC SECTOR DOMAIN

The notion that there should be an inalienable public sector role requires some justification that certain services are indeed inherently public. That justification has been provided in several forms. The most common way of justifying the public role has been through the economic characteristics of programs (Wolf, 1991). There are four conventional justifications of this type:

- Public goods. These are goods for which it is impossible to deter consumption once they are produced. For example, defense or clean air, are not marketable and therefore must be produced through government.
- Externalities. If the total social costs of creating a product are not included in its price, as with industries that produce significant levels of pollution, then government must intervene in order either to regulate that production or to force the producer to internalize those costs.
- Natural Monopolies. Some products, e.g., electricity and telephones before technological change, are best produced to service extremely large areas without competition. This characteristic in turn requires government regulation.
- Inequalities. Finally, markets tend to produce significant economic inequalities, among individuals, among regions, and across time. In most industrial democracies that level of inequality is deemed unacceptable so the public sector must intervene.

Although economic analysis has been a common way in which to understand and justify the distinctive activities of the public sector, there may also be more political and even ideological justifications for a strong role for the public sector. The problem for comparative analysis is that these justifications are often culturally specific, while the economic justifications are assumed to apply in all cases.[2] For example, water is provided privately in many European countries while this is one of the most basic public services in the United States, presumably the bastion of the private sector.

One of the most important conceptions that can guide decisions about the appropriate location of a service is the concept of "services publics" common in French discussions of this issue. These services publics are assumed to be the inalienable functions of the public sector, although there may not be the clear intellectual basis for the distinction such as that the economists provide. To some extent the public sector role is defined by constitution, or law, with those laws being justified through the appeals to more or less traditional understandings of what the role of the state should be.

Within the system defined by the concept of services publics the public administration may itself be defined by statutes, specific recruitment patterns, and by rights and obligations derived from both law and traditional practice. This distinction is most evident when there is a formal civil service system that differentiates public from private employment. Still, a traditional view of the state and its servants ascribes a clear role to those public servants and generally also confers on them relatively higher status than they have in the world of "New Public Management."

Even when the legal distinctions between public and private sector employment are not strongly established social and cultural distinctions may perform something of the same function. There are a number of studies of differences in the socio-economic roots of public and private sector employees (see Rouban, 1999; Selden, 1997), as well as of differences in their political behaviour (Blais, Blake, and Dion, 1997). In several countries the recruitment of the civil service is very distinctive, e.g., the weight of the south in Italy or (at least historically) Oxbridge in Britain. In these informal terms the public–private divide may be well-established and may function to separate the two types of employment even when public employees may be hired under private contract law.

Finally, the concept of separation remains an accepted myth for members of both sectors. The presumed separation has permitted members of the private sector to complain about mistreatment at the hands of government, e.g., by business regulators, while at the same time working more or less covertly (and cozily) with those same public officials to get what they want from government. For the public sector the norm of separation has justified some personnel and managerial practices that might not have been feasible in the private sector. Further, the norms of separation have enabled the public sector to maintain something of its capacity to exert the authority of the state over the society, and to leverage private sector resources without ceding legal authority over the programs. In reality separation may be fiction, but it is certainly useful.

Although the traditional pattern in reality did not produce the type of separation proclaimed in the formal models, the tendency in contemporary government is to accept more readily the blending of the two sectors. Indeed, many of the reforms of the public sector that have been adopted during the past several decades have tended to celebrate the melding of the two sectors rather than to attempt to maintain the separation. These reforms have, in turn, provoked some reactions that have stressed the need to maintain or reinforce the separation.

Cumulation

One of the present tendencies in defining the role of the public sector is to cumulate, and thereby to amplify, the patterns of blending together public and private sectors. For example, the creation of "quangos," or similarly autonomous organizations, to perform many of the tasks of the public sector, is not the only way in which the control of governments has been undermined. Those organizations often, in turn, provide their services through contracts or through public–private partnerships that further move away from the public sector.

Diffusion

Although there are marked cultural and structural differences among the industrialized democracies, there are also pressures toward greater conformity and the diffusion of the ideas of bridging the public–private divide. These ideas have been spread through a variety of mechanisms. Some international organizations such as OECD and the IMF have been instrumental in promoting these types of reform. Likewise, consulting firms and individual policy entrepreneurs have vested interests in promoting these reforms and in convincing decision makers that the efficiency of government can be enhanced by adopting the right reform package; given popular disaffection with existing forms of governing making that sale may not be difficult.

What is most surprising is the extent to which even countries with strong state traditions have succumbed to the fascination with making the public sector function more like a market. The French government, for example, has in one form or another adopted many of the same reforms found in the Anglo-Saxon countries that have been at the centre of reform (Bezes, 1999). The major exception appears to be Germany and systems operating within that general tradition. Even these countries have adopted some of the changes, albeit not in the comprehensive fashion found in many other systems (Schröter, 1999). Thus, although states may be able to define the nature of the public and private clearly, they may still make choices to shift the boundaries between the sectors.

Issues Raised by Hybridization

The most general phrase that can be applied to the changes in the public sector is "hybridization." Rather than having clearly defined sectors, most public activities are now delivered through mechanisms involving both sectors. Similarly, the private sector is now firmly tethered to the public sector and may be dependent upon it for financing and the favourable regulation of market entry to protect industries. In biology hybrid species are often thought to be particularly hardy. In public administration these species may well be excessively hardy, given that they are also more than a little dangerous.

Familiar Critiques:
Corruption, Capture, and Collusion

Both the political right and the political left have had their own particular worries about the ways in which the blending the two sectors tends to undermine the true purposes of both and produce outcomes that are far from optimal for the society as a whole. As one might expect, the critiques are rather different, but their common focus has been this mixture of public and private action. Further, these familiar critiques go well beyond political rhetoric to include more academic debates. Concerns about mingling the public and private sectors are well-established in political science and public administration (Mosher, 1980; Smith, 1975) but the reforms of the 1980s and 1990s have magnified these concerns and made them more relevant for the average citizen.

On the political right the arguments have been that collusion between special interests and public sector organizations tends to produce excessive levels of public expenditure and an over-production of private goods, and also perhaps an underproduction of public goods (Downs, 1960). Mancur Olson (1982), for example, argued that special interests were deeply involved in distributive coalitions with public sector organizations that tended to benefit those two actors at the expense of a more encompassing public interest. William Niskanen (1971) put forward similar arguments but put the major onus on self-aggrandizing bureaucratic organizations rather than on the interest groups. In either case, however, coalitions of interests and interested bureaucrats produce excessive public expenditures.

On the political left the arguments have been different, but much of the logical basis in the blending of public and private activities is similar. For the left the hybridization of the state is simply a means of the private sector gaining control of the power of government for its own purposes – in Lowi's (1973) terms the "private use of public power." In this version of the argument against hybridization the major negative outcome is the capture of public sector regulators by private interests, and the watering down of the intended effects of regulations on industry.

Some analysts, largely European, argue that capture actually is the bureaucracy capturing the private interests and using those private sector organizations as agents of the State. The reality, however, may not be so clear as in either version of capture and what may occur is interdependence and a weakening of the appropriate roles for both parties. Industries, for example, tend to have substantially more information than do bureaucracies and can use that asymmetry to soften the regulations that might otherwise be imposed. Likewise, the financial monopoly that government can have over third party providers, especially in social policy, means that these providers become the creatures of government and are often more concerned with pleasing the public sector funding bodies than they are in defending the interests of their clients.

Hybridization and Personnel

As well as affecting the manner in which public services are delivered, hybridization also impacts the personnel who work for government in a variety of ways. For personnel the most important manifestation of hybridizing is the end of the public service as an exclusive career, and the increasing recruitment of outsiders to major posts in the public sector. Further, public employees are no longer treated as members of a distinctive group in society that has given up some financial rewards in favour of a capacity to serve; public servants are now treated about the same as any other employees, and often rather worse.[3]

The movement in and out of government, and especially the movement of so many new people into government, is producing a variety of problems. For example, there are cultural differences around issues such as probity and confidentiality, especially when moving out of office, that create tension within organizations. Further, many of the newer employees have been hired on personal contracts rather than through the older pay and grading system, so that their salaries are often much higher; civil servants can compete for the higher-paid posts and often do so successfully, but the internal wage differentials being created are substantial (Hood and Peters, 1994).

There may also be problems for the implementation and policy-making roles of public organizations resulting from hybridization. For example, as more employees become temporary and move readily between the sectors, public organizations lose the memory and continuity. This, in turn, may result in less adequate policies being adopted, less useful policy advice, and less predictability for clients. Again, paradoxically, one of the purposes of reform was to make government a more reliable partner for the private sector in a variety of areas but the net effect may be to make government ever more arbitrary and capricious.

Schizophrenia

Related to the above problems with public sector personnel are some additional problems that might be considered as a kind of schizophrenia in government resulting from hybridization. Administrators in the public sector are increasingly being asked to implement private sector values and to use private sector instruments and many find themselves managing in ways that they had not anticipated when joining the public sector. Further, within organizations, as well as for individuals, there may be competing sets of values at work. In that context it is difficult for a manager to grasp just what the values of the organization, and the public sector, actually are.

The problems of schizophrenia may be exaggerated by the failure to make working in the public sector really like working in the private sector. In particular, many members of the public sector may be asked to administer using private sector values, and to surrender traditional benefits such as job security, while not really being able to earn the same wages as they would in the private sector. Many civil servants appear to believe that they have been presented with the worst of both worlds (Ingraham, Murliss, and Peters, 1999). If the New Public Management is attempting to motivate public employees in the same ways as employees in the private sector are motivated, there must be some means of substituting real changes in wages for some of the values that must be relinquished as the newer forms of management are implemented.

Complication

If we are to use the language of economics to describe this aspect of the problem of hybridization it would be that the transaction costs being imposed in the public sector have been increasing because of the increasing complexity of the mechanisms for service delivery and financing. Coase (1935) argued famously that firms and other hierarchies are the means of overcoming the transaction costs of the market.[4] Many contemporary reformers appear to have forgotten, or ignored, that point in favour of introducing rather elaborate bargaining and contractual arrangements that are almost certain to increase transaction costs within the public sector, and between the public and private sectors, when governments attempt to implement a program.

As well as understanding these complications in service delivery as strictly economic issues, we can also understand them as political and administrative issues. The complications that create costs within the public sector also impose external costs on citizens and on organizations that work with the public sector in providing services. Again, this result of change in government is rather paradoxical. Part of the drive for reform is to simplify services, and provide "one-stop shopping" for public services whenever possible. The blending of public and private provision may add to the number of providers and make it less clear who is the actual provider, and who is the responsible actor, for any public service.

Diffusion of Power

Another tendency has been in the diffusion of power and the loss of control from the centre of government. Part of the reform efforts of the past several decades has been to decentralize and also to empower, shifting effective political power away from those institutions that traditionally have wielded it and granting more to the remainder of the political system. In almost all cases this has meant increasing the power of subnational governments at the expense of central state institutions. That tendency, in turn, has meant that the multiple power centres created may not work together, resulting in less effective public control, or even influence, over the economy and society. Many contemporary politicians may extol that reversal of perceived excess of centralized control, but it may in reality present significant problems for governance.

Another aspect of the diffusion of power is the empowerment of the public to exert influence over policy and programs in ways that have not been acceptable in the more separated model of government. As noted the public and private sector actors had been involved in service delivery to a greater degree than generally understood in the traditional model of the state. In the reformed state the public as a whole may be empowered, through consultation and "citizen engagement" (Pierre, this volume), to play a more influential role in making and implementing policy. This may appear democratic but may in fact reduce the public nature of policy and enhance the level of private control.

Mutual Imprisonment

The increasing tendency of the public and private sectors to depend upon each other for implementing and even financing projects means that they may become mutual prisoners. For any project once begun in this manner to continue to function requires that they each participate as planned. This means that in a sort of game of "Chicken" they can exert substantial pressures on each other for concessions or changes in the bargains. The pressures may be greater on government simply because it is legally charged with delivering the service, with the arrangements for delivery being only a matter of convenience. Thus, a threat from the private sector partners to revoke the arrangement may be legally and politically threatening to the public sector.

The degree of mutual imprisonment may vary according to the type of relationship that exists. For example, financing (especially for capital projects) may be the most constraining type of arrangement, even if those constraints may be short-term. A half-built bridge or roadway is much worse than none at all; it can become a symbol of government failure. Thus, mechanisms such as the Private Finance Initiative in the United Kingdom and a growing number of similar programs elsewhere mean that governments are increasingly becoming locked into financing arrangements that constrain their autonomy (Timmins, 1999). Further, governments may be forced into patrimonial relationships with private actors that undermine the rational–legal nature of the State, and all this may not actually save government any significant amount of money.

Obfuscation

Another of the almost inevitable consequences of hybridization is an obfuscation of the public and private spheres, and with that comes greater confusion and uncertainty. This obfuscation is manifested through several aspects of the recent changes in government. For example, the reforms brought about by new public management promote a number of different goals, some of which may be contradictory, or at a minimum are not totally compatible. For example, on the one hand government employees are being held more personally responsible for actions, and are rewarded differentially based on personal performance. On the other hand they are supposed to be members of teams pursuing public sector goals through more collaborative action.

Likewise, the Private Finance Initiative (see above) tends to cloud ownership and the fiduciary relationships existing in public programs. This clouding of public sector involvement makes it difficult for the citizen or for the legislature to identify the real beneficiaries of a program, or to assess the projects being created through these private financing arrangement. While traditional standards, e.g., not co-mingling funds, may be discounted by the new breed of public sector manager, these financing arrangements violate those principles that have been crucial for maintaining financial probity and accountability in government for decades.

The obfuscation of control may be identified operating in the opposite direction as well; government may appear to privatize and to reduce its involvement in the economy, while at the same time maintaining effective control over an industry (see Wright and Parotti, 1999). This practice is often seen in programs of "partial privatization" in which the State retains a blocking minority ownership, or perhaps only a single "Golden Share," but in effect retains substantial involvement and control over the industry. Governments may benefit by raising money when the stock of these firms is sold off, but the firms are not that much less public sector organizations than they were before being partially privatized, and may not be able to operate any more efficiently.

Legitimacy

The effects of hybridization may also be perceived in the legitimacy of public programs, and of government more generally. That is, the public expects certain types of activities to be undertaken through the public sector – although these may vary in different countries – so that hybridized arrangements are almost immediately suspect. Likewise, in some cases public sector agents (especially service providers) have greater legitimacy than do the "bean counters" who have come to be central participants in making decisions about public policies. Thus, programs designed to enhance legitimacy through efficiency and lower cost may in fact diminish what has become a scarce commodity in the contemporary public sector.

The former aspect of the threats to legitimacy can be understood through the programs to privatize prisons in several countries. Even though prisons can be privatized rather easily, i.e., it is not that difficult to specify through a contract the types of activities required on the part of the private agent, the public still appears wary of this activity. They tend to think of prisons as exercising the monopoly of legitimate force held by the state, and as being exercised properly only by public employees. Likewise, the shift within the National Health Service in Britain toward more managers and perhaps fewer health care workers appears widely suspect among the public, and there are also an increasing number of public questions about using cost criteria to make medical decisions.[5]

Accountability

Finally, and perhaps most importantly, changes in the public sector are creating major problems for maintaining accountability for the actions of government. The hybridization and diffusion of power associated with recent changes in governance also creates ambiguity and a lack of transparency, and with those changes come problems for accountability. That is, as services come to be provided through complex arrangements involving both public and private sector actors it is difficult to determine who is in the end responsible. This confusion is to some extent paradoxical, given that enhancing the capacity to identify responsibility, as well as creating greater administrative transparency, have been goals of many reform projects (Reichard, 1998). For the average citizen, however, the present arrangements are confusing but he or she will probably continue to consider government to be the logical focus for accountability, even if the program is delivered by a mixed method.[6]

With the continuing sense of accountability held by the public comes the difficulty that while the actual delivery of a public service is dispersed government will probably be held to blame if there are errors. This maintenance of (perceived) responsibility without real control places government in a very awkward position. It appears that as this disjuncture has come to be implemented in a number of settings governments are also beginning to find ways to re-establish control over programs, but in the process may be creating clientelistic practices that further undermine the Weberian nature of the public sector[7] That is, if the traditional rule-based style of control is no longer viable then political leaders may opt for alternative, politicized versions of control (Rouban, 1999; Peters, 1999).

REDEFINING THE PUBLIC

Given all the changes in the process of reform, and the problems associated with those changes, what can be the way forward for the public sector? It is almost certainly politically impractical to think about returning to the status quo ante; the changes in the public sector have been too profound, and even many traditional civil servants can discern virtues in some aspects of the changes that have been implemented. While it does appear impossible to return completely to the previous pattern of governing, the difficulties – especially in accountability and in the treatment of individual public servants – appear sufficiently great to require some partial restoration of more traditional patterns of governing.

One central element in any revitalization of the public sector must be a restatement of some traditional public sector values such as integrity, fairness, and especially accountability. Private sector values such as efficiency and competition may have some place in the public sector, but not the almost exclusive position they have been accorded recently.[8] The various types of change that have been detailed already all have tended to denigrate the traditional values of the public sector. Therefore, not only have the reformers been concerned with imposing managerialist values but they also may have undermined sufficiently the values of the older public sector that for many of the more recent recruits there are no stable values for guidance other than the managerialist ideas. Given that, restoring the older culture of the public service could be a difficult task.

There is an especially pressing need to consider what reform has meant to accountability in the public sector. Traditional forms of parliamentary accountability in Westminster systems often emphasized the infrequent scandal and ignored more important questions about the average performance of government (Aucoin, this volume). Still, they did provide a means by which the elected representatives of the public could impose some control and attempt to make administration perform "in the public interest." The market reforms of government may reduce these political questions to economic ones about cost and simple economic efficiency. These economic values are indeed important but are not the only, or perhaps even the most important, values for inclusion in a system of public accountability.

Associated with the need to revitalize the values supporting the public service is the need to more clearly and consciously conceptualize just what are the appropriate boundaries for the public sector. We have noted the difficulties in developing a clear definition of the sector, and there will inevitably be some gray area between the public and the private. That penumbra has, however, been tending to expand in favour of more restrictive ideas about the proper nature and role of the two sectors. This may be in part simply a function of the ease with which hybridization has come to be accepted, and the ease therefore of avoiding political conflict over these issues. That conflict avoidance has, however, also produced a number of governance problems that are sufficiently grave – perhaps especially the blurring and loss of accountability – to justify more political battles.

Finally, any reassertion of the role of the public sector will also require a clear reassertion of the proper role of public servants in making and implementing public policies. Public servants are now generally labelled as part of the problem of the public sector, but if the hope is to promote greater efficiency and effectiveness in government then there must be more of a role for the public service as the embodiment, and guardian, of the public sector values mentioned above. To some extent the values may have to change before there is any capacity to restore the role of the public service.

NOTES

1 There were, and are, of course differences among the Anglo systems, with the United States having the clearest dominance by the private sector while Britain and Canada have ascribed greater powers to the public sector, and the public service.
2 Of course, the idea of inequality mentioned above may be perceived very differently in different societies. A level of inequality unacceptable in Northern Europe has been perfectly acceptable in the United States, or in parts of Southern Europe. See Cohen and Henry (1997).
3 Even in societies that have ascribed a high status to public employees that status has tended to fall. France may be a major exception (Rouban, 1998a; 1998b).

4 See also Williamson (1996) and Majone (1998).

5 The cost question has probably always been a concern in the NHS, but the issue does appear to have become more visible after the Conservative reforms in the 1980s.

6 The public appears to have some sense of public services even when academics and members of governments are incapable of defining them clearly. Further, they believe (rightly or wrongly) that they have more recourse with the public sector than with the private.

7 In some instances governments appear to be reverting to almost patrimonial forms of administration as ministers develop their own private staffs.

8 It is, in fact, wrong to assume that efficiency was not a public sector value. Weber, Wilson and others did talk about efficiency but simply did so in rather different ways from the market reformers in government.

BIBLIOGRAPHY

Bezes, P. 1999. The French Reinvention Exercise (1988-1997): A legitimation process between politicians and higher civil servants. Paper presented at annual Workshops of the European Consortium for Political Research, Mannheim, Germany.

Blais, A., D. Blake, and S. Dion. 1998. *Politics, Elections and Public Employment*. Pittsburgh: University of Pittsburgh Press.

Coase, R. 1937. The nature of the firm. *Economica* 4:386-405.

Cohen, E., and C. Henry. 1997. *Service public, secteur public*. Paris: Conseil d'Analyse Economique.

Downs, A. 1960. Why the government budget is too small in a democracy, *World Politics* 12:541-63.

Doig, J. 1983. "If I see a murderous fellow sharpening a knife cleverly...": the Wilsonian dichotomy and public authority. *Public Administration Review* 43:292-304.

Hood, C., and B. G. Peters. 1994. *Rewards at the Top*. London: Sage.

Ingraham, P. W., H. Murliss, and B. G. Peters. 1999. *The Higher Civil Service and Administrative Reform*. Paris: OECD.

Lowi, T. J. 1973. *The End of Liberalism*. New York: W. W. Norton.

Olson, M. 1982. *The Rise and Decline of Nations*. New Haven, CT: Yale University Press.

Page, E. C. 1994. *Political Authority and Bureaucratic Power*, 2nd ed. Brighton: Wheatsheaf.

Peters, B. G. 1998. Institutionalization and deinstitutionalization: regulatory institutions in American government. In *Comparative Regulatory Institutions*, eds. G. B. Doern and S. Wilks. Toronto: University of Toronto Press.

_____ 1999. Is democracy a substitute for ethics? Administrative reform and accountability. Paper presented at Conference on Administrative Ethics, University of Durham, March 24-26.

Pierson, P. 1998. *Dismantling the Welfare State*. Washington, DC: The Brookings Institution.

Reichard, C. 1998. The impact of performance management on transparency and accountability in the public service. In *Ethics and Accountability in a Context of Governance and New Public Management*, ed. A. Hondeghem. Amsterdam: IOS Press.

Rouban, L. 1999. *The French Civil Service*. Paris: La Documentation Française.

Salamon, L. M. 1989. *Beyond Privatization: The Tools of Government Action*. Washington, DC: Urban Institute Press.

Schröter, E. 1998. Reform of the public sector in Germany. Paper delivered at Conference on Public Sector Reform in Germany and the United Kingdom, Humboldt University, Berlin, December.

Stewart, J. 1998. Advance or retreat: from the traditions of public administration to the new public management and beyond. *Public Policy and Administration* 13:12-27.

Taylor-Gooby, P. 1998. Commitment to the welfare state. In *British and European Social Attitudes*, eds. R. Jowell et al., 15th Report. Aldershot: Ashgate.

Timmins, N. 1999. Private sector partners share government's traditional role. *Financial Times*, April 29.

Weber, M. 1958. Bureaucracy. In *From Max Weber: Essays in Sociology*, eds. H. H. Gerth and C. W. Mills. New York: Oxford University Press.

Williamson, O. E. 1996. *The Mechanisms of Governance*. Oxford: Oxford University Press.

Wright, V. 1994. Reshaping the state: implications for public administration. *West European Politics* 17:102-34.

Wright, V., and L. Parotti. 1999. *Privatization,* Vol. 11 of The International-al Library of Comparative Public Policy. Cheltenham: Edward Elgar.

Wunder, B. 1995. *Les influences du "modèle" napoléonien d'administration sur l'organisation administrative des autres pays.* Brussels: IIAS. Cahiers d'Histoire de l'Administration 4.

Relationships Between Ministers/Politicians and Public Servants: Public Service Bargains Old and New

CHRISTOPHER HOOD

This chapter is in three main parts. The first part argues that the concept of public service "bargains" can help us to identify the various points of origin from which public service reforms begin in different countries. A clearer analysis of points of origin can in turn produce a better understanding of varieties of reform, too little differentiated in the first generation of comparative writing about New Public Management developments. The notion of a "public service bargain" is taken from the work of Bernard Schaffer, and denotes a deal – explicit or implicit – concluded between public servants and elected politicians or the society at large. Such a deal is concerned with the entitlements and duties of the public service relative to other players in the polity, and is expressed in convention or formal law (typically a mixture of the two). This chapter identifies some of the main ways in which such bargains can vary, distinguishing two varieties of "systemic" bargain ("consociational" and "Hegelian") and three varieties of "pragmatic" bargain ("Schafferian," "hybrid," and "managerial").

The second part suggests there are some indications from the literature on contemporary public management reforms that pragmatic bargains are likely to be more readily changed than systemic ones, and Schafferian more readily than hybrid ones. To the extent that such a generalization is accurate, any explanation of the observed pattern would need to combine an account of the factors governing institutional design at the level of "public service bargains" with a historical account of general changes in politics, technology or organization in the era of New Public Management. No generally accepted account of either of these elements has yet been developed. One possible point of departure, explored briefly in this section, is Murray Horn's transaction-cost approach to understanding institutional choice. From that perspective it might be argued that the transaction costs of changing systemic bargains are likely to be greater than those applying to pragmatic bargains. Within the class of "pragmatic" bargains, Schafferian and hybrid bargains in principle impose higher uncertainty costs on politicians than managerial bargains, while Schafferian and managerial bargains are likely to involve higher agency costs than hybrid bargains. Perceptions of all these costs may vary over time; but given what are often claimed to be universal politicial concerns with "blame avoidance" (lower uncertainty costs) it seems surprising that Westminster-model systems starting from a quasi-Schafferian bargain have not generally moved to radical "managerial" bargains.

The third section examines public service bargains from a strategic-action perspective. It identifies some of the main forms of "cheating" by the parties that can be associated with the five main types of public service bargain identified earlier, and sketches out four polar outcomes among which politician–bureaucrat relations can shift. Exploring public service bargains from a "cheat-or-deliver" perspective raises the central questions of what makes public service bargains cheat-proof, including culture, institutions, and the capacity of the various parties to keep each other in check by tit-for-tat tactics. It may be that one of the reasons why the Westminster-model countries have not moved as a group from Schafferian to pure managerial bargains is the cheating problems that beset the managerial bargain and potentially make uncertainty costs unexportable by elected politicians, particularly if they have attempted to reduce their agency costs under a managerial bargain by cheating through backdoor interference outside the agreed framework. Shifting to more hybrid-type bargains or mixed Schafferian–managerial bargains has a lower upside on uncertainty costs for politicians but also a lower downside, and (especially when quasi-cheating opportunities for politicians are exploited) can reduce the agency costs of the pure Schafferian bargain.

The concluding section summarizes the argument and briefly considers what if any circumstances might serve to reinforce or renew the pure Schafferian bargain relative to the two pragmatic types. A return to pure Schafferian bargains seems unlikely, but so does the emergence of any single uniform type of public service bargain.

FORMS OF "PUBLIC SERVICE BARGAIN"

A vast but diffuse literature has emerged on contemporary public service reform to describe, compare, and account for developments like the "New Public Management" and "the regulatory state." But it is becoming widely accepted that a better understanding as to who applied which kind of new public management and why it was used needs to be linked to an analysis of the various points from which efforts to reform public services took off in different countries. And that in turn implies a more differentiated characterization of the "old" public management – too often equated in public-management-reform literature with a generalized traditional model of bureaucracy. This chapter aims to contribute to such understanding by developing the concept of a public service bargain as a tool for comparison and analysis of public service systems.

The notion of a public service bargain is particularly associated with the late Bernard Schaffer (1973, 252). Schaffer used the idea of a public service bargain to characterize and explain the development of the public bureaucracy in a single country (the United Kingdom) at a particular point in time (the nineteenth century). For Schaffer the u.k.'s public service bargain at that time was an implicit deal agreed between elected politicians and civil servants over their respective entitlements and duties. The parallel is with constructive or implicit contracts in legal analysis. The Schafferian bargain was expressed wholly in convention and took a draconian form: "In this ... bargain, concluded between elected politicians and senior bureaucrats in the nineteenth century, the latter exchanged overt partisanship, some political rights and a public political profile in return for 'permanent careers, honours and a six-hour working day'" (quoted in Hood and Jackson 1991, 168. A six-hour working day in the nineteenth century, in an era when many Prime Ministers and Presidents worked only a few hours a day (Savoie 1999, 19), was then a substantial time-commitment for that type of work). For their part, elected politicians exchanged the ability to appoint/dismiss public servants and change their work conditions at will for non-partisan obedience and professional competence. Schaffer's notion of the U.K. public service bargain is like a lawyer's fiction, in that the bargain he describes was implicit or constructive, not formally enacted. But implicit bargains or constructive contracts are ubiquitous in law and social life more generally, and, according to Schaffer, British politicians and public servants behaved *as if* such a bargain had in fact been concluded.

Though Schaffer originally devised the notion of a public service bargain as a U.K. – or at least Westminster model – specific concept, that concept is capable of being stretched in several directions – both for strategic analysis and for historical and cross-national comparison. At the most general level we can define a public service bargain as some real or constructive deal concluded between public servants and other actors in the political system over their respective entitlements and duties, and expressed in convention or formal law or a mixture of both. And such a concept is potentially useful not only as a means of identifying historical and cross-national variety in the different forms of bargain that preceded the New Public Management era, but also as an analytic concept, since a leading theme of contemporary political science is the understanding of strategic behaviour over bargains. Accordingly, this chapter aims to discuss both comparative and analytic ways of developing the concept of public service bargains.

To widen the notion of a public service bargain beyond the specific form it took in the U.K., it seems useful to borrow Feigenbaum and Henig's (1993) distinction (originally drawn to identify different types of privatization) between "pragmatic" and "systemic" types. A systemic public service bargain is one which is part of a fundamental (even if constructive) constitutional settlement. The obvious example is that of a system in which the public service is at the heart of a "consociational" settlement in a socially divided society. In such a settlement, members of the different social groups (ethnic, racial, religious, etc.) in the public service provide "glue" – in some cases, the only glue – to bond a divided society together. What they get in exchange is a share of administrative power in the form of overt or de facto quotas for different social groups. Many contemporary political structures, such as the state of Belgium or the European Union, are unthinkable without their "representative bureaucracy" characteristics (Page, 1997).

Another type of systemic bargain is the arrangement envisaged by Georg Hegel in the *Philosophy of Right* (1896), in which public servants provide a "trustee" or "guardian" concern with the public or collective good of the state or society or constitutional order in exchange for status honour and (for Hegel at least) material comforts and the promise of being "looked after" over a career that relieve them of the need for close attention to their own self-interest. The Confucian notion of public officials as trustees who receive high status in exchange for an obligation to put the interests of society at large ahead of their own is closely related. Though much derided by economics of bureaucracy writers like William Niskanen (1971, 193), for whom such an exchange is inherently implausible, Hegelian bargains are frequently aspired to, for example in the many institutional arrangements (such as central bank independence) that seek to give public officials an autonomous role. One of the leading examples is the constitutional guardianship role implied for the civil service under the 1949 Basic Law in Germany, obliging public servants to be loyal to the constitution rather than the government of the day. Public servants in this sort of bargain have an autonomous status as an "estate" within the constitutional structure, functioning as trustees rather than agents in the principal–agent metaphor beloved of innumerable rational-choice writers.

In contrast to systemic public service bargains, which cut to the constitutional essence or basic foundations of a society, are bargains of a more downstream or pragmatic type, concerning appropriate roles, duties, and working relationships between elected politicians and public servants. In Weaver and Rockman's (1993) terms, they are part of downstream decision-making arrangements rather than basic institutional constraints. Obviously this distinction is fuzzy and problematic at the margin, since it rests on counterfactuals on which judgments may well vary. The point is simply that whereas it is not possible to imagine entities like Belgium or the EU continuing to exist if their bureaucracies were drawn only from a single ethnic or national group, it is possible to imagine other political entities continuing to exist with bureaucratic arrangements rather different from those they have developed (such as a "spoils system bureaucracy" instead of a mandarin class career civil service, or vice versa). Hence public service bargains in those sorts of systems seem to have shallower social foundations or to be part of a narrower politician–bureaucrat settlement (much closer to the principal–agent metaphor) than in the systemic types.

There are several possible types of pragmatic public service bargain. At one extreme are "group" bargains, applying to the public service as a whole or general classes within it, and at the other extreme are "individual" bargains, where top public servants negotiate their own role, working conditions and relationships with politicians on a person-specific basis. In effect the latter is a structure in which there is no generalized public service bargain, only a set of individual ad hoc bargains with particular office holders, in which public servants enter into individual deals with politicians and obtain some personal managerial or regulatory space not subject to the day-to-day command of a politician in exchange for the obligation to accept public blame for their errors.

Most systems can be expected to be hybrid in these terms, but also to vary in their position on the spectrum. There are no pure types, but perhaps the most "groupy" form of pragmatic bargain is the "Schafferian" bargain, when public servants provide loyalty and competent service to the government of the day in exchange for trust, anonymity, merit selection, and permanent (or at least indefinite) tenure. This constructive public service bargain is unusual, in the degree to which it casts public servants as political eunuchs and the degree to which it insulates public service appointment and dismissal from the control of elected politicians. The bargain affects the public service as a class, because there is little scope for public servants to enter into individual deals with politicians over their relationship, or vice versa. At the other end of the scale are strong "managerial" or "regulatory" bargains in which terms, conditions and working relationships are person-specific and individually negotiable. Cases towards that end of the scale might include the u.s. city-manager tradition, the appointment of chiefs of staff by particular ministers, or the much-discussed New Zealand post–1986 CEO structure. Such bargains involve elected politicians trading off liability for blame in exchange for an element of "credit slippage," using Fiorina's (1986) well-known terminology.

In between the "Schafferian" and "managerial" types comes a hybrid category in which there is more scope for individual deals between politicians and public servants over their relationship than applies to the pure Schafferian bargain, but the deals take place within a broader collective public service bargain than applies with the pure managerial or regulatory bargain and blame is shared with politicians rather than transferred to individual public servants. Perhaps the classic example of such a hybrid bargain is the French (and EU) *Cabinet* system in which politicians pick their teams of trusted councillors (typically from within the public service in the French case) and work with them on a team basis.

These five general types are summarized in Table 1. This five-part classification is not intended to be comprehensive. Its purpose is simply to show that the notion of a public service bargain can be taken beyond the particular form it took up in the Westminster-model countries, and that the Schafferian public service bargain is only one out of a number of possible forms when it is viewed in comparative perspective. The classification offered in Table 1 necessarily deals, too, in pure types, whereas most public service

TABLE 1:
Five Classic Types of Public Service Bargain

Broad Type	Sub-Type	What Society or Politicians Get	What Public Servants Get	Cases
"Systemic" bargains that are central to constitutional structures	*Consociational Bargain*	"Social glue" through representative bureaucracy	Share of administrative power	Belgium, EU, Trinidad
	Hegelian or Confucian Bargain	Focus on trustee role of promoting general public good	Status (and for Hegel career-long material comfort)	Germany
"Pragmatic" bargains that relate to specific politician–bureaucrat roles and obligations	*Schafferian Bargain*	Loyalty to and competent service to the government of the day	Permanent tenure, trust by Ministers, avoidance of public blame for policy	U.K., classic Westminster-model systems
	Hybrid Bargain	Competent service with party or personal loyalty	Trust by Ministers, limited public blame for policy	French *Cabinets* Patrimonial or spoils systems
	Managerial/ Regulatory Bargain	Public servants who are blameable for regulatory or operational errors	Operational autonomy or managerial space	U.S. city-managers, chief-of-staff positions etc.

systems in practice involve some mixture of types (for example, a mix of consociational, hybrid, and Schafferian in the Canadian case or perhaps a mix of Hegelian and consociational in the Singaporean one). Even in the U.K., the Schafferian bargain applied only to a part of the public service (the regular civil service), not to the secondary public service that emerged in the form of "quangos" in the twentieth century, whose heads were hired in many cases on conditions approximating to those of the more patronage-oriented public services of other states. But the value of making the distinctions summarized in Table 1 is that they highlight or differentiate the institutional point of departure from which public service systems enter the New Public Management age. In general, we would expect the institutional entry point to the era of New Public Management heavily to shape the public service reform action (or inaction) in each political system. These issues are discussed in the next section.

VARIETY AND CHANGE IN PUBLIC SERVICE BARGAINS

In an abstract sense the politics of public service bargains can be conceived as a set of dynamic movements around the basic varieties identified in the previous section, and the many hybrids they can produce. As yet, however, we have no systematic comparative analysis of change and stability in public service bargains. Nor do we have a generally accepted basis for explaining cross-national variation and change in such bargains. But three very tentative hypotheses can be suggested: that systemic bargains seem in general to have been "stickier" than "pragmatic" bargains in the age of New Public Management; that the pure Schafferian-type bargain seems to have come under particularly heavy pressure in that period; but that weakening in pure Schafferian bargains has not in most cases led to the adoption of pure managerial bargains, but rather to hybrid ones, or at least Schafferian–managerial hybrids. To the extent that those hypotheses are true, they call for explanation.

The admittedly fragmented literature on public management reform across the affluent democracies (e.g., Barzelay, 2000 forthcoming) seems to suggest that more dramatic changes have been made to the tradition of the Schafferian bargain in the Westminster-model countries than to the other types of bargain discussed earlier. That is not to say that systemic bargains have remained completely unchanged. In Germany, for example, the tendency seems to have been to bypass the Hegelian public service bargain by building private-law entities around the public service for many state functions. And many of the fashionable managerial and service-provision doctrines seem to have been applied, at a surface level at least, across systems with different types of fundamental public service bargains. But it is the pure Schafferian type of bargain that seems to have been the most subject to frontal attack. It seems to have been assailed from two quarters, one pushing it away from the traditional permanent-tenure model of the public service towards more limited tenure (as in Australia after 1983) and the other pushing it away from the model of the career public servant as a confidential ministerial adviser entitled and obliged to give frank advice on policy towards a role as the arm's-length implementer or regulator (as in New Zealand's public service contract model developed in the late 1980s and the U.K.'s executive agencies and quasi-independent regulators).

Indeed, Schafferian bargains have weakened across many of the Westminster-model systems (and not only in respect of the "six-hour day" which Schaffer saw as part of the nineteenth-century bargain). Such bargains appear to have unravelled in several ways. Its features of permanent tenure, particularly for departmental heads, has been limited in several states (Australia, New Zealand, the U.K. for executive agencies), and the same goes for the closed-career promotion structure. The anonymity of public servants has also been reduced, with ministers unilaterally reducing the scope of their accountability away from the notionally all-encompassing nature of ministerial responsibility in classic Westminster-model doctrine, while extending their hiring and firing powers. Its feature of public service dominance of policy advice and management has been weakened by the introduction of "chiefs of staff" (as in Canada), special advisers, and regulators. Its feature of confidential service has been weakened by freedom of information legislation that works against the kind of "free and frank" written memoranda senior public servants once used to write under the protection of a thirty-year rule or some similar confidentiality arrangement. Both of the latter two tendencies work against the tradition of the permanent adviser entitled to "speak truth to power" in exchange for public loyalty and abstention from party political activity.

Not only does the general direction of the traffic seem to have been away from the Schaffer-type bargain rather than towards it, but the more Schafferian the initial bargain the more the movement has tended to be. Arguably one of the most Schafferian initial bargains within the Westminster-model countries was the case of New Zealand, in which the 1912 Public Service Act gave stronger tenure entitlements to senior civil servants than applied to the U.K., where the retention of the royal prerogative power as the basis of civil service employment allowed for summary dismissal (Hood, 1998).

Political rhetoric would suggest that the Schafferian type of bargain in several of the Westminster-model countries has been widely replaced by a "managerial" type of bargain, in which public servants are notionally given more "managerial space" or "regulatory space" in exchange for direct accountability for results. The most dramatic case appears to have been that of New Zealand, where the whole public service moved into an approximation of a managerial form of bargain in the 1980s, with chief executives directly responsible for specified "outputs" in exchange for a greater degree of managerial freedom. But this "full monty" pattern does not appear to have been generally adopted across the Westminster-model countries, in spite of managerial rhetoric. More common seems to have been a partial move towards a managerial bargain, together with a weakened form of Schafferian bargain.[1]

These hypotheses, it must be stressed, are highly tentative. A great deal of systematic empirical work is needed to underpin them. But if this rough-and-ready characterization is robust, we need an explanation of why the pure Schafferian bargain seems to have been more vulnerable than the other types in the New Public Management era and of why in most cases systems with variants of the Schafferian bargain have settled for a more hybrid form rather than moving to a pure form of managerial bargain. That means we cannot rely on any simple pendulum or politics-of-reaction theory in which every type of public service bargain produces over time unintended and unwanted effects, leading to its replacement by some other kind of bargain. Such an account would imply that all types of public service bargains were equally liable to succumb to reform pressures driven by the politics of disappointment or perceptions that "the grass is greener" elsewhere, when that is not what seems to have been happening. Any explanation that fitted the tentative observations above would need to combine an account of the factors governing institutional design at the level of "public service bargains" with a historical account of general changes in politics, technology or organization in the New Public Management era, and we have no generally accepted account of either of these elements.

One possible starting point is Murray Horn's (1995) well-known account of institutional choice from a transaction-cost basis. This assumes legislators or other institutional designers seek to achieve commitment (durability of their preferred measures over time) while minimizing agency costs (the risk that agents or administrative organizations will follow an agenda of their own and get out of control) and minimizing uncertainty costs for favoured interests (the risk that an arrangement may turn out to impose substantial costs on one or more of the players). Viewed in this light, the Hegelian and consociational type of bargain can be seen as arrangements which privilege institutional "commitment" to a particular form of ethnic–racial conflict management or constitutional position (with variable agency costs for the society or politicians depending on factors such as the ease with which the bureaucracy can be steered through the courts). The transaction costs of changing such bargains could consequently be expected to be high.

Within the pragmatic types of bargain, commitment is inherently low for both the Schafferian and hybrid cases, and variable in the managerial–regulatory type of bargain (though such institutional commitment tends to be inherently limited in Westminster-model and Parliamentary-type systems). The agency costs to elected politicians are likely to be variable in the pure Schafferian type (because permanent tenure expectations mean control has to take place through time-intensive "conversations" if the political chemistry of the minister–official link is problematic) and in the managerial type (because of the time-intensive requirement to set up agreed frameworks and work at arm's length) than in the hybrid type (where tenure is tied to specific politicians and arm's-length frameworking control is not required). The uncertainty costs to politicians are likely to be higher for Schafferian and hybrid forms of bargain (since in the former case blame is taken by ministers and in the second it is at least shared with the public service team) than in the managerial form, since in the latter case politicians can pass blame to individual public servants.

This reasoning is summarized in Table 2 below. To the extent that it is correct, it would suggest that the pure Schafferian bargain would be preferred by politicians to the other two types only if its agency costs were perceived to be lower. The pure managerial or regulatory bargain would be preferred to the Schafferian or hybrid types if uncertainty costs were highly salient or commitment concerns were important, outweighing the high agency costs of this type.

On this analysis, the conditions for a switch away from the Schafferian bargain (more salient uncertainty costs, perceived high agency costs) to some other form of pragmatic public service bargain are not severe. So what reasons are there for believing that uncertainty costs might have risen in the era of (or immediately before) New Public Management, leading elected politicians to be more concerned with "blame avoidance" and/or that the agency costs associated with the Schafferian bargain might have started to look high relative to the managerial alternative? The sort of historical change that might bring about greater general politician concern with blame avoidance (consequently putting more of the uncertainty costs of public service bargains on to bureaucrats) might include a mixture of state service expansion (more things potentially to go wrong for which politicians would take the blame), declining levels of trust in elected politicians (with less public inclination to give politicians the benefit of the doubt when things go wrong), increasing professionalization of politics and a style of post-Cold War politics in which public management itself becomes the dominant issue of politics.[2] The near-universal triumph of a particular form of capitalist democracy associated with the end of the Cold War and linked with international regimes dedicated to trade liberalization and policies of

TABLE 2:
Commitment, Uncertainty and Agency in Pragmatic Bargains

Capacity or Cost Features	Type of Pragmatic Bargain		
	Schafferian	*Hybrid*	*Managerial*
Commitment capacity	Lower (loyalty to government of the day)	Lower (loyalty to the party or minister)	Variable
Uncertainty costs to politicians of policy error	Higher (public servants "anonymous")	Higher (blame shared with team)	Potentially lower if blame successfully transferred
Agency costs to politicians of directing public servants	Variable (low set-up costs but public servants permanent, have to be persuaded through conversation)	Medium (no arm's-length framework costs, public servants tenure aligned with politicians' but need to select and appoint)	Higher (arm's-length control means upfront time commitment on frameworking and contracts)

economic rationalism (Aucoin, 1990; Dryzek, 1996, 17-34; and contrast Campbell and Wilson, 1995, who see an age of more ideological politics) may have such an effect.

But if the reasoning above is correct, politicians switching out of a pure Schafferian bargain then face a trade-off between lower uncertainty costs and higher agency costs (plus some, possibly limited, element of commitment) in the managerial bargain as against higher uncertainty costs and lower agency costs in the hybrid bargain. If relatively few systems have moved from Schafferian to pure managerial bargains, does that mean that the politicians concerned were more concerned with agency costs than uncertainty costs?

On the face of it, such a conclusion would seem to sit oddly with the blame avoidance logic often claimed to be central to contemporary politics and augmented by the sort of historical developments referred to earlier. Why then have most Westminster-model systems not moved all the way to a Swedish agency system or New Zealand type of structure? One possible answer is that the fertile opportunities for "cheating" over public service bargains complicate the analysis, either because politicians can cheat on hybrid or Schafferian bargains by shifting the blame without moving to arm's-length control, or because public servants can cheat on managerial bargains, such that uncertainty costs boomerang back to politicians whenever residual liability issues arise. Accordingly, the next section examines "cheating" within public service bargains.

CHEAT OR DELIVER?

THE POLITICS OF PUBLIC SERVICE BARGAINS

The understanding of public service bargains needs to include analysis of the incentives and possibilities available to the contracting parties to cheat or deliver on their side of the deal, since cheating may be closely related to transaction costs. Without claiming to be comprehensive, Table 3 attempts to summarize some of the main "cheating opportunities" available to the parties under the five types of public service bargain identified at the outset. Under the consociational type of bargain, in which public servants exchange the function of providing "glue" for a divided society in return for a share of administrative power, one of the main cheating opportunities for public servants is that of promoting social segmentation instead (for example through racial, national, or ethnic preference). For politicians or the society at large, cheating behaviour consists of actions like bypassing the consociational bureaucracy or biased distribution of administrative power among the different social groups. Under the Hegelian bargain, the main cheating opportunity for public servants consists of "looking after Number One" instead of trusteeship of collective good, through behaviour that can range from outright corruption to bureau-shaping and front-line abandonment. For politicians and society at large, cheating behaviour for this type of bargain consists of actions such as denial or erosion of the status attached to public service and of lifetime rewards sufficiently comfortable to remove the need for public-spirited individuals to serve special interests (including their own) in doing their jobs.

TABLE 3

Cheating Opportunities in Five Public Service Bargains

Broad Type	Sub-Type	What Society or Politicians Get	What Public Servants Get	How Society/ Politicians Can Cheat	How Public Servants Can Cheat
General social or constitutional bargains	Consociational Bargain	"Social glue" through representative bureaucracy	Share of administrative power	Covert discrimination in hiring, firing, etc.	Promotion of social segmentation
	Hegelian or Confucian Bargain	Focus on trustee role of promoting general public good	Status (and for Hegelian career-long material comfort)	Denial/ erosion of status or "alimentation"	Corruption and self-seeking behaviour
More specific politician–bureaucrat bargains	Schafferian Bargain	Loyalty to and competent service to the government of the day	Permanent tenure, trust by ministers, avoidance of public blame for policy	Party patronage in hiring, firing etc., misleading/ circumventing/ blaming the bureaucracy	Disloyalty (leaking, sabotage) or incompetence
	Hybrid Bargain	Competent service with party or personal loyalty	Trust by Ministers, limited public blame for policy	Double-crossing and failure to give reciprocal support for public servants	Disloyalty (leaking, sabotage) or incompetence
	Managerial or Regulatory Bargain	Public servants who are blameable for regulatory or operational errors	Operational autonomy or managerial space	Covert political interference in operations	Refusal to accept blame for errors/poor performance

Turning to the pragmatic forms of public service bargain, public servants under the pure Schafferian bargain can cheat by failing to deliver loyalty or failing to deliver neutral competence or both. Cheating opportunities on the loyalty dimension include "leaking" of confidential material or policy proposals to journalists or opposition parties by disgruntled bureaucrats, and other forms of policy sabotage (typically justified by invoking the rhetoric of a Hegelian public service bargain with the parliament or society at large rather a Schafferian bargain to serve the government of the day). Cheating opportunities on the neutral competence dimension include partisan bias and managerial incompetence. For politicians, cheating opportunities over the Schafferian bargain include circumvention of the career bureaucracy and partisanship in hiring, firing, and promotion. Under the hybrid form of bargain, public service cheating opportunities are similar to those in the Schafferian form, taking forms such as failure to provide partisan loyalty and commitment or failure to provide professional competence. Cheating opportunities available to politicians include failure to provide reciprocal support for public servants and double-crossing behaviour.

The pure managerial form of public service bargain offers a number of cheating opportunities to both sides. Cheating on a managerial bargain by public servants can consist of backdoor collusion with politicians or legislators outside the terms of the agreed formal framework (Barker 1998); evasion of control frameworks, as Foster (1992) argues was frequently achieved by u.k. nationalized industry boards in the era of Morrisonian public enterprise; and political lobbying activity to influence policy settings (as has occurred with Swedish agencies), with the agency as a political actor rather than an implementer of policy settings coming from elected politicians. Cheating opportunities available to politicians include unacknowledged interference in the "managerial space" – as typically happened over officially arm's-length relations between ministers and Morrisonian public corporations over forty years in the u.k. and was often seen as a key element in the downfall of that form of public enterprise and its replacement in many cases by regulated public utilities (with a new form of public service bargain between politicians and quasi-independent regulators). Such cheating has also been observable in the case of the Next Steps executive agencies in the U.K., notably in the Prison Service Agency, whose Chief Executive, sacked in 1995, subsequently went on the record with an account of extensive but surreptitious interventions by the Home Secretary in detailed matters of prison management while arguing that as a minister he had no responsibility for "operational" issues (Lewis, 1997; Barker, 1998).

Looking at public service bargains in a cheat-or-deliver frame calls attention to at least three analytic issues. The first is that the overall outcome of such bargains obviously depends on the combined strategies of the two parties, and as in the classic Prisoner's Dilemma game, the possibilities include delivery by both sides, cheating by both sides, or cheating by one side but not the other. The corresponding outcomes can range from a "cooperative equilibrium" in which bargains are adhered to by both sides, to (at the other extreme) a poker-game culture in which both sides are continuously manoeuvering, neither trusts the other, and no bargain is likely to have much credibility or stick for very long. Table 4 summarizes these possible outcomes.

Second, in such interactions, what counts is *perception* of cheating or delivery. Those perceptions may differ among the various players. For instance, during the New Public Management era, some politicians (on the basis of experience in the 1960s and 1970s) in several of the Westminster-model countries perceived that their relationship with public servants had drifted into cell (3) in Table 4, with public servants sabotaging the demands of elected politicians in order to protect their own interests and politicians unable to control their departments (see Savoie, 1994, 11-2; Polidano, 1998, 36). At the same time, many public servants perceived the relationship had drifted into cell (2), with politicians unilaterally unloading their responsibilities onto public servants with no effective quid pro quo and denying public servants' traditional entitlement under the Schafferian bargain to "speak truth to power" in confidential discussions of policy.

TABLE 4
Public Service Bargains: Cheat or Deliver?

Public Servants	Society/Politicians	
	Deliver	Cheat
Deliver	(1) "Cooperative equilibrium": high-trust public service arrangements	(2) Public servants cowed or fatalistic but apathetic or resigned
Cheat	(3) Public or politicians distrust public servants but feel unable to change the system	(4) Low-trust "poker-game" with no stable public service arrangements

A further example of lack of uniformity in who perceives what as "cheating" is the various types of ménage à trois arrangements that have developed around ministers and prime ministers in various Westminster-model countries. The traditional ministerial department in those countries comprised a minister advised by the career public service under a single departmental head (plus specialist professional advisers with independent responsibilities, like chief medical officers, in some cases). But that essentially two-person structure has been replaced by a triadic (or even four-person) relationship in several Westminster-model countries. In Canada, the introduction of chiefs of staff or special advisers in addition to departmental heads created three key figures at the top of each department (minister, departmental head and chief of staff, the "ménage à trois canadien"). In the U.K., the creation of executive agencies whose CEOs had direct responsibility for service delivery after 1988 under the umbrella of Ministerial departments produced a different sort of ménage à trois, of minister, the official head of the department, and agency chief executives hired under a variant of "managerial bargain." (Indeed, with special advisers to ministers as well, the structure was more like a ménage à quatre.) Some traditionally minded public servants evidently see the emergence of ménage à trois (or quatre) structures, with all their possibilities for bypassing games, as a form of cheating on what they conceive as the essence of the Schafferian bargain, while politicians and some other civil servants may see it as a perfectly legitimate counter to cheating in the form of subtle disloyalty by top public servants in the ménage à deux minister–permanent head structure.

Moreover (as that example illustrates), there are forms of cheating that straddle different forms of public service bargain, if elements of both are present in the same system. As noted earlier, the creation of executive agencies within the u.k. civil service in addition to the traditional departments meant that CEOs of the agencies worked under a managerial form of bargain (directly accountable to Parliament for errors in services they delivered according to a framework document agreed with ministers) while the heads of the policy departments continued to work under a form of Schafferian bargain. (Something similar applied to the creation of quasi-independent regulators for the utilities.) In the consequent ménage à trois relationship, there are incentives for departmental heads and other departmental officials to undermine the "managerial bargain" part of the structure. If in such a ménage à trois, Ministers discover there is scope for them to bypass the head of the parent department and deal directly with the agency chief executive over sensitive policy matters, the parent department's head has an incentive to protect his/her position vis-à-vis the other two members of the ménage à trois by setting up even more monitoring and second-guessing arrangements by the department over the agency, as did the Permanent Secretary of the u.k.'s Home Office in the mid-1990s as a defensive response to direct dealing between the Home Secretary and the Prison Service Agency chief executive (Barker, 1998). The result of such triadic dynamics can be paradoxical, in that public servants believing themselves to have an autonomous managerial space under the managerial bargain may in fact find themselves facing still more regulation and oversight from the bureaucracy, and thus perceive an element of cheating from elsewhere in the public service. Much of the managerialist criticism of the u.k.'s executive agency regime has focused on the failure of parent departments to let go of detailed procedural controls, in spite of the pervasive rhetoric about the need to develop more emphasis on managerial responsibility and a results-orientation (Trosa, 1994; Hogwood, Judge, and McVicar, 1998).[3] In hybrids of this type, there are more than two players who can cheat.

The third analytic issue raised by the cheat-or-deliver perspective is the question of what mechanisms can serve to prevent public service bargains drifting into the "cheat/cheat" outcome (cell (4) in Table 4). Possible and related candidates include the "usual suspects" of culture (shared attitudes and beliefs, such as a wartime ethos of solidarity), institutions and rules (such as dedicated arrangements in the form of courts, special commissioners and the like, for policing, guarding, and adjudicating on public service bargains), and the existence of mutual checking arrangements (producing an expectation that the other side will rapidly punish defection by a tit-for-tat response, of the type analyzed by Axelrod (1984), that erodes or removes any advantages to be gained from "defection" (see also Scholz 1991).

As far as culture is concerned, two world wars and a major economic breakdown in the first half of the twentieth century, in an era when professional politics as a first career was less common than it is today, seem likely to have provided general conditions more conducive to mutual delivery on public service bargains than the contemporary age. So far as rules and dedicated policing are concerned, public service bargains are only likely to be effectively policed by such arrangements if they are expressed – or expressable – in written law rather than convention, though many aspects of such bargains are unlikely to be juridifiable. And "tit-for-tattery" requires that the players are on an equal footing, play the game on an iterative rather than one-shot basis, and are able to recognize one another in subsequent play. While the latter condition is probably met for public service bargains, the first two are less likely to be.

Tit-for-tat tactics relative to politicians by public servants under the "Schafferian" type of bargain can be subtle (as in *Yes, Minister* mould), but the cumulative effect of such behaviour may be not so much to maintain the Schafferian bargain as to push politicians into a move from Schafferian to hybrid or managerial bargains. Since public servants under the managerial bargain are not in a position of privileged confidante – and in formal terms are more easily sackable – some of the classic Schafferian tit-for-tat tactics are not open to them. Indeed, some of the most powerful potential tit-for-tat responses by public servants under the managerial bargain may come *after* the managers have been sacked and have nothing further to lose from displeasing their political masters.

That is, if the elected politicians have cheated on the managerial bargain by covertly exerting hands-on control over administrative operations for which public servants are expected to take the blame, agency heads once sacked are in a position to make a "tit-for-response." Instead of falling meekly on their swords, they can create further political embarrassment by publicly attacking the ministers who have blamed them, by revealing details of backdoor ministerial interference in the agency's affairs that makes the minister's political position worse – or at least no better – than it would be under the ministerial-responsibility conventions of the Schafferian bargain.[4] Even attempts by politicians to make agency heads go quietly by the traditional private-sector approach of generous terminal financial settlements may have negative political consequences if they lead to rows about lavish payoffs to public servants (as happened for instance after the dismissal of the head of the Australian Bicentennial Authority through a generous private-sector-style tax-efficient "golden goodbye" in the late 1980s).

Accordingly, the reason why Westminster-model countries have not moved as a group from Schafferian to pure managerial bargains may either reflect politicians placing a lower weighting on "uncertainty costs" of policy or operational error relative to "agency costs" than might have been expected (as suggested in the last section), or the way that cheating costs and opportunities have been factored in to their calculations. Attempting to pass all the uncertainty costs of operational errors from elected politicians to public servants under a pure managerial bargain is a high-risk strategy that is only likely to succeed if the contractual terms are clear-cut or if elected politicians have not cheated by backdoor interference in the work of the "managers" in an attempt to cut their agency costs. Shifting to more hybrid-type bargains or mixed Schafferian-managerial bargains has a lower upside on uncertainty costs for politicians but also a lower downside, and (especially when quasi-cheating opportunities like ménage à trois arrangements are considered) can reduce the agency costs of the pure Schafferian bargain. Cheating factors may thus also help to explain why so few Westminster-model countries have gone the "full monty" to public service managerialism.

CONCLUSION

This chapter has sought to show that analysis of public service bargains can be a fruitful starting-point for understanding the different dynamics of contemporary public service reform, since the concept brings out cross-national and historical variety and highlights strategic issues of cheating or delivery over the putative bargain. Historically, public service bargains have taken different forms across the developed democracies, in spite of the tendency of much contemporary writing about public-service reform to treat traditional public administration as a uniform style. It was suggested at the outset that systemic bargains (whether of the consociational or Hegelian variety) were in general likely to be "stickier" than pragmatic bargains, but that does not mean that such bargains are impervious to change. Consociational bargains are perhaps more likely to snap suddenly in a crisis, and Hegelian bargains to erode slowly over time (but that hypothesis needs careful investigation). For the pragmatic bargains, the general direction of the traffic seems to be away from the pure Schafferian bargain, but in spite of the ubiquity of managerial language in public service reform it seems surprising that only one Westminster-model state has adopted a relatively pure form of managerial bargain. It was suggested earlier that this outcome can either be explained by politicians' relative valuation of agency and uncertainty costs or by the way that cheating opportunities have been factored into their calculations on institutional design.

If the general direction of the traffic seems to have been against pure Schafferian bargains in the era of New Public Management, are there any conceivable or plausible conditions in which such bargains might wax instead of continuing to wane? Three possible candidates for such conditions are: a major renewal of the "sleaze" preoccupations that developed across several OECD states in the 1990s; a backlash against hybrid or managerial bargains; and a general crisis of the global capitalist order.

In principle, rising public preoccupations with "sleaze" – forms of misconduct or malversation by those in public office ranging from self-serving behaviour at public expense through conflicts of interest in public office to outright corruption (Ridley and Doig, 1995) – might lead to a change of direction in public service bargains. But the widespread public concern about such issues across a number of the OECD countries in the early and middle 1990s seems to have made only limited difference to public service bargains in most cases, suggesting that only a very strong and general "sleazequake" would be likely to have any such effect. And even then much would be likely to depend on the point of origin. A (degenerate) Schafferian structure hit by a strong "sleazequake" seems much more likely to move in the direction of a Hegelian bargain (with the public service moving towards some claim of autonomy on the basis of a guardian or collective-good role) or even of a modified managerial bargain (as politicians pursued the logic of offloading blame to public officials) as of reversion to a Schafferian type of bargain.

An alternative (though related) possible candidate for producing a change of direction in public service bargains is a backlash against hybrid or managerial bargains. Such a backlash might not necessarily reflect a perceived link with "sleaze." It might reflect a perceived accountability failure of managerial bargains, as in the 1995 Cave Creek case in New Zealand when a major tragedy produced a "no-one-to-blame" outcome (Gregory, 1995; 1996; 1998); a reaction against the fragmentation of government into separate managerial "silos," or simply a reaction against patronage overload from hybrid or managerial bargains. Such conditions are far from inconceivable, and indeed problems with the managerial bargain have been recognized in countries like the U.K., New Zealand, and Sweden in recent years (Schick,

1996). But of three possibilities mentioned above, only a "patron-age overload" backlash – arguably the least plausible of the trio – would be capable of weakening both of those bargains relative to the pure Schafferian form. Extreme forms of accountability and "silo" problems seem more likely to assail the purer mana-gerial-type bargains (even then it would seem likely to need a set of major failures, or perceived failures, of Cave Creek magni-tude, occurring in a short period, to provoke a move away from managerial bargains *simpliciter* rather than a fine-tuning response). The hybrid forms seem much less likely to produce that sort of backlash.

A third possible condition that might conceivably lead to a change of direction in public service bargains is some sort of major crisis in global capitalism comparable to the slump of the 1930s – an event often forecast by economic pessimists but yet to occur worldwide in spite of the "Asian flu" of the late 1990s. In such conditions, the public service would be likely to assume a greater economic salience than it has had in the wealthy democ-racies in the recent past. But a world-shaking event of that kind, if it weakened the legitimacy of elected politicians, seems as like-ly to stimulate a Hegelian or hybrid approach to public service bargains than a pure Schafferian one. After all, in those circum-stances the skills and competencies of career public servants might well be wholly unequal to what would be likely to be need-ed for new forms of state activity, and at the same time a great deal of talent from outside the public service would be likely to be available for public service at pay much lower than that current-ly prevailing in the business sector. So even if an economic cata-clysm made the sort of stable frameworks associated with an arm's-length managerial or regulatory model even harder to achieve, it seems far from clear that it would buttress or reinforce any pure form of the Schafferian bargain as against hybrid forms.

It is of course a besetting sin of all forecasters to assume that the future will be like the past; and social scientists, like race-course tipsters, are far better at identifying the possible runners in a horse race (as this chapter has tried to do) than picking the winner. But even briefly considering the possibility of some extreme events that would mark a sharp discontinuity with the long (world war-free, at least) peace of the last fifty years in the advanced capitalist democracies seems to give no particular reason to alter the conclusion that systemic public service bargains are likely to be more robust than pragmatic bargains, and that pure forms of Schafferian bargain are unlikely to emerge or re-emerge in a general way. At the same time it seems unlikely that pure forms of managerial public service bargain will sweep the world, in spite of the view expressed by some in the New Public Management era that such bargains represent the way of the future. New Zealand's shift from a pure Schafferian to relatively pure managerial public service bargain[5] in the 1980s has its admirers (and detractors), but it has few imitators. Given the historical starting-points, the worldwide dominance of any single type of public service bargain seems no more likely than the development of uniform types of state institutional and constitutional structures.

NOTES

1 In the U.K. what seems to have happened is a differentiation of the public service bargain, with a different regime for "regular" departmental officials on the one hand (who retained traditional indefinite tenure) and executive agency chief executives and OF-type regulators on the other, on limited-term tenure (Hood, 1998).

2 Several of these trends are consistent with Michael Power's (1997) claim that the contemporary world is witnessing the development of "audit societies," obsessed with constant verification and checking up on everybody's performance by applying the apparently comforting techniques of financial audit to other domains (like education, safety, the environment). If Power is correct in identifying such general trends, elected politicians may find an attractive role as orchestrators of "audit" systems rather than "managers" of public services.

3 One senior British civil servant remarked of the executive agency program that "we thought we were empowering people who manage things but ended up empowering people who count things"

(Hood et al., 1999). Hogwood et al. (1998) go so far as to identify a pathology of excessive accountability in the executive agency regime, and Polidano (1998, 49) argues that such developments unintendedly reduce administrative responsiveness and move bureaucracies towards administrative gridlock.

4 Such was the situation faced by the British Home Secretary Michael Howard in 1995 when he sacked Derek Lewis, the chief executive of the Prison Service Agency operating under a version of managerial bargain, after some embarrassing prison escapes followed by a damning report critical of security in two jails. The response of the sacked and disgruntled Lewis was to turn the heat on his erstwhile political "principal" by legal challenge and damaging exposés of Howard's continuous interference in the operational affairs of the agency for which Howard declined to take any responsibility. Lewis's activity provided powerful ammunition for Howard's political enemies within and outside the Conservative Party and forced him on to the defensive to at least as great an extent as if he had assumed direct responsibility for prison management under a Schafferian ministerial responsibility bargain.

5 With its abandonment of a single civil service employer, strong freedom-of-information conventions, general adoption of fixed-term contracts for government employees under managerial frameworks, and the removal of all formal barriers to lateral entry.

BIBLIOGRAPHY

Aucoin, P. 1995. *The New Public Management: Canada in Comparative Perspective.* Ottawa: Institute for Research on Public Policy.

Axelrod, R. 1984. *The Evolution of Cooperation.* New York: Basic Books.

Barker, A. 1998. Political responsibility for U.K. prison security – ministers escape again. *Public Administration* 75, Spring:1-23.

Barzelay, M. 2000, forthcoming. *The New Public Management: Improving Research and Policy Dialogue.* Berkeley: University of California Press.

Campbell, C., and G. K. Wilson. 1995. *The End of Whitehall: Death of a Paradigm?* Oxford: Blackwell.

Dryzek, J. 1996. *Democracy in Capitalist Times: Ideals, Limits and Struggles.* Oxford: Oxford University Press.

Feigenbaum, H. B., and J. R. Henig. 1993. Privatization and democracy. *Governance* 6, 3:438-53.

Fiorina, M. 1986. Legislator uncertainty, legislator control and the delegation of legislative Power. *Journal of Law, Economics and Organization* 2, 1:33-51.

Foster, Sir C. 1992. *Privatization, Public Ownership and the Regulation of Natural Monopoly*. Oxford: Blackwell.

_____ 1996. Reflections on the true significance of the Scott report for government accountability. *Public Administration* 74, 4:567-92.

Gregory, R. 1995. Accountability, responsibility and corruption: managing the "public production process." Ch. 3 in *The State Under Contract*, ed. J. Boston. Wellington: Bridget Williams Books.

_____ 1996. Careful incompetence at Cave Creek? Responsibility for a national tragedy. Paper presented to the SOG Conference, Centre for Research in Public Sector Management, University of Canberra, August 1-3.

_____ 1998. A New Zealand tragedy: Problems of political responsibility. *Governance* 11, 2:231-40.

Hegel, G. W. F. 1896. *Philosophy of Right*, tr. S. W. Dyde. London: Bell.

Hogwood, B. W., D. Judge, and M. McVicar. 1998. Too much of a good thing? The pathology of accountability. Paper presented at the Political Studies Association Annual Conference, University of Keele, April 7-9.

Hood, C. 1998. Individualized contracts for top public sevants: copying business, path-dependent political re-engineering – or Trobriand cricket? *Governance*, 11, 4:443-62.

Hood, C., C. Scott, O. James, G. W. Jones, and A. J. Travers. 1999. *Regulation in Government: Waste-watchers, Quality Police and Sleaze-busters*. Oxford: Oxford University Press.

Hood, C., and M. W. Jackson. 1991. *Administrative Argument*. Aldershot: Dartmouth.

Horn, M. J. 1995. *The Political Economy of Public Administration*. Cambridge: Cambridge University Press.

Lewis, D. 1997. *Hidden Agendas: Politics, Law and Disorder*. London: Hamish Hamilton.

Niskanan, W. A. 1971. *Bureaucracy and Representative Government*. Chicago: Aldine Atherton.

Page, E. 1997. *People Who Run Europe.* Oxford: Oxford University Press.

Polidano, C. 1998. Why bureaucrats can't always do what ministers want: multiple accountabilities in Westminster democracies. *Public Policy and Administration* 13, 1:35-50.

Power, M. 1997. *The Audit Society: Rituals of Verification.* Oxford: Oxford University Press.

Ridley, F. F., and A. Doig, eds. 1995. *Sleaze: Politics, Private Interests and Public Reaction.* Oxford: Oxford University Press.

Savoie, D. 1994. *Thatcher, Reagan, Mulroney: In Search of a New Bureaucracy.* Pittsburgh: University of Pittsburgh Press.

_____ 1999. *Governing From the Centre.* Toronto: University of Toronto Press.

Schaffer, B. 1973. *The Administrative Factor.* London: Frank Cass.

Scholz, J. T. 1991. Cooperative regulatory enforcement and the politics of administrative effectiveness. *American Political Science Review* 85, 1:115-136.

Schick, A. 1996. *The Spirit of Reform: Managing the New Zealand State Sector in a Time of Change.* Wellington: State Services Commission.

Silberman, B. S. 1993. *Cages of Reason.* Chicago: Chicago University Press.

Trosa, S. 1994. *Next Steps: Moving On.* London: Office of Public Service and Science.

Weaver, R. K., and B. A. Rockman, eds. 1993. *Do Institutions Matter?* Washington, DC: The Brookings Institution.

Public Service in an Information Society[1]

IGNACE SNELLEN

This chapter is an attempt to establish the importance of recent developments of ICTs for the future of the Public Service. "ICTs" are applications of information technological (IT) devices and programs in connection with telecommunication (C), especially networks such as the internet. In the first section ICTs are recognized as core technologies of public administration. A short overview and characterization are given of the different technologies and their use in public administration. In the second section algorithmization, transparency, and virtualization are indicated as underlying tendencies of the information age. The third section demonstrates how technologies are changing the traditional practices, beliefs, and concepts of public administration as well as of administrative law. The fourth section discusses how ICTs provoke new ambitions with respect to costs, service, and democracy in public administration. When central government orientations are compared, it appears that cost considerations are still the dominant occupation of central governments when applying ICTs. The potentialities of ICTs for improvement of service and intensifying democratic participation are only gradually and partly realized.

In the following sections the possibilities and probabilities of revitalization of the public service through the deployment of ICTs are brought forward. The discussion focuses on:

- the relation of public administration with the citizen
- the relation of public administration with not-for-profit organizations
- the relation between the layers of government
- the emerging framework of public administration
- the changing role of street-level bureaucracies
- access to governmental sources of information
- public administration and the privacy of the citizen
- knowledge management within public administration

In the final section a brief indication is provided of trends in the public service in the coming ten to fifteen years.

SOME INTRODUCTORY REMARKS: ICTS IN PUBLIC ADMINISTRATION

An attempt to establish the importance of recent developments in Information and Communication Technologies (ICTS) for public administration, seen as a public service, has to take into account the role of ICTS in public administration. The principal idea in this chapter is that ICTS are the core technologies of public administration, and that fundamental changes in these core technologies will have a revolutionizing influence on the structure and functioning of the public service. The concepts which form the basis of administrative law and the public administrative discipline will also change (surreptitiously). For example, centralization and decentralization as guiding concepts will lose their meaning within the context of the transparency which is created by ICTS.

To gauge the political importance of informatization in public administration the questions have to be raised as to what ICTS are being used, and how the application of ICTS is changing the practices and beliefs of public administration.

Such ICTS as database technologies, decision support technologies, networking technologies, personal identification and tracking technologies, and office and multi-media technologies are being used extensively in public administration to maintain and enrich its knowledge repositories.

Database technologies are applied in three basic forms of information systems:

1 Object registration systems hold a general purpose registration of the population, of legal entities such as foundations, of immovables, etc. Object systems make (legally) reliable societal exchanges possible. They function as a general purpose registration. No concrete transactions are performed by the object registration systems.
2 Sectoral systems help perform basic transactions in a specific sector of public administration such as social security, health care, police, traffic and transport, etc. More and more architectures are developed for entire sectors of society which make a free exchange and linking of data throughout the whole sector possible. They can also be useful in the construction of simulation models. In the judicial and the social security sectors "chain computerization" (Grijpink, forthcoming), which parallels the value chain of public service delivery, is taking place.
3 Control systems perform and monitor expenditure of financial, human, and physical (buildings and equipment) resources within ministries and other government bodies. Control systems are playing an ever-increasing role in the transparency and accountability of governmental institutions through performance indicators. The Canadian Treasury Board publications such as *Accounting for Results 1997* are good examples of this.

Decision support technologies serve as an aid to decision-making processes by applying specific rules to individually, or collectively, entered data. Decision support systems can range from fairly simple processing (case handling) systems, based on a few production rules, to complex advisory systems and expert systems as knowledge-based systems. Automation of decision making in public administration has gradually moved from the back office to the front office. Increasingly, databases from different government departments are automatically linked to decision-processing systems in other domains. Management Information Systems (MIS) and Executive Information Systems (EIS) also belong to the category of decision support systems.

Networking technologies are developing with great speed, adding the communication dimension to the information technologies. Time and place are losing their significance. All kinds of virtuality are thereby introduced, even the "virtual state" is a concept that is discussed seriously. Networking started with local and wide area networks. Recently intranets and extranets – using internet technology – have been widely introduced in government. The networks may have a special purpose, such as is the case for police networks, or they may have a more general data communication purpose. Slowly but steadily also the number of international networks between public administrations is growing, especially in Europe where the functioning of the European market with its free movement of capital, goods, services, and people depends on a reliable public administrative context.

Personal identification, tracking, tracing, and monitoring technologies are being developed with growing sophistication and are pervading all spheres of life. General personal identification numbers, or more specific numbers such as fiscal, social security, health care or educational numbers, can be used to create virtual general databases. Smart cards, incorporating identification numbers, and other tracing or tracking devices can also be used for identification purposes by public services and to monitor the mobility of people and vehicles. Tracking and monitoring devices are becoming more and more important; they are unobtrusive, they do not require any rearrangement of workflows or routines, but adapt themselves to existing habits, and they are extremely effective for surveillance. Closed circuit television (CCTV) is a good example of this kind of technology (Webster, 1998).

Office automation and multi-media technologies are used in the core business of public administration for the generation, handling, rearrangement, and provision of information in a retrievable form. Retrievability of the information is necessary for all kinds of audits to which public administration is subjected: legal, political, democratic, managerial, and historical auditing. Office

automation serves this purpose through the use of text processing systems and other entry devices (for text, voice, and pic-
tures); storage media such as magnetic tapes, CD or CD-ROM, or
photographic films; electronic mail, electronic data interchange;
and document and text retrieval systems. The importance of
these forms of office automation is determined by precedent,
legal evidence, and audits regarding public actions.

Due to the rapid changes of ICTs, the longevity of public
records, or their "digital durability," is at stake. It appears to be a
generally underestimated problem. When the millennium *problématique* was solved, or at least survived, the problem of digital
forgetfulness – the practical impossibility to retrieve the information stored on outdated carrier material, or the obsolescence
of the programs with which the information is processed – may
lead to problems of comparable size as the millennium problem
(Bikson and Frieling, 1993).

BASIC CHARACTERISTICS OF THE INFORMATION AGE TECHNOLOGIES

The Information Age is characterized by an all-pervasive presence of Information and Communication Technologies (ICTS) not
only in society at large and in sectors of society such as public
administration, but also in sciences such as biology, in which gen-
technology is rapidly extending our knowledge of the future.

The millennium *problématique* has brought home to us the
degree to which in the Information Age that presence of (and
dependency on) ICTS in private enterprise as well as public
administration has advanced.

The three basic characteristics of the Information Age – as far
as information and knowledge are concerned – are:

1 *Algorithmization.* Every activity that can be brought into an algo-
rithm will be automated. The extent to which this is true the millennium problématique makes clear. Every date-related routine
is automated, often (almost untraceably) embedded in chips.
For public administration algorithmization may mean:

- that the main policy implementation functions of the welfare state are taken over by computers
- that legislation and the creation of the legislation implementing computer systems will coalesce, and
- that the discretion of the street-level bureaucracy will tend to disappear (Snellen, 1994)

These impacts of ICTs on developments in public administration are well researched in different national contexts. They may lead to dis-intermediation, to de-centeredness of the individual decision maker, and to possible unresponsiveness of public administration.

2 *Transparency.* Computer applications entail what Shoshana Zuboff (1988) has called "informating":

the same technology simultaneously generates information about the underlying productive and administrative processes through which an organization accomplishes its work.

Through "informating" the reflexive capacities of the Information Society have increased exponentially. Point of sales applications and loyalty programs are good examples of this "informating." The possibilities for "data-mining" are also based on the "informating" nature of ICTs.

As a consequence, the transparency of production processes and the administrative and policy aspects of those processes – down to the details of the level of the individual – as well as the transparency of the environment in relation to clients, markets, and other relevant external developments have grown tremendously (Power, 1997).

Information systems containing shared knowledge were in the first instance created within the separate departments of public administration. These forms of "island-automation" are being followed by integration of databases at the level of organizations. Internet infrastructures facilitate the sector-wide information systems that are being built for health care, social security, physical planning, the judicial system, and the police. Within Europe the systems for international policing (Schengen

Information System: SIS) and for social security (SOSENET) may be mentioned.

The control capacity – and control aspirations! – of governments have increased, and still are increasing, with the growing transparency of sectors of society.

3 *Virtualization.* ICTS create virtualities, i.e. the appearance of things which actually are not such things. Virtuality created by ICTS is, nevertheless, real, not only in its appearance, but also in its logic and its consequences. (A virtual database may actually consist of several databases located at far distant places, but to the user it (or they) appears like one single database, and provides the user with the logic and the consequences of one database.)

Because of virtualization, time and place as a corollary of time, are losing their significance. Public administration, which in its organizational dimensions, up till now, is mainly time and territory oriented, will be organized along completely different lines. Territorial governance may be replaced increasingly by functional governance (see below). New forms of service to the public may be developed everywhere. New ways of "steering" of our complex societies are attempted in many different countries.

Not only the inner partitions but also the outside walls of the organizations of public administration are being blurred. A rearrangement of public jurisdictions during the next decades is very likely to take place.

In Canada the partnerships between central government and the provinces in the framework of "renewed federalism" may be forebodings of (implicit) rearrangements of public jurisdictions.

CHANGING PRACTICES AND CONCEPTS OF PUBLIC ADMINISTRATION

Every one of the above mentioned technologies is impacting public administration practices in their fundamental legal, political, economic, and social dimensions.[2]

As briefly indicated above, examples of practices that are changing fundamentally can be found in:

- The relationship between legislation on one hand, and system development for the execution of the law concerned on the other. The legal process of legislating and the technical process of systems building will gradually coalesce. Already the requirements of the systems building are restraining the pace and scope of legislation in sectors where the execution of the laws relies heavily on computer programs.
- The relationship between local bureaucracies and local politicians in developing the political agenda. Local bureaucracies have a leading edge on local politicians, the more they have automatically created information systems at their disposal. Research indicates that the local political agenda tends to become dominated by local officials (Smith, 1998).
- The relationship between allocations for the deployment of personnel and for information and communication technology. The reorganization of Human Resources and Development Canada (HRDC), mentioned in the following section of this chapter, is a good example of the possibilities to trade in people for information technology.
- The relationship between the street-level bureaucrat as representative of public administration and the citizen. The job of the street-level bureaucrat tends to be downgraded and his/her position within the bureaucracy weakened accordingly. It means that the position of the citizen is weakened also.

Gradually, not only the practices but also the *legal and public administrative concepts,* with which public administration is studied and normatively approached, are moving in new directions. Terms like centralization and decentralization, specialization and despecialization, autonomy, delegation, etc. are used as if the underlying reality has not changed. However, ICTs introduce a basic ambiguity in centralization as well as decentralization ("decentralization in a centralizing framework"). The same kind of ambiguity is introduced in other public administrative concepts.

FIGURE 1
Basic Concepts of Public Administration.[3]

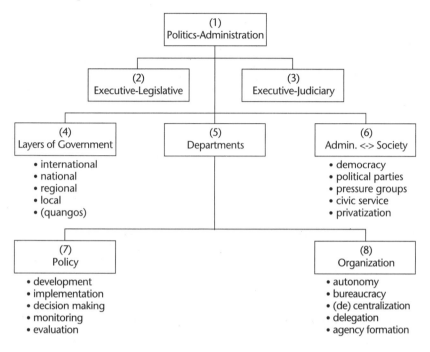

The meaning of the basic legal and public administrative concepts in an information age therefore have to be reconsidered.

The changing basic concepts of public administration I have in mind are illustrated in Figure 1.

CENTRAL GOVERNMENTAL ICT POLICY ORIENTATIONS AND AMBITIONS

Even more than most private enterprises traditional public administration is affected by *Information Age* developments. The core business of public administration is assembling, storing, processing, transporting, and providing information. ICTs have therefore become its *core technologies*. Information and knowledge (Max Weber's "Dienstwissen" and "Fachwissen": organizational knowledge and professional knowledge) about work processes and

environmental developments together form the knowledge repositories of public administration, its main basic assets. Attention to
ICT developments, and their implications for governance in the
twenty-first century, is essential for a managerial approach to a
revitalized public service. However, the attention central governments in most Western countries give to these developments is
rather one-sided, and the motives on which their attention is based
do not differ much.

In line with the increasing application of ICTs in public administration the ambitions of governments with respect to the potentialities of the public service, i.e., its cost optimum, its service
optimum, and its democratic optimum, are developing. Central
governmental ICT policy orientations with respect to the possible
significance of ICT applications for the functioning of public
administration are changing.

In the Information Age the *production function* of public
administration is changing continuously under the influence of
ICT developments. Knowledge is now recognized as a paramount factor of production. Information and communication
technologies are replacing the human production factor. The
execution of many functions of the modern welfare state would
not even be feasible without the application of ICTs to replace
people.

Through the change of the production function of the organizations of public administration its *optimal cost profile* is also
changing continuously. The pressure to make governments lean-
er and meaner therefore will be permanent.

The *optimal service profile* as well as the *optimal democratic profile*
of public administration will be affected also by changes in the
production function of public administration. The aspirations
and ambitions with respect to a more responsive and a more
democratic public administration will grow, inside as well as
outside its confines, as will be demonstrated by the examples
presented in the rest of this chapter (Snellen, 1994). The tendencies, mentioned here, are confirmed by empirical research (Lips
and Frissen, 1997). Many examples of the changing service
optimum and democratic optimum will be discussed.

The above mentioned ramifications of the Information Age in public administrations might affect the revitalization of the public service by facilitating *democratic practices,* improving *service delivery,* supporting *policy development and implementation,* and by furthering *knowledge management.*

It is, however, important to realize that every improvement of the public service through ICT applications may have its price in terms of undesirable power-shifts, loss of autonomy and / or privacy, etc.

In 1991 a comparative research project was started in seven European countries to find out what policies they followed at the central governmental level with respect to the "informatization" of their public administrations (Frissen et al., 1992). The outcome of the research is visualized in Table 1, which indicates the historical sequence of the "modes of informatization," i.e., the dominant attitudes of central governments as to the use of ICTS.

The following conclusions could be drawn from this research:

1 Whatever ministry had the main responsibility for informatization policies, the end result was an overriding interest in efficiency, effectiveness, and meta-coordination.
2 The attention of central informatization policies could be characterized as mainly internally (bureaucracy) oriented. The potentials of ICTS in a political and democratic context were only slowly beginning to be realized.
3 Ministries and other governmental bodies were eager to maintain their room for manoeuver and their autonomy. Many of the policies remained symbolic and official.
4 The interest representation in those policies reinforced their internal orientation.
5 The political involvement in informatization policies was almost negligible. Politicians considered ICTS just as tools, next to finance, personnel, and organization, and as not in need of any special political attention.

As indicated in these points only the financial and bureaucratic "modes of informatization" (see Table 1) at the central governmental

TABLE 1
Modes of informatization

	Resposible Authorities	Main Focus	Main Instruments	Represented Interests	Political Involvement
Financial Mode	Min. of Finance	Cost of EDP	Veto Plans Inventories Audits		Incidents Failures
Technical Mode	Min. of Industry	Industrial and Technical Development	Advice Subsidies Coordination	Industry Science	Industrial Share
Bureau-cratic Mode	Min. of Govern. Organization	Efficiency	Advice Plans Coordination	Sectors	(Efficiency Standard-ization)
Political Mode	Min. of Home Aff. Gov. Organization	Modern-ization	Advice Subsidies	Citizens Layers of Government	Citizens service Reduction of Bureaucracy

level were more or less developed. Only in some countries did one start to realize the important political meaning of informatization in public administration. At the moment, five years later, the situation has changed only marginally.

If we try to position the Canadian central government policy with respect to the informatization of the public service in this scheme, and to characterize its "mode of informatization," the outcome will be that the dominant attitude of central government and politicians in Canada fits mainly into the financial mode and into the bureaucratic mode. Indications for this positioning are the role of the Treasury Board and the Ministry of Finance in setting the targets for informatization by the public service. In 1994 a *Blueprint for Renewing Government Services Using Information Technologies* was published under the auspices of the Board. More specifically, the downsizing of Human Resource Development Canada, forced by the Program Review in the Spring of 1995, and to be realized before April 1998, is a good example of the way in which informatization is approached. An impressive Service Delivery Network of many thousands of kiosks and other automated self-service facilities was created to replace more than 5,000 HRDC staff. Although performance has improved, in line with improvements that can be noticed in comparable services in other countries, the main aspects of the creation of SDN are bureaucratic efficiency and economy.

As in so many automated self-service deliveries, the burden of preselecting the service still falls on the client. More of a genuine service orientation may be recognized in "Schoolnet."

ICTS AND REVITALIZATION

The following relationships qualify for revitalization of the public service through ICT applications.

The Relationships of Public Administration With Citizens as Customers, Clients, and Citoyens

The citizen as customer makes use of government services on his/her own initiative. As the case may be, the services concerned might be obtainable with other suppliers than the government. If this is the case, the citizen will only make use of the government service if it compares favourably with the service of other providers.

The citizen as *client* may be considered an "object of control," such as in prisons, or as a "case to be administered," e.g., a claimant for a social benefit. The possibilities for taking the initiative, and the power position of the citizen as client vis-à-vis the bureaucracy are very restricted.

The citizen as *citoyen* may be exercising his/her constitutional rights, as by voting, or may be acting as co-producer of policies. In modern forms of governance the citizen is more and more approached as co-producer of policies, especially at the local level of public administration. In his/her role as citoyen the citizen has the most opportunities to show initiative and is relatively autonomous.

As far as the citizen as client is concerned, ICTs play an important role in preventing bureaucracies from sending the citizen back and forth from pillar to post, which still is one of the main complaints about the functioning of public bureaucracies. ICTs make integration of files, databases, and documentary information possible, allowing the needs of the client to be satisfied at one single locality.

The necessary integration of the public services can be realized in different ways. The first way is to take the client as the point of integration. The "whole person" concept in the social security sector of the U.K. is an example. When a citizen approaches one of the many social security offices, the official is able to find out the total social security picture of the client, and to help him/her accordingly. The second way is to take the organization as the point of integration by creating a physical or virtual service counter as a front office for different departments, that can be accessed as a "one-stop shop" by the client. Products and services may be separately provided at this counter, but cross-references between them are easy to make. Routine questions will be answered immediately at the front office. More complex questions will be referred to one of the back offices. The back offices themselves remain separate. The third way is to take the back offices of different departments as the point of integration. It means that the departments will be redesigned into one (virtual) organization (Zuurmond and Snellen, 1997). This approach is the more basic one, and the most difficult to realize. The fourth way is a combination of the whole person approach and the integrated counter approach. The services of different departments are concentrated according to dominant "demand patterns" or "life events" of clients. An example of a demand pattern would be the different permits that are required in order to renovate a house. An example of a life event would be the death of a family member. In the latter case, public and private aspects of the deceased may be handled at the same counter.

ICTs used for concentrated service provision are: advisory systems, expert systems and processing systems, integrated databases, e-mail, smart cards, document retrieval systems, videoconferencing facilities, and interactive web sites. Kiosks may create an opportunity to approach public administration 24 hours a day.

To summarize, from the standpoint of the citizen as client the most important changes in public service delivery are: a 24-hour accessible "self-service government," featuring single-window access to various public information and services, faster and tailor-made public service provision, and an increasing independence of geographical locations to apply for services and information. From the standpoint of government the gains achieved are: increasing responsiveness, growing internal and external effectiveness through prevention of duplication in data, and reduction of cost in the creation and collection of data. Questions about ownership of data (especially smart cards), responsiveness and legitimacy of public service provision through ICTs, or the privacy and security of data matching and electronic formal transactions, will arise, but are for the moment still postponed (Lips and Frissen, 1997).

Questions that are raised, but are still not conclusively answered, are related to the function and role of discretion of the street-level bureaucrat on one hand, and to information security and privacy protection on the other.

As far as street-level bureaucrats are concerned, the idea is that this official's discretion is essential for a just and customized approach to the client. As a matter of fact, however, this discretion is more and more hedged in by ICT applications in his/her working environment. In routinized policy implementations bureaucracies are being replaced by "infocracies": in infocracies control is exerted not through Weberian organizational precepts but through the information infrastructure and information architecture. Control over the street-level bureaucrat is exerted by 1) the gathering of information through the network instead of by the street-level bureaucrat him/herself; 2) decision algorithms embedded in the software; 3) communication structures embedded in the software and in its authorization schemes; 4) co-ordination routinely executed by the information systems; 5) monitoring of all activities of the street-level bureaucrat and storing it in databases (Zuurmond, 1998).

By the application of the ICT devices, mentioned above, the citizen as client becomes more and more transparent and his/her privacy is at stake. In the private sector loyalty schemes fill the databases, which enterprises use to do their data-mining, and to construct "profiles" of their customers. Their ideal seems to be "one-to-one marketing." In the public sector the possible inroads into the privacy of clients is the more serious, as the citizen as client is dependent on the monopoly position of public administration as provider of services. Next to that, public administration is active in many sectors at the same time, between which personal information can be exchanged. The objective to fight fraud is often used as an excuse in this respect. Regulations with respect to exchange of information leave more and more leeway to "front-end verification" or matching with databases of other authorities.

Tracing systems, tracking systems and, administrative as well as physical, monitoring systems are making the client more and more transparent. Among the techniques used in the coupling or integration of information systems are transaction systems such as matching of databases, profiling of individuals as well as categories of the population, installation of closed-circuit television surveillance cameras, automatic photographic recognition, etc.

The introduction of "one-stop shops," mentioned above, provides another excuse to legitimate the invasion of privacy.

As far as the citizens as citoyens are concerned, ICTs facilitate forms of instant opinion polling and instant, referenda-like, interest articulations. The old ideals of direct democracy are revived. Although ICTs are nowhere used in practice to make plebiscites possible, they seem to offer an attractive, direct-democratic, alternative for forms of representative democracy. It is tempting to visualize citizens as citoyens, who on a daily basis make their preferences known with respect to certain policies. In theory such a push-button democracy would be possible. In practice it would, however, lead to a radicalized single issue approach to politics. From day-to-day inconsistent collective decisions would be taken. Coordination of policies would be practically impossible, and a more integrated approach of problems would be out of reach. As far as experience with referenda is gained, it does not appear that they eliminate deliberations between citizens. This often heard objection against referenda is not confirmed in practice. On the contrary, democratic deliberations may even be intensified, and the citizens may be more involved than under representative arrangements. But the objections just mentioned make the acceptance of positive referenda very unlikely. There is a slight tendency to introduce a kind of corrective referendum: if the legislator has passed a law, a qualified majority may reach a negative votum against it. At the same time a tendency can be noticed to gradually increase the amount of signatories required for the organization of a corrective referendum.

The prospects for other direct democracy arrangements, such as territorial and functional decentralization, vouchers, "client-based budgets" and the like, seem to be much more promising. Even if tendencies to direct democracy are not likely to be strengthened by ICTs, the indirect and substantive forms of democracy will be probably boosted by them. The practice, growing everywhere to develop performance indicators, and to let public authorities and private organizations in the public sector account for them, may strengthen this substantial form of democracy. ICTs increase the speed with which the results of performance auditing reach the electorate and political decision makers. Through this increased speed, performance auditing as a feedback mechanism may in practice develop into a feedforward mechanism for the public service.

If, but only if, representative democratic bodies are eager to profit as much as possible from the opportunities ICTs create to improve their democratic influence, ICTs could strengthen their position with respect to their opposite numbers in government and in the bureaucracies. ICT instruments available in this respect are: decision support systems, such as Geographic Information Systems, for the development of policy proposals; direct access to basic registrations available in government administrations; monitoring systems in use for policy implementation; access to automated systems for policy implementation; instant polling systems for policy evaluations; calendaring and documentary information systems for use in the representative council, etc.

As far as the relationship of people's representatives to the citizens as citoyens are concerned, expectations for ICTs such as web sites and civic networks (e.g., "Digital Cities") are high. Preliminary results of research do not (yet) confirm these expectations. Web sites are rarely used by politicians for consultation with citizens with respect to their demands and wishes. Conversations with constituents are more the exception than the rule. When "flaming" takes place, politicians tend to back out, and to end their participation in the discussion (as happened in the famous experiment in Santa Monica). Until now, web sites are mainly a replacement of (or addition to) written communications with the same content. The updating is often neglected. Only a certain elite of young male internet addicts is reached. They participate in the discussion mainly as passive onlookers. As far as politicians make use of the internet to reach their constituents or the rank and file in their party they tend to limit themselves to top-down communication.[4]

The Relationships With (Not-for-Profit) Organizations

In the last decade, autonomous developments within public administration itself, as well as in the relationship between public administration and organizations in the public sector, have set in motion new regimes of governance of the public sector. Different motives were behind these autonomous developments. The major ones were the felt need to economize on the expenses of the welfare state and the lack of effectiveness and efficiency of public administrations in handling the complexities of modern society. Apart from the different shades of autonomization (agency formation, e.g., in the form of special operating agencies, outsourcing, privatization, etc.) new concepts of governance were introduced. These new concepts of governance are phrased in terms of the application of transaction principles. Applications of ICT, such as databases, spreadsheets and GISs, make it feasible to form the indexes and indicators, that are necessary to administer those principles.

The principles are applied to the transactions within four trajectories: the trajectory between central government and other levels of government, between these other levels of government and care-providing organizations, between care-providing organizations and professionals, and between professionals and clients.

A central concept in the new governance is disciplining. In the first trajectory, central government disciplines the other layers of government by the allocation of a fixed budget. In the second trajectory, these layers will negotiate sharply with the competing care providers because every deficit would have to be financed by themselves. Therefore, these layers of government will press the care providers to compete pricewise and quote their lowest price. In the third trajectory, the care providers are confronted by the professionals. These are more and more involved in the responsibility of management for an economical stewardship of the care-providing organizations. In addition, they are forced to accept kinds of protocols and best practices, which are based on comparisons and averages derived from sectoral information systems. In the fourth trajectory, the professionals are confronted by clients who are put into a bargaining position. If vouchers are made available to them, their bargaining position is strengthened. This is even more the case when "client based budgets" are put at their disposal.

So, the transparency that will be created by ICT applications, together with autonomization of the care-providing parts of public administration, will put an end to the information asymmetry which dominated the relationships in many public sectors. Central government takes the existing budgets as point of departure and economizes on them till the other layers of government protest too vigorously. And even then, central governments have done their homework by adopting a horizontal perspective in their reviews, and by organizing "partnered" reviews (Treasury Board, 1997, 12).

The other governmental layers, for their part, stimulate the competition between the care providers to get the best or at least a realistic price. They make horizontal analyses of the operations of the care providers and develop comparative indicators to fend off their claims. The care providers make the same kind of analyses where the professionals are concerned. For example, by drafting protocols and formulating "diagnosis related groups" managers succeed in tying the medical doctors to the hospital budget. In principle the professional is rewarded according to the parameters of the protocol.

As a consequence, central governments together with the controlling and financing institutions may discipline the different sectors of the welfare state. The citizen may profit from the transparency that will be created along the road. Benchmarking and index figures will not only discipline the service providers and professionals, but also will be of use for the customers or clients, as the experiences with the "Citizen's Charter" in the u.k. make clear.

A negative consequence, however, might be that the innovative capacities of providers and professionals will get into a tight corner. The care providers, who make available to the professionals all kinds of useful information and communication technologies, reinforce their management control. Transaction systems and databases make it possible to check meticulously the workload, the methods of working, and the cost factors of the professionals, to compare them with the averages of their counterparts in the sector, and to correct them. When advisory or case-processing systems are made available the discretion of the professional may be reduced implicitly.

In the end, not only the discretion of the professional but also the autonomy of the care-providing organization is in jeopardy.

The Relationships With Lower Layers of Government

Comparable developments, as mentioned with respect to not-for-profit organizations, might appear in the relationship between central and regional or local government. Decentralization, devolution, and burden sharing are taking place in a framework of continuous centralization and in a sphere of growing transparency.

In some sectors, central governmental oversight with the help of ICTS leads to *policy-rich* forms of inspection. In other sectors a more policy-poor kind of inspection may prevail. A policy-rich form of oversight is characterized by active interference of the oversight authority in the patterns of activity of the overseen organizations. In a policy-poor form of oversight the overseeing authority limits itself to boundary-setting control, without aspirations to develop new ways of behaviour with the overseen organizations. Whatever the dominant mode of inspection, the relative importance of information and informatization in the power division between layers of government is increasing. Applications of ICTS make the policies of lower layers of government more transparent. In the domains where policy-poor kinds of inspection prevail, the mere existence of ICT-supported ways of surveillance suffices for lower layers of government to anticipate on possible interference by higher layers of government. Policy-rich forms of inspection, which are required in modern policy domains, such as environment, are facilitated by ICTS as well. Empirical research confirms these trends (Zeef, 1994).

The Emerging Framework of Public Administration

The relationships between jurisdictions, between authorities, and with executive (street-level) offices are in constant flux in many countries. Also here, the increasing transparency of the activities of different governmental bodies leads to a growing insight in the interdependencies between them, and to the aspiration to coordinate policies and activities. The relevant structural developments (or tendencies), that might result from this, are aptly described in the (British) Parliamentary Office of Science and Technology (POST) Report 110 of February 1998. The report starts from the supposition that:

Government would be organized quite differently if it were designed "from scratch" today, while the existing system reflects much more the unorganized evolution of structures and functions laid down many years ago before computers were even imagined.

Four scenarios of possible future structural outcomes, in line with developments in ICT applications, are indicated in this report. Applying Business Process Redesign, two different customer bases are distinguished: an external customer base consisting of people, businesses, etc., and an internal customer base consisting of ministers and senior officials.

The external customers are provided with services through:

- receipt of revenue
- enforcement of regulations
- delivery of products (passports, etc.)
- provision of grants and benefits
- procurement of goods and services
- provision of information

All ministries and agencies are engaged in at least three of these processes and the similarities between the activities of those departments and agencies engaged in the same process are great.

The internal customer base is engaged in policy development, and needs skilled and experienced advisers. The supporting processes in the areas of information analysis, budget management, policy presentation, staff development, legal advice, etc. are very similar across the departments.

In view of these considerations a *first scenario* for restructuring central government could be: A set of relatively small "policy" departments. These departments would focus on the delivery of policy-related services to ministers and senior officials. Officials would have access, through technology, to decision-support information (for preparation of analyses and options). They would be supported by common, technology-based processes for resource and budget management, and for communication (i.e., a central consultation process unit would allow departments to tap into sophisticated and extensive consultation resources that would be expensive and difficult to justify individually). Such a structure would be flexible and could readily be altered to reflect changing political demands.

A *second scenario* for reframing public administration could be: A set of agencies engaged in delivering the six process-based services to the citizen and business could be grouped together. There would be a single agency for each type of process or, more probably, there would be a group of agencies for each type of process. These groups would share all common process elements, so that eventually all common operations are performed optimally, and only once. The agencies would buy services from other agencies, or the private sector, for those operations which are not core to their business. Such a structure would effectively end direct departmental ownership of agencies. They would work to, and be measured against, service level agreements prepared by policy departments requiring services.

A *third scenario* for the reframing could be: Common elements to policy operations (such as legal advice, technological support, etc.) in departments could be brought together to serve more than one department. A common information infrastructure shared by the departments, and connecting the departments with the executive agencies would be necessary to forge an overall process-based structure.

A *fourth scenario* could be: The interaction between government and citizen could be rearranged according to different main "life events" (Child Age, Adult Age, Third Age) of citizens. This could lead to a re-grouping of parts of departments (the most radical option), but in the first instance to a clustering of information provision and services in "one-stop shops."

Elements of all four scenarios are discernible in the new structures that are being developed in most Western countries. ICTs, and the "virtual realities" they create, are playing a very important facilitating role in those scenarios.

The Changing Role of Street-Level Bureaucracies

Within the context of such structures the role and function of the *street-level bureaucracies,* and especially the street-level bureaucrats are changing fundamentally. The growing transparency of the work situation and the progressing automation

of administrative decision making erode the power and discretion of the street-level bureaucrat. The four dimensions in which
this erosion is taking place are:[5]

1 In the process dimension: the steps in the processing of a case.
   Starting with the back office and eventually reaching the front
   office various tasks have been taken over by the contact functionary's computer. In recent years, computer applications
   provide increasingly automated assessment of cases without
   the involvement of a contact functionary. Retracting the role
   of the street-level bureaucrat occurs gradually from back
   office to front office.

2 In the scope dimension: the percentage of cases handled
   automatically instead of by the street-level bureaucrat. In the
   first phase of automation, the functionary still maintains the
   possibility of entering data in such a manner that a particular
   outcome is inevitable. In a later phase, the system advises the
   functionary, but his/her personal judgment is not completely
   ruled out. A busy functionary who wants to play safe will
   follow the advice of the system. In a third phase, the system
   selects the "smooth" cases it handles by itself, and will leave
   only the complicated cases to the functionary. In a fourth
   phase, the system will handle all cases and assumes a monopoly for certain steps, if not all steps, of the decision process.

3 In the assessment dimension: the rule density that limits the
   room for decision. Generally, discretionary freedom is limited
   by laws and regulations, and by more detailed policy and
   organizational rules. This discretionary space cannot be fully
   "organized away" with traditional juridical and organizational means. Automation of the decision process is changing
   this. Even help desks, that are supposed to assist the user
   with the technical system, may steer the user in terms of content of the decision.

4 In the accountability dimension: the justification of the decision. More and more automated processes make use of standardized justifications composed of prefabricated texts. In
   this regard two developments are relevant for street-level

bureaucrats. First the composition of standardized justifications is increasingly done without them. Sometimes software companies even provide subscriptions for the updating of texts in view of changes in jurisprudence. A second development is that the street-level bureaucrat is increasingly limited to standardized justifications only. This, too, results in a lack of awareness of developments in jurisprudence.

The outcome of the changes in those four dimensions, which are implications of the progressing automation of the work of street-level bureaucrats, is that the decision-making premises of the street-level bureaucrat are increasingly determined outside his/her sphere of influence. In many sectors of public service, the traditional kind of street-level bureaucrat will sooner or later disappear.

The Accessibility of Governmental Sources of Information

Quite a lot of barriers have to be cleared before the accessibility of the sources of information, of which governments dispose, will be effected. Freedom of Information Acts, with their restriction to documents, are as well a hindrance as a help for the citizen, to get the information he/she wants about the *faits et gestes* of the government. Loyalty to the profession (laymen should be kept at a distance), to the organization (internal conflicts of opinion should not come into the open) and to the member of government (the minister should be kept out of trouble) makes the public officials reluctant to share their information with members of the public. There are also legal grounds why the information of the government is not always accessible (readable). The wording of the information has to be legally correct, without creating false expectations. The possible establishment of precedent leads to guarded expressions. The decisions of the administration have to be immune to objections and appeals. And politicians are not eager to indicate clearly what the opportunity costs of a decision are, and who has won or lost.

Notwithstanding the frequent occurrence of these barriers, the sources of information with the government are increasingly made available to the public. ICTs are playing a very important facilitating role in this respect. Web sites are mushrooming. The discussion about freedom of information, however, is rather limited. It focuses mainly on accessibility of documents which are related to public policy making, and on the commercialization of the data (especially geo-data) which governments have available, and are tempted to commercialize themselves in competition with private enterprise.

In many countries, access to information for parliamentarians, the media, interest groups, and even other parts of public administration, about what is happening, or has happened, in public administration, is at least as important as the commercialization of information, but does not get the same attention. A coherent policy with respect to accessibility of information from the government will have to consist of the following components.

Telecommunication Infrastructure   Privatization of the telecommunications industry leads to fierce competition with sophisticated facilities in some parts of the country, but not in the commercially less interesting parts of the country. As a consequence governments are restricted in their opportunities to provide equal access to governmental services in those backward parts of the country. Governments have to assure that minimum conditions for a democratic use of the telecommunication infrastructure are met in all parts of the country (Taylor, 1994).

Account Management   Many citizens are doubly handicapped. They are practically "linguistically illiterate" and they are "computer illiterate." Moreover, they do not have access to the required bureaucratic competence (the ability to get your own situation across in terms that are manageable for the public service). These citizens need an account manager as a personal address.

Interactive Web sites   Although web sites are mushrooming, many public organizations do not have a clear picture what they want with this new medium. They just duplicate the written information which they provide in their brochures. In that case, unique opportunities are missed in the co-production of policies (Demchak, Friis, and La Porte, 1998).

From Documents to Information to Data   Most Freedom of Information Acts are dependent on the accessibility of documents that have a substantive relationship with certain governmental policies. In that respect they relate to an era in which it was almost impossible to make the information (used and unused!) available, which the government had at its disposal at the time a policy was framed, or a decision was taken. The ease with which databases can be opened up leads to a growing pressure to enable the citizens and their interest groups, to make their own analyses on the data (Beers, 1992).

Meta-information   In line with the development "from document to data," people, pressure groups, and parliamentarians may want to know what kind of information the government has available. The controlling function of parliaments especially might be improved, if such kind of meta-information is put at their disposal.

Optimization in Networks   The more that central government departments cooperate with other public and private organizations, the more this cooperation is dependent on shared information. As indicated in the first part of this chapter, in many sectors of the welfare state, sector-wide information infrastructures are created. The accessibility of government information, therefore, has to be seen in the context of the informatization in the sectors as a whole. Optimization of information relations will improve the efficiency of the sectors themselves and their transparency for the citizen.

Public Administration and the Privacy of the Citizen

The principles formulated in the OECD "Guidelines on the Protection of Privacy and Transborder Flows of Personal Data" of 1980 are still, notwithstanding the technological developments of the last decades, an internationally recognized testbed for national forms of privacy protection. The principles can be divided roughly into two categories. The first category considers the quality of the personal data and the conditions under which they may be processed. It contains the *collection limitation principle,* the *data quality principle,* the *purpose specification principle,* and the *security safeguard principle.* The second category views the legal position of the registered person. It contains the *openness principle* and the *accountability principle.*

Although these principles have retained their validity, as a just balance between the interests of the registrar and the registered, they need to be specified and operationalized for every separate ICT application. The focus of attention of privacy protection, as far as ICTS are concerned, has shifted from the *registration* of personal data to the *processing* of personal data. The invasion of personal privacy may be feared, especially because of the enormous growth in the capacity to analyze masses of data (data-mining), while other ICT applications support the surveillance capacity of public and private organizations, and the retrieval and storage capacity of masses of data, based on administrative and visual surveillance.

Privacy protection is under great pressure. To fight fraud, governments in many countries are allowed to couple databases, to make profiles, and to match databases. In some countries the legitimacy of the tax system and the social security system is supported by such fraud detecting techniques. In addition to this, citizens may have to make a choice between informational safety and physical safety. Many people are readily prepared to trade in informational safety for physical safety through surveillance technologies.

Surveillance technologies have some characteristics in common. They pass barriers of physical distance and darkness. They pass also barriers of time. They are unobtrusive for the observed person. They observe normally without formal permission. They are normally more focused on prevention than repression. They may have a built-in hidden bias. They necessitate self-control in the observed persons.

One of the basic tasks of the state is to guarantee the safety of its citizens. It is impossible to imagine the execution of this task without surveillance technologies. Private enterprise also relies more and more on them to protect their property. And the public at large realizes that through surveillance technologies the public space may be given back to them. The challenge will be to stick to the principles of privacy and to profit from the possibilities of information and communication technology. Privacy-enhancing technologies – aiming at driving out the Devil through Beelzebub – are advocated by some, but seem not yet the answer.

The Future of Knowledge Management: How to Exploit the Knowledge Repository?

The "informating" capacity of ICTs is already mentioned. Basic registrations, transaction systems, geographic information systems, are instrumental in the building up of the knowledge repositories of public authorities. By the coupling of databases, data-matching, data-mining, profiling, and other such approaches, the knowledge base of public authorities is growing continuously. Knowledge management is becoming a separate field of specialization for all kinds of authorities, beyond the sectors of police, the military, or taxation.

For public administration in general, knowledge management is closely related to Human Resource Management. The knowledge generated, or stored, by the use of ICT applications can only be retrieved when certain human resource conditions are fulfilled. If personnel does not have the required attitude and capacities, knowledge repositories built up by public administration are of no avail. For example, when personnel are not prepared to share information, or when they are computer illiterate, the knowledge repositories within public administration will have to remain undisclosed.

Another basic condition for effective knowledge management is that the difference between data, information, and knowledge has to be taken into account. Knowledge management, the special care for a combination of "Dienstwissen" (organizational knowledge) and "Fachwissen" (professional knowledge), as Max Weber called them, is a matter of course in public administrations. Much of the knowledge of public administrations is consolidated in legal rules and regulations, and in policy and organizational rules. Public administrations are constantly monitoring situations in society. As Klaus Lenk states: "The information gathered through the monitoring of society is not only used for operational purposes in more or less pre-defined primary processes. Such information may just be kept for some future, still unknown purpose."[6]

The massive introduction of ICTs, however, gives knowledge management even more importance. All components of knowledge management get extra dimensions, possibly as new opportunities as well as new threats, in public administration. The components of knowledge management are 1) knowledge creation, 2) knowledge acquisition, 3) knowledge transfer, 4) loss of knowledge, and 5) the handling of ethical dilemmas, related to the automation of knowledge applications.

Knowledge creation through the use of ICTs was discussed in a former paragraph, where the notion of "informating" (developed by Shoshana Zuboff) was referred to. We have seen that the creation of knowledge is a constant side effect of the use of ICT applications. Automation of the execution or control of physical or administrative processes leads inherently to retraceable knowledge about the processes themselves and their content. Normally, public administrations are obliged by law to record their internal processes in a retraceable form. This "informating" nature of ICTs applied in public administration makes an *almost unlimited acquisition and storage of knowledge* possible. Transaction systems used in the administrative processes, such as student allowances, rent allowances, social housing, etc. feed the process and decision parameters into databases, on which all kinds of so-called "data-mining" techniques can be applied. The same knowledge acquisition techniques can be applied to databases that are filled with data from tracing, tracking, or monitoring systems. A further step in knowledge acquisition is set when databases are coupled or matched on an ad hoc basis.

The *knowledge transfer* in public administration has made a quantum leap through the installment of internet, intranets and extranets on one hand, and the creation of advisory systems, expert systems, and processing systems on the other. Not only time and place are losing their importance in the communication of knowledge, but new economies of scale and scope come into being also.

Loss of knowledge, however, is also an aspect of ICTs that has to be taken into account by knowledge management. The more knowledge-based systems are introduced in public administration for the automation of decision making, the greater the temptation will be to downgrade the function of street-level bureaucrats, to economize on their salaries. In many highly automated parts of public administration deskilling of professional personnel is taking place. In a certain sense, loss of knowledge is also occurring, where automated tracking, tracing or monitoring systems are installed. These systems tend to focus only on quantitative dimensions of processes and activities, and to neglect qualitative dimensions. In as far as their use leads to loss of autonomy of the monitored organizations, the locally available knowledge will dry up, or will be underutilized.

The most important way in which public administrations will lose knowledge, however, is through neglect of the problems related to digital durability of their archives. ICT developments are so fast and so drastic, that knowledge on outdated electronic carriers is – for all practical purposes – not accessible any more. That is not only a problem in view of the accountability obligations of public administration – legal, political, democratic, operational accountability, and accountability to the cultural heritage – but also in view of the management of the knowledge, that is in principle available in public administration.

This brings us to the *ethical aspects* of knowledge management in public administration. In former paragraphs, different ethical aspects – be it not under that denominator – of the applications of ICT were mentioned. The loss of discretion of the street-level bureaucrat, the loss of autonomy of not-for-profit organizations, the possible immunization of public services through automation of assessments and justifications of administrative decisions, and many other aspects could be referred to.

A more general ethical aspect of ICTs is, that they may lead to what a philosophical colleague of mine calls "epistemic enslavement," becoming the slaves of computer systems (Van den Hoven, 1995). He describes such a situation as follows: "Users of these systems are often working in an *artificial epistemic niche* (highly computerized work environments of which air traffic control towers, control rooms of nuclear power plants, offices of highly informatized government agencies are good examples) from which they cannot escape. The users are severely limited with respect to the beliefs they can *acquire,* and they are severely limited with respect to the options open to them to *justify* their beliefs once acquired. Non-compliance with the system constitutes a form of risk-taking the user cannot justify at the moment of his dissidence. Once he has given in, he has lost the resources that could provide him with good reasons to opt out."

Such ethically problematic situations may be even aggravated if electronic networks are involved (Rochlin, 1997). A further route of entrapment is followed as soon as a loose coupling of a long-linked technology is replaced by a tight coupling. This is exactly what is happening when communication technology is introduced in the world of personal computers. Out of economic and efficiency reasons, and on the basis of managerial considerations, it is tempting to create integrated databases, informational infrastructures across sectors of society – such as social security, labour market, housing, etc. – and to give shape to all kinds of virtual realities, such as virtual organizations, virtual memories, virtual meetings. Such a continuous tightening of couplings between police, prosecution, court procedures, probation and prisons, and such a creation of virtual realities are taking place in the sphere of, for instance, criminal justice. The virtual realities that are created may lead in the long term to a situation in which decision makers become accustomed to losing sight of their own decision making, or to making their decisions in a hyper-reality. These are important ethical challenges public administration will have to cope with in governance of the twenty-first century.

SUMMARY OF TRENDS IN THE PUBLIC SERVICE

As far as the ambitions of governments and public administrations are concerned, cost reductions will remain the dominant orientation.

The state apparatuses will, for the years to come, continuously be decreased in size. The orientation on *improvement of service,* such as through the creation of "one-stop shops" will have more a symbolic than a real importance. Only when governments are prepared to develop "proactive" uses of their information systems – government information being actively used to find and approach (accumulated) problem groups or problem areas, instead of waiting for the initiative of the groups or areas concerned – will a substantial improvement of the service level be achieved. Shortsighted considerations of cost reductions may hamper the full development of the democratic potentialities of ICT. Apart from the strengthening of market democracy through the introduction of vouchers, client-based budgets and the like, the ambition to expand the *democratic influence* of citizens and their organizations will play a minor role, and the possibilities of ICTs will be scarcely deployed.

As far as the relations between bureaucrats and politicians are concerned, ICTs will strengthen the power position of the bureaucrats – certainly at the lower levels of government – to the detriment of the position of the politicians. Bureaucrats dispose increasingly of transaction information, data-mining programs, and other marketing research techniques, making it possible for them to articulate interests of groups of the population – the constituencies of the politicians – and to create a firm basis for the political agenda on the information they have available. Geographic information systems, in which administrative data are stored, will probably play a major role in the powershift between bureaucrats and politicians. Bureaucrats may even develop into a new class of democratic intermediaries. In that case, politicians may limit themselves to "steering at a distance" with the help of performance indicators.

As far as the internal developments within the governmental bureaucracies are concerned, fully automated processing systems are taking over the policy implementation of the welfare state and, gradually, also decision making in the judiciary. Major parts of the welfare state policies are not implementable without automated decision making of routine cases. The overload of cases before the courts forces public defence as well as judges to rely more and more on knowledge-based systems, which replace traditional forms of discretion. Coupling of databases between different authorities will lead to further erosion of discretion. Those couplings are growing into sectoral, national, and international information infrastructures, which will increasingly determine the outcome of governmental decisions in individual cases.

As far as the overall framework of the Public Service is concerned, territorial and sectoral jurisdictions will become rearranged along functional lines of demarcation. As indicated above, policy development and policy implementation are being separated from each other, and policy implementations are being placed under independent agency headings. Financial, juridical, informatics, and organizational staff functions, related to policy development, tend to be regrouped into virtual staff organizations. Policy implementation functions, such as provision of information, allocation of permits or allowances, inspection, etc., tend to be regrouped, as well, into separate logistical organizations. The conditions of the information age allow the outsourcing of many activities without forfeiting detailed control of the activities concerned. The increasing amount of information that is systematically available stimulates an integration of policies concerning safety, youth, incomes, old age, and the like. This may lead to a rearrangement of ministerial departments along the lines of those more project-like integrated policies.

As far as knowledge management through ICTs is concerned, opportunities are there as well as threats. There are opportunities to democratize substantially the access of interest groups to the information held within public administration, and to further increase the transparency of the public service. There are also threats to the systems of checks and balances between branches and sectors of public administration, and for the discretion of the public servants, who are hedged in by infocracies. The knowledge management that is required to provide the public with the latest forms of electronically mediated services may well put the interests of the citizens as client, customer, or citoyen in jeopardy.

NOTES

1 I am grateful to Marc Denis Everell, Assistant Deputy Minister, National Resources Canada, and to Roger Jolly, Erasmus University Rotterdam, for their stimulating comments on a draft of this paper.
2 Federated structures with inbuilt checks and balances and their strict separation of powers, also between the layers of government, appear to be more resistant to ICT-induced changes than (decentralised) unitary states such as the U.K. and the Netherlands, an environment in which the separation of powers and the balance of powers are less strictly maintained, and in which the autonomy of lower levels of government is less well-guarded than in federations.
3 It is not feasible to give a complete overview of all the relevant research on ICTs' implications for public administration within the limits of this paper. The interested reader will find a recent and more elaborated overview of the subject matter in Snellen and Van de Donk (1998).
4 For further information on this subject, based on empirical research in some European countries, the reader is referred to Van de Donk, Snellen and Tops (1995).
5 This part is a short reproduction of Snellen (1998).
6 K. Lenk, Information as a key concept in the theory of public administration, lecture at Twente University, Enschede, 27 April 1995

BIBLIOGRAPHY

Beers, A. A. L. 1992. Public access to government information towards the 21st century. In *Information Law Towards the 21st Century*, eds. W. F. Korthals Altes, et. al. Deventer, Boston: Kluwer, 177-214.
Bellamy C., and J. A. Taylor. 1997. The case of the U.K. criminal justice system. In Taylor, Snellen, and Zuurmond, 37-53.
Bikson, T. K., and E. J. Frieling. 1993. *Preserving the Present. Toward Viable Electronic Records.* The Hague: Sdu Uitgeverij.
Demchak, Chr. C., C. Friis, and T. M. La Porte. 1998. Reflections on configuring public agencies in cyberspace: a conceptual investigation. In Snellen and Van de Donk, 225-244.
Donk, W. B. H. J. van de, I. Th. M. Snellen, and P. W. Tops, eds. 1995. *Orwell in Athens: A Perspective on Informatization and Democracy.* Amsterdam: IOS Press.

Frissen, P. H. A., V. J. J. M. Bekkers, B. K. Brussaard, I. Th. M. Snellen, and M. Wolters, eds. 1992. *European Public Administration and Informatization. A Comparative Research into Policies, Systems, Infrastructures and Projects.* Amsterdam: IOS Press.

Grijpink, J. Forthcoming. Chain-computerisation: non-Intrusive information infrastructure for interorganisational public policy implementation. In *Information Infrastructure and Policy*, Volume 6.

Hoven, M. J. van den. 1995. Information technology and moral philosophy: philosophical explorations in computer ethics. Diss. Erasmus University Rotterdam.

Lips A. M. B., and P. H. A. Frissen. 1997. Wiring government. Integrated public service delivery through ICT. In *Iter/NWO* vol. 8:67-164. Alphen a.d. Rijn: Samsom.

Organization for Economic Cooperation and Development. 1980. *Guidelines on the Protection of Privacy and Transborder Flows of Personal Data.* Paris: OECD. http://www.oecd.org//dsti/sti/it/secur/prod/ PRIV-EN.HTM.

Parliamentary Office of Science and Technology. 1998. *Electronic Government – Information Technologies and the Citizen.* London: POST. http://www.parliament.uk/post/egov.htm.

Power, M. 1997. *The Audit Society: Rituals of Verification.* Oxford, New York: Oxford University Press.

Rochlin, G. I. 1997. *Trapped in the Net: The Unanticipated Consequences of Computerization.* Princeton: Princeton University Press.

Smith, C. 1998. Political parties in the information age: from mass party to leadership organization? In Snellen and Van de Donk, 175-187.

Snellen, I. Th. M. 1994. Automation of policy implementation. *Informatization and the Public Sector* 3, 2:135-149.

_____ 1998. ICT and street-level bureaucrats. In Snellen and Van de Donk, 497-505.

Snellen, I. Th. M., and W. B. H. J. van de Donk, eds. 1998. *Public Administration in an Information Age: a Handbook.* Amsterdam: IOS Press.

Taylor, J. A. 1994. Telecommunications infrastructure and public policy development: evidence and inference. *Informatization and the Public Sector* 3, 1:63-73.

Taylor, J. A., I. Th. M. Snellen, and A. Zuurmond, eds. 1997. *Beyond BPR in Public Administration: Institutional Transformation in an Information Age.* Amsterdam: IOS Press.

Treasury Board Secretariat. 1997. *Accounting for Results*. Ottawa, Ont.: Public Affairs Branch, Treasury Board Secretariat.

Webster, C. W. R. 1998. Changing relationships between citizens and the state: the case of closed circuit television surveillance cameras. In Snellen and Van de Donk, 79-95.

Zeef, P. H. H. 1994. *Tussen Toezicht en Toezien. (Between Overview and Onlooking)*. Rotterdam: Phaedrus.

Zuboff, S. 1988. *In the Age of the Smart Machine: the Future of Work and Power*. New York: Basic Books.

Zuurmond, A. 1998. From bureaucracy to infocracy: are democratic institutions lagging behind? In Snellen and Van de Donk, 259-272.

Zuurmond, A., and I. Th. M. Snellen. 1997. From bureaucracy to infocracy: towards management through information architecture. In Taylor, Snellen, and Zuurmond, 205-224.

The Dialectics of Accountability for Performance in Public Management Reform

PETER AUCOIN

RALPH HEINTZMAN

INTRODUCTION

Accountability is a cornerstone of public governance and management because it requires that those who hold and exercise public authority *be held to account*. Although accountability regimes vary in important respects among political systems, taken collectively they encompass processes whereby citizens hold their governors to account for their behaviour and performance directly through elections; the representatives of citizens in legislative assemblies hold political executives and public servants accountable through mechanisms of public scrutiny and audit; political executives hold their subordinate officials accountable through hierarchical structures of authority and responsibility; and, among other things, courts and various administrative tribunals and commissions hold legislatures, executives, or administrative officers accountable to the law (constitutional, statutory, and administrative). In some of the above respects, various other institutions and mechanisms perform important functions that support accountability processes, including independent audit agencies, ombudsmen, and access to government information regimes.

The purposes that accountability are meant to serve are essentially threefold, although they overlap in several ways. The first is to *control* for the abuse and misuse of public authority. The second is to provide assurance in respect to the effective use of public resources and adherence to public service values. The third is to encourage and promote learning in pursuit of *continuous improvement* in governance and public management. At a minimum, accordingly, accountability relates to policy, organizational, and management performance.

Because accountability is an integral dimension of governance and public management it cannot be affected by the extent to which governance and public management are subject to ever increasing complexity (Thomas, 1998). Governments everywhere are under increasing pressures to be both more productive and more effective, that is, to achieve not only the greatest degree of economy and efficiency possible but also to secure desired outcomes in respect to economic and social development. Global forces are placing relentless pressures on governments to manage their public households in ways that enable their economies to be competitive. Social transformations on a global scale are requiring governments to be more effective in securing social cohesion. The two sets of dynamics, moreover, are inexorably related (Peters and Savoie, 1995; Mulgan, 1998).

At the same time, all governments must now govern in a context where there are greater demands for accountability for performance on the part of a less deferential citizenry, more assertive interest groups and social movements, more aggressive and intrusive mass media and, more generally, the emergence of an "audit society" (Power, 1997). While it varies in its particulars, the phenomenon of democratization is a universal force. It encompasses demands for greater transparency in the conduct of public business by political and administrative officials, increased public access to government information, more explicit standards of public service entitlements and rights, enhanced citizen consultation and engagement in policy development and in the design and delivery of public services, and, among other things, public reporting on the performance of government in producing "results that citizens value" (Barzelay, 1992).

Central to the processes of accountability are the changes in both governance and public management that have been instituted as governments have sought to respond to these several imperatives and demands. At least three broad sets of changes – or reforms – are critical in this respect.

The first are initiatives to introduce a greater degree of devolution or debureaucratization in the management of public affairs. These initiatives raise crucial questions for accountability precisely because authority and responsibility are no longer concentrated at the top of the hierarchy as a result of deregulation, delegation, or decentralization. The second are initiatives to introduce a greater degree of shared governance and collaborative management in the conduct of public business. In these instances, governments and government organizations enter into partnership or integrated service delivery arrangements with a wide variety of "others" – various private sector parties (commercial and voluntary), other governments, and other departments and agencies within the same government. The interorganizational dimensions of these arrangements have obvious implications for public accountability. The third are initiatives to improve the ways by which governments are managed and report on their performance. Increasingly, this means managing to outputs and outcomes and reporting on a comprehensive set of performance measures, including reporting on how well outputs contribute to the achievement of desired outcomes. The allocation of responsibilities, and the determination of accountability, between political officials (in both the executive and legislative branches of government) and the public service bureaucracy is especially critical in the context of these changes.

This chapter examines these three sets of change in light of what we deem to constitute the dialectics of accountability for performance, that is, the inherent tensions that exist between the three purposes of accountability in the context of public governance and management. We do not subscribe to the thesis that improved accountability and improved performance necessarily pull in opposite directions. We recognize that this issue is often stated in this way and we acknowledge that failure to attend to the construction of an adequate accountability regime when designing new approaches to public governance and management in order to improve performance often leads to this very result. Although all efforts at synthesis or balance must always be a work in progress, what we propose is required is greater attention to those dimensions of performance where accountability should matter most and can be secured. The reason is that accountability can, and should, be a major force for improving performance.

CHANGES IN GOVERNANCE AND PUBLIC MANAGEMENT

This is not the place to discuss the above noted changes in governance and public management at great length. However, in order to situate the implications of these changes for accountability and later to discuss how accountability can help to address issues of improved performance, we need to outline the ways by which these changes themselves are meant to improve performance in governance and public management. Only then can we assess the importance of the dialectics of accountability in relation to performance.

Devolution and Debureaucratization

In a comparative perspective it is obvious that different political systems have different starting points from which to institute reforms that entail devolution and/or debureaucratization. In part, the differences arise because of the differing ways by which various governance and management structures have sought to secure performance and accountability.

For instance, the devolution of authority for the management of financial, human, and related administrative resources has been a major focus of reforms in the main Westminster systems of government precisely because they have emphasized executive-centred command and control systems in order to promote performance and accountability. Most of the continental European systems, including those with reform programs to debureaucratize public management, have not had to go the same route, because they had never instituted the same kind of centralized command and control systems. They pursued the same ends through other means including, especially, the use of comprehensive administrative law regimes. Or, in the case of the United States, these ends are pursued through command and control systems among others, but in these cases they are as much the products of independent legislatures as they are the designs of the executive branch of government (Kettl, 1998).

But even among political systems that share a common set of structures and traditions there have been different approaches to change. The Westminster systems, for instance, have not all proceeded in the same direction, in part because they had different starting points. Britain and New Zealand opted to resort to new forms of government organizations, as alternatives to the traditional integrated ministerial department for the purposes of improving public management, while Australia and Canada have sought to devolve greater managerial authority within the context of the traditional departmental form (Aucoin, 1995).

How higher orders of governments have sought to devolve, or debureaucratize, management and, in some cases, governance authority in respect to lower orders of government has also varied. In some instances, such as France, decentralization has had important consequences for enhancing local control because of new relations between the lower echelons of the national bureaucracy in the field and the local governments within their regions. In some cases, such as Canada and the United States, higher orders of governments have devolved (or "off-loaded") responsibilities to lower orders of government – federal to provincial/state, provincial/state to municipal/local. In some instances, especially Britain and certain state governments in Australia, debureaucratization has amounted to compulsory market-testing schemes to promote the contracting out of the delivery of municipal government services.

And, of course, devolution and debureaucratization have prominently included initiatives to contract out the delivery of public services, encompassing services to citizens as well as services internal to government, and to commercialize the structures and practices of those public enterprises not privatized (the ultimate expression of debureaucratization). Debureaucratization is a form of devolution for our purposes, primarily because contracting out and commercialization (or corporatization) constitute methods for reducing the extent to which those providing public services are subject to the centralized command and control systems that corporate management authority in government impose over traditional service delivery organizations.

What has transpired in the comparative experience of reform, therefore, is a mix of different approaches. In every case, nonetheless, the aim has been to diminish what is perceived to be the imposition of centralized corporate command and control systems, including laws, regulations, and policies – in short, to "banish bureaucracy," as popular American rhetoric succinctly puts it (Osborne and Plastrik, 1997). The objective virtually everywhere, even if it is not everywhere the sole objective, is to enhance efficiency. In addition, devolution has been pursued in order to achieve greater public service accountability, as in the case of Britain and New Zealand, or to promote greater legitimacy for the state, as in the case of France. The assumption that increased devolution or debureaucratization is always driven by an increased concern for accountability obviously does not hold in all cases.

But even where the operative assumption is that increased discretion and a removal of centralized controls will invariably lead to improved performance, especially improved efficiency, one cannot assume that more than lip-service, if that, will be paid to the place of accountability in whatever new structures are designed "to let the managers manage." More than one system has experienced this shortcoming in seeking to promote "managerialism" without altering its accountability regime. Those systems which have sought "to make the managers manage" and have avoided this particular shortcoming have done so only because enhanced managerial accountability constituted a central objective of devolution or debureaucratization in the first place. Whether their new accountability regimes have been up to the task is, of course, another matter.

Devolution and debureaucratization, as a general approach to reform, constitute essentially a rejection of the ideal of uniformity and standardization in public administration, as established and enforced through a hierarchical and corporate structure of authority and responsibility. As an ideal, these features of Weberian bureaucracy have been subject to a particularly strong, or at least persuasive, criticism over the past two decades. While this is not the place to discuss the criticism at length, or to enter the debate, it does need to be noted that the result in relation to accountability for performance has been the bifurcation of the concept or understanding of "performance." This bifurcation has taken place in two ways.

On the one hand, insofar as performance is defined in terms of "efficiency," and many of the early managerial reforms were defined almost exclusively in this way in some systems, efficiency has come to be viewed not merely as one measure of performance but as an objective that stands against other objectives, including those which are meant to be secured via uniformity and standardization. The implication, explicit or implicit, is that there is not an efficiency dimension in the pursuit, for example, of due process, natural justice, impartiality, or employment equity. In the pursuit of the most efficient input–output ratio, accordingly, these elements of the "output" come to be regarded as separate considerations; they are the non-productive or politically imposed "add-ons" that complicate the work of managers in the public sector and which, as much as possible, should become subject to managerial discretion.

On the other hand, insofar as performance is defined in terms of "results" or "outcomes," performance has also come to mean something other than the objectives meant to be secured through uniformity and standardization. In this case, the bifurcation is perhaps even more significant in its implications for accountability. The reason is simple. In this view, how power and resources are used in the management of government operations is deemed merely the means to an end. This means–end dichotomy ignores the fact that in public governance and management some "means" are, and are perceived to be by citizens, "ends" in themselves; that is, they constitute integral dimensions of the public policies that govern the activities of government. Indeed, in some dimensions, they are part and parcel of constitutional or statutory law. They are, in short, integral to any definition of "results" or "outcomes." They are not merely means, or, for that matter, simply "constraints."

It follows, accordingly, that reforms which seek to devolve authority, or otherwise debureaucratize public management, inevitably give rise to questions of accountability, especially in terms of its control and assurance dimensions, whenever one or the other of these bifurcations leads to an unacceptable understanding and practice of governance or management. This is not to suggest that central command and control systems, establishing and enforcing uniformity and standardization, are the only way to promote and secure the public service values that are deemed essential at any point in time. It does mean, however, that how these objectives are achieved in a devolved or debureaucratized regime requires that an appropriate accountability regime be in place.

Shared Governance and Collaborative Management

In the case of the several initiatives that can be placed under this general heading, all of which fall within the broad Canadian definition of "alternative service delivery," there is obviously a great variety of experiences in the comparative context. Shared governance and collaborative management have come to the fore in recent years, nonetheless, for a number of reasons relevant to the contemporary period. They have also taken a number of different but related forms.

The two most important innovations in this regard are partnerships and structures for integrated service. In the case of the former, there is a recognition not only that governments cannot do everything but that effective governance and management often requires the cooperative efforts of other levels of government and/or the private sector, broadly defined to include both commercial and voluntary organizations. In these regards, a government may not have sufficient resources, expertise, or legitimacy to proceed on its own. It is, in this sense, that even some instances of contracting out fall into this category, as strategic alliances, although legally they constitute merely a contractual relationship and are not technically a partnership. Structures for integrated service constitute mechanisms of collaboration between different governmental departments and agencies that are established in recognition of the need to provide seamless service to citizens by way of "single windows," "one-stop service delivery," "joined-up services" or "case management," wherein the coordination of services is undertaken by public servants and is not the responsibility of the citizen or business client. In addition to integrated service on a horizontal basis, that is across the organizational boundaries of a government, integrated service delivery can also constitute a partnership if other levels of government are involved. Shared governance and collaborative management initiatives, in short, come in a wide variety of different mixes of organizational options.

Shared governance and collaborative management constitute an acknowledgement that there are critical limits to the capacity of the state either to unilaterally dictate the course of public affairs, to marshal the full range of resources to tackle complex or serious problems, or to secure the necessary compliance without engaging citizens and business in the co-production of public services and regulations. They also recognize that the advantages and requirements of organizational specialization in policy development, program design, and service delivery must not become impediments to the effectiveness of government in dealing with issues that cut across the organizational boundaries of the state apparatus. The fragmentation that is essential to specialization, in others words, needs to be rejoined, integrated or connected in order to effect horizontal, or "whole of government," coordination. This is hardly a new issue of governance or management. But its increasing salience comes from the ever-expanding complexity of horizontal policy challenges as well as the ever-expanding use of information technologies not only for managing in government but for service delivery itself, including the capacities of citizens and business to engage in co-production, even self-service.

There are at least two ironies, or paradoxes, that emerge with the increased phenomenon of shared governance and collaborative management. The first is that partnerships amount to a belated recognition that a reduced role for the state in the range of activities financed by government need not rule out a more proactive role for government in the governance of society and economy. In our view, it is a mistake to think of this development purely in terms of a separation of the "steering" and "rowing" roles of government. The transformation in many systems is much more complex, nuanced and, in several respects, fundamentally different than what is suggested in this neat and tidy, but essentially simplistic and inevitably misleading, concept (Osborne and Gaebler, 1993). Not only are governments still rowing, in some cases with even greater vigour, as proactive "brokers" of information for example, they are also, and even more importantly, sharing the steering role with partners! Through partnerships, the capacities of the state for steering and rowing are actually enhanced; they not confined to a kind of "board of directors" role. Accountability will be secured in such arrangements, however, only to the extent that we recognize just what has been transformed in the exercise of authority and responsibility in the unfolding of these new arrangements (Canada, 1999).

The second irony, or paradox, is that integrated service amounts to a belated recognition that the improved management of operations requires more than simply the creation of single purpose or stand-alone organizations – the "agency" model of public management. The logic of this model lies precisely in "the greater specification of operational tasks, combined with greater clarity in authority, responsibility, and accountability" (Aucoin, 1996, 14). In some, if not many, instances, however, reformers assumed that the specification of tasks, as outputs to be managed and delivered efficiently, constituted the end point of reform. This tendency is not an unexpected result, especially in those cases where the outcomes to be achieved are taken to be one and the same with the outputs produced. In these instances, the services in question are not subject to searching analysis as to their ultimate purpose and the question of their connections to other services, as one among many outputs with an effect on achieving desired outcomes, is mute. However, the greater specification of tasks and clarity in mandates ought to be the starting, and not the end, point of reform. In other words, the agency model can be the means whereby agencies constitute the "building blocks" of service integration given their capacity to have greater specificity of purpose. In this context, the requirements of integrated delivery are "more likely to be better understood and thus facilitate management coordination" (Aucoin, 1996, 14). This issue is critical to the interorganizational dimensions of accountability for integrated delivery.

Managing to Outputs and Outcomes

Managing to outputs and outcomes represents a change in public governance and management insofar as governments have explicitly sought to exert greater political control over the direction of government policies in relation to their public service bureaucracies; to make public service managers manage to specifically agreed targets, standards, and measures of performance in exchange for greater managerial authority; to set explicit contracts for public services delivered by third parties; to establish the common goals and objectives of partnerships; and, among other things, to respond to demands for greater transparency, credibility, and relevance in public reporting within various accountability forums.

In moving in this direction governments have varied in their intentions. In some instances, governments have explicitly attempted to overcome or avoid what political leaders, at times supported by public service advisors, viewed as the pathologies of bureaucracy. These pathologies include the assumed tendencies for political decision makers to be captured by their public service bureaucracies and their interests; for political goals to be displaced by public service organizational goals in the process of policy implementation; and for public service bureaucracies to become inward-looking and process-oriented in managing inputs (money and staff) and in complying with rules and regulations.

In other instances, governments have sought to be more positive, that is, to approach the matter of reforming bureaucracy by re-designing its systems so that public servants could be empowered. In these cases, the efforts have been to promote citizen-centred service by adopting an outward-looking (or an "outside-in") orientation, to promote productivity by focusing on the production of outputs that citizens themselves value and by using alternative service delivery systems to provide these outputs, and by utilizing more strategic approaches to determine what creates public value in the pursuit of desired socio-economic outcomes.

Whatever the determinants and philosophies of reform, there has emerged a universal emphasis on performance, or results-based, management that has enhanced the attention given to outputs and outcomes. Although the legislative and administrative regimes vary in the comparative experience, there is now some considerable agreement that a number of elements constitute an effective performance regime. These include the need for: greater clarity, coherence, and specificity in strategic, business, and service improvement plans; published performance targets and standards of service; performance measures and indicators for outputs and outcomes; public reporting on performance in relation to outputs and outcomes; auditing of performance and assurance on performance reports; and performance reviews and effectiveness or outcome evaluations. In some systems, such as in New Zealand and the United States, there are elaborate legislative frameworks governing the performance management or reporting regime; in other cases, there are government commitments to such regimes. In the evolution of these regimes a number of dynamics are working their way through governmental systems.

For one thing, the focus on outputs and outcomes has required political leaders, especially political executives, to be more forthcoming in articulating their policy goals. Not only does doing this run against the grain of political leadership in certain respects, even in those instances where the political leadership has insisted on a more outcome-focused approach it has proven exceptionally difficult to get beyond very general statements of objectives across the full agenda of a government. This accounts, in some measure, for the fact that some governments are more interested in sticking to an output-focused approach, with political executives "purchasing outputs" from public service or third party providers. But, here too, establishing the policy goals to guide the setting of targets and standards has not been an easy task across the full range of government outputs. Managing the state from both these perspectives, nonetheless, has at least made many political executives more attuned to the complexities of public policy and thus more appreciative of the critical importance of policy research, analysis, and evaluation.

As part of the recent evolution, accordingly, the functions of policy research, analysis, and evaluation have regained at least some of the ground lost to operational management in the earliest rounds of public management reform. This is especially the case obviously in those systems which moved furthest away from the traditional understanding of governance as statecraft towards a private sector model of governance that views governance as essentially managing the provision of services and service delivery in a contestable marketplace. This dynamic is clearly evident, for instance, in recent efforts by the British and New Zealand governments to focus ministerial and public service attention more explicitly on outcomes.

But even in systems where managerialist approaches did not gain complete dominance, there have been efforts to rebuild the policy capacity of government. Canada is a case in point and here there is a major initiative to enhance the role of the policy research network within government and to develop more effective linkages between this network, or networks, and the external research community (Bakvis, 2000). The Canadian case in this regard is illustrative of a phenomenon found in a number of systems, namely, the perceived need to revitalize the public service by enhancing its capacity to serve as a principal, if not exclusive, source of policy advice to political leaders. In part, this development stems from the increasing recognition that many, if not all, of the key policy issues facing governments cannot be addressed within the confines of vertically structured government organizations, even when the state architecture is not highly fragmented and mandates are fairly comprehensive. Rather, the big issues cut across the boundaries of numerous organizations, in many cases being "whole of government" issues.

A second dimension of this evolution has been changing relationships between central agencies and line organizations. The logic of managing to outputs and outcomes requires, in theory, that central agencies reduce the degree to which they command and control the management of line departments or agencies in exchange for the latter's acceptance of the dictates of a performance management regime. The emphasis, in other words, shifts from the centre enforcing rules and regulations respecting inputs and processes to line managers ensuring that attention is given to managing to outputs and outcomes. In the process, central management agencies move from being command and control centres to being "management boards," that is, establishing the frameworks necessary to promote performance, encouraging and advising on best practices, reviewing performance reports for the purposes of continuous improvements, and holding managers to account for performance.

In several cases, there are continuing complaints on the part of line departments or agencies that, notwithstanding the rhetoric, central agencies are still too much into command and control, although virtually everywhere there is recognition that some change for the better has taken place. More importantly, perhaps, there are criticisms in some cases that central agencies are seeking to promote performance by dictating the instruments to be used, most notably by insisting that line managers contract out for services or service delivery (especially in respect to outsourcing for certain internal services) and/or by mandating the competitive market testing of services. Managers who are critical of these approaches argue that they, and not the centre, should have the authority to make such "management" decisions according to the circumstances of their particular organizations and operations. The tensions here are central to questions about the respective accountabilities for performance of central agencies on the one hand and line organizations on the other. It is also the case that where managing to outcomes, rather than to outputs, has received greater attention, there can be important implications for the relative power of central policy agencies vis-à-vis central management agencies.

A third consequence of the installation of performance management regimes is the increased importance attached to performance auditing (OECD, 1996; Barzelay, 1997) and various kinds of performance inspection and review. The result is that audit, inspection, and review agencies generally have become more important in the overall accountability process. The reason is simple. Although there are variations across different systems, the tendency is for these agencies to have shifted their focus from auditing, inspecting, and reviewing for *compliance*, with legislative or central executive and administrative regulations, rules, and processes, to assessing and evaluating *performance*, as measured by some combination of managerial efficiency and program effectiveness, and to providing assurance in respect to *performance information* as reported by those subject to the performance reporting regime.

By virtue of this change in focus, however relative in some cases, the issue arises as to the fundamental role of such agencies in the accountability equation. In one sense, audit, inspection, and review can be integral dimensions of administration, as in the case of internal audit for instance, or as in Sweden where the national audit agency has taken on administrative responsibility for coordinating financial management reforms. In another sense, these functions are essential to accountability, as in the case of external audit. The issue is partly institutional: to what institution of government do these agencies report their findings and what constitutes their mandate? In a more nuanced way, however, the issue is essentially about the relative priority they attach to each of the three purposes of accountability: control, assurance, and continuous improvement.

One of the greatest challenges in the implementation of an approach that manages to outputs and outcomes is to avoid the tendency, perhaps even temptation, to substitute a performance measurement regime that is so tight, with respect to output and outcomes "measures," that the flexibility required to exercise political or professional judgment in the pursuit of high performance is no more present than in a command and control regime. And the reason is essentially the same, that is, it is assumed that the strategies, conditions, and practices to achieve high performance can be established at the front end of the process; in short, the assumption that government can be put on automatic pilot. In particular, of course, it assumes that the causal connections between outputs and outcomes are known. Governing by political conviction, with biases in favour of particular instruments and methods over others and with a low tolerance for debate and dissent, invariably constitutes a recipe for a performance management regime wherein managing to outputs and outcomes becomes as rigid and formulistic as anything produced by the traditional bureaucratic model. In this context, accountability amounts to little more than control.

ATTENDING TO THE ACCOUNTABILITY DIALECTICS

Attending to the dialectics of accountability in the context of the above three developments in governance and management requires a recognition that different constitutional regimes are affected differently by each of these changes. But the changes themselves do not introduce entirely novel phenomenon. All systems, for instance, have had to assume some measure of devolution, as discretion is invariably exercised in the political and bureaucratic administration of public affairs; governments have long had to cope with the need to coordinate certain kinds of services, given the inevitable specialization required in governments as complex organizations; and political and administrative officials, especially those on the front lines of public service delivery, have always paid attention to the purposes of what they seek to do and do even when, at times, they appeared to be overwhelmed by systems and rules.

What is relatively new, nonetheless, is the extent to which there is a greater demand for accountability, broadly defined.

The diminished reality of anonymity and the enhanced exposure of political leaders and public servants, particularly the latter, as a consequence of the new information age and the emergence of a more intrusive mass media constitutes one dimension of this demand. A second is the decreasing deference to authority and expertise. This is a function of the fact that while we know more about the interconnectedness of our socio-economic order, we have less confidence in our knowledge of causes and effects as they relate to what governments do or could do to tackle the most pressing issues on the political agenda. There are thus increased demands for justifications of policy and program undertakings. Finally, a number of factors, including globalization, the proliferation of services industries, and the new information technologies, have increased the extent to which government performance is compared within and across individual political systems as well as to private sector organizations. A scorecard mentality cannot but produce pressures for governments to account for their performance, including shortcomings, in comparison to others.

These demands are unlikely to diminish in the near future. At the same time, it is unlikely that the changes we have discussed will become less critical, even though other developments will invariably be added. What is required, accordingly, is an appropriate alignment of accountability processes with these demands and changes. In this respect, we need to consider the balance between the three purposes or functions of accountability.

Accountability as Control

The control function of accountability lies at the heart of democratic accountability in all major constitutional models because each, in its own way, seeks to ensure that the authoritative and coercive powers of the state are not abused or misused. In all systems, accordingly, an array of accountability processes and mechanisms serves to control the exercise of power. Some systems, however, have been predicated on a greater assumption of trust in elected and appointed officials than others where suspicion of officialdom is a central feature of institutional design, as in the United States for example (Behn, 1999). In any event, all three developments outlined above can be seen to run counter to traditional notions of control. Devolution and debureaucratization increase discretion; shared governance and collaborative management disperse responsibility; and managing to outputs and outcomes gives preference to results over compliance with input controls and prescribed processes.

In each of these cases, however, there need not be diminished attention to the control over important factors. Control can be secured, even enhanced, by ensuring transparency in operations and reporting; access to information on the part of citizens and the media; complaint and redress procedures with independent appeal mechanisms; legislative institutions organized and staffed to scrutinize and investigate executive and administrative behaviour; and by comprehensive mandates for independent audit, inspection, and review agencies. Internal to executive government, central management agencies can foster the required control by ensuring that standards are set for broadly defined comptrollership and that public service values respecting state – citizen and management – staff relations are clearly enunciated, and by exercising management prerogatives when necessary to take corrective or disciplinary action.

Stating the conditions for control in this manner might appear to suggest that nothing is changed in the accountability dialectic: control remains central and centralized. Yet, this is to miss the point, which is that ultimately there must be control in democratic government and public administration. What can be changed is the way that authority and responsibility and accountability are delegated, shared, and defined. Devolution and debureaucratization, for example, must be accompanied by clearly expressed spheres of discretion or flexibility; expressed another way, the deregulation of central corporate rules must be accompanied by an explicit recognition of those matters where uniformity and standardization are no longer required as a matter of law or policy. In the case of shared governance and collaborative management, agreements or contractual-type arrangements must provide for ways whereby each party's responsibilities for promoting and protecting the public interest will be secured either through processes of mutual adjustment or through recourse to independent dispute resolution mechanisms. Performance management regimes focused on managing to outputs and outcomes must define "results" in ways that encompass the necessary public service values such as probity, fairness, and impartiality. In each of these instances, those with authority and responsibility are accountable and thus must be subject to control.

Some argue that the three developments in question, especially devolution/debureacratization and managing to outputs/ outcomes, which are considered the defining features of the "new public management," cannot be accommodated by traditional systems of accountability but that a new system of accountability has yet to be designed (Stone, 1995). We do not accept this view, primarily because we think that the characterization of new public management as essentially a scheme to "empower" public servants to be "entrepreneurial" misses an important point. While we acknowledge that some of the rhetoric in the new public management does indeed put the issue this way, especially where private sector management constitutes the inspiration and the frame of reference, well-designed reforms need not diminish attention to accountability. In our view, reforms are required because traditional approaches that relied primarily on centralized command and control systems, and focused exclusively on securing compliance with input control and process, became, at least in some large part, ineffective not just in securing performance but also accountability for performance.

It is the case that traditional approaches were effective in several respects. For instance, they helped to ensure the establishment of non-partisan, merit-based and professional public services in modern democracies. The regimes put in place to achieve this requirement of good public governance and management varied across political systems. Yet, everywhere there was the recognition that staffing the public service had to constitute a separate administrative function, that is, exercised with some independence from what otherwise would constitute an integral part of the executive authority in administration. These approaches also helped to ensure that the increased spending and regulatory powers of the state accompanying the establishment of the modern administrative state did not result in corrupt or unsound practices on the part of either political executives or bureaucratic officials in the administration of public services writ large.

In one sense, command and control systems with their application to inputs and processes were not primarily meant to secure accountability from those to whom they were implied; rather, they were deployed in place of conferred or delegated authority and responsibility. They served an accountability function in the sense of control, to be certain, but they meant to restrict the need for, or possibility of, discretion down the line. This is what "error-free" administration means; errors are meant to be eliminated by not allowing for discretion but rather by prescribing in ever-increasing detail what must be done or not done. The great advantage of this approach is that authority and responsibility are concentrated; accountability can thus be (more) easily attributed to those at the centre who establish and enforce the regime. This is especially the case in the Westminster or other executive-centred systems compared to those systems where authority and responsibility are divided and shared, as in the United States for instance.

Their great disadvantage, of course, is that they reduce the extent to which political or professional judgment can be exercised in pursuit of desired results or improved performance when what is commanded or prescribed does not appear to do so. And, of course, the pursuit of good public governance and management, as sound administration, can only occur to the extent that the constraints that flow from this traditional approach are, in fact, clear, coherent, and consistent. To the degree that they are not, the pursuit of sound administration requires that those charged with administering public affairs, political executives and public service managers alike, create the necessary organizational space and administrative slack to cope with the constraints applied by this regime. While this does not necessarily imply any attempt to subvert the regime, it runs the risk of leading to resistance to centrally prescribed rules, selective compliance, or policy distortion. The more extensive the details of commands and controls, the more likely that the rules are not clear, coherent or consistent. Micro-management from the centre, in other words, works well only when the details are minimal. In few places, however, has this state of affairs been the experience for some time. Centrally imposed command and control systems have become discredited as the principal means to sound administration not because executives or managers necessarily reject the public purposes of public service values meant to be served by the constraints in question, but rather because this method of control is no longer viewed as achieving these purposes in an efficient or effective manner.

Governments have responded to these criticisms by reducing the weight of micromanagement. The streamlining of centrally imposed commands and controls, in the pursuit of debureaucratization, has been virtually everywhere an initial response. What the centre had constructed, it could dismantle. Yet, streamlining the regime does not necessarily advance the public purposes that constraints are meant to promote and secure; it merely reduces the burden on executives and administrators. Increased discretion might well be appreciated by those to whom it is conferred, but discretion exercised in the absence of constraints is hardly a recipe for sound public administration. On its own, "letting the managers manage" has never been a credible alternative to centralized commands and controls. Systems of devolved authority and responsibility work well only when accompanied by other mechanisms of constraint, such as comprehensive systems of administrative law, backed by judicial or administrative review, transparency and full disclosure, strong legislative oversight, or the disciplines of the market or professional codes.

It is for these reasons, that governmental systems have sought to enhance accountability by adopting performance management and reporting regimes for managing to outputs and outcomes. While there are a number of limits inherent in these regimes (Hood, 1998), it is important to stress that the issue ought not to be seen as entailing a trade-off between accountability and improved performance, defined as either efficiency or results. Put most simply, diminished attention to probity, fairness, and impartiality, as illustrative of critical public service values, ought not be traded-off for improved performance narrowly defined as economy or efficiency. This is not to deny that some public service values, at some times, will be in tension and judgment is required in decision making. Yet, the key to sound public governance and management within the context of current management reforms is greater attention to risk-planning and risk-management and thus accountability for the performance of these tasks. Risks in respect to the realization of critical public service values are not thereby eliminated, of course, but it needs to be recognized that no system of control, including centralized systems, can eliminate risk. Indeed, we need to remind ourselves that many, if not most of, the disasters and scandals, as instances of maladministration, with which we are familiar have occurred under regimes that are, or were at the time, highly centralized in their controls.

From the perspective of accountability as control, the most critical dialectic is thus the need to attend to risk-planning and risk-management without resorting to excessive micromanagement from the centre of government or by legislative imposition. The responsibilities of central management agencies in government as well as of those legislative bodies and their agencies which conduct oversight and review functions in a system of greater devolution/debureaucratization and shared governance/collaborative management are thus to ensure that plans and systems to attend to risk are formulated, approved, and monitored regularly. The advantage of this approach is that risks differ with different policies, organizational designs, and management environments and, accordingly, need to be tailored to be most efficient and effective in managing to outputs and outcomes. Accountability as assurance has a function to perform here, but equally, if not more, important is the need for the centre of government and/or legislatures to control for the performance of this function in governance and management. There is no substitute if public service values, and thus the public interest in sound administration, are to be given the attention they require.

Accountability as Assurance

Citizens, legislatures, and governments need to be assured that public authority and state resources are used in ways that adhere to public service values and best practice in the administration of public affairs whatever the distribution of authority and responsibility. This constitutes a major dimension of accountability precisely because it is assumed that citizens cannot govern directly in respect to most matters, that elected representatives in legislatures cannot govern simply by legislating, and that even political executives, however the executive power is arranged, cannot themselves govern without reliance on a more or less permanent body of appointed officials. In the language of traditional political theory, a good deal of "indirect government" is inevitable in the modern state. In the language of "agency" theory, sets of "principals" must rely on sets of "agents" to accomplish their objectives in institutional contexts where the former inevitably must place a degree of faith or trust in their agents to behave in ways that advance the objectives and secure the best interests of their principals. However the matter is expressed, the bottom line is that an effective system of accountability is necessary to provide assurance to principals that their agents are fulfilling their responsibilities as intended. Otherwise there is an "accountability deficit."

Accountability as assurance obviously increases in importance given the three trends and developments at issue. Furthermore, it is unlikely that reliance simply on traditional approaches to assurance, however important they remain, will suffice. Not surprisingly there are several innovations respecting assurance that have been introduced in many, if not all, political systems. And, while there is a tendency to convergence, as systems learn from one another, there are also interesting swings in individual systems; for instance, systems that tended not to rely on legal assurance are moving in that direction and systems that relied less on political assurance are doing more of this (Cooper, 1995). It is also the case, of course, that advances in information technology are making possible the development of assurance instruments that previously were not technically or economically practical on a broad scale, including various kinds of performance management and reporting information systems and citizen and client, and even staff, surveys.

Audit, inspection, and review processes and mechanisms have long been used, both internally and externally, to provide assurance, especially in respect to compliance. Each of these approaches has been enhanced in recent years, as noted, in that the scope of what is audited, inspected, and reviewed has expanded. In part, this is a function of a more expansive agenda of public service values and best practice, notwithstanding the downsizing, deregulating, and privatizating that have taken place. In part, as well, however, it represents an attempt to attend to the accountability consequences of each of the developments at hand. Because all three have been accompanied by efforts to specify, among other things, goals and objectives, service entitlements and standards, best management practices, and performance targets, there is a good deal that must be audited, inspected, and reviewed from the perspective of assurance. There are two important requirements of assurance that need to be recognized if accountability for performance is to be improved.

The first is that assurance must encompass more than simply compliance with formal performance systems, including both management and reporting systems. Important as compliance is in this respect, the critical issue for assurance is that performance itself, as examined in various ways, is assessed. This requires that those responsible for assessing performance go beyond simply checking for adherence to mandated processes. Otherwise, a focus simply on performance management and reporting "systems" amounts to merely a substitution of one kind of formality for another, based on an assumption that the new system, because it claims to address "results" rather than "process," actually gets at the question of substantive performance. This is not to deny that changes in systems do affect the incentives under which those with authority operate and thus how they behave. But no system of incentives can be devised to eliminate opportunities for those with authority to behave in ways that do not secure the desired performance or improvements in performance. Both organizations, as institutional designs, and policies, as program or service plans, must be managed by individuals. This means that individuals, when acting alone or in collaboration, must be held accountable for their individual performance.

In many circumstances, it is exceedingly difficult to assess individual accountability; hence the frustrations of citizens, legislators, executives, or managers in often not being able to hold "anyone" to account for major breakdowns in performance when things go awry. Blaming the "system," or whole organizations, is regarded as less than satisfactory, especially when it is assumed that individuals who should be held to account are able to escape any personal consequences. An equally, perhaps even more, perverse outcome occurs when superiors shift the blame to subordinates, by pushing accountability down to the lowest levels in the hierarchy, or, in the case of shared governance and collaborative management, to partners or third parties. No process of accountability can completely eliminate the possibility of these outcomes, especially where the issues of performance become highly politicized or judicialized and thus contentious judgments of organizational or policy dynamics are at play. Yet, accountability as assurance suffers when the processes of assurance do not seek to assess the personal accounts of those individuals with authority and responsibility in respect to their decisions and actions as opposed to simply their compliance with formal systems. In these instances, the processes of accountability do not sufficiently address issues of assurance respecting the actual behaviour and thus performance of individuals who function as the "agents" of "principals." The latter are not assured that the former are, in fact, exercising authority and responsibility properly or effectively. Form triumphs over substance.

From the perspective of public service accountability, assurance that processes of accountability actually address issues of performance so defined is especially critical given the need to secure and maintain, and in some cases to rebuild, public confidence in the institution of a professional and non-partisan public service. Even with reduced anonymity, a phenomenon that varies across different political systems, public servants are less exposed to public scrutiny than are elected officials in the normal course of events. However, it is usually the managers in the public service who have the greatest impact on the performance of government in *managing* policy implementation, contracts with third parties, organizational systems, and financial and human resources, and supervising the staff of the public service. As the lead in a recent *Economist* review of a set of studies on the determinants of organizational performance succinctly put it: "It's the managers, stupid" (August 8, 1998, 54). Providing assurance as to the quality of public service management is a critical requirement of those who "manage the managers." The greatest challenge in this regard, especially given the trends in question, is to assure citizens and their elected representatives that those responsible for managing the managers, namely, public service leaders at the centre of government, do ensure that accountability for individual management performance counts.

Management boards at the centre of government, however structured, must have the capacity to provide this assurance through mechanisms of audit, inspection, and review. A focus on individual management accountability does not mean that managers should not foster collegial, or team, management in their organizations; it does not mean that managers should not foster horizontal management across vertically based organizations; and, it does not mean that managers should not foster partnership arrangements with third parties. These are critical dimensions to good public management in pursuit of high performance. However, it does mean that peer evaluations are rigorously pursued as a function of assurance. While this inevitably must entail a large measure of judgment in what are often ambiguous issues, there is no other way to make performance count. No profession allows its individual members to decide on their own whether they have met and upheld professional norms and values in the practice of their profession. On the contrary, they are held accountable to their peers who are collectively responsible to provide assurance for their clients as principals.

To the extent that the professional public service in any jurisdiction does not provide for this assurance, others will and they will use political criteria to assess performance (Sutherland, 1991; Polidano, 1999). In no jurisdiction is the public service afforded the opportunity to be as self-governing as the traditional professions. Everywhere the public service is constitutionally subordinate to political executives and/or legislatures, albeit in different ways in different systems. But a public service is professional, and thus non-partisan, only to the extent that judgments about management performance are determined by professional standards. The responsibility of public service leaders, however structured to perform this required management board function, is to establish these standards and to provide assurance that individual managers are held to account against them. The use of more contractual-type employment contracts, especially for the most senior public service leaders who function at the political–bureaucratic interface, need not diminish the professionalism of the public service. But great care is required to ensure, and to assure citizens, that professional competence in the leadership ranks of the public service is not diminished as a result.

A second requirement of quality assurance entails the need to provide, to use the current language, a "balanced scorecard," that is, to ensure that all critical dimensions of performance are encompassed within the processes of accountability (Kaplan and Norton, 1996). The objective here is not merely to "balance" what is assessed in terms of performance, although the issue is usually expressed in this way in part because of the perceived tension between different elements of performance, but rather to ensure that the full range of elements which ought to be assessed in terms of performance is, in fact, actually considered. Two developments in the context of providing assurance illustrate the importance of complete coverage.

On the one hand, there is an increasing acknowledgment that the provision of assurance concerning individual management performance should entail a process where individual managers are assessed not only by their superiors or by those who operate at the same level in the hierarchy but also by their subordinate staff. The need for such assessments is driven by several factors. Public service leaders need to provide assurance that managers manage their staff well in order to retain high quality and highly motivated staff in the public service at a time when there are greater opportunities for career mobility for the very best and a diminished loyalty to organizations. Public service leaders also need to provide assurance that poor performance on the part of managers in managing staff does not diminish quality public service, including quality policy advice, at a time when there are increased pressures to be productive and effective. Further, of course, public service leaders need to provide assurance that managers adhere to public service values and ethics in their management of staff, especially where managers have enhanced discretion and there is reduced reliance on prescribed rules (Canada, 1996). And, finally, increased expectations about accountability generally have led to a decline in the willingness of staff simply to accept poor management as a function of deference to authority (Duxbury, Dyke, and Lam, 1999). Staff assessments of managers, as a normal course of good management practice, are as necessary as the practice of university students evaluating the teaching performance of their professors.

On the other hand, assurance respecting the quality of public services must not only be provided by the use of client surveys and other instruments that seek to ascertain client evaluations of the services they receive as users of public services (assurance that is by no means universally provided as yet), it must also extend to efforts to provide assurance that citizens generally are given opportunities to evaluate the quality of public services from the perspective of the broader public interests in public services, including regulatory services. While these instruments may be used for other purposes as well, from the perspective of accountability they address issues of assurance by providing a measure of independent assessment of the quality of public services by citizens and clients rather than relying exclusively on the claims that emanate from the partisan-political process or from the public service itself. Hence, the importance of independent audits of the methodologies used in performance reporting.

Accountability as Continuous Improvement

Accountability as continuous improvement constitutes the process whereby assessments of performance become demands or stimuli that promote improvements in policy, organization, or management. There is nothing automatic about this, of course, as assessments may be challenged, what is learned may be ignored, or the political pressures on the system may not be sufficient to bring about improvements even where the lessons are accepted in whole or part. However, the challenge of achieving the purpose of accountability as continuous improvement is no different than the challenge of achieving the other two purposes of accountability; in neither of these cases are the purposes always served well or secured in every respect.

It is now fashionable to depict this third purpose of accountability as the most important, in large part because control and assurance are regarded as excessively preoccupied with the negative or inhibiting functions of "blaming" and "compliance," neither of which is viewed as making a positive contribution to improved governance and public management. Indeed, in some interpretations, accountability, as continuous improvement, is explicitly or implicitly set against accountability as control and as assurance, that is, as a reform to accountability itself. This view is accorded prominence especially in those quarters where it is assumed that continuous improvements will be forthcoming only to the extent that public managers are permitted, even encouraged, to innovate, take risks, or be entrepreneurial, and, therefore, where there must be a willingness to tolerate and accept errors or failures as a normal and necessary part of the experimental or learning process. Accountability as continuous improvement, in this view, is seen as the positive side of accountability, foregoing naming and blaming or nitpicking on compliance with process. Everyone in the accountability process is meant to reinvent themselves as management consultants!

There is an element of justification for the emphasis on continuous improvement as a central purpose of accountability. Too great a focus on control or assurance can serve to undermine this third purpose of accountability, and, in the process, to diminish the capacity of the state and the public service to improve both governance and public management. This is especially the case where an excessive focus on the first two purposes is driven primarily by partisan-political forces serving their own ends in either the legislative or executive branches of government; by central agencies in the public service seeking to maintain their own bases of power and influence; by audit, inspection, or review agencies searching for any and all evidence of maladministration to justify their own importance in the system; or, by mass media intent on sensationalizing or exaggerating incidents of improper conduct or shortcomings in public services essentially to promote their own wares. An emphasis on accountability as continuous improvement is thus part and parcel of an effort to reinvent both political behaviour and political culture as essential to a larger reinvention of government.

While this third purpose of accountability has an element of idealism, in some instances even naiveté, about it, political and administrative leaders do have incentives to use accountability as continuous improvement as the means to promote their objectives. Requiring the use of benchmarking in performance reporting, for instance, is increasingly regarded by political leaders as an effective means to promote improvements in various kinds of public services, including internal services, particularly where one can have some confidence in the credibility of the comparisons in question, such as when the services are undertaken by a sufficient number of comparable organizations in a single political system, for example, municipal or state/provincial governments. In these instances, benchmarking can be used to provide political legitimacy for particular policy, organizational, or management options. A similar logic can be applied to program evaluations or to various kinds of performance reporting requirements, such as a requirement that organizations report on progress in relation to mandated service improvement plans. In these instances, accountability as continuous improvement constitutes a way to apply pressure without directly intervening in governance or management. It is in this manner, for example, that those who undertake external audits, inspections, and reviews – if they focus on performance in the broadest sense – can be effective in promoting continuous improvement even if they lack any power to direct the organizations whose performance they assess. They use as their bases of assessment a universe of "best practices" – a form of benchmarking itself.

Accountability as continuous improvement is necessarily a process of learning, and learning is never simple nor without struggle (Canada, 1994). As Sutherland argues, for instance, the Westminster principle of responsible government "builds heavily on a retrospective cycle of discussion, evaluation, argument and blame, so that parliamentarians have the opportunity to educate themselves about the outcomes of legislation and policies now in effect, as well as the quality of all ministers' administrative leadership of their departments" (1996, 2). Her view of the Westminster model as "a learning organization" dovetails with Kettl's argument that performance management and reporting in the American system ought best to be regarded fundamentally as a process of "communication," and not simply measurement, that "occurs within a broader political process, in which the players have a wide array of different incentives" (1994, 45).

The public character of accountability is especially prominent in the use of program evaluation where such evaluations must be published. Program evaluations are perhaps the leading edge of public accountability because they address the causal connections between the outputs of governments and desired outcomes; in short, they serve to constitute a form of public knowledge about the effectiveness of legislative and executive action. While they may have limited utility in helping to shape political priorities in the short term, in the budgetary process for instance, given the limits of applied research in drawing definitive conclusions in most areas of public policy, they serve to focus discussion on the merits and shortcomings of particular approaches to public policy. To the extent that public knowledge constitutes the basis of such discussion, however, two consequences need to be considered. One is the extent to which it is desirable to have public servants engage in public discussion directly or indirectly; the other is the extent to which others are willing to address the constraints inherent in public management as governance.

To the degree that governments, including their legislative branches, enhance their capacities to undertake policy research, analysis, and evaluation on the assumption that greater effectiveness in governance depends upon increased policy knowledge, a broader range of participants is the likely outcome. Citizens increasingly demand that they be consulted, even engaged, in the policy process and, in any event, governments cannot ignore the wider arena of public knowledge that encompasses think tanks, consulting groups, universities, international research organizations, some media, and even other governments. At issue, accordingly, is the willingness of governments to allow, even encourage, their own public servants, as knowledge workers, to engage with others in public forums, lest the work done inside government not be exposed to the scrutiny and review of the wider arena. The capacity of public servants "to speak truth to power" increasingly means not merely to speak to those to whom confidential advice is given but to those attentive publics who seek to frame public discourse on public policy directions but who do so in ways that cannot be expected to flow exclusively from a disinterested perspective of the public interest. What a professional and non-partisan public service means in the context of increasing openness, and the increasing prominence of policy networks that extend out from government to the larger arenas of public knowledge, is one of the major transformations taking place in contemporary governance. Public accountability in this context is also transformed.

This transformation in public accountability, however, also demands that those with whom public servants interact have an obligation to address the constraints that are inherent in public management as governance. In particular, it means that accountability processes which are focused on continuous improvement be conducted in ways that acknowledge the limits to public service authority and responsibility, even where devolution/debureaucratization and shared governance/collaborative management are the norm and public servants are expected to manage to outputs and outcomes. These changes in governance and public management are significant developments but they have not reinvented either governance or public management to the point where public servants are freed completely from the constraints that flow from legislative or executive policy or regulation or public service values. While there is an inevitable tension in the dictates of the three purposes of accountability, the pursuit of the purpose of continuous improvement demands that those who audit, inspect, and review public service management do so in the broader context of benchmarking and program evaluation where the impacts or effects of these constraints should be identified, as clearly as possible, as factors that affect the realization of outputs and outcomes and over which public servants have, and should have, little or no control (Aucoin, 1998). To the degree that this obligation is not met, the purpose of accountability as continuous improvement is undermined; the public interest in full communications is not served by incomplete, and thus misleading, performance scorecards or evaluations, or by the inevitable temptation, thereby perversely encouraged, of public servants either to manage merely to the limits of "contracts" for specified outputs (Schick, 1996) or, on the other hand, to become political advocates of the policies of their political masters.

CONCLUSION

The dialectics of accountability for performance are obviously not a recent phenomenon. Regardless of the particulars of the various accountability regimes in different political systems, there have always been tensions between the three purposes of accountability. Notwithstanding recent efforts to give priority to the second and third purposes, especially the latter, accountability as control continuously, albeit sporadically, comes to the fore when scandals break out, disasters occur or major conflicts erupt (Gregory, 1998). In the Westminster systems, in particular, there is much angst about the efficacy, even the meaning, of traditional mechanisms of accountability, centred as they are on the concept and principle of ministerial responsibility (United Kingdom, 1996; 1997).

In our view, the debate over how to incorporate new mechanisms and methods of accountability needs to be situated within an understanding of the dialectics of accountability for performance as entailing the tensions between the three purposes of accountability. The issue is not fundamentally about tensions between accountability and performance. If it were so then we would have to assume that the democratic principles of accountability are somehow antithetical to the pursuit of efficiency or results-based management, that is, one can have either accountability or performance but not both, at least not both in the same measure. We acknowledge that this issue is often put this way, explicitly or implicitly, whether it be in arguments for more business-like or entrepreneurial management, for greater responsiveness to citizens as clients, customers or consumers, or for a more contractual and competition-based approach to public service delivery.

Pitting accountability against performance does not, in our view, address the issue in the most constructive manner. Greater understanding and improved practice require that we address the tensions between accountability as serving the purposes of control, assurance, and continuous improvement in relation to the changes to governance and management reforms which are meant to improve performance. Improving accountability arrangements does not necessarily improve performance, but the proposition that there can be improved performance in the absence of improved accountability is a proposition that cannot be sustained.

Improving accountability for performance constitutes an important agenda for revitalizing public service but it requires more than simply an acknowledgment of the tensions involved in accountability dialectics. In addition to the initiatives noted in our discussion, we conclude by drawing attention to two critical requirements.

First, improved accountability requires that the public service possess the capacity to perform its core public administrative functions, especially those relating to monitoring, control, review, and evaluation. This capacity, or "capability" as the New Zealand government has expressed it (Upton, 1999), demands more than the institution of appropriate accountability systems.

It also requires the staff resources, within both the executive and the legislative branches of government, to fulfil the objectives of these systems. Achieving this capacity demands that the resources committed to accountable management and oversight – in central management agencies, operational departments and agencies, and legislative review and audit agencies – not be viewed as merely "bureaucratic overhead" (Gow, 1997). Rather, they need to be seen as representing the necessary long-term investment in good governance if new public management regimes are to realize their purposes without introducing "accountability deficits."

Second, improved accountability requires political and public service leadership on at least two fronts. On the one hand, there must be a commitment to transparency on the part of those with executive and administrative responsibilities. Beyond any legislated requirements in this respect, this demands a willingness to communicate and share information in ways that enable those with responsibilities for securing accountability to perform their functions not only efficiently but also without recourse to the confrontations that invariably raise doubts about the credibility of performance reporting. On the other hand, there must be a commitment to continuously enhance meaningful communications on the part of those with oversight, review, and audit responsibilities. Facts rarely, if ever, speak for themselves, especially in the political arena, even when conscious efforts are made to develop a shared understanding of the uncertainties and choices that apply to contested issues of public policy and management. Disagreements and debate are inevitable in the politics of accountability. Accountability is most effectively secured, nonetheless, when those who have the responsibility to evaluate and assess performance engage in honest dialogue with those whose performance is the subject of accounts.

BIBLIOGRAPHY

Aucoin, Peter. 1995. *The New Public Management: Canada in Comparative Perspective*. Halifax: Institute for Research on Public Policy.

_____ 1996. Designing agencies for good public management. *Choices* 2, 4:5-19. Montreal: Institute for Research on Public Policy.

_____ 1998. Auditing for accountability: the role of the auditor general. Occasional paper. Ottawa: Institute on Governance.

Bakvis, Herman. 2000. Rebuilding the policy capacity in an era of the fiscal dividend. *Governance* 13, 1 (January):71-104.

Barzelay, Michael. 1992. *Breaking through Bureaucracy: A New Vision for Managing in Government.* Berkeley: University of California Press.

_____ 1997. Central audit institutions and performance auditing: a comparative analysis of organizational strategies in the OECD. *Governance* 10, 3 (July):235-260.

Behn, Robert D. 1998. The new public management paradigm and the search for democratic accountability. *International Public Management Journal* 1, 2:131-164.

Canada. Auditor General. 1999. Collaborative arrangements: issue for the federal Government. *Report of the Auditor General of Canada to the House of Commons.* Ch. 5. Ottawa: Minister of Supply and Services Canada.

Canadian Centre for Management Development. 1994. *A Strong Foundation: The Report of the Task Force on Public Service Values and Ethics.* Ottawa: CCMD.

_____ 1994. *Continuous Learning.* Ottawa: CCMD.

Cooper, Philip J. 1995. Accountability and administrative reform: toward convergence and beyond. In *Governance in a Changing Environment,* eds. B. G. Peters and D. J. Savoie. Montreal and Kingston: McGill-Queen's University Press.

Duxbury, Linda, Lorraine Dyke, and Natalie Lam. 1999. *Career Development in the Federal Public Service: Building a World-Class Workforce.* Ottawa: Treasury Board of Canada Secretariat.

Gow, James Iain. 1997. Managing all those contracts: beyond current capacity. In *New Public Management and Public Administration in Canada,* eds. Mohamed Charih and Arthur Daniels. Toronto: Institute of Public Administration of Canada, 235-261.

Gregory, Robert. 1998. A New Zealand tragedy: problems of political responsibility. *Governance* 11, 2 (April):231-240.

Kaplan, Robert S., and David P. Norton. 1996. *The Balanced Scorecard.* Boston: Harvard Business School Press.

Kettl, Donald F. 1994. *Reinventing Government: Appraising the National Performance Review.* Washington: The Brookings Institution.

_____ 1998. *Reinventing Government: A Fifth-Year Report Card.* Washington: The Brookings Institution.

Mulgan, Geoff. 1998. *Connexity: Responsibility, Freedom, Business and Power in the New Century*. London: Vintage.

Mulgan, Richard. 1997. The processes of public accountability. *Australian Journal of Public Administration* 56, 1 (March):25-36.

OECD. 1996. *Performance Auditing and the Modernization of Government*. Paris: OECD.

Osborne, David, and Ted Gaebler. 1993. *Reinventing Government: How the Entrepreneurial Spirit Is Transforming the Public Sector*. New York: Plume.

Osborne, David, and Peter Plastrik. 1997. *Banishing Bureaucracy*. Reading, MA: Addison Wesley.

Polidano, Charles. 1999. The bureaucrat who fell under a bus: ministerial responsibility, executive agencies and the Derek Lewis affair in Britain. *Governance* 12, 2 (April):201-229.

Power, Michael. 1997. *The Audit Society*. New York: Oxford University Press.

Peters, B. Guy, and Donald J. Savoie, eds. 1995. *Governance in a Changing Environment*. Montreal and Kingston: McGill-Queen's University Press.

Schick, Allen. 1996. The spirit of reform: managing the New Zealand state sector in a time of change. A report prepared for the State Services Commission and the Treasury, Wellington, New Zealand.

Stone Bruce. 1995. Administrative accountability in the Westminster democracies: toward a conceptual framework. *Governance* 8, 4 (October):505-526.

Sutherland, Sharon. 1996. Does Westminster government have a future? Occasional paper. Ottawa: Institute on Governance.

Sutherland, S. L. 1991. The Al-Mashat affair: administrative responsibility in parliamentary institutions. *Canadian Public Administration* 34, 4 (Winter):573-603.

Thomas, Paul. 1998. The changing nature of accountability. In *Taking Stock: Assessing Public Sector Reforms*, eds. B. G. Peters and D. J. Savoie. Montreal and Kingston: McGill-Queen's University Press, 348-393.

U.K. Public Service Committee. *1996 and 1997 Ministerial Accountability and Responsibility*. London: House of Commons.

Upton, Hon. Simon. 1997. Address to the 1999 Public Service Senior Management Conference, State Services Commission, Wellington, New Zealand.

Organizing for Service Delivery: Criteria and Opportunities

JONATHAN BOSTON

INTRODUCTION

Prompted by a range of fiscal, social, administrative, and ideological imperatives, many governments since the mid-1980s have been experimenting with new forms of service delivery. In particular, there has been a general shift away from the previous reliance upon relatively inflexible, bureaucratic, in-house modes of delivery, such as the traditional ministerial department, and a significant expansion of external contracting, the use of semi-autonomous agencies and the formation of interagency or intergovernmental partnerships. Many governments have also corporatized or fully privatized certain kinds of services, especially those deemed to be of a largely commercial nature. Trends of this nature pose a host of important and complex issues.

One of these concerns the principles and values which should be used to determine the choice of policy instrument to achieve particular public purposes. For instance, in what circumstances might a departmental mode of delivery be preferable to an agency, Crown company, or private contractor? To put the point differently, what criteria should be employed to guide decisions over institutional design? Further, are there any bodies of theory or empirical evidence which might assist in determining the best institutional mechanism for delivering specific kinds of services, whether these be correction services, childcare services, revenue collection, secondary health care, libraries, public transport or scientific research?

Another set of issues relates to the economic, social, and political consequences of the recent period of institutional experimentation in various countries, perhaps most notably Australia, Britain, Canada, and New Zealand. For instance, how have the new forms of service delivery and the greater reliance on external contracting affected governmental and institutional performance? More specifically, what empirical evidence is there concerning the impact of recent institutional reforms on key performance measures, such as productive efficiency, labour productivity, service quality, consumer satisfaction, and the extent to which government programs are effective in meeting their intended outcomes? Equally important, how have the new forms of service delivery affected accountability in all its various forms (i.e., political, managerial, legal, financial, and professional), and, more generally, what has been the impact on the role of the government in society and the relationship between the state and citizens? Also of interest in this context are the policy lessons which can be gleaned from the recent experimentation with new institutional forms and modes of service delivery. For instance, what particular institutional changes appear to have worked best, and why? Conversely, what has not proved to be successful, and why? Further, what are the risks associated with partnerships or external contracting, and how can these be minimized? And how can the interests of *citizens* and *taxpayers* be protected when so much emphasis is being placed on *consumers* and *clients*.

The purpose of this chapter is to explore these and related issues. First, it surveys the existing instruments for service delivery and the relevant theoretical and empirical literature relating to institutional design. Second, it outlines the new forms of service delivery being employed within the OECD, giving particular attention to the establishment of new agencies and the growth of competitive tendering and contracting. Third, it explores some of the wider policy issues generated by such developments, including the limits to contracting out, the proper role of citizens in the design and delivery of tax-funded services, and the issue of risk management. Finally, a number of suggestions are made for rethinking and revitalizing the delivery of public services.

Given the immense scope of the topic it is impossible to do justice to all the issues in a single chapter. Accordingly, the following discussion focuses almost exclusively upon developments within the OECD, and especially within the Anglo-American world. Likewise, attention is given primarily to the state's role in delivering and purchasing tax-funded services; issues surrounding the justifications for governmental funding and the state's regulatory responsibilities are correspondingly ignored, as are the arguments for and against user charges. Furthermore, the emphasis is upon services to citizens and taxpayers, not to ministers. Hence, issues relating to the organization and provision of policy advice are not addressed in any detail. Lastly, little consideration is given to corporatization, privatization, and the relative merits of for-profit versus non-profit organizational forms.

INSTITUTIONAL DESIGN:
GENERAL ISSUES AND PRINCIPLES

National and subnational governments fund and provide (through various mechanisms) a huge range of services. It would take considerable space merely to list such services, let alone describe their defining characteristics (i.e., in terms of fiscal cost, quantity, quality, location, mode of delivery, etc.). In terms of public expenditure, the most significant services in most jurisdictions include: income support (i.e., the payment of welfare benefits, pensions, allowances, grants, and subsidies); health care; education and training; housing (e.g., in the form of targeted allowances and subsidized in-kind provision); defence; policing; the criminal justice system (including courts and correction services); active labour market programs; social services (such as social work, counselling, family resolution, rehabilitation, etc.); scientific research; conservation and environmental protection; urban and regional planning; and the provision of infrastructure assets and public utilities. Additionally, many governments devote significant resources to the arts, broadcasting, and communications, the protection of indigenous peoples and their culture, and development assistance.

Over the years governments have developed a plethora of organizational forms (many with a distinctive legal structure or separate statutory basis) for carrying out tasks and functions of this nature. Common amongst these have been ministerial departments, secretariats, public enterprises, statutory boards, regulatory agencies, courts and tribunals, authorities, commissions, councils, institutes, foundations, and advisory bodies. Considerable emphasis is often placed on the legal status and attributes of the organizations in question. For instance, in many jurisdictions there are distinct legal entities known as corporations, and these in turn can be subdivided into limited liability companies, corporations created under their own statutes, and incorporated societies. Likewise, different kinds of unincorporated structures based on contracts can also be distinguished, such as partnerships, joint ventures, strategic alliances, franchises, and distributionships. However, the precise legal form of the organization may be less important in many instances than other variables, such as governance, financing, leadership, industrial relations and institutional culture, not to mention the regulatory and political environment within which the organization operates (see Hikel, 1997, 78).

An examination of public sector organizations within the OECD reveals significant institutional regularities and continuities at the national level. That is to say, individual bureaucracies have generally developed a set of distinct and often specialized organizations with each different type of organization carrying out different kinds of functions. Against this, there are major variations across the OECD in the preferred type and mix of institutions, the product, no doubt, of contrasting bureaucratic traditions, constitutional arrangements, political imperatives, and economic circumstances. For instance, during the twentieth century ministerial departments were used to a much larger extent for the provision of public services in countries with relatively centralized political systems, such as Britain, France, Ireland, Italy, Japan, and New Zealand, than in countries with more devolved systems, such as Denmark, the Netherlands, Sweden, and the United States. Likewise, whereas in some jurisdictions regulatory functions have been undertaken mainly by departments, in others they have primarily been the responsibility of semi-autonomous agencies. Another major difference lies in the scope and scale of public enterprise: whereas in some countries, most notably the United States, relatively few commercial functions have been undertaken within the public sector, in others, public enterprise has been a major policy instrument.

Differences of this nature contribute to the significant variations which are evident across the OECD in the way specific public services – whether child care, compulsory education, health care, correction services or labour market programs – are purchased and delivered. To illustrate: correction services are variously administered within the OECD by separate departments (e.g., an interior ministry or "Home" office), business units (or agencies) within departments, semi-autonomous agencies, and private firms on contract. Much the same applies to the conduct of scientific research. Similarly, in the case of compulsory education there are major differences in funding mechanisms, the pattern of school ownership, governance structures and regulatory arrangements. In some countries, schools are funded at the national level and largely self-managed. In others, schools are primarily funded and managed by local authorities. In most countries, the bulk of schools are publicly owned and operated. In others, most notably Belgium and the Netherlands, a high proportion of schools are privately owned but publicly funded.

Distinguishing Institutional Forms

At least three problems arise in distinguishing the various kinds of institutional forms (including the different types of contract) that can be used for the delivery of public services. The first is simply the extraordinary variety of institutional devices available to policy makers. As Thomas and Wilkins (1997, 110) point out, there is apparently "no limit to the ingenuity of governments to invent new structural arrangements." Exactly how some of these arrangements should be classified is not always clear.

Issues of terminology pose a second difficulty. Terms such as "department" or "ministry," while used in most jurisdictions, do not necessarily mean the same thing. In some cases, for instance, the terms are used interchangeably; in others, such as New Zealand, the word "ministry" generally refers to small organizations primarily dedicated to the provision of policy advice to ministers, whereas departments tend to be larger, multi-purpose organizations with significant delivery responsibilities. By contrast, in Belgium, Denmark, Finland, and Portugal, the word "department" typically refers to a branch or separate division within a ministry. Likewise, commercial enterprises fully or partially owned by the state are variously referred to as public enterprises, Crown corporations, state-owned enterprises, state trading companies and nationalized industries. However, in some jurisdictions (e.g., Finland and Sweden) a distinction is drawn between "state-owned enterprises" (which are commercial bodies in which the state is the majority share holder) and "public enterprises" (which are financially self-supporting and in administrative terms lie somewhere between a traditional government agency and a state-owned enterprise, OECD 1993, 91).

Third, there are significant variations in the way organizations with an apparently similar legal form, ownership structure, and system of governance actually operate in practice. For instance, a ministerial department is typically defined as an organization established by Crown prerogative or executive fiat for the purposes of servicing the needs and will of a cabinet minister; it is thus characterized by a direct accountability relationship between its political and administrative heads. Normally such organizations receive most, if not all, of their funds from the government via the budget process. Yet there is a world of difference between a ministerial department operating in a highly centralized, heavily regulated bureaucratic context (e.g., with comprehensive and detailed input controls) and the same organization operating in an environment of substantial administrative devolution (especially with respect to human resource management and financial management). Thus, the typical criticisms of departmental modes of service delivery – namely, that they are inflexible, inefficient, and unresponsive to consumer preferences – may not apply, or at least may not apply to the same extent, when the department (and its senior management) enjoy a significant degree of administrative autonomy over the selection and allocation of inputs (staff, capital, information technology, etc.). Indeed, in some cases ministerial departments may have greater managerial flexibility and operating "space" than supposedly more autonomous public agencies and trading companies. In New Zealand, for instance, since the public sector reforms of the late 1980s departments have had almost as much flexibility with regard to their internal management as most Crown entities (which typically operate at an arm's-length relationship with ministers). Indeed, they also appear to have significantly greater autonomy in relation to inputs and financial management than many of the new agencies in Canada.

The nature of the bureaucratic controls and constraints on departments is thus a critical factor to consider in determining the relative merits of such organizations for the delivery of various kinds of services. The same point, of course, applies equally to other institutional forms, including agencies, boards, statutory corporations, and public enterprises. Accordingly, it oversimplifies matters to suggest, as is not uncommon in the public administration literature (see Thomas and Wilkins, 1997), that there is a readily identifiable continuum of organizational forms – for instance, from ministries (or departments), through agencies, to statutory corporations, public enterprises, and finally to private organizations. This does not mean that organizations cannot be placed along a number of policy-relevant and analytically distinct continuums (e.g., according to their reliance on public funding, their relative political independence, their level and scope of delegated authority, or the degree to which they are bound by civil service rules covering such matters as remuneration and the hiring and firing of staff). However, as indicated above, there is no simple one-to-one correspondence between the particular title given to a public sector organization and its location along such dimensions.

In short, in considering the most appropriate organizational form for the delivery of certain kinds of publicly funded services it is necessary to examine not merely the relevant structural characteristics of the organizations in question, but also the wider constitutional, political, cultural, and administrative context in which they are operating. Preferring an agency over a department may make perfect sense in certain circumstances – for instance, if greater operational flexibility is deemed desirable and the use of an agency would facilitate this. At the same time, it might be possible to achieve equally desirable results by easing some of the administrative or budgetary constraints within which departments operate, undertaking internal organizational re-engineering, appointing new senior staff, introducing new technologies and information systems, or implementing more exacting performance management systems (including the development of clear service standards). Such approaches may also have the advantage of incurring lower transitional costs and avoiding major change–management problems.

Criteria for Selection

Having cleared some of the ground, it is now possible to move to the central issue of organizational design, namely the problem of determining what kind of organization is best suited for carrying out particular tasks and, in relation to this chapter, the more specific issue of choosing the best way of delivering various kinds of public services. Even a cursory reading of the relevant literature indicates that there is significant disagreement amongst scholars on issues of this nature. To the extent that any emerging consensus can be detected it is that the field of institutional design should not be regarded as an exact science, that there are no eternal laws, and that Taylorist mechanistic analogies and propositions (e.g., that there is "one best way") are seriously flawed (see Aucoin, 1998; Wilson, 1989). Equally, there is as yet no unified or general theory which can either explain the existing pattern of organizational forms within public bureaucracies or provide policy makers with clear normative guidance (Schick, 1996, 38). Indeed, to date there have been relatively few attempts to provide an overarching theory of institutional design in the public sector (see Horn, 1995).

Against this, there is no shortage of "administrative doctrines," as Hood and Jackson (1991) call them, relating to institutional design. Prominent amongst these are the doctrines that "form should follow function" (i.e., the organizational form should reflect the nature and attributes of the service being performed), that "like should be put with like" (i.e., services with similar characteristics should be grouped together), that commercial and non-commercial functions should be separated, and that the tasks of purchasing and provision should be undertaken by different organizations. Drawing on the analysis undertaken by Hood and Jackson, Table 1 sets out some of the competing sets of doctrines and the kinds of normative justifications which are offered in their defence.

While there is no general theory of institutional design, there are of course various theories, such as agency theory and transaction cost analysis, which can assist (at least to some extent) in explaining various kinds of institutional choice (e.g., the degree of administrative delegation, the procedures for administrative decision making, the form of governance, and the structure of rewards and sanctions, see Horn, 1995). Such theories also provide criteria which can be used for determining the relative merits of different institutional options, such as whether particular activities (e.g., revenue collection or rubbish collection) are best undertaken in-house or via external contracting.

For instance, transaction cost analysis suggests that in-house provision (i.e., the use of a public sector organization) is likely to be preferable (in terms of productive efficiency, effectiveness, and accountability) when there is limited contestability in the relevant market and when contract specification, monitoring, and enforcement is difficult (e.g. due to problems of specifying and measuring the desired level and quality of outputs) (see Boston et al., 1996, 23-24; Bryson and Smith-Ring, 1990; Gorringe, 1996;

TABLE 1
Institutional Design: Key Administrative Doctrines and Their Justifications

Administrative Doctrines	Typical Justifications
1 *Public versus private organization*	
1.1 Prefer public	Enhances public control, accountability, and equal treatment
	Enhances allocative and productive efficiency
	Improves long-term planning and investment
1.2 Prefer private	Enhances allocative and productive efficiency
	Minimizes political interference
	Enhances economic freedom
2 *Kinds of public organization*	
2.1 Prefer ministerial department (classical public bureaucracy)	Increases ministerial control and responsibility
	Enhances parliamentary oversight and political accountability for administrative action
	Highly adaptable organizational form
2.2 Prefer non-departmental forms (statutory companies, trusts, universities, etc.)	Reduces ministerial control and responsibility; boards, commissions, publicly owned facilitates local democratic control
	Facilitates recruitment of specialist or more representative personnel
	Increases managerial autonomy and administrative flexibility, thereby enhancing efficiency and effectiveness
	Facilitates organizational autonomy and independence from government
3 *Kinds of private organization*	
3.1 Prefer for-profit organization	Enhances managerial incentives and financial accountability
	Efficiency benefits of transferable property rights
3.2 Prefer non-profit, independent or voluntary organization	Reduces opportunism
	Enables more diverse delivery of services and greater client sensitivity
	Use of volunteers reduces costs

continued

4 *Scale of organization*

  4.1 Prefer large scale
      Enhances systematic learning and innovation
      Enhances coordination, priority setting, and integrated planning
      Reduces influence of narrow, parochial interests
      Enhances productive efficiency (due to economies of scale)

  4.2 Prefer small scale
      More "human," improves worker motivation
      Better administrative oversight; minimizes span of control problems
      Enhances productive efficiency (due to diseconomies of scale and greater contestability of supply)
      Greater adaptivity and responsiveness

5 *Functional scope of organization*

  5.1 Prefer multi-purpose
      Enhances coordination and a holistic approach
      More efficient due to economies of scope

  5.2 Prefer single-purpose
      Narrower and sharper focus improves managerial oversight, external monitoring, and accountability
      Facilitates a more unified organizational culture and mission

6 *Degree of uniformity*

  6.1 Prefer uniform administrative structures
      Enhances predictability and uniformity
      Facilitates interagency comparisons, enhances monitoring, performance assessment & control of customers

  6.2 Prefer pluriform administrative structures
      Optimal organizational form depends on function and context

7 *Inclusive versus divided responsibility*

  7.1 Prefer inclusive ("single roof") organization
    7.1.1 via horizontal integration across
      Enhances productive efficiency and flexibility-related activities (or across the portfolio)
      Facilitates unified political responsibility
      Minimizes transaction costs and improves consumer convenience via "one-stop shops"
      Improves policy coordination

continued

7.1.2 via vertical integration (e.g., of policy making and execution, purchasing and provision etc.)	Minimizes transaction costs Enhances oversight and control Improves security of supply Improves policy coordination and quality of advice
7.2 Prefer divided responsibility	Minimizes conflicts of interest Minimizes bureaucratic "capture" Reduces the concentration of power; facilitates more checks and balances Enhances clarity of organizational mission Facilitates contestable provision, decentralization of responsibility, and greater client responsiveness

8 Single source-supply versus multi-source supply

8.1 Prefer single-source supply	Enhances productive efficiency by minimizing duplication, waste, and transation costs Facilitates specialization and scale economics Enhances effectiveness by minimizing potential confusion, deadlocks, and inter-agency rivalry
8.2 Prefer multi-source supply	Enhances productive efficiency by facilitating contestable supply Facilitates multiple advocacy Enhances consumer choice

9 Combine like activities versus combine unlike activities

9.1 Prefer like with like (e.g., on the basis of purpose, process, clientele, or area)	Homogeneous organizations operate more effectively Facilitates greater specialization
9.2 Prefer administrative pluralism	Diversity facilitates creative synergies Avoids excessive concentrations of power over sensitive functions

10 Long versus short hierarchies

10.1 Prefer long	Enhances motivation by providing more incentives Enhances command and control functions
10.2 Prefer short	Improves information flows Reduces duplication Improves accountability and reduces buck-passing up the chain of command

Source: Boston et al., 1996, 74-5. Based on Hood and Jackson, 1991, 71-100.

Kettl, 1988; 1993; Lane, 1993, 176-88; Treasury, 1987; Vining and Weimer, 1990; Williamson, 1985; Wilson, 1989). Such conditions are most likely to apply when the operating environment is characterized by high levels of uncertainty, a significant risk of opportunism by agents, complex and frequent transactions, high asset specificity, and small numbers bargaining. Conversely, contracting out is likely to be the preferable option when the opposite conditions apply, i.e., when the supply of the good or service is highly contestable and when transaction costs are relatively low (due to tight constraints on opportunism, a small number of relatively simple transactions, a high degree of certainty, etc.). In practice, many goods and services fulfill neither set of criteria. For instance, the supply of the good or service in question may be partially contestable, and the transactions costs may be neither very large nor negligible. In such circumstances, the relative merits of in-house provision versus external contracting may be difficult to determine.

It should be borne in mind, of course, that there are practical limits to the application and effectiveness of "classical" contracts (i.e., formal, written, signed contracts), irrespective of whether these are employed between or within organizations (Hardin, 1992; Stewart, 1993). Many matters simply cannot be expressed or specified adequately within formal contracts; nor is enforcement necessarily straight-forward. Accordingly, both in-house provision and outsourcing depend to one degree or another on implicit, obligational or "relational" contracts, as Williamson (1985) calls them. Put differently, the success of much contracting – whether internal or external – is heavily dependent on the maintenance of high levels of commitment, goodwill, integrity, trust, and reciprocity. In making institutional choices, therefore, it is important to consider how the proposed arrangements will affect "specific assets" of this nature.

Three other aspects of institutional design are important to stress. First, questions of institutional design are not solely technical in nature; they also pose significant normative issues. As Cameron argues:

Alternative ways of organizing an institution represent choices among competing values. This applies to all organizations, governmental or non-governmental ... Organization is instrumental of values in two respects. First, values may be secured or rejected directly, insofar as they are or are not embodied in the organization itself. Values such as participation or professional autonomy, for example, are related direct-ly to the way in which an institution is organized. Second, values may be advanced or retarded indirectly, insofar as the organization is or is not conducive to their attainment (1992, 167).

In determining the best way of undertaking a particular activity there are potentially a large number of values to take into account. Some are more generally applicable than others. For instance, in most situations values such as productive efficiency, cost effectiveness, and accountability will be relevant. The appli-cability and significance of other values – such as institutional autonomy, customer responsiveness, cultural appropriateness, procedural justice, equitable access, uniformity of treatment, minimizing fiscal risks, the desirability or otherwise of participa-tory governance, stakeholder representation, power-sharing and political devolution (or the principle of subsidiarity), the protec-tion of indigenous rights, and so forth – will depend on the nature of the particular task in question (including, where rele-vant, the attributes of the service being provided) and the public purposes which it is intended to serve.

Given this situation, the choice of organizational form can be expected to vary, amongst other things, according to: 1) the val-ues which are deemed relevant; 2) the way these values are weighted; and 3) which of the organizational options available is thought most likely to facilitate the realization of the desired values. Needless to say, given the possibility of significantly different weightings, not to mention the uncertainty often sur-rounding the relationship between means and ends, policy makers in different contexts and at different times may well end up making highly divergent choices over how best to deliv-er particular services. Thus, those committed to radical demo-cratic principles and vigorous public participation in the design and delivery of public services are likely to favour strongly decentralized organizational forms, with many services (like schools and hospitals) being managed by locally elected boards. By contrast, those who doubt the wisdom of direct democratic control (perhaps because of the risks of insufficient administrative competence, inadequate oversight, "capture" of the policy process by sectional interest groups, or other forms of democratic failure), are likely to prefer greater reliance on organizations which are managed by appointed boards.

Second, and related to this, organizational design in practice will necessarily be influenced by a range of constitutional, political, economic, and administrative constraints. Plainly, one of the critical issues which needs to be addressed is the appropriate or desired level of ministerial involvement, control, and responsibility. Where ministers want relatively direct control of an activity – perhaps because of the magnitude of the government's funding role, the difficulties specifying outputs and assessing performance, or intense political interest and sensitivity – then it will probably be necessary to undertake the activity via a ministerial department (or at least within an agency which is closely coupled with a department). Conversely, where a significant measure of institutional autonomy is deemed desirable – as for instance in the fields of higher education and scientific research – then a non-departmental form is likely to be preferable. Issues of this nature have – very appropriately – figured prominently in the so-called "prior options" process that has been used in Britain since the late 1980s to determine whether to place particular departmental functions within an executive agency, and if so, what kind of agency to establish.

Third, institutional choice must take into account the interdependencies between organizations within the public sector, as well as any interdependencies between the different levels of government. Departments, agencies, and other public bodies are not independent, isolated, self-contained units; rather, they form part of a large, constantly changing, and integrated bureaucracy. The performance of a single agency is thus affected to one degree or another by the performance of other parts of the public sector within which it operates. In considering questions of institutional design, therefore, it is necessary to examine not merely the merits of a particular organization form for undertaking a specific function (or set of functions) but also the overall mix of organizational forms (e.g., the appropriate mix of single-purpose versus multi-purpose organizations), the mechanisms for achieving interorganizational (and intergovernmental) cooperation and coordination, and the wider implications of any particular organizational choice on the performance of other parts of the bureaucracy. For instance, there may be good reasons for hiving off various departmental service delivery functions to a series of single-purpose, semi-autonomous agencies, but such action runs the risk of exacerbating interorganizational (and perhaps even intergovernmental) coordination problems while making strategic policy management and systematic, intersectoral policy development all the harder. Accordingly, where major organizational changes are instituted, especially those which decouple policy making and implementation (or purchasing and provision), considerable care should be taken to ensure that adequate interagency linkages are put in place and that there are robust feedback loops linking those responsible for policy delivery with those responsible for policy evaluation and policy development (see Ewart and Boston, 1993; Mintzberg, 1996).

In evaluating the relative merits of a single-roof, vertically integrated organization combining both policy advice and policy delivery functions as compared to a decoupled arrangement, at least four criteria are important to consider:

- the extent to which the policy work is largely operational in nature and whether advisers need a detailed day-to-day knowledge of operational issues in order to supply sound, relevant, and timely advice;
- whether it is in the public interest (e.g., for reasons of confidentiality, security, efficiency, equity, procedural justice, etc.) for a government department directly accountable to a minister to undertake the provision of the service;

- whether there is scope under existing technologies for contestable provision;
- whether any additional transaction costs arising from an organizational split (or contracting out) are likely to be compensated for through savings in production costs.

Given the various considerations outlined above – including competing values, uncertainty, changing technology, and organizational interdependence – it should be evident that there is unlikely to be a single best organizational solution for each and every kind of delivery activity (or indeed any kind of governmental activity). This is not to infer that better ways of providing public services can never be identified or implemented. But it does suggest that the quest for optimal solutions is misguided. In fact, there is a strong probability that some of the preferred solutions at one particular historical moment will become the perceived problems at another.

ALTERNATIVE SERVICE DELIVERY:
ISSUES AND OPTIONS

As noted, many OECD countries have been experimenting over the past decade or so with new ways of delivering publicly funded services. The goals of such experimentation have been multiple (Aucoin, 1995; 1998; Langford, 1997; Seidle, 1995; 1997). In most cases greater efficiency, cost-effectiveness and fiscal savings have been important aims. But other objectives have often been equally, if not more, significant: encouraging innovation; improving the quality of services; reducing compliance costs; enhancing the responsiveness of services to citizens' (or consumers') needs; facilitating greater cultural diversity; fostering greater democratic control and public participation; empowering and motivating employees; rebuilding trust in public institutions; and reducing the overall role of the state. No doubt in some cases the key imperative has simply been to overcome existing bureaucratic inertia or circumvent the rigid input controls and other civil service constraints applying to ministerial departments.

The new forms of service delivery have been defined and categorized in numerous ways. In Canada, for instance, the term "alternative service delivery" (ASD) has been widely employed since the early 1990s to refer to the various administrative innovations which have occurred at the federal and provincial level. Unfortunately this term does not, as yet, have an agreed meaning, and appears to embrace a disparate range of policy initiatives (Langford, 1997, 60). For instance, the Canadian federal Treasury Board Secretariat has defined ASD as "the most appropriate means of providing programs, activities, services and functions to achieve government objectives. This concept includes a wide range of instruments and arrangements used directly by government or in cooperation with other sectors" (quoted in Langford, 1997, 62). Yet presumably "the most appropriate means" might include a relatively traditional ministerial department, and while this is a policy alternative in one sense it is not the kind of alternative which most reformers usually advocate. A rather different definition was advanced by the IPAC conference in 1997. Under this approach, ASD is regarded as "a creative and dynamic process of public sector restructuring that improves the delivery of services to clients by sharing governance functions with individuals, community groups and other government entities" (quoted in Ford and Zussman, 1997a, 6). Yet this definition is even more problematic. For one thing, many of the recent innovations in service delivery have not involved "sharing governance functions." For another, not all recent changes have brought undisputed improvements in the quality or quantity of public services available to clients.

Efforts to achieve greater definitional clarity with respect to the nature of ASD will doubtless continue. In the meantime, it is important to recognize that the options for improving service delivery within the public sector are not confined simply to changes in organizational structure and administrative processes (see Borins, 1995; Privy Council Office, 1996). While by no means complete, Table 2 outlines some of the options available under eleven separate headings. Needless to say, many other classifications are possible (see Langford, 1997, 63), and additional policy options can be identified within each general category. Further, none of these options is new, and few are mutually incompatible. Thus, a huge range of permutations and combinations is possible (e.g. enhanced service delivery might be pursued via the simultaneous establishment of a new agency, changes in the method of service delivery, the introduction of new technology or improved systems of quality management, a degree of contracting out, etc.). Of course, if a service were to be full privatized in terms of both its funding and provision then it would cease to be "public." The state may nonetheless believe that some form of regulation is needed in the public interest.

It is impossible, in my view, to develop a simple rule of thumb, formula or template for determining which particular option (or combination of options) is likely to provide the best method for delivering (or improving the delivery of) any specific service. Numerous relevant criteria can, of course, be identified, but their application, as noted earlier, will depend on a wide range of constitutional, legal, political, administrative, cultural, and economic considerations. Accordingly, policy makers are probably best advised in most instances to treat each case separately and develop a program improvement plan which is most suitable given the particular context and service characteristics in question (see Treasury Board Secretariat, 1995).

Since it is not possible to examine all forms of alternative service delivery in this chapter, attention here will be focused on two specific developments, namely the formation of executive agencies (of various kinds) and contracting out.

The Agency Approach

Semi-autonomous agencies have long been a vehicle through which all manner of public services have been delivered. In some jurisdictions, most notably Sweden, agencies ("authorities" or "boards" as they are variously called) have been the preferred mechanism for service delivery for over two hundred years (Fordin, 1996; Larsson, 1995, 58-69; Petersson, 1994, 99-101). Thus, at the central government level most key services, such as

TABLE 2
Ways of Improving Service Delivery

---

1 *Internal management changes & organizational re-engineering:*
   - administrative delegation & decentralization (e.g., in relation to HRM)
   - relaxation or removal of certain input controls and constraints
   - new systems of performance management, including rewards and incentives
   - establishment of internal business units

---

2 *Establishment of wholly new organizations:*
   - new (non-profit) service agency (or Crown corporation)
   - corporatization

---

3 *New services and methods of service delivery:*
   - case management
   - more accessible services (e.g., re. proximity, physical access, hours of provision etc.)

---

4 *Improved standard setting, quality management, and performance monitoring:*
   - new monitoring and review bodies
   - TQM
   - benchmarking
   - citizens' charters, performance targets, service standards, and service guarantees
   - more specific purchase contracts and performance agreements
   - better information, complaint procedures & opportunities for redress

---

5 *Closer cooperation and partnerships between organizations:*
   - single-window service and one-stop shops (via horizontal and/or vertical integration)
   - co-location
   - joint ventures
   - partnerships (consultative, contributory, operational, etc.)
   - sharing common services

---

6 *Devolution and power sharing:*
   - devolution to subnational government
   - devolution to a tribal authority
   - new, more participative or representative, governance structures

---

7 *Contracting and franchising:*
   - market testing
   - competitive tendering
   - full contracting out
   - franchising

---

continued

8 *Funding changes:*
  • partial cost recovery (via user charges)
  • full commercialization

9 *Applications of information technology:*
  • computerization, electronic delivery, use of internet, etc.
  • on-line transactions
  • mobile offices
  • "electronic town hall meetings"

10 *Regulatory initiatives:*
  • occupational and industry self-regulation
  • licensing of providers
  • replacing direct provision with regulatory instruments

11 *Privatization:*
  • different methods (share giveaways, competing tendering, etc.)
  • partial or full transfer of ownership and control

education, housing, policing, and active labour market programs, are administered by boards rather than departments. Currently, Sweden has in excess of 270 such boards.

Since the mid-to-late 1980s the use of agencies for program delivery has become increasingly fashionable in many other jurisdictions, including Australia, Britain, Canada, New Zealand, and the Netherlands, but to a lesser extent in Japan, the United States, and central and southern Europe (Aucoin, 1998; Peters, 1997). In Britain, for instance, the "Next Steps" initiative launched by the Conservative Government in 1988 had resulted in the establishment of 138 agencies by October 1997 (Office of Public Service, 1997). These bodies now employ around three-quarters of those working in the civil service. The approach in Canada, at both the federal and provincial level, has been more gradual (KPMG/IPAC, 1997; Seidle, 1995, 82-86; Wright and Waymark, 1995). Nonetheless, there are now a significant number of new agencies, variously referred to as Special Operating Agencies (SOAs), delegated administrative organizations (DAOs), alternative service units (ASUs), scheduled agencies and legislated agencies. Some operate exclusively at a single

level of government; others – like the Canadian Food Inspection Agency – involve intergovernmental cooperation (see
Doering, 1996; Moore and Skogstad, 1998). For instance, the
Canada Business Service Centres have brought together some
21 federal departments, provincial and territorial governments, and the private sector to provide one-stop access to a
wide range of services (Ford and Zussman, 1997a, 13). Despite
the generally slower pace of "agencification" in Canada than
in Britain, Manitoba – to take but one province – is expected to
have up to 40 SOAs by the year 2000 (Thomas and Wilkins,
1997, 114). In addition to the creation of new delivery units,
there have also been efforts in many countries to improve the
service delivery of existing agencies. For instance, in the United States under the "reinventing government" program certain
agencies have been designated as Performance Based Organizations and given greater operational independence (Ingraham, 1997).

The nature of the new agencies which have been formed
varies considerably (e.g., in terms of their legal status, governance structures, range of functions, powers, source of funds,
and degree of autonomy), as does the regulatory context within which they are required to operate. For instance, some are
stand-alone entities; others (especially in Britain and Canada)
are subordinate to other organizations (usually a ministry or
department). Some have separate empowering legislation (as in
the case of several of the most recently established agencies in
Ottawa); others operate within existing legal instruments or
executive prerogative. Some have multiple, and often substantial, functions; others have a single, often narrowly focused,
mission. Some are heavily involved in the provision of policy
advice; others are predominantly operational in character.
Some provide services almost exclusively to other public agencies; others deal directly with members of the public. Some
employ their own staff; others do so only via delegated authority. Some are fully government funded; others receive only a
small proportion of their funding via the budgetary process.
Some are wholly non-commercial in orientation; others are

essentially commercial and self-funding. Some have considerable financial discretion; others do not. Some are governed by boards of directors; some have advisory boards; yet others are managed solely by a chief executive who reports directly to the head of a ministry (or in some cases a minister). Where governance functions are undertaken by boards, their size and composition varies. Some are wholly appointed (usually by the relevant portfolio minister), some are wholly elected, and some comprise both appointed and elected members. Thus there is no standard, generic agency model.

A common motivation for moving service delivery functions from traditional line departments to agencies has been the opportunity for greater administrative discretion and managerial autonomy, particularly with respect to staffing, remuneration systems and financial management. Hence, in most cases the managers of the new agencies have been bound by fewer civil service controls than under previous arrangements. This applies even when the agency has been formed within a department – as in the case of the British executive agencies – rather than as a stand-alone entity. As a direct counterpart to this greater managerial discretion and the removal of various input controls, improved systems of performance management have generally been instituted to ensure that the new agencies are appropriately accountable for their activities. Common instruments for achieving such accountability (and greater hierarchical control) have included various "contractualist" devices (e.g., charters, purchase agreements, performance agreements, framework documents, statements of corporate intent, business plans, strategic plans, etc.), together with more exacting monitoring and reporting mechanisms (in relation to both financial and non-financial performance). New, more flexible, performance-oriented remuneration systems have typically been introduced, certainly at senior levels within the agencies, with top managers often employed on fixed-term, performance-based contracts.

Given the diversity of structural and governance arrangements, the relationship between ministers and agencies varies both within and across jurisdictions. In some cases, ministers appoint a board of directors but have no role in management appointments, this responsibility lying with the board. In other cases, ministers appoint both the board and the head of the agency. In yet other cases, where there is no board (or perhaps only an advisory board) the appointment of the head of the agency may be either the responsibility of a minister or a civil service department (or a combination of the two). Differences of this kind obviously create a range of distinct principal–agent relationships. In some cases the head of an agency may, in effect, serve two or more principals – a board, a supervising ministry, and a portfolio minister. In other cases, there is a much simpler straight-line accountability from an agency head to a board and from the board to a minister. Having said this, in practical terms the day-to-day working relationship between ministries and agencies, or between ministers and the heads of agencies, may not correspond to the formal accountability structure. Hence, although on paper the relationship between an agency and the relevant portfolio minister might be expected to be the responsibility of the board, in reality it is the agency head who manages the political relationship. This of course highlights the importance of the informal, as well as the formal, structures and networks when considering issues of institutional design and organizational performance.

Evaluation of Agencies

Despite the substantial literature documenting the expansion of delivery agencies since the late 1980s, the evidence concerning the impact of this development on organizational performance, service quality, accountability, and other relevant measures remains relatively limited, partial, and incomplete. For instance, a detailed KPMG/IPAC study of ASD in Canada in 1997, much of which focused on the establishment of new agencies, contained no comprehensive hard data on the costs and benefits of agencification (though various ad hoc examples of improvements were noted). Thus, there was little evidence on the costs of implementation or the impact of the new structures on public sector employment, public expenditure, the costs of service provision, productive efficiency, labour productivity, and service quality, let alone any wider social and distributional implications or the effectiveness of the new agencies in achieving broader policy outcomes. As one of the contributors to the KPMG/IPAC volume noted:

At the moment, we have little good disinterested information on the actual outcomes of individual ASD projects and consequently, little information about the overall impact of ASD at the level of single jurisdictions or for the country as a whole (Hikel, 1997, 83).

A similar lack of comprehensive hard data is evident in overviews of the Next Steps program (and related developments) in Britain (e.g., Greer, 1994; O'Toole and Jordan, 1995; Pollitt, Birchall, and Putman, 1998), and the structural reforms in both Australia (e.g., Alford and O'Neill, 1994; Considine and Painter, 1997; Weller, Forster, and Davis, 1993) and New Zealand (e.g., Boston et al., 1996; Halligan, 1997; Schick, 1996).

This relative lack of hard data is due partly to limited research and partly to methodological and measurement difficulties. The latter problems should not be underestimated. For instance, it is often hard to isolate the effects of particular organizational changes, such as the establishment of an agency, from the numerous other management changes which may be occurring at the same time (including the introduction of new technology, a greater reliance on external contracting, or changes in public funding, human resource management, financial management, etc.). Thus, if better performance is identified, it may be difficult to determine the respective contributions of structural reform and other management changes.

Against this, there are some very useful independent and government-sponsored case studies of the performance of specific agencies. These generally point to positive outcomes as a result of the move to an "agency" status. For instance, such studies include evidence of:

- cost savings
- staff reductions (including at senior levels)
- improvements in service quality, as measured for example by the speed, accuracy, and reliability of delivery, easier access to services, fewer complaints, etc.
- the development of a stronger customer/client focus and orientation
- greater opportunities for experimentation and innovation
- significant changes in organizational culture, including a clearer organizational identity and sense of purpose
- generally positive assessments by managers, employees, consumers, and politicians; and
- agencies meeting a clear majority of their key output (or performance) targets (see Bellamy, 1995; Hunt, 1995; Petrie, 1998; Pollitt, 1997; Schick, 1996; Seidle, 1995; Trosa, 1994; Wright and Waymark, 1995)

A typical summary of the benefits brought about by the establishment of agencies is provided by Thomas and Wilkins (1997, 120) in their analysis of SOAs in Manitoba:

Employers have been empowered through clear mandates, delegated authority, training and incentives to expose their professional capabilities to a doubting public, media and bureaucracy. Attitudinal surveys and needs assessments have shown a clear growth in the commitment of employees to the success of their agency and to their related job satisfaction. This has translated into better service, cost savings for the government, and a confident, motivated workforce. The special status accorded SOAs has created a kind of "Hawthorne effect" in organizational performance.

On the negative side of the ledger, many studies also reveal evidence of:

- greater interorganizational conflict
- organizational fragmentation having negative effects on policy coordination and policy learning

- higher levels of employee stress
- significant additional transaction costs generated by the new contractualist policy instruments and performance management regimes
- a mismatch between the aims and objectives of agencies and their key performance indicators
- excessive interference by control departments (or parent departments)
- inappropriate use of political patronage in the appointment of agency boards or chief executives
- concerns about a decline in political accountability and responsiveness (e.g., see Aucoin, 1998; Boston, 1995; O'Toole and Jordan, 1995; Thomas, 1998)

The issue of accountability has attracted repeated attention. On the one hand, many commentators have noted the gains in managerial accountability as a result of more rigorous systems of performance management and financial management which have generally been associated with the new agencies. For instance, citizens and legislatures frequently have available to them much better information on what the agencies produce, the expected standards of performance, and the extent to which these standards have been achieved. Against this, there have been concerns in many jurisdictions about the possible loss of political accountability, with ministers often being less willing to take overall responsibility for the operations of the new agencies which fall within their portfolio (see O'Toole and Chapman, 1995; Chapman, 1997). More specifically, critics have argued that while ministers gladly take the credit for improved performance, they show greater reluctance to accept responsibility for substandard performance. There have also been concerns about the apparent loss of political control over the activities of certain agencies (especially those operating outside a departmental framework), evidenced by the difficulty which ministers have had in some instances in fine-tuning their operational discretion and ensuring that agencies act in accordance with government policy. In short, it seems that certain kinds of agencification may run the risk of impairing a government's "steering" capacity (Pierre, 199, 52).

Significantly, in cases where questions about the political accountability of specific agencies have surfaced, similar problems were often evident under previous structural arrangements. This suggests that it is not necessarily the specific institutional form which is at fault but rather that the activity in question is highly complex or inherently controversial. Moreover, concerns about the accountability and control of agencies exist in widely differing political systems, including Sweden which has had several centuries to perfect the agency model (Fordin, 1996; Larsson, 1995, 65-66). This highlights the absence of any ideal models for the governance and management of agencies undertaking service delivery functions.

It is sometimes suggested that moving service delivery functions out of departments and into agencies (or into separate departmental business units) facilitates a clearer delineation and assignment of responsibilities: ministers become responsible for policy while public servants are responsible for implementation. Such a proposition, however, is flawed both in principle and practice (see Schick, 1996, 42; Trosa, 1994, 24-25). In a parliamentary democracy operating under the doctrine of individual ministerial responsibility, ministers are vicariously responsible for the public organizations and policies for which they have political oversight. This includes both explanatory and amendatory responsibilities. (In Sweden, incidentally, the doctrine of individual ministerial responsibility does not apply in the same way as in other parliamentary democracies and agencies are accountable to the government as a whole rather than to individual ministers.) Further, it is impossible in many instances to eliminate all confusion over lines of responsibility or to avoid overlapping responsibilities (especially when there are multiple principals). Equally, as Schick (1996) has argued, efforts to specify and delineate accountabilities in a very precise fashion run the risk of narrowing the focus of administrators and reducing their broad sense of responsibility.

Lessons

Turning to some of the lessons from the recent experimentation
with agencies in various countries, a number of matters are
worth highlighting. First, there is no need to hive-off the delivery
functions of departments and place them in separate, stand-
alone, arm's-length agencies in order to improve service delivery.
As the public sector reforms in Australia and New Zealand have
demonstrated, it is possible to achieve significant additional
management flexibility and improved performance within a
departmental framework if appropriate changes are made to the
relevant bureaucratic controls on human resource management,
financial management and administrative practices (see Boston
et al., 1996; Henry, 1995; Petrie, 1998; Seidle, 1995, 58-60). Likewise, few net gains can be expected from agencification if structural reforms are not accompanied by corresponding changes to
incentive structures, performance management systems, and
administrative controls.

Second, the success of new agencies in undertaking their
delivery functions depends on a range of variables including, as
Thomas and Wilkins (1997, 116) have argued, their "mandate,
strategy, leadership, structure, process, culture, conflict and
power." Of these, the importance of leadership must not be
underestimated (see Petrie, 1998). After all, in a devolved managerial environment much will depend on the calibre, competence, drive, and vision of the head of the agency. This includes
the capacity to recruit and retain a strong, dynamic senior management team, the ability to oversee the process of change while
retaining the confidence, enthusiasm, and dedication of staff (not
least those on the front line of service delivery), the ability to
inspire a vigorous, performance-oriented and customer-
focused organizational culture, and the capacity to work with
ministers of widely differing priorities and perspectives. In
order to secure capable, effective, and stable leadership careful
attention must be given to the methods of appointing and
remunerating agency heads, as well as the issue of succession

planning and the nurturing of future senior managers. To rely on the capacity of the "market" to produce such leadership would be imprudent.

Third, there are some definite advantages in institutional specialization. That is to say, a relatively narrow mandate – i.e., a single main purpose or function – appears to be more conducive to improved organizational performance than the coupling of multiple (and potentially conflicting) purposes or functions. This is not to suggest, however, that regulation and delivery, policy and operations, and purchasing and provision, should always be separated (see Aucoin, 1998; Howden-Chapman and Ashton, 1994). Indeed, a rigid, vertical split between policy and operations has well-known drawbacks in terms of reduced policy coordination and policy learning, while the horizontal decoupling of discrete service-delivery functions into separate agencies may have negative implications for service users (e.g., in terms of accessibility, convenience, and higher compliance costs). Thus, where a strategy of institutional disaggregation is being pursued, care needs to be taken to ensure that adequate horizontal and vertical coordination mechanisms are put in place and that agencies have adequate incentives to cooperate where appropriate.

Fourth, while it is difficult, if not impossible, to determine whether one particular kind of agency model is preferable to another, no single agency model is equally applicable for delivering each and every kind of public service. Instead, as Schick (1996, 38) argues, in delivering services governments are likely to be "best served by a variety of organizational forms." These will include publicly owned companies (or Crown corporations) that operate in contestable markets, as well as non-commercial agencies, some of which operate independently of government departments and some of which are separate departmental business units. Nor, according to Schick (1996, 38), is there much value in seeking absolute consistency in design for each separate institutional form.

In selecting the appropriate kind of agency, the following criteria are relevant:

- the nature and extent of the government's "purchase interest"
- the degree of market contestability
- the desired level of political independence or impartiality, as well as the likely extent of ministerial involvement
- the extent to which outputs and outcomes can be tightly specified, observed, and monitored
- the desired level of stakeholder or citizen representation in matters of governance
- the nature and level of the political risk associated with the activity in question, and the need to ensure a close alignment of political risk and political responsibility (see Gregory, 1997; Wilson, 1989)

Clearly, where close ministerial control and oversight is deemed desirable, where the services are largely tax-financed and non-contestable, and where outputs and/or outcomes are difficult to observe, having the activity located within a departmental framework is likely to be preferable, other things being equal, to alternative institutional options. Conversely, where significant independence is desired, a more arm's-length relationship with ministers is likely to be preferable. The potentially greater political and financial risks associated with such an arrangement will thus have to be accepted as an inevitable by-product of the quest for greater autonomy; one cannot have it both ways.

Fifth, regardless of the preferred institutional arrangements, where there is a desire to bring about rapid improvements in the quality of service delivery and sharpen the customer focus of an agency, there can be significant advantages in selecting, and then emphasizing, a small number of key performance measures which have a clear user orientation. A good example would be to set a precise and demanding goal for reducing the waiting time for access to a particular service, such as elective surgery, or the time taken to process applications for passports, welfare benefits, pensions, and so forth. Strategies of this nature, of course, run the well-known risk of "goal displacing" behaviour. Nevertheless, they can be useful, certainly on a short-term basis, for encouraging innovative thinking and bringing positive changes to the internal culture of an organization. Over the longer term, there is plainly merit in having proper, comprehensive service standards (or "charters") and for these to be integrated with each agency's performance management system.

Sixth, with respect to governance: controlling agents and holding them accountable is generally easier to ensure under straightforward, single-line principal–agent relationships rather than in situations where agents serve multiple, and potentially competing, principals. Where governance responsibilities are shared between two or more principals (e.g., several levels of government, several departments, or public–private partnerships) there are likely to be higher agency costs, as well as greater political risks and coordination problems. At the same time, shared governance may be unavoidable in certain situations (e.g., because of the cross-jurisdictional issues involved). In such circumstances, it is essential to clarify the precise nature of the powers and responsibilities which are being shared (e.g., program design, financing, regulation, staffing, service definition, etc.) and the exact lines of accountability between management and the governing body.

Seventh, and related to this, moving service delivery from traditional line departments to agencies raises important issues about the process by which the boards and/or chief executives of the new bodies are appointed. Where ministers are directly involved in making such appointments, appropriate safeguards should be instituted to ensure that good advice is received on suitable candidates and that the risks of politically motivated appointments are minimized. The creation of a Commissioner for Public Appointments, as occurred in Britain in 1995 in response to a recommendation of the Nolan Committee, or the establishment of an independent appointments' commission, are amongst the options worthy of consideration (Skelcher, 1998).

Finally, the formation of agencies is likely to necessitate new systems of external monitoring and reporting. In this context, a balance needs to be struck between ensuring, on the one hand, that the reporting framework is sufficiently comprehensive and exacting to enable adequate control and the management of risk, while, on the other hand, avoiding a regime which is unduly costly and interventionist.

Contracting Out

Most national and subnational governments in OECD countries have contracted out a range of tax-funded services for decades, if not centuries. Since the early 1980s, however, there has been renewed interest in competitive tendering and contracting (CTC) in most jurisdictions as a means of improving service delivery and securing fiscal savings. It is possible here to comment on only a few of the policy issues raised by the increase in public sector contracting and to provide only a brief review of the substantial empirical evidence surrounding the relative merits of in-house provision and external contracting.

In terms of the scope and scale of CTC by public institutions and agencies, a number of broad observations can be made:

1   While it is difficult in many jurisdictions to determine the exact volume of external contracting (e.g., in terms of public expenditure), the extent of such contracting appears to vary significantly across the OECD with a greater reliance on private provision in countries like Australia, Britain, and the United States than in many continental European countries.
2   The extent of CTC in some jurisdictions (e.g., the state of Victoria in Australia, and local government in Britain) has greatly increased in recent times as a result of governments setting targets or making it mandatory for a certain percentage of services to be contracted out (or at least subject to market testing and competitive tendering).
3   The prevalence of contracting out varies significantly across policy sectors: it is much more extensive in areas like health care, scientific research, training, and the design, construction and maintenance of public infrastructure than in policing, diplomacy, prison management, revenue collection, policy advice, and the payment of welfare benefits. However, more and more publicly funded services are being opened up to

competitive tendering, with contracts now being awarded for services which previously were largely, or even exclusively, the domain of public sector providers.

4 In some jurisdictions there has been a shift from the use of open-ended and untied grants to legally binding contracts. Thus, many non-profit organizations which previously received grants are now required to bid for contracts. In effect, this has meant a shift from relational to classical contracts.

5 Considerable variation exists with respect to the nature, comprehensiveness, specificity, and monitoring of the new forms of contracting which have developed. For instance, whereas in Britain a high proportion of the contracts in the health sector are not legally binding, in New Zealand there has been a strong preference for legally enforceable contracts.

The Cost and Benefits of Contracting

There is a wealth of empirical literature examining the costs and benefits of the CTC of publicly funded services. With little doubt, the most comprehensive and detailed study to date has been that produced by the Australian Industry Commission in 1996. This not merely reviews a large number of international empirical studies which explore the effects of contracting but also considers many of the wider policy issues generated by the greater use of CTC (e.g., the potential barriers to fair and effective competition, the merits or otherwise of allowing in-house bids, the problems of determining contract design and service specification, the impact on accountability and ethics, the problems of quality assurance and performance monitoring, etc.). Among the key lessons to emerge from this analysis are the following:

• It is vital to structure CTC in a way which ensures clear and accurate specifications, effective competition so that the best provider is chosen, and adequate monitoring of the contractor's performance.

- A major benefit of CTC is that it forces agencies to review
  what they are doing and whether their current activities are
  effective in meeting underlying policy goals.
- The focus of CTC needs to be on service outcomes [or outputs
  where this is not possible], rather than inputs.
- Successful CTC requires a cultural change in government and
  a new mix of skills. It has to be supported by Ministers /
  Councillors, driven by senior management, and handled in
  close consultation with staff and their representatives, as well
  as clients and the community at large (Industry Commission,
  1996, 1).

With respect to the impact of CTC on accountability, costs and
service quality, the Industry Commission offered the following
observations and judgements:

- Whatever the method of service delivery, a government
  agency must remain accountable for the efficient performance
  of the functions delegated to it ... CTC inevitably involves
  redefining responsibilities and relationships between key
  stakeholders, and introduces a new player – the contracted
  service provider – into the chain (1996, 4-5). The study reported evidence of both enhanced accountability and a blurring of
  accountability under CTC. It also noted the potential for a loss
  of accountability as a result of reduced opportunities for
  redress and administrative review, and a loss of transparency
  due to the need to protect commercial confidentiality (see also
  Audit Office, 1994; Martin, 1995; Mulgan, 1997).
- While there are instances where costs have increased through
  its use, CTC can and generally does reduce the ongoing costs
  of agencies' service provision. Seventy-five per cent of surveyed Australian and overseas empirical studies found that
  CTC reduced the ongoing costs of service provision: savings
  ranged from 10 to 30 per cent in over half of the services
  studied. The savings from CTC can vary widely and do not
  appear to be strongly related to the type of service considered (1996, 11).

- The report noted evidence of both improvements and reductions in quality arising from CTC. It observed that "agencies may encounter difficulties in specifying and measuring quality, particularly when the future needs of individual clients cannot be predicted ... However, the Commission is not persuaded that these difficulties are necessarily exacerbated by CTC. Nor are they necessarily overcome by agencies delivering services themselves" (1996, 7).

Overall, the Industry Commission's findings confirm the results of many other studies which have indicated that CTC offers the potential for significantly improving the performance of publicly funded services (at least under certain conditions). It is important, however, not to exaggerate the gains from CTC or to ignore the fact that CTC is inappropriate for some kinds of service (e.g., front-line policing). For instance, Hodge (1998) provides an important note of caution arising from his use of the technique of "meta-analysis" to assess the economic effects of contracting. From an evaluation of the data in some of the most methodologically rigorous studies of contracting out (with a sample size of over 20,000 separate measurements), Hodge concluded that the average cost reductions were around 8–14 per cent, significantly lower than those reported by the Industry Commission and by other general reviews of the empirical evidence (1998, 21). Moreover, he found that cost savings occurred under both external contracting and in-house contracting, and that the gains (on a range of measures) varied significantly across different services. Unsurprisingly, perhaps, the most substantial improvements were found for standard, relatively competitive services like maintenance, refuse collection, and cleaning, while generally insignificant improvements were common for services such as police/security, health, fire, training, and transport services (1998, 23).

The Limits to Contracting Out

One of the many policy issues posed by the recent increase in the use of CTC by public sector organizations concerns the proper limits to external contracting. Are there, for instance, any services which should never be contracted out and what principles should be used to guide decisions in this area? Despite the obvious importance of this issue – in constitutional, political and administrative terms – there is a remarkable dearth of literature on the subject. Nor do most jurisdictions have clear constitutional or statutory limitations affecting the kinds of activities that external contractors can undertake. Moreover, at a technical level (and leaving the public interest to one side) there is potentially no limit to the range of services which can be contracted out. After all, mercenaries can be recruited to fight wars, and private companies can be contracted to manage prisons, collect taxes and customs, and provide welfare benefits and social services.

To date, perhaps the best analysis of the proper limits to external contracting has been provided by the u.s. General Accounting Office (GAO) (1991). In a report examining the use of external contractors by federal government agencies, the GAO sought to assess whether contractors were undertaking functions which could be regarded as "inherently governmental" in nature. Part of the problem in answering this question was, of course, the difficulty of defining "inherently governmental" and determining what kinds of functions fall within this category. For instance, few would disagree with the proposition that the making of foreign policy is an inherently governmental function. After all, only governments, by definition, can have foreign policies and no organization or institution other than the government should be responsible for determining the nature of these policies. Yet if the making of foreign policy is an inherently government function, does this mean that only elected officials and public employees should be involved in the "conduct" of foreign policy (e.g., negotiating with other governments, providing advice, etc.)? Presumably the answer here is "no," or at least "not necessarily." In other words, it would be perfectly acceptable for a government to seek advice on a matter of foreign affairs from experts outside the public sector (e.g., from universities or think-tanks). Nor would it be unreasonable in certain circumstances for a government to send a private citizen to hold talks on its behalf with a foreign power. The "conduct" of foreign policy, therefore, need not be a function undertaken exclusively by public officials.

In determining which of the enormous range of functions and activities undertaken by governments should or should not be contracted out to private providers, the GAO argues that the issue is fundamentally political or ethical rather than simply technical in nature. Moreover, the critical question is not whether external contracting is technically feasible (even if potentially risky or costly), but whether it is in the public interest. In applying the test of the public interest, the GAO identifies two main principles or criteria (in addition to the standard questions of efficiency, cost-effectiveness, etc.). The first is that a government must always retain control over the process of policy formulation and implementation, as well as the management of public organizations:

A key criterion in determining whether service contracts are appropriate is whether the government maintains sufficient in-house capability to be thoroughly in control of the policy and management functions of the agency... This includes the capacity to adequately direct, supervise, and monitor contracts (1991, 30).

The second principle is that only governments and public employees should have the authority to exercise discretion or make value judgments.

The first principle, in my view, is largely uncontroversial. Plainly, if the government loses control to an external contractor – perhaps because it ceases to have the capacity to be a "smart buyer" – then it places both itself and citizens at significant risk. The second principle, however, is less compelling. Presumably one of the objectives of contracting out is to facilitate greater managerial flexibility, discretion, and innovation, and in many cases the use of such discretion will entail contractors making certain kinds of value judgments. Accordingly, the GAO's second principle is simply too broad as it stands and requires greater specificity (e.g., perhaps concerning the kinds of value judgments which should only be made by elected officials or public employees).

In considering the application of principles of this nature to specific services – such as correction services, tax collection, childcare or the provision of policy advice to ministers – several matters are important to stress. First, technology is continuing to advance. Accordingly, some services which may at one time have been inefficient to contract out may, as a result of technological innovations, become amenable to contracting (i.e., from a narrow economic standpoint). Likewise, changes in technology may alter the capacity of policy makers to maintain adequate control under both in-house and external provision.

Second, there appears to be a range of services which are readily amenable to external contracting but where it may be desirable for governments to retain a significant in-house capacity. The provision of policy advice and correction services almost certainly fit this category. In both cases, it is perfectly feasible, if not often more efficient, for governments to engage in external contracting: consultants and think-tanks can be employed via competitive tendering arrangements to supply large amounts of advice on a wide range of issues; and the empirical evidence suggests that the application of CTC to prison management (as well as construction) can be beneficial (though it is not without certain risks and drawbacks). In both cases, however, there would be major risks for governments if they lacked professional in-house advisers and public prisons. For instance, in the absence of in-house advisers with expertise across all the key areas of public policy, the government would have little capacity to assess the quality of the advice being purchased externally, let alone the capacity to integrate this advice properly into the policy-making process (see Boston, 1994). Similarly, in the case of correction services, it is one thing to contract out the management of low-to-medium security prisons, it is another to contract out the management of facilities holding dangerous criminals. Further, the number of prisoners at any given point in time is dependent on a range of factors that are outside the control of government. Given the significant variability in prison musters, it may be to a government's advantage to bear the risk of managing fluctuating muster levels via in-house facilities rather than paying private providers a large risk premium to do the same thing.

ENGAGEMENT OF CITIZENS IN
CHOICES AND DESIGN

Another important policy question posed by the introduction of new methods of service delivery and the greater weight which has been placed on consumer responsiveness and client satisfaction concerns the proper role of citizens in the design and delivery of tax-funded services (see Pierre, 1995). This obviously touches upon significant issues in the realm of democratic theory, as well as philosophical questions concerning firstly, the rights and responsibilities of citizens, and secondly, the relative merits of politics and markets as social-choice mechanisms. For instance, advocates of what Barber (1984) refers to as a "strong" democracy (i.e., a democracy in which citizens are active participants in the process of policy making) tend to favour an extensive role for citizens in the design of service delivery and in the governance of public delivery agents (e.g., via the use of elected boards to run schools, hospitals, early childhood centres, etc.). They are also likely to place greater weight upon the interests of citizens relative to those of consumers and clients of public services. By contrast, advocates of "thin" democracy give more attention to the role of high-level representative institutions and delegated authority rather than direct democracy or civic participation in agenda-setting, deliberation, and policy implementation. Accordingly, they generally favour appointed, rather than elected, boards and place more weight on economic rather than political empowerment.

Quite apart from these broader questions of democratic theory, there are other principles and considerations regarding citizen engagement in service delivery which needed to be underscored. First, the interests of individuals as citizens and subjects are not identical to their interests as consumers of particular public services (although in most cases these interests overlap).

This has two implications. On the one hand, there must be processes for mediating any conflicting interests and determining where the public interest lies; this is, of course, one of the central roles of the political system. On the other hand, it is not sufficient to rely solely on the "signals" sent by consumers (e.g., via exit or voice) to the suppliers of public services to determine what kinds and levels of service ought to be provided – and this applies irrespective of the level of marketization or user charges. Bear in mind, too, that many public services are "consumed" involuntarily and do not involve a two-way exchange. For such reasons, they differ fundamentally from typical market transactions.

Second, and related to this, under conditions of parliamentary sovereignty it is Parliament which is the ultimate principal when dealing with publicly owned, funded, or managed services, not the direct users of these services. Thus, it is for Parliament to determine, at least in broad terms, the range and forms of service which citizens are entitled to receive or, in some cases, forced to consume.

Third, as Alford (1998), amongst others, has stressed, citizens are not merely consumers or clients of many public services but very often they are also co-producers. That is to say, the successful delivery (or production) of various services depends, either partly or substantially, upon the active (generally voluntary) cooperation and participation of individual citizens. For instance, the provision of safe, good-quality public housing requires that tenants take proper care of their rented accommodation and any shared facilities, and refrain from various kinds of anti-social behaviour. Equally, the maintenance of an effective, efficient, and fair tax system is dependent upon not just citizen compliance or passive abstention, but also positive actions, including the maintenance of accurate records, the truthful reporting of income, and the timely lodging of returns.

While recognizing the controversial nature of citizen participation in the design and execution of service delivery, there are in my view a number of broad principles which are applicable irrespective of the kind of service in question:

1 Citizens should be properly informed about the nature of the services being provided, including the standards of service to be expected and the government's intended policy outcomes. Further, citizens should have the right to access all relevant performance information, including annual reports and the reports of external monitoring agencies. Such information should be provided in a comprehensible fashion.

2 There should be appropriate avenues for the investigation of complaints (e.g., via ombudsmen or independent commissioners) and the provision of compensation for substandard service.

3 Citizens should be consulted whenever a significant change in the delivery of public services is planned, and there should be appropriate opportunities for citizens to make submissions and influence policy outcomes. Where appropriate, the views of citizens should be sought via the use of focus groups, advisory panels, and citizens juries.

As noted, there has been considerable disagreement over the appropriate role of citizens in the governance of public institutions and agencies. For instance, whereas there is often strong support for parents and other lay representatives to be involved in the governance of childcare centres and schools, the inclusion of elected lay representatives on the governing bodies of public hospitals, housing agencies, and research institutes is typically more contentious. In my view, there is no "correct" or optimal solution. There are, however, a number of general principles or criteria which should be considered in determining whether direct citizen participation in governance is appropriate. These include:

- the complexity of the "business" and the nature of the competencies required to ensure effective oversight and scrutiny of management
- the extent to which elected lay representatives may enhance the quality of the service by virtue of their particular expertise or experience

- the degree of institutional autonomy which is deemed desirable (and the potential risks to such autonomy if all members of the governing body are ministerial appointees)
- the extent to which the public body in question is involved in significant, and possibly contentious, allocative decisions
- the extent to which citizens have other means available for expressing their preferences and influencing the policies of the bodies in question (e.g., via consultative panels, etc.)

MANAGING RISK

The many innovative approaches to the provision of public services in recent years have brought both gains and losses. One of the main downsides has been, at least in some instances, an increase in various kinds of risk. Yet as has often been pointed out, "there can be no experimentation without risk. Ministers and senior officials must accept some of the uncertainty implicit in giving up a degree of control. Not every experiment will be a success. Some honest mistakes will be made. This needs to be understood and accepted" (Bourgon, 1997, 26). This does not mean, of course, that all risks are acceptable or that efforts should not be made to minimize the likelihood of failure.

Accordingly, when alternative delivery options are being considered, careful attention should be given to the kinds and levels of risk which might be encountered. Such risks include (OECD, 1994, 13-17):

- moral hazard (e.g., risks arising from the failure of one or other of the parties to a contract to carry out their obligations perhaps because of asymmetrical information, difficulties in detecting non-compliance, or the absence of effective sanctions)
- technological risks (e.g., risks arising from uncertainty surrounding the technical feasibility of a new method of service delivery)
- fiscal risks (e.g., risks arising from poor investment decisions, unanticipated cost increases, or the bankruptcy of a private partner or contractor)

- political risks (e.g., risks arising from an uncertain political environment, the controversial nature of the proposed policy initiative, or the political costs associated with the previously mentioned possibilities actually occurring)

Having identified the nature of the risks at stake, a proper analysis needs to be undertaken of how they might be reduced or even eliminated. Obviously, certain kinds of alternative service delivery (e.g., partnerships with private companies for the provision of expensive or complex services) are likely to entail greater risks than others. Where two or more entities are involved in the provision of a service, the sharing of any financial risks needs to be clearly identified and properly addressed in the relevant contractual and/or accountability documents.

THE WAY FORWARD

Despite a degree of marketization and privatization since the 1980s, governments in OECD countries continue to fund, purchase, and deliver a vast array of services. There is every reason to believe that this state of affairs will continue. Consequently, it will be important for governments – not merely for fiscal or efficiency reasons, but also in the interests of maintaining public confidence and democratic legitimacy – to continue to explore the most appropriate ways of providing and improving those services for which they are responsible. This poses many serious and continuing challenges for both politicians and their senior civil service advisers. One such challenge is to ensure that there are adequate opportunities for policy learning from the numerous reforms which have been instituted over recent years. This, in turn, requires an appropriate investment in policy-oriented research and evaluation (both comparative and country-specific). As it stands, there is a dearth of hard data and reliable analyses of many of the recent endeavours to improve organizational performance. This lack of in-depth research needs to be rectified.

Aside from more and better evaluation, the preceding discussion has highlighted a range of other matters which need to be underscored when considering how to revitalize the public service and enhance the delivery of publicly funded services. First, choosing between institutional forms is typically a complex matter. It requires that attention be given not merely to the specific attributes of the service in question, but also to the broader constitutional, political, economic, and administrative context in which the service is provided. Furthermore, it is imperative to be clear about the values which are at stake and the respective effects of different institutional arrangements on the realization of these values. This is only possible by means of detailed, systematic, case-by-case analyses.

Second, many policy makers, especially in the Anglo-American world, appear to place great faith in "structural solutions" to policy problems. Thus, if a particular department or agency appears to be delivering substandard services, the preferred political response is to "restructure." Correspondingly, there is a bias against undertaking reforms of a primarily non-structural variety within existing organizational boundaries. Now, there is undoubtedly a time and place for "restructuring," even "radical restructuring." But it is also evident from the experience of the past few decades that significant improvements in performance can be achieved without major changes in the formal structure, governance, or legal status of organizations. For instance, it is possible to enhance the efficiency and quality of services produced by government departments by easing input controls, enhancing performance-management systems, and giving managers greater autonomy with respect to staffing, remuneration, administrative procedures, contracting options, and budgetary arrangements. Accordingly, hiving-off particular delivery functions into wholly new agencies is not the only, or necessarily the most desirable, way of enhancing organizational performance. Indeed, although classic ministerial departments have had a relatively "bad press" during recent decades, they remain a remarkably flexible, politically responsive, and administratively robust vehicle for achieving a multiplicity of public purposes.

Third, and related to this, there is a large menu of options – as outlined in Table 2 – for improving the delivery of public services. The appropriate option, or combination of options, needs to be determined on a pragmatic basis and in reference to a range of competing administrative doctrines. Accordingly, any assumption that "one-size fits all" must be rejected. Irrespective of the particular service in question, it is imperative that public service managers be given the incentive and opportunity to experiment with new forms of service delivery, initiate pilot schemes, pursue interorganizational partnerships and exploit the benefits of new technologies. Creativity and innovation, however, carry various risks, not least political. While proper risk-management strategies should always be adopted, these will never be foolproof. It is important for this to be understood by policy makers and citizens alike.

Finally, delivering high-quality public services requires high-quality, well-trained staff – at all levels. This applies irrespective of whether services are produced by public bodies or contracted out to private providers. Protracted fiscal restraint in many jurisdictions during the 1980s and 1990s has tended to reduce the level of expenditure by government agencies on staff training, as well as making it difficult for the public sector to maintain competitive salaries and employment conditions. If these issues are not addressed, then there is every likelihood that either the quality or quantity of public services (or both) will fall. This in turn points to one of the fundamental dilemmas facing attempts to revitalize the public service: will citizens be prepared to pay the price of having quality public services or will the quest for smaller government and lower taxes prove dominant? Upon such questions hangs a good deal.

BIBLIOGRAPHY

Alford, J. 1998. A public management road less travelled: clients as co-producers of public services. *Australian Journal of Public Administration* 57, 4:128-37.
Alford, J., and D. O'Neill, eds. 1994. *The Contract State: Public Management and the Kennett Government.* Geelong: Deakin University Press.

Aucoin, P. 1995. *The New Public Management: Canada in Comparative Perspective*. Montreal: Institute for Research on Public Policy.

_____ 1998. Restructuring government for the management and delivery of public services. In *Taking Stock: Assessing Public Sector Reforms*, eds. B. G. Peters and D. Savoie. Montreal & Kingston: McGill-Queen's University Press.

Audit Office. 1994. Employment of consultants by government departments. In *Report of the Controller and Auditor General: Third Report for 1994*. Wellington.

Barber, B. 1984. *Strong Democracy: Participatory Politics for a New Age*. Berkeley: University of California Press.

Borins, S. 1995. Public sector innovation: the implications of new forms of organization and work. In *Governance in a Changing Environment*, eds. B. G. Peters and D. Savoie. Montreal & Kingston: McGill-Queen's University Press.

Boston, J. 1994. Purchasing policy advice: the limits to contracting out. *Governance* 7, 1:1-30.

_____ ed. 1995. *The State Under Contract*. Wellington: Bridget Williams Books.

Boston, J., J. Martin, J. Pallot, and P. Walsh. 1996. *Public Management: The New Zealand Model*. Auckland: Oxford University Press.

Bourgon, J. 1997. *Fourth Annual Report to the Prime Minister on the Public Service of Canada*. Ottawa: Privy Council Office.

Bryson, J., and P. Smith-Ring. 1990. A transaction-based approach to policy intervention. *Policy Studies* 23:205-29.

Cameron, D. 1992. Institutional management: how should the governance and management of universities in Canada accommodate changing circumstances? In *Public Purse, Public Purpose: Autonomy and Accountability in the Groves of Academe*, eds. J. Cutt and R. Dobell. Halifax: Institute for Research on Public Policy.

Chapman, R. 1997. *The Treasury in Public Policy-Making*. London: Routledge.

Considine, M., and M. Painter, eds. 1997. *Managerialism: The Great Debate*. Melbourne: Melbourne University Press.

Doering, R. 1996. Alternative service delivery: the case of the Canadian food inspection agency. Paper prepared for a presentation to the Department of Justice, "Alternative Service Delivery Workshop," November 25.

Ewart, B., and J. Boston. 1993. The separation of policy advice from operations: the case of defence restructuring in New Zealand. *Australian Journal of Public Administration* 52:223-240.

Ford, R., and D. Zussman. 1997a. Alternative service delivery: transcending boundaries. In *Alternative Service Delivery: Sharing Governance in Canada*, KPMG/IPAC. Toronto: KPMG/IPAC.

_____ 1997b. Conclusion. In *Alternative Service Delivery: Sharing Governance in Canada*, KPMG/IPAC. Toronto: KPMG/IPAC.

Fordin, Y. 1996. Autonomy, responsibility and control: the case of central government agencies in Sweden. In *Performance Management in Government*. PUMA. Occasional Papers No. 9, Paris: OECD.

General Accounting Office. 1991. *Government Contractors: Are Service Contractors Performing Inherently Governmental Functions?* GGD-92-11, Washington.

Gorringe, P. 1996. Government and institutions. Unpublished paper. Wellington: State Services Commission.

Greer, P. 1994. *Transforming Central Government: The Next Steps Initiative*. Buckingham: Open University Press.

Gregory, R. 1997. The peculiar tasks of public management. In *Managerialism: The Great Debate*, eds. M. Considine and M. Painter. Melbourne: Melbourne University Press.

Halligan, J. 1997. New public sector models: reform in New Zealand and Australia. In *Public Sector Reform: Rationale, Trends and Problems*, ed. Jan Erik Lane. London: Sage.

Hardin, I. 1992. *The Contracting State*. Open University Press: Buckingham.

Henry, D. 1995. Reform of a major service delivery agency – not platitudes but action. *Administration* 43, 1:16-35.

Hikel, R. 1997. Alternative service delivery and the prospects for success: political leadership and erformance measurement. In *Alternative Service Delivery: Sharing Governance in Canada*, KPMG/IPAC. Toronto: KPMG/IPAC.

Hodge, G. 1998. Contracting public sector services: a meta-analytical perspective of the international evidence. Paper prepared for a conference on "Public Policy and Private Management," the Centre for Public Policy, Melbourne University, February 19-20.

Hood, C., and M. Jackson. 1991. *Administrative Argument*. Aldershot: Dartmouth Publishing.

Horn, M. 1995. *The Political Economy of Public Administration.* Cambridge: Cambridge University Press.

Howden-Chapman, P., and T. Ashton. 1994. Shopping for health: purchasing health services through contracts. *Health Policy* 29:61-83.

Industry Commission. 1996. *Competitive Tendering and Contracting by Public Sector Agencies Report No. 48.* Melbourne: Australian Government Publishing Service.

Ingraham, P. 1997. The policy/operations dichotomy in the u.s. federal government. In *Policy and Operations.* Ottawa: Canadian Centre for Management Development.

Kettl, D. 1988. *Government by Proxy: (Mis?) Managing Federal Programs.* Washington, DC: Congressional Quarterly Press.

_____ 1993. *Sharing Power: Public Governance and Private Markets.* Washington, DC: The Brookings Institution.

KPMG/IPAC. 1997. *Alternative Service Delivery: Sharing Governance in Canada.* Toronto: KPMG/IPAC.

Lane, Jan-Erik. 1993. *The Public Sector: Concepts, Models and Approaches.* London: Sage.

_____ ed. 1997. *Public Sector Reform: Rationale, Trends and Problems.* London: Sage.

Langford, J. 1997. Power sharing in the alternative service delivery world. In *Alternative Service Delivery: Sharing Governance in Canada,* KPMG/IPAC. Toronto: KPMG/IPAC.

Larsson, T. 1995. *Governing Sweden.* Stockholm: The Swedish Agency for Administrative Development.

Martin, J. 1995. Contracting and accountability. In *The State Under Contract,* ed. J. Boston. Wellington: Bridget Williams Books.

Mintzberg, H. 1996. Managing government, governing management. *Harvard Business Review* May-June:75-83.

Moore, E., and G. Skogstad. 1998. Food for thought: food inspection and renewed federalism. In *How Ottawa Spends, 1998-99,* ed. L. Pal. Toronto: Oxford University Press.

Mulgan, R. 1997. Contracting out and accountability. *Australian Journal of Public Administration* 56, 4:106-116.

OECD. 1993. *Public Management: OECD Country Profiles.* Paris: OECD.

_____ 1994. New ways of managing infrastructure provision. Occasional Papers, No. 6, Paris: OECD.

_____ 1997. *Issues and Developments in Public Management.* Paris: OECD.

Office of Public Service. 1997. *Next Steps Briefing Note.* London: Cabinet Office.

O'Toole, B., and R. Chapman. 1995. Parliamentary accountability. In *Next Steps: Improving Management in Government?*, eds. B. O'Toole and G. Jordan. Aldershot: Dartmouth.

O'Toole, B., and G. Jordan, eds. 1995. *Next Steps: Improving Management in Government?* Aldershot: Dartmouth.

Peters, B. Guy. 1997. Separating policy and operations: a summary of national responses. In *Policy and Operations.* Ottawa: Canadian Centre for Management Development.

Peters, B. Guy, and D. Savoie, eds. 1995. *Governance in a Changing Environment.* Montreal & Kingston: McGill-Queen's University Press.

Petersson, O. 1994. *Swedish Government and Politics.* Stockholm: Fritzes.

Petrie, M. 1998. *Organization Transformation: The Income Support Experience.* Wellington: Department of Social Welfare.

Pierre, J. 1995. Marketization of the state: citizens, consumers, and the emergence of the public Market. In *Governance in a Changing Environment,* eds. B. G. Peters and D. Savoie. Montreal & Kingston: McGill-Queen's University Press.

_____ 1997. The policy-operation divide in Sweden: a report from Utopia. In *Policy and Operations.* Ottawa: Canadian Centre for Management Development.

Pollitt, C. 1997. The separation of policy and operations in government: the U.K. experience. In *Policy and Operations.* Ottawa: Canadian Centre for Management Development.

Pollitt, C., J. Birchall, and K. Putman. 1998. Letting managers manage: decentralisation and opting out. In *The New Management of British Local Government,* ed. G. Stoker. Basingstoke: Macmillan.

Privy Council Office. 1996. Report of the deputy ministers' task force on service delivery models. In *Deputy Ministers' Task Forces: Final Reports.* Ottawa.

Schick, A. 1996. The Spirit of Reform: Managing the New Zealand State Sector in a Time of Change. Wellington: State Services Commission.

Seidle, F. Leslie. 1995. *Rethinking the Delivery of Public Services to Citizens.* Montreal: Institute for Research on Public Policy.

_____ 1997. Responsiveness and accountability: the drivers of alternative service delivery. In *Alternative Service Delivery: Sharing Governance in Canada*, ed. KPMG/IPAC. Toronto: KPMG/IPAC.

Skelcher, C. 1998. Reforming the Quangos. *The Political Quarterly* 69,
1:41-47.

Stewart, J. 1993. The limitations of government by contract. *Public
Money and Management* 13:7-12.

Thomas, P. 1998. The changing nature of accountability. In *Taking Stock:
Assessing Public Sector Reforms*, eds. B. G. Peters and D. Savoie. Montreal & Kingston: McGill-Queen's University Press.

Thomas, P., and J. Wilkins. 1997. Special operating agencies: a culture
change in the Manitoba government. In *Alternative Service Delivery:
Sharing Governance in Canada*, ed. KPMG/IPAC. Toronto: KPMG/IPAC.

Treasury. 1987. *Government Management*. Wellington: Government
Printer.

Treasury Board Secretariat. 1995. Framework for alternative service
delivery. Ottawa.

Trosa, S. 1994. *Next Steps: Moving On*. London: Office of Public Service
and Science.

Vining, A., and D. Weimer. 1990. Government supply and government
production failure: a framework based on contestability. *Journal of
Public Policy* 10:1-22.

Weller, P., and G. Davis, eds. 1996. *New Ideas, Better Government*. St
Leonards: Allen and Unwin.

Williamson, O. 1985. *The Economic Institutions of Capitalism: Firms, Markets, Relational Contracting*. New York: Free Press.

Wilson, J. Q. 1989. *Bureaucracy: What Government Agencies Do and Why
They Do It*. New York: Basic Books.

Wright, J., and G. Waymark. 1995. *Special Operating Agencies: Overview
of the Special Operating Agency Initiative, Management Practices*.
Ottawa: Canadian Centre for Management Development.

Externalities and Relationships: Rethinking the Boundaries of the Public Service

JON PIERRE

The pendulum movement between state and market domination which has characterized much of the twentieth century has had a distinct and direct impact on the public service.[1] Much of the state's exchange with civil society is conducted through the public service; it is the public bureaucracy which has seen its domain expanding in times of growing state encroachment of the surrounding society and, by the same token, it is the bureaucracy which tends to become the prime target for aggressive cut-back political campaigns, as the Australian, British, Canadian, and New Zealand experiences show (Hood, 1995; Savoie, 1994). The rhetoric of offering "pink slips and running shoes" to civil servants, or "put another civil servant on the barbie, mate" – a phrase used to describe the current Howard government's fervent reform efforts vis-à-vis the Australian public service – testifies to the ways in which the civil service comes to be seen as "the evil of all evils" by neo-liberal regimes and their followers.[2]

The focus in this chapter is on how recent cutbacks and reconfigurations of the public service in the Western democracies have reshaped the boundaries of the public service. The analysis progresses through an examination of different developments both within the public service and in society which challenge our traditional notions of those boundaries. The overall pattern suggests that in several important respects the public service has lost much of its previous organizational and normative specificity by which should be meant norms, rules, patterns of behaviour, structures, and role expectations that are distinctly different from those of other sectors in society; political institutions are developing new points of contact with the surrounding society, encouraging new channels for citizen input on political and administrative matters. But rather than bemoaning these trends and developments they should probably be seen as a restructuring of the public service in order to respond to citizens' changing image of public services and their right to be involved in political and administrative deliberation and decision making.

These issues would probably have been less complicated to address a couple of decades ago. Interestingly, a substantive portion of administrative reform during the 1990s has either explicitly been aimed at blurring or downplaying the public–private distinction or has had that consequence, although that was not the stated purpose of the reform. We are currently witnessing two parallel developments which both, albeit in different ways, prompt us to rethink the significance of the historical boundaries of the public service. One development is manifested in the search for new governance structures which are gradually complementing or replacing previously used policy instruments. These new governance structures represent alternative instruments and channels for the state to articulate and pursue the collective interest. What sets them apart from more traditional structures and instruments is not so much their targets as their lesser reliance on compliance but stronger emphasis on cooperation, shared resources, and societal inclusion (Peters, 1996; Peters and Pierre, 1998; Pierre and Peters, 2000; Rhodes, 1997). By creating public–private partnerships and other forms of joint projects, the public service taps into resources to which they previously had no access. In many countries – particularly those with a strong corporatist tradition – so-called "third sector" initiatives aiming at giving voluntary associations a clearer role in public service delivery have been a common feature. Thus, this strategy rests on the notion that much is to be gained by fusing public and private resources, broadly defined, instead of keeping them apart.

The other trend also relates directly to exchanges between the public and private but runs counter to the emergence of new forms of governance, i.e., it sees new forms of societal encroachment of the state. These new or emerging forms of societal input on public policy and public administration include new models of citizen engagement and political articulation in policy making. An important objective characterizing these new channels is not just to offer citizens a new avenue to political influence but also to increase the legitimacy of the public service.

The main argument coming out of the analysis is that both of these developments – again, in different ways – should be seen as an organizational adaptation to the society it is serving in the late 1990s and, more importantly, as what Maier (1987a, 17) refers to as "a rediscovery of the political." The new models of governance we see emerging are the result of a gradual transformation of institutional roles and policy instruments which, in turn, reflect a transformation of the state to meet the challenge of governance in the political and economic milieu of the late twentieth century. Similarly, new, emerging forms of citizen engagement and other societal encroachments of the public service could well be seen as proof of a genuine civic interest in matters of the state although, as will be discussed in greater detail below, this is a type of involvement which normally is characterized by non-partisanship, disaggregation, and localism.

DEFINING THE BOUNDARIES OF THE PUBLIC SERVICE

A first cut at defining the boundaries of the public service can be to look at two idealized models of public service political and administrative specificity. It should be noted that the debate on these boundaries in and of itself suggests that a significant change has taken place in our perceptions of the public service and its role in society; the current emphasis on the accessibility and transparency of the public service should be seen as a manifestation of changing values and perspectives with regard to the role of the state and the public service. Table 1 compares the institutional system of a public service with sustained

TABLE 1
Institutional Models of Public Service With Different Degrees of Public Service
Specificity

Policy Functions	Sustained	Blurred
Policy formulation	Political parties Departments	Citizen engagement Think tanks
Policy implementation	Departments Subnational governments	"Third sector" arrangements Public-private partnerships Quangos Agencies

boundaries with that of a public service characterized by blurred boundaries.

The public service model with "blurred" boundaries which is our main interest here is characterized by selective, ad hoc channels of policy input such as citizen engagement and think tanks. Similarly, policies are implemented through a wide variety of organizations, many of which are designed in order to facilitate joint, public–private coordination of resources and leverage. The emergence of selective policy and blended structures of implementation could in part be thought of as a deinstitutionalization of representative structures and *Rechtstaat* value systems. However, the advocates of these developments tend to describe them more as complementary structures than as a rejection of traditional systems of policy input and implementation. This has been the case not least in the Canadian debate on citizen engagement.

Certainly, one could argue that blurring the public sector specificity is a "good thing" from a democratic point of view since it allows more broadly for new and more spontaneous forms of citizen involvement in the public service and the political sphere. Architects of administrative reform in much of the Western world have seen greater public sector transparency and openness towards its external environment as a key recipe for reinvigorating the public service and also to strengthening the legitimacy of the public service (see Peters and Savoie, 1998). In the u.k., "Citizens' Charters" and "Citizens' Panels" seek to encourage more direct communication between citizens and the public service. In the Scandinavian countries where public sector transparency is part of the political culture (Peters, 1984) there has been a search for alternative models of exchange between the public service and the citizenry. As will be discussed below, similar strategies of administrative reform can be seen in France and Germany.

In order to understand the changing boundaries of the public service we will depart from three different approaches to defining the public service. The first and perhaps most natural approach is to apply a legalistic perspective on these issues; the public service can be defined in legal or constitutional terms. Legal frameworks pertaining to the public service define much of the structure as well as the internal procedures and decision-making processes of the public service, according public sector institutions norms and values which set them apart from other organizations in society. The public service in this perspective comprises those organizations which operate under the Public Administration Act or any functional equivalent thereof. These institutions constitute the core of state authority and are subject to the same (or similar) rules and legal frameworks and they derive their resources largely from the same sources. The legal framework defines institutionalized procedures of administrative and/or political accountability for decisions and actions taken inside the public service. This approach views the boundaries of the public service as the limits of the jurisdiction of public office and constitutional law.

This perspective on defining the boundaries of the public service made more sense in an era when the issues under investigation here were not very salient. Two decades or so ago, a legalistic definition provided a definition of the public service with great accuracy. With the emergence, and increasing popularity, of quangos, agencies, publicly owned corporations, and public–private partnerships, it makes less sense to think of the boundaries of the public services in this rather static perspective. This, however, is an observation of considerable significance in and of itself; it makes less and less sense to think of the

boundaries in terms of which legal framework defines and regulates any given organization.

If the legalistic approach defines steering systems and processes in the public sector as well as an enumerated definition of
public organizations, an alternative approach to uncover the
boundaries of the public service is to treat these borders as primarily institutional, i.e., to look at the structural arrangements of
the state (cf. Olsen, 1991). This perspective yields an image of the
public service as a set of institutions which can be altered at any
given time. The public service is defined as the sum of public
organizations which, in turn, are defined by enumeration. While
there is a recognition that public organizations differ from private ones with regard to management, accountability, resource
bases, tasks, relationships to clients/customers, different
economies of scale, etc., the institutional approach attaches no
normative or political sentiments to this observation. Again, this
way of delineating the public service was much less complicated
some time ago before the wide array of borderline institutions
and organizations emerged. While this approach may help give
reasonably valid accounts of the public service at any particular
time, it is of little help in generating an understanding of the
changes of the boundaries themselves. Also, this approach says
nothing about the normative or organizational specificity of the
public service; it merely provides a list of organizations and institutions which, at any given point in time, could be seen as elements of the public service.

A third and final way to think about the boundaries of the public service is to define functions that in different respects could
be described as critical to society – law enforcement, basic services, some degree of coordination and governance, and so on
– and then investigate to what extent public or private organizations carry out the tasks associated with each particular function. The functional approach to defining the boundaries of the
public service may also serve as an economic model for assessing to what extent services should be public or private, i.e.,
market failures which cause collective action problems in the
economy that market actors themselves have no incentive to

resolve on an individual basis. Such problems include the development of infrastructure, education and training, and selected welfare programs like health care. A functional approach based in economic theory defines these functions as critical to society, yet no individual corporate actor has an incentive to fulfill them. It is in that economic, functional perspective that services are defined as collective.

This approach does not make any prejudgments about the status of different service-producing organizations; it merely defines what roles the state and the public service actually play and the functional domain of the public service in society. This strategy has the advantage of bringing out two things. First, it helps us show the range of what states actually do, or at least the range of the state's responsibilities. Also, the functional approach accommodates the wide variety of roles which the public service can play in service delivery, i.e., regulating, financing, monitoring, and evaluating the process of public service delivery.

While these different aspects of the public sector boundaries sound fairly straight forward in theory they offer tremendous problems when applied to real-world public services. Defining public and private organizations, for example, is difficult not least since many organizations can be characterized as a mix of public and private (Peters, 1988). Indeed, much of the institutional reform in the public service during the past couple of decades has deliberately sought to create organizations which in different ways bridge or transgress the public–private boundary, partly in order to allow political institutions to tap into resources controlled by private or corporate actors (Peters, 1998), partly – as mentioned earlier – in order to develop new governance channels and instruments (Pierre and Peters, 2000; Rhodes, 1997).

We can now assess the three ways to think about the boundaries of the public service according to three clusters of "variables"; accountability, forms of policy input and participation, and finally, the degree of specificity vs. integration of the public service which the three models suggest. Table 2 summarizes this analysis.

The legalistic approach to defining the boundaries of the public service – which in these respects can serve as an idealized model of the role of the public service in a democratic system of

TABLE 2
Approaches to Understanding the Changing Boundaries of the Public Service

| | Analytical Themes | | |
Approaches	Specificity vs. Integration	Source of Accountability	Policy Input and Participation
Legalistic	Specificity	Public office	Citizenship
Institutional	Some integration	Political, democratic	Political parties
Functional	Generic view on sectors	Service providers, "stake-holderism"	Consumers, users, clients

government – rests on systems of accountability, policy input, and institutional specificity which are explicated in constitutional and other legal frameworks. Thus, accountability is directly associated with public office (elected or administrative), not with individual persons. Policy input is open to all citizens, and the high degree of public service specificity is deliberately sustained in order to ensure that collective decisions and actions can be subject to a specific type of scrutiny and assessment.

In the institutional model, public service organizations and organizational change are directly controlled by elected officials. Given this strong political presence in the management of the public service, accountability for public services is perceived more as a political than a bureaucratic issue. The specificity of the public service is less marked in this approach, compared to the legalistic model, for two reasons. First, the desire to keep public services "public" is in part political, but this does not mean that public service managers see much in the private sector which deserves to be incorporated into public service delivery. Secondly, this type of politically controlled public service often (but not always) tends to see ever-expanding service commitments for the public sector, something which over time generates problems with both public sector expenditures and revenues. This, in turn, sets the public–private pendulum discussed earlier in motion towards the "market" end of the pendulum swing.

In the functional approach, finally, the issue of whether public services are produced and delivered by public or private, for-profit organizations is a managerial much more than a political matter. Accountability is a complex issue in this model but tends to be defined primarily in terms of customer satisfaction and is thus ultimately associated with those who deliver the services. Policy input in this model is selective; public service decisions are either guided by consumer behaviour in the market, or by direct, individual or group input on an ad hoc basis.

Together, the three different ways of thinking about the boundaries of the public services describe a development of values and norms driving administrative reform, from the legalistic approach over the institutional approach towards the functional model. However, a quick comparative assessment of administrative reform suggests that most of what has happened has not been a series of clear and conscious choices between different philosophies about how the public service should relate to its external environment but rather a number of incremental decisions about how best to blend the three models of the public service (Aucoin, 1990; Peters and Savoie, 1998). Thus, public service providers in most Western democracies have not had to face a distinct choice between either downplaying or sustaining the public–private distinction. Administrative reform throughout the Western world suggests that administrative reform has followed a fairly pragmatic "both/and" type of strategy. Core values of the public sector such as legality, impartiality, etc. have not been explicitly called into question or compromised. However, the increasing emphasis on efficiency has placed the public service in a position where it must make a de facto choice between which goals and values to compromise.

THE POLITICS OF CHANGING THE BOUNDARIES OF THE PUBLIC SERVICE

The process of changing – or blurring – the boundaries of the public service is not just an organizational or managerial process; it is primarily a political process. Much of the current debate on these issues, not least the New Public Management literature (Osborne and Gaebler, 1992) focuses almost exclusively on the managerial aspects of public service production. To the extent that the analysis goes beyond those aspects of the public service, the perspective is primarily functional (see below); there is a rejection of a public sector specificity and what is at stake is the production of services in a generic perspective (Self, 1993). However, political institutions exercise political power and their programs are collectively financed, hence we need to be aware of how the changing boundaries of the public service impacts on political control and accountability. This is not to suggest that reforms aiming at blurring the public–private distinction in and of themselves are necessarily suspect, undemocratic projects, but recognizing such changes as political projects means that we must assess them in terms of what alternative channels for collective control and democratic accountability they offer.

An important aspect of the decreasing significance of the public–private distinction relates to new or emerging channels of communicating policy ideas and input into the political process. While this input nearly always draws on demands and expectations from civil society and pressure groups, a number of countries are currently experimenting with designing channels for citizens to play a more active role in the policy process. The drivers of these developments are in many jurisdictions found both inside and outside the public sector with different motives for devising these new channels of participation on different sides of the border. For the state, encouraging citizen engagement is often seen as a way to strengthen the legitimacy of the political process; for the groups of citizens pursuing this new form of participation an important objective is to bring in actors to monitor the process critically in order to prevent abuse of political power or public financial resources and to safeguard a truly democratic process.

From Consultation to Participation   Over the past several years, and with substantive cross-national variation, there has been a growing emphasis in administrative reform on developing new forms of participation. A wide variety of institutional means have been employed in these efforts but the common denominator is to provide means for citizens to play a more active role inside the public service than hitherto. In New Zealand and the Scandinavian countries, for instance, there have been extensive reforms in the public education sector aiming at increasing citizen participation in the management of schools and in the development of curricula. Similar reforms have been implemented in several other public service sectors such as daycare centres for small children and in the physical planning process in Germany and Sweden. Furthermore, a large number of countries have restructured their public service in order to grant citizens easy access to the public service. Thus, in France a reform in the early 1990s introduced a new form of partnerships between the central state administration and local authorities in order to create new structures for citizens' contact with the public service, particularly in socially turbulent urban districts (Meininger, 1998). These *maisons des services publics* provide public services based on a one-stop office model.

There is an interesting element of path-dependency in how the public service – and the surrounding society – seem to think about how best to organize the exchange across the public–private border. In the Anglo-American democracies, with their emphasis on individualist values in political life, new modes of such exchange are typically devised in the shape of communication between individuals and the public service. In more collectivistic or corporatist political cultures such as Austria, Germany, and the Scandinavian countries, there is a much stronger emphasis on developing new forms for organizations to be players in the policy process. Historically speaking, citizen engagement was conducted through political parties and interest organizations. The "remiss" procedure in Sweden is a system in which almost all reports from Royal Commissions are circulated to public service authorities but also to interest organizations and voluntary associations which might be affected by a Commission's proposal. These organizations are invited to submit comments on the Commission Reports, which are summarized and, presumably, incorporated in the Government Bill. While we see some signs of a growing interest in opening up new channels for individual citizens to approach the public service, for instance as a result of the new information technology, the collectivist legacy remains strong in these cultures.

These new forms of participation and deliberative democracy play many different roles such as bridging the public–private border, facilitating input from those who use different public services and engaging customers in the delivery of the public service. We have little knowledge about exactly how much difference these new models of participation in the public service make in terms of the services delivered. While the new forms of citizen involvement are likely to enhance the support and legitimacy for the public service we need yet to see the evidence that services delivered under this new model of management are more positively received compared to previous service delivery models.

As the public service becomes functionally delineated in this way, another problem appears in the management of the tensions between professional groups and citizens' expectations on substantive input to the public service. Professionals must be prepared to allow citizens/customers to have a real say on the matters which are being deliberated, otherwise these new models of participation will breed frustration and critique. "Citizens" in these models of participation are for the most part individuals with great expertise in decision making (see below) and are not likely to be content with an involvement in the public service which appears to serve primarily as a hostage for cut-backs in public expenditures.

We must also assess the degree of compatibility between the new models of participation and traditional models of public service decision making with regard to how they safeguard political equality. There is much to suggest that participation in the public service will display a similar selection bias as traditional modes of political participation, i.e., this is an activity which seems to come more naturally to middle-class professionals than to other social groups.

A third general problem associated with the new modes of participation is that while all customers are citizens, not all citizens are customers. As long as public services are overwhelmingly financed on a collective basis there is a need to ensure that all citizens have some institutionalized means of influencing public service production (Peters and Pierre, 1998; Pierre, 1995).

New Forms of Citizen Engagement If citizen participation in the public service marks a new way of thinking about the boundaries of the public service, citizen engagement represents one step further in the efforts of "bringing the citizens in." Citizen engagement, however, takes a broader, more critical view on representative government and political parties and takes its point of departure in the political significance of citizenship and derives to a large extent (but not entirely) from a distrust of government. The overarching objective is to allow citizens to review public policy at a close viewpoint, to provide genuine input on policy proposals, and to bring perspectives and values which representative structures do not seem to bring to the discussion. Thus, advocates of increased citizen engagement do not see this form of involvement as merely another channel for promoting narrowly defined policy demands but rather as a new means of promoting the public interest. Thus, citizen engagement is predicated on an activist notion of citizenship (Sears and Schulman, 1998). Citizen engagement is perceived as a safeguard against abuse of political power and inadequate measures to resolve societal problems. It is also believed to be a viable alternative or complement to the type of political representation which is provided by the political parties.

These new forms of citizen engagement have gained attention in several Western democracies but primarily so in Canada. They represent an implicit rejection of political parties as representative structures; party membership and activism has decreased dramatically in most west European countries where mass membership in political parties has a long history. Thus, only 5 per cent of the German population are today members of a political party, to be compared with the 25 per cent of the Germans who are members of a sports club (Klein and Schmalz-Bruns, 1997). Similarly, in Sweden only 8 percent of the population are currently members of a political party (Petersson et al., 1998). Despite this crisis in the representative channels, however, citizen engagement has not received much attention either in Germany or in Sweden.

If we broaden the definition of citizen engagement slightly we can see that reforms with a similar overall objective have recently been implemented in several jurisdictions. In Austria, the Parliament passed legislation in September 1998 which put an end to the privileged position of MPs in promoting petitions for referenda and in nominating presidential candidates. Previously, referenda were initiated if eight MPs or 10,000 ordinary citizens signed the petition. Under the slogan "one man, one vote," the Parliament has now declared that all signatures should be given an equal weight. Indeed, MPs alone can no longer initiate a referendum. Instead what is now required are signatures by one per mill of the Austrian population or about 8,100 signatures. Similarly, nominating presidential candidates previously required 6,000 signatures or support from five MPs; in the new system, 6,000 signatures are required and the privileged position of MPs has been abolished.

A slightly different aspect of citizen engagement is found in reforms aimed at increasing the number of elected offices at different levels of government. In Germany, a system with elected mayors has recently been introduced. A similar system has also been created to elect a mayor for the Greater London area with plans to apply the same system in all cities in the U.K. In a similar vein, several large cities in Scandinavia have introduced (or are planning to introduce) systems with elected neighbourhood councils with extensive authorities within their area.

It is interesting to note that jurisdictions that have gone far down the NPM road, such as Australia, Britain, and New Zealand, have implemented only minor reforms to establish new points of citizen input in the policy process.[3] The functional perspective on the public service – which is the essence of the NPM philosophy in these respects – produces an ambiguous view on citizen engagement. As Boston and his colleagues (Boston et al., 1996) argue, reforms like privatization and corporatization tend to deprive citizens of some of their traditional, representative channels of policy input since these reforms ultimately aim at reducing political control over the public service and "letting the managers manage" (Osborne and Gaebler, 1992). At the same time, however, NPM aims at providing customers with market-style choice, something which gives at least those who use a certain public service some compensation for the loss in political control.

These new channels of policy input are good examples of the blurring of the boundaries of the public service. However, as a policy instrument they probably fit better in some political cultures than in others. In most west European countries different forms of citizen engagement are part of the political culture and tradition; we need only think of the Swedish "remiss" procedure which is a broad consultation process of most Royal Commission reports, the ombudsman institution (incidentally another Swedish invention), or the system of mass membership parties characterized by a (nominally speaking, at least) high degree of internal democracy and a deliberation process which accords individual members the right to put forward motions on almost all political issues. That having been said, the decline in some of these representative channels could well prompt reform similar to what has happened recently in Canada.

Public–Private Partnerships Partnerships between public and private actors are perhaps the most apparent manifestation of the blurring of the boundaries of the public service and a functional approach to public service organization (Pierre, 1998a; Walzer and Jacobs, 1998). In Europe as well as in North America, public–private partnerships at different institutional levels have a long history, but they seem to have become increasingly popular as the public service explores new governance instruments. This type of partnership enhances the capability of political institutions by allowing for a fusion of public and private resources. At the same time, partnerships are said to obstruct democratic control and accountability and obscure the collective interest. The democratic dilemma of public–private partnerships is that while they are often deemed necessary to enhance the leverage of local authorities these types of coalitions are less susceptible to democratic, political control than organizations that are strictly public. Partnerships can do things which political authorities are prevented from doing by themselves, but, as Peters (1998) points out, that is precisely why they were created in the first place. Thus, assessing the values of partnerships in a democratic perspective is a complex task; the reduction in political and democratic control has to be weighed against increased leverage.

Public–private partnerships are most common in areas where there is a mutual interest in cooperation across the public–private distinction, for example in local economic development. From the point of view of private business, forging a partnership with local authorities is a means of securing access to city hall and the political elite; for the city, a partnership allows local officials to enter a dialogue with the corporate sector on mutual development projects, sometimes with businesses as significant sponsors while authorities secure the political and administrative side of the project. These partnerships bring together the political and economic elites of the city behind a narrow, pro-growth agenda, an arrangement which raises questions both about transparency but also about the political influence of the ordinary citizen (Molotch, 1976). Thus, public–private partnerships in some ways run counter to the citizen empowerment which is the purpose of new forms of citizen engagement. Bringing in citizens or interest groups into the policy process will not resolve this problem as partnerships, by design and default, tend to be secluded from traditional models of political steering, control, and transparency.

New, Emerging Models of Accountability   Not very surprisingly, the relaxation of the legal boundaries of the public service have posed tremendous problems and ambiguities with regard to the accountability of public service actions. The main problem here is that a high degree of public sector specificity defined fairly clear channels of accountability; bureaucrats were accountable to elected officials who, in turn, were accountable to the polity in general elections. In the system we now see emerging in many

national contexts, civil servants cannot be held accountable by
elected politicians because the operative institutions are either
agencies enjoying considerable discretion or for-profit organizations operating under contracts. The 1995 Cave Creek disaster in
New Zealand where 14 people died as a scenic viewing platform
constructed by the Department of Conservation collapsed, or the
breakout of three IRA convicts from a high-security facility in the
Isle of Wight in 1995 are two examples of a large number of incidents which caused considerable confusion with regard to who
should be held accountable in the final instance. While recent
reforms have addressed core problems in the public service such
as management, efficiency, and a direct exchange between service providers and customers with some degree of success, much
less has been said on how accountability is to be guaranteed in
these new service systems. What has happened in many cases is
a separation between management and control on the one hand
and responsibility and accountability on the other, something
which is a sure recipe for confusion.

Part of the problem is that in many jurisdictions there is a lin-
gering ministerial accountability although public service agents
are corporatized, converted into agencies or even privatized. In
a public service system reformed according to NPM ideals, traditional models of accountability can only review the appropriateness of the decisions to lift a particular public service out of
the traditional legal framework, e.g., by converting prison management into an agency, or contracting out a sector of medical
care. Since the very essence of market-driven administrative
reform is to detach service production and delivery from tight
political and bureaucratic control, traditional political accountability should not, and cannot, include specific cases of acci-
dents or maltreatment, the possibility of which elected officials
could be assumed to have had some degree of knowledge.
Furthermore, since the managers leading NPM-style service-
delivering organizations are not subject to the legal frameworks
associated with traditional public office, this argument applies
also to many of the traditional models of bureaucratic accountability.

On the more positive side, blurring the boundaries of the public service has in many ways helped increase the transparency of the public sector which is a precondition to accountability (Moncrieffe, 1998). In addition, market-based administrative reform advocates argue that the creation of market competition will not weaken but in fact strengthen citizens' access to accountability through consumer choice. There may be some truth to that but the accountability problems we have seen emerging over the past decade are not so much related to continuous choices between different service providers but have manifested themselves more discretely, as the New Zealand and British experiences mentioned earlier substantiate.

There are probably several different ways in which accountability can be sustained and accommodated in reformed public service systems. One way ahead could be to explore an accountability system operating on and between two levels, the ministerial level and the managerial or the operational level. On the ministerial level, accountability can only be meaningful if elected officials have a fair amount of detailed information about the production of public services. Such information is normally obtained by a monitoring of service performance in relationship to the service level stipulated in contracts. On the managerial and operational levels, accountability for actual performance rests with managers. Thus, this is a simple model of accountability which operates in two steps; one interaction of accountability is between citizens (or, more correctly, the electorate) and elected ministers, and another interaction exists between ministers and service providers. Ministers and service producers in this model should only be held to account for factors over which they have been the decision makers, i.e., ministers are not accountable for specific cases of poor and unsatisfactory public services unless they are legally contained within the service contract. Similarly, service-producing managers are not held responsible for complaints which refer to service regulations not laid down in a contract. Thus, the key difference between managerial and ministerial accountability is that the former is primarily performance-based, the latter is based in a legal definition of jurisdiction.

Obviously, there are many other models which could help resolve the accountability problem in modern public service systems. Most departments who have contracted out services tend to monitor very closely to what extent services delivered are in accordance with the contract. What is needed is a broader framework defining responsibilities at different organizational levels and how these areas of responsibility relate to each other.

Changing Public Sector Values and Ethics Public sector ethics have been a topic of intensive debate over the past five to ten years. The Weberian bureaucracy model prescribed an ethical code which has been challenged by recent administrative reform such as decentralization, "empowerment" of citizens and civil public sector employees at different levels, and increased emphasis on efficiency rather than implementation of decisions made by elected officials. The discussion about a distinct set of values and ethics for the public sector is predicated on relatively robust boundaries of the public service and, as the present analysis argues, there is a growing body of evidence testifying to the decline of the specificity of the public service. What does that mean in terms of redefining the ethics of public employment and the public service? What consequences does the increasing emphasis on efficiency and pay-for-performance have on core public sector ethical values such as fair and equal scrutiny and treatment? To what extent does managerialism introduce a new and potentially conflicting set of values in the public service?

A quick glance at administrative reform in the Western democracies suggests that there is a growing awareness about these issues in many jurisdictions. However, the core values of this ethical code are rarely addressed; instead, the main focus is often on redefining liabilities and accountability. While this certainly is important (see above), the big questions concerning to what extent the traditional code and ethics of public employment can be sustained are rarely addressed. Blurring the boundaries of the public service has created a regulatory "void" in these respects; previous legal and ethical frameworks describing proper bureaucratic behaviour is becoming increasingly irrelevant and outdated, yet no coherent framework has come in its place.

There is also much to suggest that there has been an erosion of the pride and reputation of the public service. Public employment is much less prestigious today than it was a couple of decades ago and citizens' trust in public employees is low. The overall decreasing support for the public sector plays a great role in explaining this development. Furthermore, in some countries public employment no longer enjoys a special legal framework; there has been a fairly widespread tendency to equate public and private employment in terms of labour market legislation.

Changing Relationships With Media   The previously secluded public bureaucracy has opened up to media (or perhaps more correctly, has been opened up by the media) during the past decade or so. An integrated element of administrative reform has been to increase transparency. To this end several countries such as Australia have recently passed new or revised freedom of information acts, offered a stronger protection for whistle-blowers, etc. Much of the changing attitude among the media vis-à-vis public sector experts, however, is explained not so much by the public service but rather by changes in the journalists' profession. Following a period of fairly submissive reporting – subtle editing, allowing experts to elaborate without interruption, presenting "the official story," etc. – there was a clear shift towards more a more assertive coverage in the 1970s and early 1980s (Djerf-Pierre, 1996; 1998). These changes, in turn, reflected changes in how journalists perceived their own role and that of the media in society; emphasis now focused much more on critical scrutiny and revelations of improper behaviour than on providing official reports of current events. More recently, the competition now facing most public service media corporations from commercial networks seems to have played down some of the criticism previously common, at least in the west European milieu. All of this suggests that since much of the media's approach to the public sector is more reflective of indigenous professional and cultural norms and beliefs than of the public service itself there is not very much the public service can do to manage its relationship with the media.

Interestingly, the blurring of the boundaries of the public sector and the subsequent transparency it produces has not weakened the significance of the public–private distinction among the media. If anything there are today higher demands and expectations placed on public service employees than on corporate representatives.

CONCLUSIONS

Some time ago, Charles Maier, in discussing the changing nature of public–private exchange, noted that

> ...the present moment...seems rich in contradictory possibilities. On the one hand, there is a rediscovery of the political, a renewed insistence upon collective will and power. The belief in "decisionism" emerges after the disappointment with welfare state functionalism and disillusion with the belief that bureaucratic settlements or technological fixes can replace politics. But as politics in turn falls short of its promises, what seems to emerge is not a renewed civil service functionalism, but a yearning for intermediate institutions (family and religion), or programmed routines and social science protocols that would make politics unnecessary (1987a, 17).

Bringing Maier's observations up to date, we can say that the "yearning for intermediate institutions" has to some extent been funnelled back into the public sector, only now with a new, emerging mode of involvement. What Maier saw as a tendency to look for other institutional structures which could serve as vehicles for the pursuit of collective interests — there is an implicit communitarian notion in his predictions — was interrupted by a resilient civic view that the state and the public service still matter, but that in order to enjoy enduring political support the public service must adapt to the changing types of demands and expectations placed upon it. Furthermore, as the state has abandoned many of its previous, imposing policy instruments and placed greater reliance on less coercive and more cooperative instruments, the public service must restructure to serve as the administrative vehicle for this new or emerging type of political coordination.

The main arguments explored in this chapter can be summarized in three general points. First, over the past decade or so there has been a downplaying or blurring of the boundaries of the public service in most Western countries. This could be described as a progression from relying primarily on a legalistic definition of the public service over an institutional definition towards a functional delineation of the public service. Today, the legal specificity of the public service is rarely mentioned. Instead, there is a strong emphasis on transparency, efficiency, serving the customer, entrepreneurialism, and collaborative institutional structures such as partnerships.

Secondly, the decreasing specificity of the public service is the outcome of forces within as well as outside the public service. The key indigenous drivers are related to the utilization of new policy instruments which, in turn, sustain emerging forms of governance. Also, the fiscal pressures of the public sector have propelled the search for new ways of producing and delivering public services. Furthermore, many countries have witnessed a search for administrative reform which could help restore societal confidence in the public service. Improving the public service's capacity to respond to citizens' expectations of the public service has been an important element of this strategy. The external pressures towards change stem from citizens' frustrations with bureaucratic inertia. Also, the overall normative shift towards the market has portrayed the public service as a rigid legacy of times past.

Finally, the new or emerging points of contact between the public service and its external environment reflect new modes of involvement and pursuit of interests which are no less political than the traditional models of exchange. There is probably still a notion of the public service as a political entity insofar as it regulates collective matters. But the legitimacy of the state and the public service rests to a considerable extent on civic notions of consent and efficiency (Rose, 1984), hence the public service must respond to external changes in the ways in which policy demands are explicated and in citizens' expectations in terms of administrative expediency and service. That having been said, however, the emerging forms of interest articulation represents a disaggregation of input to which the public service – and the political system at large – yet has to respond. For instance, it is essential that emerging forms of citizen engagement do not exacerbate inequalities among citizens in terms of their efficacy in communicating with public authorities.

The obvious question, as we bring this discussion to a conclusion, is whether the declining specificity of the public service is, normatively speaking, a "good thing" or a problem. Ironically, the blurring of the public–private border in society raises intruguing questions about what that distinction represents. Why, for instance, should privatization be such a salient political objective if no significant differences existed between the public and private spheres of society?[4] As the preceding analysis has shown, most of the changes in these respects seem to be appropriate responses by the public service to changes in its external environment, not least what appears to have been a search for new representative channels and new linkages between the public service and key societal actors in order to create new levers and governance instruments.

But if these are appropriate responses to the external changes, does that mean that the future will see the development of public service becoming less dictated by what policy makers and civil servants believe to be appropriate solutions and more governed by external pressures? Are we, to phrase this differently, likely to see the public service becoming less "public" strictu sensu – which is the essence of sustaining the specificity of the public sector – and instead evolving into a more generic organizational creature, and, if so, what does that mean in terms of the role, the legitimacy, the leverage and the status and prestige of the public service? The bottom line here is that the public service cannot stand as a rigid and fixed structure in a dynamic and transformative society; adapting to what seems to be an ever-increasing pace of change will be one of the biggest challenges for the public service in the future. Building and sustaining a highly adaptive capacity – and not so much a governing capacity – is therefore critical to the public service. Also, we should remind ourselves that much of what we may believe stands above the "winds of change," as The Scorpions sing, and has proven surprisingly vulnerable.[5] This should tell us something about the permanence of many other features of contemporary societies.

NOTES

1 I am most grateful to Barbara Liegl and Luc Rouban for providing updates on administrative reform in Austria and France respectively. Also, this paper has benefitted from comments from the participants in the "Revitalizing the Public Service" seminar and also from an anonymous reviewer.
2 "In Context," March 9, 1998, CCMD.
3 However, in Britain the Citizens' Charter, which was introduced in 1991 could be seen as a way of strengthening the position of the citizens vis-à-vis the public service; see Pierre, 1995 and the literature cited there.
4 I owe this insight to a comment raised by the anonymous reviewer.
5 For an older generation, "winds of change" would allude to Harold Macmillan's speech in 1960 regarding African independence movements.

BIBLIOGRAPHY

Aucoin, P. 1990. Administrative reform in public management: paradigms, principles, paradoxes and pendulums. *Governance* 3:115-37.
Boston, J., J. Martin, J. Pallot, and P. Walsh. 1996. *Public Management: The New Zealand Model.* Auckland: Oxford University Press.
Catt, H. 1996. The other democratic experiment: New Zealand's experience with citizens' initiated referendum. *Political Science* 48:29-47.
Djerf-Pierre, M. 1996. *Gröna Nyheter* [Green News]. Gothenburg: Department of Journalism and Masscommunication.

Djerf-Pierre, M. 1998. Changing regimes: journalist culture and the popularization of TV news in Sweden. Paper presented at a EURICOM conference on media tabloidization, London, September 9-11.

Hood, C. 1995. "Deprivileging" the U.K. civil service in the 1980s: dream or reality. In *Bureaucracy in the Modern State*, ed. J. Pierre. Aldershot: Edward Elgar, 92-117.

Kettl, D. F. 1993. *Sharing Power: Public Governance and Private Markets*. Washington, DC: The Brookings Institution.

Klein. A., and R. Schmalz-Bruns, eds. 1997. *Politische Beteiligung und Buergerengagement in Deutschland*. Bonn: Bundeszentrale fuer politische Bildung.

Maier, C. S. 1987a. Introduction. In *Changing Boundaries of the Political?*, ed. C. S. Maier. Cambridge and New York: Cambridge University Press, 1-26.

_____ ed. 1987b. *Changing Boundaries of the Political?* Cambridge and New York: Cambridge University Press.

Meininger, M-C. 1998. Public service, the public's service. In *About French Administration*, ed. F. Gallouédec-Genuys. Paris: La Docmuentation Française.

Molotch, H. L. 1976. The city as a "growth machine." *American Journal of Sociology* 82:309-30.

Moncrieffe, J. M. 1998. Reconceptualizing political accountability. *International Political Science Review* 19:387-406.

Olsen, J. P. 1991. Modernization programs in perspective: an institutional perspective on organizational change. *Governance* 4:125-49.

Osborne, D., and T. Gaebler 1992. *Reinventing Government*. Reading, MA: Addison-Wesley.

Peters, B. G. 1984. *The Politics of Bureaucracy*. New York: Longman.

_____ 1988. *Comparing Public Bureaucracies*. Tuscaloosa: University of Alabama Press.

_____ 1996. *The Future of Governing: Four Emerging Models*. Lawrence, KS: University of Kansas Press.

_____ 1998. "With a little help from our friends": public-private partnerships as institutions and instruments. In *Partnerships in Urban Governance: European and American Experience*, ed. J. Pierre. London: Macmillan, and New York: St. Martin's Press, 11-33.

Peters, B. G. and J. Pierre. 1998. Governance without government: rethinking public administration. *Journal of Public Administration Research and Theory* 8:223-42.

Peters, B. G., and D. J. Savoie, eds. 1998. *Taking Stock: Assessing Public Sector Reform.* Montreal & Kingston: McGill-Queen's University Press.

Pierre, J. 1995. The marketization of the state: citizens, consumers, and the emergence of the public market. In *Governance in a Changing Environment.* Montreal & Kingston: McGill-Queen's University Press, 55-81.

———. ed. 1998a. *Partnerships in Urban Governance: European and American Experience.* London: Macmillan, and New York: St. Martin's Press.

———. 1998b. Public consultation and citizen participation: dilemmas of policy advice. In *Taking Stock: Assessing Public Sector Reform,* eds. B. G. Peters and D. J. Savoie. Montreal & Kingston: McGill-Queen's University Press, 137-63.

Pierre, J., and B. G. Peters. 2000. *Governance, Politics and the State.* London: Macmillan.

Pollitt, C. 1990. *Managerialism and the Public Service.* Oxford: Basil Blackwell.

Rhodes, R. 1997. *Understanding Governance: Policy Networks, Governance, Reflexivity and Accountability.* Buckingham: Open University Press.

Rose, R. 1984. *Understanding Big Government: The Programme Approach.* London: Sage.

Rouban, L. 1998. La modernisation de la gestion des collectivités locales de plus de 10,000 habitants. Paris: CEVIPOF.

Savoie, D. J. 1994. *Thatcher, Reagan, Mulroney: In Search of a New Bureaucracy.* Pittsburgh, PA: University of Pittsburgh Press.

Sears, A., and D. Schulman. 1998. Civic literacy: building blocks for effective engagement. Mimeo. Ottawa: CCMD.

Self, P. 1993. *Government by the Market?* London: Macmillan.

Thomas, P. G. 1998. The changing nature of accountability. In *Taking Stock: Assessing Public Sector Reform,* eds. B. G. Peters and D. J. Savoie. Montreal & Kingston: McGill-Queen's University Press, 348-393.

Walzer, N., and B. D. Jacobs, eds. 1998. *Public-private Partnerships for Local Economic Development.* Westport, CT and London: Praeger.

PART FOUR

VISION OF PUBLIC SERVICE

Managing at the Top

JACQUES BOURGAULT

DONALD J. SAVOIE

In recent years a veritable plethora of measures have been introduced in many Western countries to strengthen the senior civil service. OECD countries, in particular, have been busy on this front and there is every reason to believe that more of the same is in store for us. One might well say, "I don't know if we are on the right road but we're making good time." It takes only a cursory look at some OECD documents to see that many roads have been taken to reform the conditions of employment, the appointment process and even the power and responsibilities of senior public servants.[1]

The purpose of this chapter is to review some of these measures and to explore the issues on which further action may be taken. By senior civil service we mean executives operating at senior levels in the public service. In the case of Canada, for example, it means members of the "executive" (EX) group and deputy ministers. Our main objective is to identify the areas which hold promise and to begin developing a road map so that getting on the right road rather than "making good time" drives future efforts, recognizing, of course, that the right road depends on who is doing the driving.

There are powerful forces already at play shaping the work of senior public servants. For one thing, the roles of elected and permanent officials appear to be evolving. Public servants are increasingly being called upon to "read" the public mood through a series of measures, including special consultative mechanisms. Politicians meanwhile appear to be taking a much stronger interest in machinery of government issues and in how public services are delivered. Politicians are no longer content to set the broad policy agenda and establish new policies and then let public servants sort out their implementation. In Canada and in other parliamentary systems of government, the system is largely based on the good faith of those who work in it. In other words, the roles of politicians and of senior public servants are not clearly spelled out in any document. They do evolve and do change. This chapter seeks to understand the nature of this most recent change and then to offer advice to the senior public service as to how to position itself to meet future challenges.

What, then, are the key questions and issues for senior government executives? Recent measures introduced in some national civil services have sought in some instances to break with career tenure and automatic career progression, to strengthen executive development and training efforts, to promote mobility in order to create a higher-quality executive group, and introduce new performance-related pay schemes. At the same time, senior government officials have been faced with mixed signals from political leaders about what is expected of them – the continuing debate between the need for "doers" rather than "thinkers" and the need to separate "policy" from "operations." In addition, the pressure to be responsive to the wishes of political leaders may have, to some extent, compromised the ability of senior executives to focus on management and human resources matters.[2] Similarly, there is an increasing tendency to involve a number of departments in addressing a particular issue: "horizontality" and "coordination" have become priorities (Bourgault, 1997).

For the above reason we decided to consult senior government of Canada officials, including three current cabinet ministers, to identify the key questions which need to be answered and the areas of concern which need to be explored. Accordingly, their views, in no small measure, have shaped the findings of this study. All of the fourteen respondents we interviewed were in the executive branch. Though we had a series of set questions, the interviews were, for the most part, open-ended. In all cases, the respondents were invited to raise questions and deal with other issues. We made no attempt to draw a representative sample which would have been impractical for the purpose of this study. Rather, respondents were selected on the basis of their expertise and we made every effort to ensure a cross-section of officials from central agencies and line departments. We also submitted our findings to a group of ten senior government officials at an especially convened meeting to discuss "managing at the top" issues. In our consultations, we made every effort to look ahead ten years in an attempt to identify what will be the underlying forces shaping approaches not only to managing in the public sector but also managing the senior executive category of the public service itself. We sought to identify what was needed for the thinking, doing, and managing tasks of senior executives.

We decided to bring a comparative perspective to the study, on the grounds that we can learn more by comparing the experiences of different public services rather than by focusing exclusively on our own.

We began the interviews with the following questions:

- How much time do you spend on departmental matters? How much time do you spend on government-wide or horizontal issues?
- Looking ahead ten years, could you speculate on what will be the key responsibilities of senior public servants? To what extent will they differ from today?
- What knowledge and skills will be needed in future to make it to the top of the public service?
- If you could change one thing to facilitate the work of senior public servants, what would it be?

COMPARING EXPERIENCES

It may appear alarmingly quixotic for two academics to set out to offer a road map to guide the senior public service. So bear in mind that much of our findings are based on questions we put to government officials themselves. But a series of specific questions does not necessarily elicit straightforward replies – for example, should development measures be geared to strengthening the policy advisory capacity of senior government managers or their management abilities? Should development and training measures be produced in-house or in conjunction with the private sector? The list goes on. In any event, at times we got very different answers from different respondents.

About the only point of agreement that cuts across countries is that most national public services are in a "period of transition" (Halligan, Mackintosh, and Watson, 1996).We write mainly because a number of countries have not embraced public service reforms, at least, reforms under the New Public Management (NPM) banner. Continental bureaucracies, for example, notably those in Germany and France, have not gone down the NPM road. But this is not to suggest that they have stood still.

Countries that have embraced the NPM model have sought sweeping changes and have turned to positive rhetoric to sell their reform measures, including evocative phrases like "empowerment," "reinvention," and the like. Countries that have not embraced the NPM model have sought to reform government operations in a more incremental, consultative, and consensus based fashion.[3]

It is important to bear in mind that NPM initiatives can never be implemented in a vacuum. How a country's public service is structured is vitally important. As is well known, there is a great variety of systems and structures ranging from *les grands corps en France,* career public services in Canada and Australia, the "spoils" system in the United States, and so on.[4] In addition, new developments everywhere are also shaping new measures whether they fall under the new public management banner or not. These developments include new emphasis in parliamentary systems on holding public servants accountable before Parliament, a desire everywhere to strengthen performance measurement, and a willingness to promote a greater "horizontal perspective" on the policy and the decision-making processes. Some countries have been more successful than others on these fronts as other chapters in this book make clear.

It is not at all clear what model or models will ultimately emerge to hold sway. But we do know of a number of factors which will influence the shape of the new model. The first is "the lack of esteem in which national public services are held."[5] It is widely believed, particularly in Anglo-American democracies, that the private sector is inherently superior to the public sector.[6] It became accepted wisdom in many quarters in the 1980s, and well into the 1990s, that market forces were much better at allocating resources than the public sector. The solution then appeared to be straightforward – shift activities from the public to the private sector.

Private sector management practices were also considered to be superior to those of the public sector. Accordingly, management practices from the business community were imported to strengthen government operations.[7] This, however, met with varying degrees of success.[8] Still, the desire to speak the language of business continued: increasingly, we heard about empowerment, contracting out, management for results, performance pay, and the like.

It is in this environment that we conducted our review of government literature and carried out our consultations with senior government of Canada officials. At the risk of repetition, public service reforms now cut across national boundaries. Many Canadian officials readily acknowledge that they make it a point of keeping abreast of reforms in other countries. As one observed, "lessons learned is an important part of our business. No sense reinventing the wheel at every turn. We know that Britain, New Zealand, and Australia have all been particularly active in reforming their public service. They have become excellent labs for us. We can look at what works, what does not, what we can pick and choose, and tailor measures to accommodate our requirements."[9] Developments abroad led senior Canadian government officials to ask questions about the role of deputy ministers in portfolio management, in reporting to Parliament, and in managing agencies.

What then have they been seeing abroad? They have seen in various countries a number of similar measures designed to strengthen the senior executive category of national public services, particularly since the early 1980s. In many countries, for example, authority in the personnel management field has been shifted to departments and agencies, which has led to an enhanced managerial attention of senior civil servants to human resources; internal mobility has been encouraged; new management development courses have been introduced; and attempts have also been made to refine the objectives of the selection and appointment process.[10] Of course, not all of these efforts have been successful. Mobility, though much talked about, is hardly more evident today than, say, fifteen or twenty years ago. Cuts in the number of managerial positions, reluctance to release good people and unfavourable pay levels compared to the private sector have inhibited measures to promote mobility. Similarly, linking pay increases to performance has hardly been significant in dollar terms and has not been as straightforward in its implementation as might have been first envisaged (OECD, 1997).

New skill requirements have also been identified as necessary for senior public servants: it is clear that there is now a general recognition across most countries that senior public servants have special development and training needs. These needs, the argument goes, are different from those of other public or private sector managers. Some countries, notably Canada, Australia, the Netherlands, and the United Kingdom, have established a distinct office or agency to oversee new management development measures. Still, there are exceptions. Sweden, for example, makes no formal distinction in skills training between senior and lower-level public service managers.[11]

But no matter the structure, governments have been busy in recent years putting in place measures to strengthen management practices in their operations. They have developed courses to promote leadership abilities, management and networking skills, and policy development capacities. Governments have, over the past fifteen years or so, invested considerable amounts of money in management development, precisely at a time when they have also had to reduce their overall expenditure budgets. This suggests a recognition on the part of the political authority allocating scarce resources that managing at the top of the public service was in need of repair or an understanding that conditions were changing so rapidly that the senior public servants needed to be kept up to speed.

Though no doubt both reasons play a part in the growth of management development measures, the political rhetoric suggests that, if anything, the former probably held more sway than the latter (OECD,1997). By the 1980s, it became clear that political leaders wanted their senior public servants to be multi-talented; they wanted policy advisors who would be highly responsive to political direction, as well as possessing strong management skills and capable of cutting costs and managing like their private sector counterparts. Senior government executives meanwhile welcomed management development measures if only to understand the changes they were being asked to cope with.

The world of senior government executives has changed considerably over the past fifteen years. For one thing, the higher public service is smaller and in many countries (e.g., the United States, Australia, Canada, and New Zealand) the decision to cut the size of the senior public service had as much to do with ideology as the need to reduce government spending.[12] The role of the senior public service also changed to reflect the wishes of political leaders. A senior government official in New Zealand captured the political mood of the 1980s and 1990s when he observed, "*Yes Minister* is seen as a comedy by the public, a documentary by public servants, and a tragedy by ministers."[13] Thus, we saw the role of the senior civil service change by contract, performance pay, privatization, make or buy tests, and the decentralization of management decisions. We also saw a tendency on the part of elected officials to test the policy advice of their senior public servants against outside sources or expertise.

The question then is how much change has been introduced and has it taken root? The answer varies by country. In Britain, we are informed that it has been more cosmetic than real; in Canada and Australia, there have been changes in both the values and management practices in the higher public service, while in New Zealand very real changes have taken root on many fronts.[14] In countries where change has taken root, we see a great focus on results in terms of efficiency, effectiveness, and quality of service. Countries like Australia and New Zealand, for example, have also implemented measures to replace highly centralized hierarchical structures in government operations with decentralized management environments. But, as the old saying goes, every reform is its own problem. OECD reports in its *Governance in Transition* document that decentralized management environments can weaken "policy coherence and public accountability and erode traditional public service values such as equity and integrity."[15]

WHAT NOW?

There is little indication to suggest that less change lies in the years ahead. It is still at the top of many government agendas.

The Clinton administration recently unveiled its desire to cut the Senior Executive Service (SES) in half. It declared that it would tighten the definition of SES positions so that those who do not perform managerial functions would be moved into other groups. In addition, the administration made it clear that it wanted to shift the SES group to a "high-risk, high-reward" orientation. Joyce Edwards, head of the Office of Personnel Management, declared that "there is no room for any poor "performances" (OECD,1995). She added that senior executives would also be encouraged "to move among programs and agencies, so that executives develop a broad base of experience."[16]

The Canadian government meanwhile recently established a "leadership network." Prime Minister Chrétien declared that the network was "a new horizontal organization" designed "to meet the challenge of building a modern and vibrant Public Service able to use fully the talents of its people."[17] One of the organization's principal tasks is to support "the collective management of Assistant Deputy Ministers," the level immediately below the deputy minister or permanent secretary level.

The new organization was established through an Order-in-Council and designated as an agency with its own spending estimates. It reports to the clerk of the Privy Council and the Committee on Senior Officials (COSO). The clerk explained that assistant deputy ministers were "being asked to play many roles – that of expert manager, strategist, and visionary leader. You are also expected to operate in an environment where issues are increasingly horizontal and service delivery must be seamless."[18]

Under the collective management approach, new assistant deputy ministers are appointed to level, not to a position. "Corporate exercises" are conducted to prequalify candidates, who can self-identify or be nominated by a deputy minister and are assessed against leadership competencies. There is now one "corporate pool" of assistant deputy ministers so that "Assistant Deputy Ministers in the Department of Foreign Affairs and International Trade will be considered for assignments outside the Department. Conversely, Assistant Deputy Ministers will be considered for assignments in the Department of Foreign Affairs and International Trade" (PCO, 1998).

The decision to shift to a collective management of the assistant deputy minister community and to promote to level rather than to a position is a significant development for the public service. For one thing, it means a fundamental shift away from the classical Weberian public service organization. Weber insisted that the requirement of the position was of paramount importance. For him, everything turned on the job, not the individual. Under the new approach, everything turns on the individual who prequalifies and not on the requirements of the position. The approach, the argument goes, favours generalists over specialists.

The "generalist" category, however, is in many ways a catch-all category. At a minimum, it means that generalists have a general knowledge of policy and government operations, but do not bring technical or specialized knowledge to public policy issues. This is not to suggest, however, that generalists started their careers as generalists. Someone with, say, a Ph.D. in biology can start his or her career in, say, the Department of Fisheries and Oceans, but then decide in mid-career to assume managerial positions.

To be sure, the senior official can no longer function as a "departmental" or "sectoral" specialist as was the case in the 1950s and 1970s. The various background documents published in support of the new approach speak to this issue through many references to the need for "diversity of experience" and to "work in an environment where issues are increasingly horizontal" (Weber, 1947). Accordingly, in future, more senior officials will make it to the top after going through a diversity of front-line level experiences, because of their general knowledge of the system, their ability to manage difficult situations, and their capacity to work with the centre of government. Specialized knowledge of a particular sector or the policies and programs of a given department will likely become less important.

LOOKING AHEAD

The Big Picture

The above leads to a vexing question – what is the proper role of a national government in society? That question has been debated time and again in recent years not just in political parties, in policy think-tanks, but also inside government. There is a view that somehow, or somewhere, a definitive answer can be provided and that once the answer is in hand, the world will be a great deal more simple for everyone, not least, the national public services. All of this has promoted a certain "hype" about getting on the road to government reform (PCO, 1998). A profound belief in the superiority of the private sector was the one guide to the road map that became common to governments in Anglo-American democracies.

A number of respondents believed that the future senior public service will continue to look much as it has done over the past fifteen years or so. That is, elected officials will continue to insist on a more responsive public service in defining the public policy agenda. The need to strengthen management practices will continue to be felt at all levels of the public service.

Still, respondents and seminar participants reported that new skills will need to be introduced and existing ones to be sharpened to deal with a rapidly changing public policy environment. One theme that came up time and again was the need for "a new ability to interact with the public." Arthur Kroeger, a long-service senior federal public servant, explains that in the years ahead, "the public service will have to become less faceless. We have prized our anonymity, but it is fading."[19] Respondents identified two powerful reasons to explain this development.

First, governments have to make the transition from leading the "uninformed" to leading the "informed." As the Canadian population becomes better educated and more knowledgeable about public policy and government operations, senior civil servants have to develop a capacity to meet the public to discuss and persuade. Leadership of the uninformed was different in that one could rely, as Harland Cleveland (1995) argued, on "vertical structures of command and control" to provide direction. Leadership of the informed will not take place through an "authoritative" and "command" approach. It will require strong listening and communication skills, and a capacity to partner, to cooperate, and to encourage.

In addition, many respondents noted that the information revolution is fundamentally transforming how public policy issues are defined and managed. The information revolution, one respondent argued, is "empowering both citizens and front-line workers. The public servant delivering a service in St. John's, Newfoundland, can function quite well now without having to deal with Ottawa. He can have access to all the policy and program information on the internet. For that matter, so can the citizen. It can provide instant knowledge to the citizen and he can turn to that knowledge to influence government. I can assure you it was not always so. But what it means is that the relationship between head office and the region and between the government and the citizen is changing. It also means that we have to adjust."[20] Again, this speaks to a greater capacity on the part of senior managers to reach out and assume a more visible role.

The information revolution is also posing a new challenge for the federal government. As its services are increasingly being delivered via the internet and third parties, how can it continue to make its presence felt since it has to rely less and less on "bricks and mortar" to be visible to citizens?

On the face of it, one might be tempted to conclude that the impact of the information technology (IT) revolution will only be felt by mid-level and front-line managers operating points of service. But the impact is and will continue to be broadly felt at the most senior management levels. The IT revolution could well change how democracy works, as Snellen argues in an essay in this book. Indeed, one Canadian observer insists that because of IT developments, "democracy, as we know it, will be finished." The IT generation is much more accustomed to open discussion and immediacy and it will have different expectations from national political and administrative institutions.

In addition, new information technology can never be fully implemented in isolation from the organizations it is expected to serve. Senior level management will need to rethink their organizations to take full advantage of developments in information technology. A recent assessment of new information technology in France concluded that "the great productivity gains result from changes to organizational structures and procedures are too often neglected. This is true for applications within ministries, but even more so for applications that affect several ministries."[21] Accordingly, senior officials will need to keep abreast of new developments in the information technology field. It will no longer be possible to leave the field to hired guns or consultants brought in to deal with a specific problem or a crisis.

The impact of globalization on the senior public service was highlighted by several participants. They argue that, though one might think the opposite, globalization actually slows down policy and decision making. The government can no longer act on a major issue without first gaining a full understanding of how the proposed measure will impact on the competitive position of Canadian firms and even individual Canadians.[22] This, in turn, means that senior public servants will have to hone their "consultative" skills and deal more and more with provincial or state governments, private firms, and key individuals, not only to secure information but also to persuade.

Senior public servants reported that it was difficult to provide a specific breakdown on the amount of time they spend on departmental matters as opposed to government-wide or horizontal issues. A departmental matter can quickly become a government-wide issue; thus, one can hardly establish a neat and tidy definition dividing issues between two camps. One deputy minister, for example, observed that all major issues in his department are horizontal or government-wide. When he was asked by the Secretary to the Cabinet to make a presentation to a meeting of all deputy ministers to outline his departmental priorities, he began by saying that his department had no priority because all the priorities were tied one way or another to the policies and programs of other government departments. It is clear that horizontal management is not just another flavour of the month in Ottawa. At least in the government of Canada, numerous initiatives have been introduced over the years to promote a horizontal perspective. These include cabinet committees, mirror committees of deputy ministers, retreats of deputy ministers, "updates" for all assistant deputy ministers, and the list goes on. It may well be, however, that the introduction of New Public Management measures will make it more difficult to promote a horizontal perspective. A senior government official may well be torn between pursuing a level of performance to secure a performance bonus on the one hand and embracing a horizontal perspective on the other.

Assuming, one argued, that you could actually divide one's work on a percentage basis, then it is clear that the "horizontal" or "government-wide" issues will gain in importance in the years ahead. But, he added, the important point is not by how much it will increase, but rather "how" senior public servants will go about their work. Many respondents believed that in future issues will be resolved through "networking." The federal government of tomorrow will operate as a kind of clearing house where issues are brought in to be resolved not by a single government department, but rather by several departments as well as the provinces, private firms, and interested parties.

The above implies that "core government" will be considerably smaller a decade hence. One respondent, for example, speculated that the core administration of the federal government in ten years may only amount to 15 per cent of the entire government's current size. She argued that "steering rather than rowing" will become the guiding principle in future decisions concerning the machinery of government. Programs and services, she added, will be delivered by arm's-length agencies or corporations, by the private sector or by provincial governments. The core government will essentially consist of a policy advisory and coordination function.

Notwithstanding the above, a number of respondents insisted that there are still a number of common principles or ideas linking the public service, broadly defined. The challenge then, in their opinion, is to apply these principles while providing sufficient operational autonomy to agencies or to program specialists to enable them to deliver services and activities in the most efficient manner possible. They also argued that identifying these common principles will be crucial to ensuring that the public service continues to enjoy a level of "legitimacy" with Canadians. Indeed, some suggested that the issue of legitimacy will gain in importance in the years ahead, as contracting out and new forms of partnerships with various organizations take root. As Canadians look for stability and legitimacy in public service, only "common principles" will be able to provide them.

Respondents insisted that policy advice will regain importance. But so will a capacity to monitor and evaluate policies and programs. Most practitioners see little merit in separating completely the rowing and steering functions in government. Departments and agencies will need to strike the proper balance between the two so that the policy advisory and program implementation functions can draw insights and experiences from each other.

Skills

What knowledge and skills then will be needed in future to make it to the top of the federal public service? A number of respondents believed that senior executives will need to develop a capacity to manage through culture and vision, rather than through administrative prescriptions. They will need to have a proven track record of working in teams and in reaching out to policy actors outside of their own departments.

Strong communication skills will be valued, in future, even more than they are at the moment. In the past, communication was too often seen as an "add-on" to the policy formulation process rather than as an integral part of it. One senior official pointed to recent reforms in the unemployment insurance program as a case in point. It became clear that to have any chance of success, or to win the approval of the politicians, the policy proposals had to be accompanied by a convincing communication strategy.

The above also suggests that it is the fixers who will be highly valued in senior government circles in future. One respondent observed that "fixers capable of delivery and getting things done in consultation with partners" will have greater opportunities for promotions in the public sector. To be sure, political fixers have always been highly valued in government operations, particularly during the past twenty years or so. But as decision making becomes ever more complex and involves a growing number of "partners" or outside groups, and as constraints of one kind or another – ranging from environmental concerns to tight fiscal circumstances – must be reckoned with, those who can cut through obstacles and bring partners onside will in future steal the stage, particularly with elected officials.

Senior officials will also require a strong capacity to work with elected officials. One deputy minister maintained that this can only be learned by doing and by looking to role models. He claimed that, contrary to popular beliefs, senior public servants are now less able to work with elected officials and interpret their objectives than was the case fifteen or twenty years ago. Politicians, he explains, now get policy advice from a variety of sources, including lobbyists and politically appointed advisors and assistants. He adds that senior officials have less time to brief ministers than they used to have, in that they actually spend more time managing down, because of the current emphasis on management issues and implementing program review decisions, than on managing up. He adds that senior officials are increasingly at risk of losing their capacity to manage up.

In future, he and other respondents suggested, senior public servants will need a capacity to manage up, down, out and in. That is, they will need a capacity not only to understand the goals of elected officials but also to motivate their employees. They will need a full understanding of Canadian society, its challenges, its place in the global economy, and be able to communicate this to people outside government. In addition, they will need to be able to bring the views of outside experts and citizens into the government policy-making process so that new policies will be well grounded in what is possible. In brief, understanding the "big picture" rather than managing the details of the day will dominate the work of senior public servants in future.

This, in turn, will require still more emphasis on management development measures for senior level managers. A few years back, Honeywell studied how its senior managers learn. The study concluded that managers learn to manage based on 50 per cent on-job experience, 30 per cent relationships, and 20 per cent from formal training. Yet, their managers reported that they spend less than 1 percent of their time in training (Zemke, 1985). One can easily speculate that things are not much different for senior managers, at least in the case of the government of Canada. Learning from role models who have "been there, done that" was probably better suited to a command and control management approach to fast-changing circumstances.

Establishing informal procedures and new means of communications requires, in the jargon of the management development world, "continuous learning organization" and "learner-centred development measures."[23] It also means that senior managers will need to block off some time to read and to attend seminars and conferences. This will be no small task. As is well known, the urgent will very often crowd out the important in senior levels in government when time is always the rarest of commodities.

Attitudes

The future senior government officials, to be successful, will not only possess particular skills, but also, according to one respondent, require to have "several winning attitudes." He or she will have an open mind, be flexible, and willing to look at totally new ideas to solve problems. One respondent singled out the recent successful negotiations between Ottawa and Quebec on human resources development. Had federal government officials stuck to "old references and attitudes," no deal would have been possible. This, in turn, suggests that government officials will need to embrace "continuous learning" not just in words, but also indeed as part of their management development planning.

They will also need to sharpen their ability to juggle their various roles and responsibilities. To be sure, they will still have corporate responsibilities. But they will also increasingly be drawn into the work of their line departments or agencies and will need to develop a capacity to relate to the requirements of their outside partners. In other words, the successful officials will have developed a capacity to react instinctively to issues from both the horizontal (government-wide) and vertical perspective.

They will be risk-takers. But, much as always, they will be rewarded only if they do not create problems for their political masters or if their actions do not draw them into a heated public debate. Having a solid judgment about what constitutes the public interest while also being confident of what can work without entailing a political debate will be the hallmark of the successful senior public servant in years to come.

The Career of the Future

In future, there will be two distinct career paths for government officials. One path will be for the "specialist," the individual who has a strong background in a particular sector. He or she will be able to become a "senior specialist" and enjoy a fairly healthy monetary reward. In other words, they will not have to join the managerial ranks to enjoy a well-paying position. The reason is straightforward: as issues and sectors become more complex and more interwoven, those persons possessing the right mix of knowledge and expertise will be indispensable to the smooth operating of government departments and agencies. Some current officials believe that this development cannot come soon enough. Many have recognized for some time that "the best and the brightest" do not always make the best or even competent managers. The best and the brightest, however, have often been slotted in management positions if only to pay them enough to retain their services.

The second career path will be a management one. Indeed, some respondents are convinced that, in future, governments will make every effort to establish an "early management" stream and try to attract candidates from a variety of sectors – large municipal governments, provincial governments, not-for-profit organizations and, if possible, the private sector. As already noted, senior managers will be expected to have held a variety of management jobs and the most senior levels will be reserved for those who have gained field experience.

Senior managers will have strong interpersonal skills and a capacity to master "soft skills." By soft skills, respondents meant the ability to deal with subordinates with a "human touch." One thirty-year veteran of the public service reported that he "was never treated like a person, by a person. I always felt treated like a member of the system." Public servants, he added, "will stay in government, even if salaries are lower, if they feel like they are treated well by top managers."

OBSTACLES

Respondents identified a number of obstacles inhibiting the work of senior public servants. Spending cuts in government operations are still being made and there is now precious little left to cut. Salaries have not kept pace with those in the private sector and there are now fewer and fewer opportunities for promotion. In such an environment, they argue that it is exceedingly difficult to manage through culture and to motivate employees. In addition, as already noted, Canadians generally no longer hold the federal public service in high esteem, contrary to what was the case some forty years ago. This, too, constitutes an important obstacle to motivating public servants down the line.

The senior public service of the future, as already noted, will need to be flexible and to adjust to changing circumstances. There are, however, difficult hurdles within the system itself to be overcome, if the new approach is to prevail. For one thing, the current practice at the senior levels is for managers to hire "clones," or as one respondent labelled the convention, the "Russian doll syndrome." Junior-level officials identify "mentors" in the senior ranks and then make every effort to be like them and to model their behaviour accordingly. This tendency, it is argued, still exists and it will invariably inhibit an effort to bring about change. This matters, because diversity of views will be more valued in future both in society and, by ricochet, in government.

Respondents also reported that we have had far too many reform measures from Increased Management Authority and Accountability (IMAA) to PS2000, all designed to fix the public service and all failing to live up to expectations. There is now a strong culture of disbelief in the federal public service, with many public servants reacting rather cynically to new reform initiatives. It has also created instability and even insecurity over possible further job losses and confusion among staff over the purpose and direction of the organization. One respondent explained "henceforth we should just introduce a new measure and ensure that it is properly implemented. We should not announce another grand scheme. There is simply no appetite for it any more."[24]

A number of respondents also maintained that past reform efforts did not pay sufficient attention to promoting strong management labour relations. In the past, senior managers have all too often looked to the labour specialists in central agencies to deal with unions. This, given the current move to empower departments and agencies, will need to change.

However, the biggest obstacle inhibiting both the work of senior public servants and real change is the apparent inability of political institutions to embrace change and to make it stick. We have reached the point, at least at the federal level in Canada, where senior public servants have done most of what they can do to reform their institution. Future reforms such as turning the public service into a small policy advisory core is a decision that can only be made at the political level. Similarly, only elected officials can address the visibility issue regarding the delivery of services.

To involve outside experts, to manage information "in" and "out," to encourage public participation are all issues requiring political attention. The question as to where Parliament or even Cabinet fit in the new information age, how they operate and remain relevant in a global economy, can only be established by elected officials. Until they do so, senior public servants will be left to play at the margins, trying as best they can to adjust once again their own institution and cope with a variety of often conflicting demands. In brief, the time has come for elected officials to recall the biblical injunction: "heal thyself." It is crucial that they look to their own institutions. Every government is being affected by the information revolution and the global economy. Yet, Parliament and Cabinet still function much as they did twenty years ago.

Perhaps the most stubborn obstacle to be surmounted is the "control lobby." This includes the media, the office of the auditor general, the opposition, and other "watchdog" organizations. This lobby is constantly on the lookout for missteps in government operations and always at the ready to pounce on government officials to lay blame, if possible. Yet, many reform measures are designed to encourage government officials to take risks and to innovate. At some point, the control lobby will need to recognize that it cannot have it both ways.

Elected officials now must take the lead in defining the road map. Any decisions that could be taken by senior public servants have, by and large, already been taken. It is the big picture that now needs to be addressed, and it is up to our elected representatives to do so.

It is not at all clear that political leaders are prepared to look at their own institutions to strengthen national governance. The OECD has sponsored numerous studies on public management and concluded that "the challenge for governance at the end of the twentieth century is one of institutional renewal." It adds that "outdated institutions and practices need to be redesigned or replaced with one that better matches the realities and demands of dynamic market economies with the objectives and responsibilities of democratic systems" (OECD, 1995). Its own studies and efforts, however, have only been directed at the public service and the internal organizations of government departments and agencies. Little is said about political institutions.

Assuming that political leaders will recognize the need to "heal thyself" and fix their own institutions, what ought to be the role of senior public servants in their process? Public servants, more than most, know how political institutions work, their strengths and weaknesses. They also have an intimate knowledge of how government operations work and how administrative realities and requirements connect to political institutions. They ought not to stay on the sideline if political leaders truly decide to review political institutions and their role in society.

NOTES

We would like to thank Martine Etier, research assistant, for her contribution and assistance in producing this chapter.

1 See, for example, Benita E.C. Plesch et al., *The Senior Civil Service: A Comparison of Personnel Development for Top Managers in Thirteen OECD Member Countries.* Paris: OECD, June 1997.

2 See Canada, Discussion Paper on Values and Ethics in the Public Service. Ottawa: Canadian Centre for Management Development, 1996.

3 See, among others, Christopher Pollitt, "Justification by Works or By Faith? Evaluating the New Public Management," *Evaluation,* vol. 1, no 2, 1995, pp.133-54.

4 Jacques Bourgault, "La gestion de la performance dans la haute fonction publique : quelques cas issus du modèle de Whitehall." In Marie-Michèle Guay, ed., *Performance et Secteur Public.* Quebec: Presses de l'Université du Québec, 1996, pp.194-213.

5 Ibid., 93.

6 See, among others, Donald J. Savoie, *Thatcher, Reagan, Mulroney: In Search of a New Bureaucracy.* Pittsburgh: University of Pittsburgh Press, 1994.

7 See, among others, B. Guy Peters and Donald J. Savoie, *Reforming the Public Sector: Taking Stock.* Montreal & Kingston: McGill Queen's University Press, 1998.

8 Ibid. See chapters by Christopher Pollitt.

9 See, among others, Christopher Pollitt and Geert Bouckaert, *Public Management Reform: A Comparative Analysis.* Oxford: Oxford University Press, 1999.

10 Consultations with a deputy minister, Government of Canada, Ottawa, September 1998.

11 See, for example, Patricia W. Ingraham, James R. Thomson and Ronald P. Sanders (eds.), *Transforming Government: Lessons from the Reinvention Laboratories.* San Francisco: Jossey-Bass, 1998, chapters 1 and 6.

12 See, among others, Jacques Bourgault et al. "Performance Appraisals of Top Civil Servants: creating a corporate culture." *Public Administration Review,* 53, 1:73-80.

13 See, among others, Patricia Ingraham, "Managing Public Policy: The Changing Role of the Higher Civil Service." In Peters and Savoie, eds., *Reforming the Public Sector: Taking Stock.*

14 Quoted in ibid. p.170.

15 See, among others, Christopher Hood, "Deprivileging the u.k. Civil Service in the 1980s: Dream or Reality?" In Jon Pierre, ed., *Bureaucracy in the Modern State: An Introduction to Comparative Public Administration.* Aldershot: Edward Elgar, 1995, 110-17; and Jonathan Boston et al., eds., *Public Management: The New Zealand Model.* Melbourne: Oxford University Press, 1996.

16 ses Could be Cut in Half. *AMS Horizon,* Washington, DC, April 30, 1998, p.2.

17 Ibid.

18 Ottawa, Release, Prime Minister Announces Creation of the Leadership Network. Office of the Prime Minister, Ottawa, June 4, 1998, p.1.

19 Consultation with a senior federal government official, Ottawa, October 1998.

20 Quoted in *Governance in Transition,* p.61.

21 Jim Mitchell, a former senior federal government official, made a similar observation in his "What We Can Expect for the Government and Society in the Near Future," notes for an address to the 1995 Real Property Conference, Ottawa, November 15, 1995, p.6.

22 See, among others, R. Bruce Dodge, *Learning in an Organizational Setting: The Public Service Context.* Ottawa: Canadian Centre for Management Development, 1992.

23 Consultation with a senior federal government official, Ottawa, September 1998.

BIBLIOGRAPHY

Jacques Bourgault. 1997. Horizontal integration at the top. *Optimum,* 27, 4:12-24.

Cleveland, Harland. 1985. The twilight of hierarchy: speculations on the global information society. *Public Administration Review,* 45, 1 (January-February).

Halligan, John, Ian Mackintosh, and Hugh Watson. 1996. *The Australian Public Service: The View From the Top.* Canberra: University of Canberra, 78.

Kroeger, Arthur. 1998. Some thoughts on the future. The Second Annual George Davidson Memorial Lecture, Treasury Board Secretariat, May.

OECD. 1995. *Governance in Transition.* Paris: OECD, 7,16.

_____ 1997. *The Senior Civil Service: A Comparison of Personnel Development for Top Managers in 13 OECD Countries.* Paris: OECD, June 19-20.

Privy Council Office. 1998. *Supporting Excellence in the ADM Community: An Overview of the New Collective Management System.* Ottawa: Privy Council Office, May.

Tapscott, Don. 1997. *Growing Up Digital: The Rise of the Net Generation.* Toronto: McGraw-Hill.

Max Weber. 1947. *The Theory of Social and Economic Organization.* New York: Oxford University Press.

R. Zemke. 1985. The Honeywell studies: how managers learn to manage. *Training,* August.

Public Employment and the Future of the Public Service

PATRICIA W. INGRAHAM
B. GUY PETERS
DONALD P. MOYNIHAN

INTRODUCTION

At the heart of much of the debate and discussion of public service reform and its impact is this question: Does government now perform more effectively and efficiently than in its unreformed state? In most nations, serious evaluations of that question are only now beginning. Of the many dimensions to be explored, the effective use of human resources must be close to the top of the list. The recent focus on Human Resources Management recognizes the same bureaucratic shortcomings that earlier reforms generally tackled in the 1980s. Enabling better public performance was typically addressed by a series of structural reforms, by altering the shape and functions of the public service.

The purpose of this chapter is to examine the key effects of public sector reforms across the globe, in an effort to provide insights into the personnel issues facing governments today, and to determine for us what these issues suggest for the future of public employment. Personnel issues have rarely been given in-depth attention, with reformers often assuming that by decentralizing the personnel function and increasing the flexibility of managers, such issues would no longer be of central concern. Greater discussion on personnel matters is needed to gauge the full implications of these reforms on public sector employment in the twenty-first century.

There are at least four factors that will affect the capacity of the public service to perform the central tasks in governance that it has in the past. Virtually all reform efforts that have occurred since the 1980s have reflected one or more of these different aspects. Understanding these different factors helps us to begin to frame a picture of where public sectors are at this point and where they appear to be headed. These reform factors also provide the background necessary for us to consider the most pressing issues and dilemmas facing governments. Although we discuss each of these four factors separately, it is important to note their interactions and synergies.

Downsizing

One of the dominant factors affecting the capacity of government to perform is the downsizing of the public sector. Although there are marked variations in the success of political leaders in reducing the size of the public sector (see Gregory, 1998 for an extreme example) many major governments have reduced public employment. Table 1 demonstrates the contracting role of government employment and the public service, in selected countries. In some instances, reductions have been performed with attention being given either to the particular types of employees to be eliminated or the functions to be abolished. In other cases there have been across the board reductions in the public work force. Far from viewing government as the employer of last resort – as it was once considered in some societies – many citizens and politicians now appear willing to see just how far the public sector can be reduced. It is important to look at whether the capacity of governments to perform crucial functions has been diminished and if so, to what extent. Related issues include: Has downsizing removed the next generation of senior public servants and led many others to question their commitment to government as a career? Will new reward structures create the ability for government to recruit and retain employees whose skills will match future demands? Do the "new" public services reflect the societies they serve in demographic and broad social terms? The downsizing questions, in short, are not just of short-term savings in personnel costs, but ones of long-term capacity of government to govern well.

Restructuring

As well as being downsized, the public sector has been restructured to meet the demands of its political masters and to conform to prevailing ideas of management and good governance (Peters, 1996). In some cases the two activities have been components of the same reform in the public sector, as in contracting out. This translates to fewer public employees, but also means that there are fewer public employees of a particular type, often lower-skilled employees. Such a move to making the public service more white-collar poses specific management challenges. Other forms of restructuring, e.g., the widespread use of the "agency model," also tends to reduce the size of the core organizations of government.

Another style of restructuring – flattening public organizations and reducing levels of management within them – exacerbates some of the problems of downsizing mentioned above. That is, reducing these layers of middle management government may be eliminating the next generation of more senior managers, unless there is the intent to rely much more heavily on external recruitment. Eliminating middle-management positions also reduces the clarity of a career structure in government and clearly has implications for communication and management capacities of public organizations.

Finally, we should mention the aspects of restructuring having to do with public personnel systems themselves. As noted, governments may be losing some of the distinctiveness of their career structures. Further, these changes may link state and society more closely than in the past, and in the process create a better understanding of each "side" by the other. That having been said, however, the question of career structures and the capacity to gain the commitments required for public service must be raised.

Change in Labour–Management Relations

A third change in the public service with implications for its future is the change in labour–management relations. The position of unions in the public sector is at present somewhat paradoxical. On the one hand, unions are now much less powerful in many countries than in the past. On the other hand, the public sector appears to be the most unionized part of many economies in the late 1990s.

The decline of unionization as a force in the public sector has been the result of political action to some degree. This is perhaps especially true for the United Kingdom in which Mrs. Thatcher made a concerted effort to break the power of the unions. In other cases, downsizing and the loss of nationalized industries has significantly reduced the role of organized labour in government. In France and Spain, however, unions appear almost as strong as ever. In the United States, the Clinton Administration has viewed labour as a key player in its reinvention activities and has worked to develop links between reformers and unions, most notably through the National Partnership Council. Given that, union opposition has been a key factor in stopping comprehensive human resources reform.

The reduction of union influence may be important for management in the short term, but it will also have long-term consequences. In particular, unions (especially those specifically for the public sector) may, through the bargaining process, create some sense of belonging to government. Put in another way, unions may have helped reduce the individualization that appears to be a part of much of the modern economy for public employees. Further (although their motives may have been less than altruistic) service unions have been powerful advocates for their clients. This may become ever more relevant with unions called on to provide extra – though often insufficient – protection for members, as traditional civil service protections are stripped away or core civil service jobs are contracted out.

The Changing Composition of, and Demands on, the Public Sector

The public sector now looks much different than it did several decades ago. There are several reasons for this. In the midst of the downsizing, there have been attempts to alter the gender and, in some instances, the ethnic composition of the public service. As a result, while it is smaller, the public sector in most countries is now also more representative of the society that it governs than at any time in the past. Women, in particular, have taken many more jobs in government. The overall age of members of the public service has decreased, as downsizing encouraged retirement or early retirement for many.

Maintaining diversity will continue to be a challenge to managers in the public sector, however. That diversity is important for demonstrated moral reasons, but it is also important for the effective implementation of many programs for whom a significant proportion of the recipients are members of key demographic groups. Given the lead role that the government employment has always played in terms of opportunity for under-represented groups in society, the simple fact of reduction in size poses a special challenge.

For future purposes, government, in addition to being smaller, will have to be more expert and more able to contend with difficult scientific and social scientific issues. Unfortunately, the experience of the 1980s and 1990s has been of shedding many scientists, policy analysts, and other technical experts with critical skills for future capacity. Even if such "expertise" is contracted out, the management skills needed to manage such contracts effectively and to retain core expertise in the public service are daunting.

If the public sector continues to change as it has, public management may well become the management of third-party actors through contracts, loans, and a variety of other indirect mechanisms (Kettl, 1993). This will require a very different type of managerial expertise than that which has been developed to cope with the direct provision of public services. It is not clear, despite the accumulation of examples and evidence, that governments have come to think seriously about the straightforward managerial implications of the "tools" they have selected to implement their programs.

The above discussion of recent changes in the public sector is crucial in providing the background from which key issues for the public service of the future will emerge. Ultimately, these issues will be best addressed by developing an agenda that will deal with them comprehensively, as a coordinated strategic human resources effort. It is the intent of this chapter, using the data available on contemporary public employment, to consider how these issues combine to create a series of personnel dilemmas for governments everywhere.

The fundamental issue is whether government now has the right people for its tasks. This is by no means a simple question, as it involves a clear understanding of just what government intends to do, and the type of personnel that will be required to perform those tasks. The impact of reforms has not served to strengthen this understanding. Rather it has raised questions regarding the validity of traditional personnel processes and procedures without providing guidelines for what, if any, replacements are necessary. The previous discussion of the effects of recent changes in the public sector indicates some skepticism about the composition of government and its ability to recruit and retain the quality of personnel. Notable efforts such as La Relève notwithstanding, that concern appears to be well justified.[1] If, for example, the future of government is to be less in recruiting its own personnel and more in contracting and the use of temporary and part-time employees, is government prepared to manage such a workforce? And, what does a public sector with such characteristics imply for the efficiency and equity of service delivery, and the probity and commitment of the service delivery personnel?

Even if we assume that reformed governments do have the right people, and are effective at recruiting more of them, are there carefully considered strategies to ensure the retention of these employees? If the experience of different downsizings is an indicator, it appears not. Most downsizing strategies were not carefully targeted or designed to retain outstanding individuals. Many reduced without consideration as to the extent to which the skills of those who remain match the challenges government faces, an issue only now being considered.

Finally, even if the right people are hired, are they in the right place? The potential of any workforce will not be fully realized until it is aligned correctly with the structure of the organization and the work processes that it utilizes. In some nations, structural reforms and human resources reforms have been matched and simultaneous. In others, they were not. In still other countries, public services with decentralized operations and national–provincial–local relationships face the question of where skills are needed in different terms.

These key issues might be captured in a challenge to: "Recruit and retain the right people, and put them in the right places." An underlying quandary is whether government can – or should – be a model employer, given the numerous other demands being imposed upon it. Will governments continue to emphasize diversity? Will governments still be more tolerant of unions and labour–management negotiations than are most contemporary private sector organizations? Will government attempt to maintain a fair and equitable pay system for all personnel, while coping with the economic pressures to cut costs and to reduce the size of the public sector? These are all important questions, even in an age in which government is supposed to operate like a private sector enterprise.

REFORMING HUMAN RESOURCES: A SUMMARY OF EXPERIENCE

National efforts to reform human resources provide a broad spectrum of choice and strategy. At one end is the United States, where the National Performance Review (now the National Partnership for Reinventing Government) has argued that while management and civil service reforms are necessary, reform can proceed incrementally and without legislative foundations. It appears to be fair to say that this attitude has been moulded in part by the realization that efforts to pass comprehensive legislative reform – such as the Federal Personnel Systems Act of 1996 – were likely to be unsuccessful. The New Zealand perspective was different; that nation addressed the issue early and head-on in its 1988 State Sector Act reform. Following this legislation, the State Services Commission was reconfigured from a strongly standardized central personnel agency to a much more modest consultant and adviser.

Evidence is beginning to emerge from other nations, however, that some of the "eye-glazing" HRM issues delegated, decentralized, or ignored in earlier reform activities are now recognized as central to effective performance. The Canadian initiative La Relève is intended to address issues of recruitment, retention, development, and compensation in the national public service. It grew from what the Clerk of the Privy Council described as a "quiet crisis" resulting from downsizing, limited pay, and consistently increasing demand for public services. The Canadian Universal Classification Standard (UCS) reform also provides an example of very broad-based HRM reform. It operates from the fundamental premise that more strategic utilization of human resources is a critical component of effective performance. "UCS," a senior Treasury official noted recently, "is now understood to be the key to all the other reforms" (OECD Focus, 1998). The Universal Classification Standard will replace the 1967 system that places employees of the national government into 72 different classifications; this system is now viewed as counter-productive to effective individual and organizational performance. The intent of the new system is to work directly towards the achievement of results, recognizing changes in the workplace such as the use of teams, the increase in contract work, cross-government partnerships and the impact of new technology. The key goals of the UCS are simplicity (reducing the number of classifications to 29), universality (in that it embraces all work done by government), and gender neutrality. It is also intended to foster employee mobility, a multi-skilled workforce, and better client service.

The Australian overhaul of the public service based on the Public Service Bill, and on the 1996 Workplace Relations Act, has a similar purpose to the Canadian effort, but is even more sweeping. As a prelude to the Bill, Australia delegated most remaining HRM authority away from the Public Service Commission (now called the Public Service Merit Protection Commission) to the agency level. Australia has also recognized the need for additional reform. The Public Service and Merit Protection Commission's *Re-engineering People Management* (1997) emphasized not only efficiency measures, but the alignment of key human resources with major organizational objectives. Classification reform is a key part of the effort.

EMERGING PERSONNEL DILEMMAS

The efforts of these governments illustrate a clear acknowledgment of the fact that if public organizations are to function well and to perform at high levels, they must have the capacity to recruit, hire, and retain the right people for the jobs to be done. This new "right people in the right place at the right time" criteria has itself become a performance standard against which broader organizational performance can be judged (Ingraham and Kneedler, 1999).

This standard can be disassembled into underlying questions, questions largely unaddressed by 1980's reforms.

- What does the "right people" mean?
- Does government have a system in place to think about, and plan for, the skills and capacities it needs now and will need in the future?

While the above questions can be a theme in thinking about the design and performance of government organizations and employment systems, the long-term effect of 1980's structural reforms make them more complicated. The following sections address the changes that accompanied such reforms, with a view to tracing the observable effects on the public service.

DOWNSIZING: WHO LEFT AND WHO STAYED?

One major influence on both the number of employees and the environment in which they work has been the downsizing of government, described in Table 1. Although precise comparisons are difficult, two conclusions emerge from a comparative analysis of downsizing activities in the past decade. As Table 1 indicates, many major nations engaged in some downsizing activity. Much of this was directed at the core national bureaucracy. Second, although there was some targeting in this regard – the higher service was reduced in Canada, mid-level "control" positions were the (unsuccessful) target in the u.s., administrative support staff were the targets of the German "Lean State" reforms – in most cases, downsizing was a blunt instrument. It reflected what Hogwood (1998) has called "changes in nature of government," rather than careful workforce planning directed at current and future human resource needs. Ironically, strategic planning, one of the tenets of careful human resources management, was generally sacrificed for the priorities of the reform efforts. The intent was to reshape the structure, the content, and the intent of core public administration, but – apparently – to think about the people part of the equation later.

The extent of the downsizing of the central core varies dramatically from nation to nation. In New Zealand a "crashing through" strategy produced dramatic results: if only permanent staff are included, the reduction is slightly over 50 per cent. If temporary staff are added, the reduction between 1985 and 1997 increases to 61 per cent of the core workforce (Gregory, 1998, 9). The overall reduction, while real, covers significant variation from function to function in New Zealand. Central agencies and Treasury have declined substantially; the Department of Social Welfare has increased slightly. The changes in these numbers have triggered other changes. At the same time that Treasury's

TABLE 1

Employment in the Central/Federal Services for Selected Countries
(in thousands)

	1985*	1995**	Percentage Change
Australia	429	360	-16.1%
France	1,527	1,699	11.3%
Germany	858	546	-36.4%
United Kingdom	268	163	-39.2%
Sweden	811	731	-9.9%

*1988 for France. **1994 for Australia and France.*
Source: The Changing Structure of Employment and Pay in the Public Service Sector, 1998.

permanent staff decreased, for example, utilization of contracts and consultancies increased rather steeply, accounting for 6 per cent of total Treasury expenditure in 1988 and rising to 21.5 per cent in 1996/97. (Gregory, 1998, 11).

Canada has also achieved significant reductions. As Figure 1 indicates, the period 1993 to 1998 saw a 29 per cent reduction in full-time equivalents. Certain occupational groups have borne the brunt of downsizing, with Clerical and Regulatory, General Labour and Trades, Secretarial Stenographic and Typing, and General Services accounting for half of reductions since 1995. Other groupings have been less affected by reductions and have grown in relative terms during the downsizing period, signifying a shift in the composition of the public service towards more knowledge-based workers. Employees in the Executive, Scientific and Professional, and Administrative and Foreign Service Categories now constitute 52.7 per cent of Canadian federal employees compared to 43 per cent in 1993 (Treasury Board of Canada Secretariat, 1998).

Hogwood (1998) describes a different pattern in the U.K., where privatization, the creation of Next Steps agencies, and other activities have reduced total numbers of employees in the traditional core. This has been accompanied, however, by rather large increases in health and education employment, and by large increases in temporary and part-time employment. Germany presents yet another model. In an effort to

FIGURE 1
Changes in Canadian Federal Employment

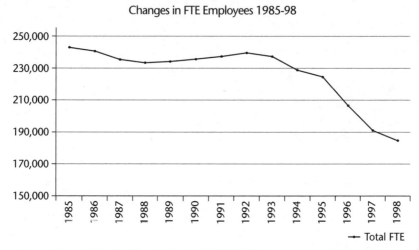

Source: Treasury Board of Canada Secretariat 1995, 1998.

return to pre-unification employment levels and public sector costs, the federal government does not have nearly as far to go as do the Länder and local governments, where size and cost have increased by nearly 50 per cent in a twenty-year period (Lean State Advisory Council, 1997). Downsizing in Germany is targeting these governments; Bavaria and the free state of Bremen are examples of early reductions. Although some question the German commitment to substantial downsizing and reform, citing past examples of lack of political will (Derlien, 1996), both political and economic influences have changed.

Governments seeking to reduce the size of their public personnel have drawn from a number of different downsizing strategies, in some cases with specific parts of the public service targeted. The most commonly used strategies and targets are:

- Privatization/Contracting Out
- Involuntary Reductions
- Voluntary Reductions through early retirement, buyouts

- Targeting the Core for Reductions
- Targeting Specific Levels of Personnel System for Reduction

Downsizing activity has been widespread, with governments adopting a variety of targets and strategies simultaneously, often with differing degrees of emphasis. A good example is the United States, where all of the above strategies and targets were adopted, with the exception of involuntary reductions. The emphasis on voluntary reductions damaged any sense of strategic downsizing and served to frustrate the other goals of targeting core middle-level managers for downsizing (u.s. Office of Personnel Management, 1998). In the u.s., and elsewhere, we can expect that the nature of government's downsizing approach will have differential impacts on capacity, making it an important item for future reform research.

THE CHANGING NATURE OF PUBLIC EMPLOYMENT

How does the public service in different countries look after a sustained period of reform? To answer this question we have to consider what has changed about the structures, working conditions, and demographics of public organizations. An underlying conceptual and methodological problem also emerges from this question. How to determine what is "core government," how to categorize employees who are supported by government but are contract or outsourced resources, and how to think about the "right" balance are now important items in reform research agendas. In a recent chapter, Hood, et al. (1998) argue that the conflicting perspectives on public employment contained in the core public bureaucracy model and those contained in the more market-based, contracted-out model may represent a fundamental cultural shift in views of government and its responsibilities. Different issues have been raised in the "hollow government" literature (Milward and Provan, 1991; Milward, 1996). Here, the concern is with the extent to which government is able to retain critical capacity and essential expertise as it contracts away – frequently with little forethought or analysis – many government activities and functions. The increased fragmentation in the delivery of traditionally governmental services may also in the long-run raise accountability and visibility issues as it becomes more difficult to discern what government is doing, and who is doing it.

For our purposes, the issue is somewhat different, though still related. If key "right" people and skills are contract or temporary employees, are they building longer-term government capacity? In a reformed setting, is that issue no longer so critical? Without any question, some level of contracting for both basic and highly expert skills makes sense. It is the connectedness of these employees to government organizations, values, and long-term capability that is of concern here. Traditionally, the size of government and government employment issues were most often addressed in terms of civil service status. But, as the OECD recently noted, "...the far-reaching changes that have affected public services since the late 1980s will probably make that distinction inoperative in more and more countries." (1997b, 4). Additional issues are raised, in this regard, by the use of total authorized personnel figures versus total filled and by part-time employee counts.

Despite the inability to generalize about capacity of government after downsizing, it is clear that some important characteristics of public employment have changed. Leaving the "core–contractor" issue aside for a moment, the increased use of part-time and temporary employees is a common factor across reformed central governments. New Zealand, not surprisingly, is an exception. Gregory reports the following: "By 1987 there were only about 2,000 temporary public servants in New Zealand, as compared with 18,200 the previous year. By 1997, there were none." (Gregory, 1998, 10). Because there has been limited analysis of the employment patterns of the Crown Sector Corporations, however, this statement may be somewhat misleading.

The New Zealand case notwithstanding, temporary employment is often seen not only as a cost-cutting device (temporary employees rarely have the benefits that accrue to full-time members of the public service) but as a strategic workforce planning measure as well. Surges in demand, in needs for special expertise, seasonal requirements, and in geographic reallocations can be quickly and tidily met with temporary workers. In the United States, when the Federal Aeronautical Administration was excepted by Congress from most central personnel rules and authority, one of the agency's first actions was to simplify temporary hiring procedures to facilitate their use (FAA, 1996). Both the Internal Revenue Service and the Department of Defense also rely heavily on temporary appointments in the U.S.

In the U.K., on the other hand, part-time employment is the story. Part-time employees now account for a much larger piece of the total employment, largely because of substantial increases in the health and education sectors. Hogwood reports that one in ten British civil servants are now part-time and that the number of part-time workers has nearly trebled in twenty years (Hogwood, 1998, 23). Interestingly, he also observes that one impact is on the number of women in the core service: 91 per cent of part-time workers are women. In Germany, where part-time employment is expanding rapidly, it is also raising some concerns. Here the issue is related to the relatively young age of many part-time workers and the adequacy of the salaries they receive. While the measure does in fact save money, it may also cause young German officials to be paid at very low rates.

The complicated mix of permanent full-time core employees, part-time employees with benefits, temporary employees with few or limited benefits, and contract employees with private sector pay and benefits make it extremely difficult to draw conclusions about the state of "public" employment generally. It is problematic to accurately gauge the size of public employment and it would be desirable if governments attempted to develop some type of aggregate measures of the services that they provide and the human resources they employ, broken down by core/part-time/temporary and contract employees. The fragmented mix of employees from different sectors also raises issues of capacity in terms of ability to bridge across the different kinds of employees and the purposes they serve in the broad public employment picture. Additionally, it places other specific issues on national human resource management agendas and redefines some of them. Composition of the workforce, compensation of public employees, and labour–management relations in this polyglot environment all require some rethinking. We now turn our attention to these issues.

COMPOSITION OF THE PUBLIC WORKFORCE

Diversity among public employees and equal opportunity for public jobs have been objectives of most national governments for over forty years and speak to concerns of representativeness. But overcoming the weight of historical hiring patterns, educational paths to public service, veterans' preference, and strong cultural norms has been more daunting than many anticipated. The long-held civil service tradition of "growing your own" leadership only exacerbated the scope of the problem. It could – and did – take years to move through the ranks and promotions to get to the top. For many nations, the top looked much the same after diversity initiatives as prior to them. While external hiring emphases for the senior service and for many of the reformed Next Steps, Crown Corporation, and other public agency CEOs have addressed this problem somewhat, the concern for greater diversity remains.

One of the areas in which comparable cross-national data is available is that of numbers of women in the senior public service. Most national reforms targeted at the higher service and at executive capacity in the organizations created by reform have emphasized the use of extensive external recruiting and hiring procedures. While this had the intent of "freshening" the senior executive ranks, it has also served to change their composition, with the increase in numbers of women being the most notable change. As Figure 2 demonstrates, in some cases this change has been dramatic.

The extent to which these trends are reflected in the broader management of the public service is difficult to measure over a sustained period due to lack of detailed comparative data. This is the area in which downsizing might have taken its toll,

FIGURE 2
Women in the Senior Public Service

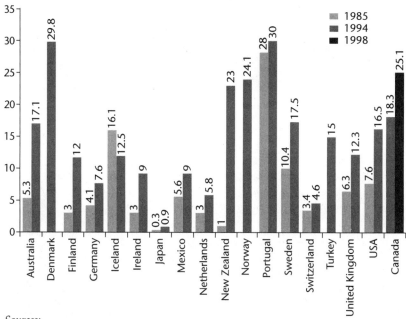

Sources:
OECD, 1997c.
Canada: Treasury Board of Canada Secretariat 1995 and 1998.
Germany: 1987 and 1994.
Netherlands: Central Administration only.

because to the extent that seniority provisions governed downsizing activities, the most recently hired – women and traditional minorities – would be the first to go. On the other hand, in cases where retirement and attrition governed the reductions the total numbers of white males would most likely be reduced. Figure 3 illustrates that with the Canadian experience at least, females and minorities have seen reductions, but at a much lower rate than the downsizing average for the public service.

In three nations where comparable data in relation to female representation in the civil service was available for the past

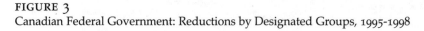

FIGURE 3
Canadian Federal Government: Reductions by Designated Groups, 1995-1998

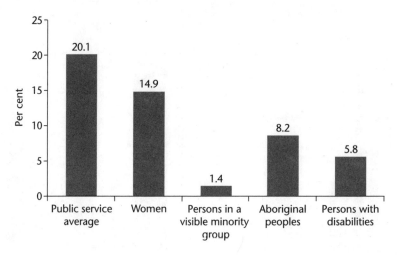

Source: *Treasury Board of Canada Secretariat 1998, p70.*

decade (Table 2) two trends are confirmed. The first is that absolute numbers of women in the civil service are declining after the early 1990s. However, the second trend is that the overall proportional representation of women is increasing. This suggests, that in these three countries at least, women as an overall proportion of the civil service have fared better than their male counterparts as government numbers are being reduced by various methods.

Finally, in relation to diversity (as narrowly defined here) it is important, once again, to note Hogwood's analysis of the emerging trend in Britain. The changing nature of the core of government, the changing patterns and choices for employment that is public sector related, and the continued high entrance rate of women into the employment pool create large areas of uncertainty for future conditions. In the past, large public organizations were most demographically representative at the bottom. Diversity initiatives dealt with mid- and upper-level entrance procedures, lower-level career development and promotion,

TABLE 2
Representation of Women in the Total Civil Service for the United States, Australia and Canada

	United States				Australia				Canada			
Year	Males	Females	Females % of total	Female change from previous	Males	Females	Females % of total	Female change from previous	Males	Females	Females % of total	Female change from previous
1988	1228049	897099	42.21%		96921	72477	42.79%					
1990	1223255	927104	43.11%	3.34%	86700	74683	46.28%	3.04%				
1992	1231412	944167	43.40%	1.84%	85771	78707	47.85%	5.39%	117714	107905	47.83%	
1994	1147332	896117	43.85%	-5.09%	78356	71503	47.71%	-9.15%	121412	109980	47.53%	1.92%
1995	1095954	864623	44.10%	-3.51%	75822	69017	47.65%	-3.48%	107379	100598	48.37%	-8.53%
1996	1058566	831840	44.00%	-3.79%	70361	64713	47.91%	-6.24%	97201	97193	50.00%	-3.38%
1997					64196	62088	49.17%	-4.06%	91803	95380	50.96%	-1.87%
1998												

Sources: USA: United States Office of Personnel Management, 1997:28.
Australia: Australian Public Service Statistics Report, Public Service and Merit Protection Commission, located at http://www.psmpc.gov.au/publications97/apssa96table1.htm.
Canada: Treasury Board of Canada Secretariat for 1995, 1996, 1997, 1998.

and the creation of bridge occupations. Even if the hiring of women and traditional minorities improves at the very top, there is still the potential for groups to "get stuck" in part-time jobs, creating a new problem. This reflects the lack of smoothly functioning career chains, which were severely disrupted by downsizing and restructuring. It suggests that there remains a dysfunctional institutional process in dealing with the issue.

In one of the few analyses of changing mobility patterns, the Australian Public Service found that women and other underrepresented groups – with the exception of those with disabilities – had significantly higher mobility patterns than other members of the service. In all cases, however, mobility appeared to decline with age and tenure of service. Overall, in the ten years analyzed (1987–1997), mobility in the service decreased; this is attributed to lack of promotional opportunity (PSMPC, 1997c). A similar phenomenon, with regard to representation at different age levels, has also been observed. Canada offers a good example: females constitute the clear majority of public service workers in the earlier age categories, but age has an easily observable negative relationship with female representation. As a result, females make up an increasingly smaller proportion of the workforce at the higher age bands, where the most senior jobs have been traditionally concentrated.

COMPENSATION OF THE PUBLIC SERVICE

The OECD recently noted that the need to reform public sector pay determination has been recognized by many OECD members, including Australia, Finland, New Zealand, Sweden, and the U.K. The analysis concludes that "...since the beginning of the 1990s, the countries that have reformed their pay systems are the ones that are most successful in holding down their wage bills (Australia, Canada, Finland, the Netherlands, and the U.K.). However, certain countries with relatively centralized systems have also succeeded in controlling their wage bills" (OECD, 1997, 7). The same analysis concluded that pay reform had slightly more effect than reducing staff numbers in reducing

FIGURE 4
Canadian Federal Government: Gender Representation by Age

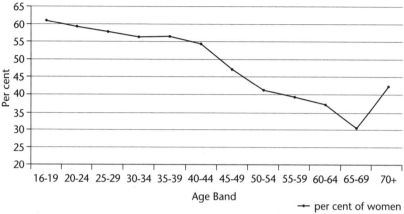

Source: Treasury Board of Canada Secretariat 1998, p15.

total cost. Table 3 displays the current total compensation costs as a percentage of government consumption expenditure for selected nations.

Cost reduction is not, of course, the only purpose of public sector pay reform. Many nations have used the reform as a means of facilitating recruitment, as a way to differentiate rewards for different levels of performance, and, in many cases, to place public sector compensation and benefits closer to par with the private sector.

Generally, there are four main themes that resonate across national pay reforms: tying pay to performance and establishing standards and benchmarks against which to assess performance; limiting the total amount by which compensation costs can increase; introducing greater flexibility into pay schemes or delegating greater decision responsibility in that regard downward; and altering the nature and scope of benefits packages available to members of the public service.

A closely related set of developments are those connecting industrial relations and unions to the discussions of pay and benefits changes. In some cases, such as Canada, collective

TABLE 3

Total Compensation Costs as Percentage of Government Consumption
Expenditure for Selected Nations

	1994	*1995*	*1996*
Australia*	48.1	47.9	49.1
Austria	58.8	59.1	58.7
Canada *	56.1	55.5	—
Czech Republic	31.0	34.2	37.0
Denmark	70.4	70.3	—
Finland	72.7	71.4	71.6
France	66.1	67.5	—
Germany	52.8	52.1	—
Hungary	—	46.7	—
Ireland	80.0	78.7	78.9
Italy	57.4	56.7	—
Netherlands	58.8	58.3	—
New Zealand	68.0	65.3	65.0
Poland	68.3	71.9	—
Portugal	77.8	78.7	78.4
Spain	70.2	70.2	—
Sweden	66.2	66.2	—
Switzerland	76.8	77.7	—
United Kingdom	54.1	53.2	52.8
United States *	49.8	50.1	50.1

When compensation costs are not available, figures refer to the pay bill.
Source: Public Sector Pay and Employment Data Base, OECD and National Accounts,
OECD.

bargaining was suspended while major downsizing and budget
cutting occurred. In New Zealand, one aspect of the early
reforms was the removal of unions from the discussions of the
most far-reaching reforms. In both cases, some limited "recon-
necting" is now occurring.

The United States presents a different kind of example. From
its earliest stage, those involved with reinventing government
and the National Performance Review worked closely with the
largest federal labour unions. The National Partnership Council was a formal mechanism for ensuring ongoing discussion
and collaboration. The fundamentally tenuous nature of the
partnership was tested, however, when the unions essentially

abandoned ship on the administration's proposed civil service reforms. The pay issue – specifically implementation of the Federal Employees Pay Comparability Act (FEPCA) of 1990 – has again called the relationship into question. The Act was intended to allow for "catch-up" pay increases if the public pay lagged behind private counterparts, but it contained provisions that limited increases as long as budget deficits were a serious issue. With the balanced budget, that time would appear to have been 1998. The White House announced, however, that the administration is "rethinking" the formula used to calculate such increases. The president called the formula "flawed" and argued that its use would increase federal personnel costs dramatically. *The Washington Post* observed: "While the decision focuses on arcane statistical techniques, it will likely reinforce widespread perceptions among federal workers that their pay system has broken down" (August 10, 1998, A15). In 1998 and 1999, Congress pushed for higher federal employee pay, albeit much less than would have been awarded if FEPCA was being implemented. This allowed the administration to point out that Congressional action had determined pay, and enabled it to continue to avoid paying FEPCA-mandated increases. As long as the White House succeeds in avoiding these increases, unions will continue to complain that they are not being fairly treated and are falling further behind private sector counterparts.

The Australian Public Service, while at an early stage of its compensation and benefit reform, provides an overall framework for a comprehensive package:

1 Wage and pay improvements must be linked to productivity gains and be consistent with maintaining low inflation;
2 Portable leave and benefits should be part of the package to enhance mobility;
3 Pay arrangements should be flexible to the extent that such flexibility meets agency needs;
4 A rationalized classification structure should be clearly linked to service-wide benchmarks for performance, with specific fitting to agencies as needed;

5 Salary-related running costs will be indexed and limited;
6 There will be no taxing or redistribution of one agency's savings to pay the costs of another.

The Australian assumption is that industrial relations and collective bargaining will be an important part of the discussions and agreements that will lead to the reforms.

CHANGING INDUSTRIAL RELATIONS
IN THE PUBLIC SERVICE

As noted above, the role of industrial relations is integrally related to pay reform efforts. Perhaps a broader and more fundamental issue with regard to industrial relations is the retreat of many governments from their (once) stated desire to be "model employers" and the possibility of a more remote role for public sector unions in many countries. Most governments in industrialized democracies had looked rather favourably on labour unions and had permitted, or even encouraged, the organization of public sector workers prior to the beginning of the major reform cycles in the 1980s. The emphasis on reducing costs, the individualization implied in many managerialist approaches in public personnel management, and the hostility of political conservatives to the public sector in general have since combined to produce numerous overt and covert attacks on unions in the public sector.

Perhaps the most overt case of these attacks was in the United Kingdom during the Thatcher years. Much of the change there revolved around public sector pay and the principle of comparability, but the attacks went further. Not only was the system of pay determination based largely on comparability abrogated, but the more general pattern of consultation under the Whitley Councils was essentially terminated. The general pattern of industrial relations appeared to change from cooperation to confrontation, provoking a number of strikes and the reorganization of civil service unions (Blackwell and Lloyd, 1989).

Further, the decentralization of most public sector employment into a number of semi-autonomous agencies has made continuation of the traditional pattern of industrial relations almost impossible (Fairbrother, 1994). There is much less sense of government as a single employer, meaning that bargaining over wages and conditions of service must also become more decentralized. The increasing use of private contracts for hiring has also reduced possibilities for effective organization.

Public sector unions have been under attack also in the Antipodes and in some European countries. Here the confrontation between government and the unions has been less overt, with the downsizing of the public sector, and especially the elimination of a number of public enterprises, reducing the relevance of unions for government. As in the United Kingdom, the decentralization and deconcentration of government services has reduced some of the organizational capacity for public sector unions. Even for those areas in which government remains directly involved contracting out and the use of a variety of partnerships means that the major personnel management functions have moved to the private sector.

Of course, in some European countries public sector unions have been able to maintain their powerful positions, although not without struggle. This is perhaps most evident in France, where the strikes in the autumn of 1995 made it clear that the unions continued to have the capacity to mobilize their members and to employ their power to affect public policies as well as the conditions of work. Similarly, the virtual draw between the public sector unions and the government in Denmark in 1998 meant that unions there would continue to exert a good deal of influence. Even in many of these cases, however, the ideas of managerialism are beginning to reduce the collective powers of unions.

Given these changes in industrial relations, what is the likely impact on personnel management and the recruitment and retention of employees in government in the coming years? On one hand, it appears clear that in most countries the trade unions have lost a good deal of their political power. This is not seen just in their ability to influence their own working conditions but also in their capacity to influence public policy more generally. Further, adoption of management techniques such as pay-for-performance and a more significant role for performance evaluation in general may lessen the capacity of unions to bargain for public employees as a group. The people of the public service may continue to be important, but they may be so more as individuals than as a collectivity.

On the other hand, the public sector remains perhaps the most unionized sector in many economies. At the same time that traditional unionization has been under attack in both the public and the private sectors, white-collar unionization and unionization of service workers has been increasing. In some countries such as the United States, unions in the public sector, e.g., the AFSCME, are the only unions that are increasing membership and other unions such as the Teamsters are increasingly active in this sector. The unions with which governments will have to contend may be different, but there still will be unions in the public sector. Indeed, the bargaining may be more difficult given that the newer patterns of organization are less familiar and the workers being organized are more marginalized than in the past.

In addition, a second thrust in the reforms of the public sector has been in the direction of greater consultation with workers as well as with the public. This concept of consultation appears particularly important in Canada and figures prominently in La Relève. Although public sector unions per se are not mentioned, these organizations form an obvious mechanism for some aspects of the consultation. And it is not just Canada in which consultation will be one of the central drivers in future public sector reform; the more general concern with how to involve employees while at the same time stressing performance and accountability will be central to continuing reforms in a number of settings.

What will the impact of these changes be? They may actually enhance the capacity of the public sector to recruit the best and brightest. Individual employees, especially those in the upper echelons, will be able to bargain for their own pay and perquisites, and may well be better off economically than under previous systems, and hence the system may be able to attract more of the best and brightest – at least those interested in financial compensation. At the same time, the average employee in the public sector may not be as well off economically, or in terms of the capacity to influence his or her conditions of employment. It may be, therefore, that much like the rest of the economy and society there will be a more marked differentiation between the top and bottom of the economic ladder in the public sector. Further, the basis of involvement in government may shift from a concern about public service and the intrinsic attraction of the career to more utilitarian concerns about rewards. That would not be a positive development, in part because government will never be able to match the salaries being offered in the private sector.

Information Technology and Knowledge Workers

A key question being raised, as increased attention is turned to developing personnel policies, concerns which skills, needs, and expertise are necessary in the new configuration. Only by addressing this fundamental concern can governments begin to give thought to what it considers to be the desired role and profile of public servants for the future. This question is put into sharp perspective when considering the role of Information Technology specialists. There is scant aggregate knowledge on the use of Information Technology within government systems. Of late, assessments of government performance have begun to ask how IT integrates within public organizations to improve capacity and performance, e.g., the Government Performance Project of Syracuse University. It is difficult to judge, however, if governments have availed themselves of the full potential of IT-related improvements. Private sector companies can effectively use IT to develop competitive advantage, and it is probable that private companies that are not attuned to the capabilities of IT will be eliminated in many industries. The monopoly situation of government organizations does not subject it to the type of guidance that membership of a competitive framework offers its actors. It will not go out of business if its systems are inefficient. This makes the need for government to be strategic in its use of IT all the more important.

Perhaps the most serious concern for governments in relation to IT is in terms of getting value for money. Vast amounts of money can be spent on public projects that are characteristically large, technically complex, and difficult to plan. The returns on these investments are often poor and even non-existent, and may have been accompanied with cost overruns without marked performance improvement (GAO, 1999). This suggests the need for governments to consistently define and properly organize IT processes. Government employees tend to understand that IT is important and will enhance performance in some way, but cannot understand the process by which IT will achieve the goal of improved performance. The purchaser of an IT system has to understand how it is related to a performance goal and how employees will interact with the new system to achieve these goals.

A key factor in the ability to improve the relationship between goals and IT processes will be the ability to recruit and retain IT specialists. The case of Ireland illustrates the tensions involved, where government IT specialists have been paid large "loyalty bonuses" that circumvent the rigid traditional civil service pay structure. The lesson that many governments are coming to understand is that the traditional model of public employment, and especially the traditional notions of compensation, are inadequate to recruit and retain workers with IT skills.   The options for public employers are to: make IT and other high-demand knowledge workers an exception to rigid pay systems; rethink and reform those systems with an emphasis on flexibility and competitiveness; contract out the bulk of IT requirements. The last option, the outsourcing of IT needs, has become increasingly common, but with little questioning of the wisdom of this option. The special nature of many government projects, and the long-term expenses of outsourcing, may force governments to conclude that developing more comprehensive in-house expertise will be a worthwhile investment.

Overall, governments need to begin to exploit more effectively the possibilities offered by Information Technology for

improved performance. Front-runners in the use of IT have uti-
lized it to integrate and improve the accessibility of government
services (OECD, 1998). The manner in which they do this, and
how they incorporate IT knowledge workers in this process, will
have serious implications for personnel policies. However, governments must also understand that an increase in the use of
technology does not mean that the traditional importance of
other types of knowledge workers is no longer relevant. Efforts
to downsize based on the premise that IT-related productivity
gains will take up the slack will often be erroneous. Some
knowledge will simply not be replaced by IT improvements. A
lack of willingness to maintain knowledge workers can be costly; the technical skills of such workers can be essential for overseeing many jobs in expensive programs (GAO, 1999).

THE FUTURE OF THE PUBLIC SERVICE

The Implications of Contracting Out

One of the common patterns that has been observed in efforts to
reform government has been an enthusiasm for contracting out of
governmental functions. This practice has multi-faceted implications for public sector management in terms of downsizing, the
shape and composition of government, and the manner of service
delivery. Most pertinently it can be seen in personnel terms,
where it also has serious implications for the skills required of the
public sector. The ability to create, monitor, and enforce contracts,
both for individual workers and for larger contracting companies,
is going to prove crucial in the future of the public service. This
necessitates that government employees have a clear idea of who
will best deliver performance. These are not skills that have been
fostered in the traditional civil service or have been given sufficient attention by reformers. While the creed of reform has called
for more empowerment, the necessities of contract management
will see a core civil service that cannot afford not to be focused on
ensuring compliance – ironically producing further red tape for
the public managers. Contractors will be challenged to specify

sufficient detail to guarantee compliance with public goals, while providing enough flexibility to ensure that public red tape is not being unnecessarily exported to the private sector.

Assuming that the trend of contracting out is not reversed, the following fragmented public sector model presents itself:

- The contractors: a core civil service with increased responsibility for managing contracts of the service delivery part of government. The traditional public policy advice function is declining, with politicians enjoying a wide range of policy analysis and advice from non-governmental sources. The contractors need essential skills in terms of 1) dealing with their political masters, especially in agreeing on what goals are to be set; 2) deciding the process needed to reach these goals; and 3) managing that process through contracts and measures of progress.
- The contracted: the disparate elements that combine to deliver the services funded by the central government; this group includes more local levels of government, private sector companies, employees who work under short-term or part-time contracts.

The dichotomy becomes blurred when we discuss those who work within the civil service but under individual contract arrangements, who fall into both divisions. The significant qualification of this model is that those in the core, especially the upper elements of the core, may be subject to contracts themselves that may be even more rigorous than other contracted actors. There is, however, a need to differentiate between the managers and the managed elements of public sector delivery. Hence we arrive at a situation where the core is distinguished by the fact that it is managing service delivery by proxy, and may be doing so in the context of a declined policy advice role. Stripped of this role, and the traditional bureaucratic job security, the core public servant is a public manager in the most literal sense. He or she is a manager first and foremost, and what he or she manages happens to be public.

One of the implications of this change is that to retain skilled managers under contract the government will have to be willing to offer salaries competitive with the private sector in order to ensure institutional memory and long-term capacity. Indeed this may not be enough. Turning the core public sector into a collection of contract agents raises some serious concerns, not only about the skills required to do the job, but also about the long-term attractiveness of this type of role for future employees. A role that is shorn of policy-advice responsibilities and hands-on management of public services does not send out a call to arms to those passionate about public service, or even just those demanding interesting and rewarding work. The Report from the Wye River Conference gave the views of public sector leaders in the United States, and emphasized the challenge involved in recruiting and retaining managerial talent for the public sector. A key element in meeting this challenge was recognizing that managerial talent was "human capital" and needed to be treated as an investment to be developed with an expected return (Ingraham et al., 2000, 55).

Employees receive appropriate rewards, incentives, and development opportunities; they give back necessary expertise, solid capacity, and higher performance. The interactive responsibility of this commitment and exchange is frequently missing in the current environment. If greater value is to be placed on human capital management and performance is to become the driver in the system, the mutual responsibility link must be created.

Treating employees as human capital also means going beyond simple compensation strategies and recognizing that the future public employment system "will proceed from the fundamental position that public work is valuable, challenging, and a contribution to effective government" (Ingraham et al., 2000, 56).

Another insight that arises from this fragmented public sector model is that the specification of goals, in conjunction with politicians, offers strong guidance for successful contract management. Simply put, it is easier to manage contracts when you can specify and measure what you are contracting for. However, experience in the United States suggests that clear advance specification of goals between public service partners has been problematic (Ingraham et al., 2000, 56):

In most cases, however, there has not been adequate attention to front-loading common goals, expectations, or means of evaluating the effectiveness of the partnership. Furthermore, accountability for quality and effectiveness of service has become less clear.

Increased emphasis on performance management, as exemplified by the Government Performance and Results Act (GPRA) in the United States, offers substantial opportunities for combining the goal-setting and contracting process, but it is recognized that the nature of political involvement in the process will be critical. There are also implications about governmental capacity in dealing with contract management situations. If government does decide to contract out, it must consider what is the most effective way to do so; what skills are best acquired through contract relationships; and what skills are desirable to retain and foster within the core. The conclusion of what these necessary skills are may differ radically from country to country, but at least such conclusions should be made on the basis of careful deliberation rather than as the result of purely budgetary choices.

Discussion of contract in relation to government suggests a more abstract use of the term. Contracting out is one of a number of public sector reforms. All of these reforms, in turn, reflect and affect a broader contract: that democratic contract between a government and its people. A greater emphasis on customer orientation, a tenet of many of the reforming governments, is a clear way in which the terms of a democratic contract is being fulfilled. There is a sense that the structural reforms of many governments are reflective of the flux and transitory status in which the democratic contract now finds itself. As the incorporation of clear and specified goals helps orient the contracting out process, an awareness of what vision a government has for its democratic contract will help orient the wider reform process.

Asking and Answering Human Resources Questions

A number of issues emerge from a discussion of the future of public service employment, in the aftermath of often radical reform that is still a continuing process in many countries. An inescapable point is that Human Resources Management is emerging as the key to long-term success for public sector reform. Reform that directly impacts the environment, size, composition, and functions of the public sector is incomplete without careful attention being given to personnel implications. Many of the early and most radical reformers seemed to regard these personnel implications as an afterthought; a problem that would take care of itself as functions were devolved, or something that could be dealt with after the heavy lifting of structural reform had taken place. It has become increasingly clear that government reform that fails to consider how personnel capacity needs to be directed may be ultimately self-defeating. Greater governmental attention to the issue of Human Resources Management is an acknowledgment of this, even though that is no guarantee that governments have the right answers to the thorny personnel problems that arise in a reformed workforce.

The reason that policy makers may not have the answers at hand is that the governmental structures and functions they now deal with are far different and more complex than previously. It is true to say that, to a great degree, many governments find themselves in unfamiliar territory. Changes and efforts to improve human resources are occurring within the confines of a restructured and reconfigured public service. This new public service is disaggregated to a much greater extent into core, part-time, temporary, and contracted-out workers. This raises questions regarding the level to which government can, or should, concern itself with developing centralized personnel policies for these vastly differing areas.

Indeed, the most difficult question of all may be: "How can we tell if government does have the right people, or that it is contracting for the services of the right type of people?" Some of the evidence needed will come from within the public sector, especially as governments are increasingly engaged in monitoring quality and performance, e.g., through GPRA in the United States and a host of service quality programs implemented elsewhere (Pollitt and Bouckaert, 1995). Some of the evidence also will come from the workforce itself, its morale and its overall satisfaction with work conditions, and with the challenges and rewards of employment. Still other pieces of evidence will come from the public, either directly or through the political process. Even so, attempting to say that there is an appropriate mixture of skills and an adequate level of capability is a very difficult practical exercise.

At the beginning of this chapter we considered whether government is still considered the employer of last resort. The answer from reforming countries, while perhaps not representative of all governments, is a resounding "No." In many developed nations politicians are more likely to make political hay by preaching against bureaucracy than promising to create public jobs. In addition fiscal considerations and economic orthodoxy prohibit governments to undertake large-scale public employment programs. For those that see public employment as a method to strategically provide government services, this is good news. In what appears to be a declining number of nations, where there is an expectation that government will not tolerate a certain level of unemployment, it will be surprising if the "provider-of-last-resort" model of public employment will not continue to be relevant. Perhaps a more pertinent question for developed nations is with regard to the government's obligations as an employer. Is government a model employer? Should it be? It may be that government is no longer a model employer but that it is becoming more reflective of employment norms in the rest of society. Does there remain with government some obligation to guarantee a type of stable, predictable work environment that provides strong worker protections? If public organizations look more like private, do they still carry the responsibility to reflect the democratic concerns of representativeness and equity?

As many countries have shifted away from the traditional bureaucratic model they find few ready answers that can provide a comprehensive blueprint for what will follow. At this point there is still a need to develop the right questions to give direction to these answers. Questions posed in this chapter are designed to facilitate this process, outlining a research agenda for those interested in how governments have restructured their functions, and how they may most effectively organize their workforces to align with new structures and new challenges.

Revitalizing the Public Service

The traditional model of the public service has been questioned, in very practical terms, by the reforms seen across the globe. The role of public service employees has been reconceived in terms of the relationship with their direct employer – the government – and their ultimate employer – the people of that nation. Of course this traditional model of hierarchical bureaucracy, with lifetime employment and a consistent pattern of compensation and promotion, is a generalization of a variety of different experiences across the world. Descriptions of the future of the public sector are also going to be generalizations, with as wide a deviation from this new model of public service as there was from the old. So far the evidence suggests a fragmentation of the nature of public employment in the future, with different types of work, workers and conditions, all loosely falling under the rubric of the public sector. Even those who remain in the "core" are likely to perform different functions under different conditions. An important realization that follows from this point is that a discussion of the public service that seeks to really examine the functions that a government performs must necessarily look beyond the traditional core bureaucratic model. Perhaps one of the key elements for the revitalization of the public sector may be to clearly define what is meant by the public sector, and how the different fragmented elements contribute to public goals. In order to think about Human Resources Management governments need to consider a fragmented, yet comprehensive, strategic approach to the different elements of public service provision.

We can begin to prepare, and even welcome, a different profile for the public servant. Increased employment flexibilities and higher lateral entry will make the public sector merely one option in a multi-track career. With the decline of the job-for-life concept, governments need to take advantage of their flexibility to hire, but also to ensure that government is perceived as a dynamic place to work for highly skilled professionals who are comfortable stepping between the public, private, and non-profit sector. This model of public employment has the advantage of breaking the bureaucratic malaise and producing more rounded public servants. This should be illustrative of the fact that public sector reforms can, and must, be structured in such a way as to offer the maximum possible advantage for the part that public employment will have to play in contributing to governance in the twenty-first century.

NOTES

1 "La Relève," or Renewal of the Public Service, has been launched by the Privy Council Office as a program to renew interest in the public service of Canada and revitalize its internal functioning.

BIBLIOGRAPHY

Barr, Stephen. 1998. Administration rethinking pay formula. In *The Washington Post*, August 10:A15.

Blackwell, R., and P. Lloyd. 1989. Industrial relations in the Thatcher years. In *Industrial Relations in the Public Sector*, eds. R. Mailey et al. London: Routledge.

Derlien, H. U. 1996. Germany: the intelligence of bureaucracy in a decentralized polity. In *Lessons From Experience: Experimental Learning in Administrative Reforms in Eight Democracies*, eds. J. P. Olsen and B. G. Peters. Oslo: Scandinavian University Press.

Elliot, R. 1998. The changing structure of employment and pay in the public service sector. Unpublished OECD Briefing Paper.

Fairbrother, P. 1994. *Politics and the State as Employer*. London: Mansell.

Federal Aviation Administration. 1996. 1996 FAA Strategic Plan. Washington DC: Government Printing Office.

Gregory, R. 1998. The changing face of the state in New Zealand: rolling back the public service. Paper prepared for presentation to the Annual Meeting of the American Political Science Associations, Boston, September 3-6, 1998.

Hogwood, B. W. 1998. Reinventing public employment? The restructuring of public sector employment in Britain. Paper prepared for presentation to the Annual Meeting of the American Political Science Associations, Boston, September 3-6, 1998.

Hood, C., D. King, B. G. Peters, and B. Rothstein. 1998. Working for government: rival interpretation of employment change in public services. Paper prepared for presentation to the Annual Meeting of the American Political Science Associations, Boston, September 3-6, 1998.

Ingraham, P. W., S. C. Selden, and D. P. Moynihan. 2000. People and performance: challenges for the future public service – the report from the Wye River conference. *Public Administration Review.* January/February 2000, Vol. 60. No.1:52-58.

Ingraham, P. W., and A. E. Kneedler. 1999. Dissecting the black box: toward a model of government and management performance. In *Advancing Public Management: New Developments in Theory, Methods, and Practice,* eds. J. L. Brudney, L. O'Toole, and H. G. Rainey. Washington DC: Georgetown University Press.

Kettl, D. F. 1993. *Sharing Power: Public Governance and Private Markets.* Washington DC: The Brookings Institution.

Lean State Advisory Council Resolutions. Presented at "Lean State Rewards the Future-oriented Administration." Congress in Düsseldorf, February 19-20, 1997.

Milward, H. B. 1996. Symposium on the hollow state: capacity, control, and performance in interorganizational settings – Introduction. *Journal of Public Administration and Research Theory* 2:193-197.

Milward, H. B., and K. G. Provan. 1991. Institutional-level norms and organizational involvement in a service implementation network. *Journal of Public Administration and Research Theory* 4, 391-417.

Minister of Public Works and Government Services Canada. 1998. La Relève. Ottawa: Minister of Indian Affairs and Northern Development.

OECD. 1998. Modernizing the human resources framework of the Canadian public service: the universal classification standard. *Focus,* July.

_____ 1997. *Trends in Public Sector Pay in OECD Countries.* Paris: OECD.

_____ 1997b. *Measuring Public Employment in OECD Countries: Sources, Methods and Results.* Paris: OECD.

_____ 1997c. *Managing the Senior Public Service: A Survey of OECD Countries.* Paris: OECD.

_____ 1998. *Information Technology as an Instrument of Public Management Reform: A Study of Five OECD Countries.* Paris: OECD.

Peters, B. G. 1996. *The Future of Governing: Four Emerging Models.* Lawrence, KS: Kansas University Press.

Pollitt, C., and G. Bouckaert. 1995. *Improving the Quality of European Public Services: Cases, Concepts and Commentaries.* London: Sage.

Public Service and Merit Protection Commission. 1997. *Re-engineering People Management.* Canberra: Public Service and Merit Commission.

_____ 1997b *Australian Public Service Statistics Report.* Canberra: Public Service and Merit Commission.

_____ 1997c. *Mobility in the Australian Public Service.* Canberra: Public Service and Merit Commission.

Treasury Board of Canada Secretariat. 1995. Employment Statistics for the Federal Public Service April 1, 1994 to March 31, 1995. Ottawa: Minister of Public Works and Government Services.

_____ 1996. Employment Statistics for the Federal Public Service April 1, 1995 to March 31, 1996. Ottawa: Minister of Public Works and Government Services.

_____ 1997. Employment Statistics for the Federal Public Service April 1, 1996 to March 31, 1976. Ottawa: Minister of Public Works and Government Services.

_____ 1998. Employment Statistics for the Federal Public Service April 1, 1997 to March 31, 1980. Ottawa: Minister of Public Works and Government Services.

United States Office of Personnel Management. 1997. *THE FACT BOOK–Federal Civilian Workforce Statistics–1997 Edition.* Washington DC: U.S. Office of Personnel Management.

_____ *Downsizing in the Federal Government.* Washington DC: U.S. Office of Personnel Management.

PART FIVE

CONCLUSION

The Future of Reform

B. GUY PETERS

We have now come full circle. We began this series of three books inquiring how governments were responding to the rather profound changes occurring in their social, economic, and political environments. That first exercise was retrospective, but as we now look into the future some of the same questions become apparent. The first, and most fundamental, question is whether government can continue to govern in anything like its former manner and, if not, what role will it have in the future? Second, as the social, economic, and political environment continue to change and to present new challenges, how can government be organized to be most effective? What sort of instruments should government use to reach its policy goals. Finally, what role will the public service play in the emerging model of governance, and what type of public service will be needed to perform the tasks of governance?

The authors of the chapters for this third book in the series each have addressed a part of these questions about the future. As we conclude this volume we will attempt to examine these questions (and especially the third) in light of those contributions, as well as some more general ideas about change that emerged in our discussions and which appear embedded in those articles. Understanding change, and especially predicting it, is an extremely difficult task for the social scientist, so our attempts here may appear somewhat inexact and preliminary.

There are so many variables involved, and so many possible choices, that predicting the future of governing usually produces subsequent embarrassment. Still, it is crucial to consider seriously what the future will look like, and then attempt to prepare for it or, if possible, also to shape it.

There appear to be two basic conceptions of change embedded in the studies contained herein. The first, and most common, is that of a linear development from a known past to an uncertain future. This notion of change need not be teleological, but it does appear to imply that once we (as individuals or as societies) move through one mode of organization, or one way of doing things, we do not go back. We subsequently learn new and better ways of performing our needed tasks and we progress. For example, economic production has moved from a craft basis to the production line and then to a team basis. Public sector management may have progressed in a similar direction, having moved from hierarchical organizational structures to either market or participative styles of governing (Peters, 1996), with little likelihood of returning to the older formats (but see Wright, this volume). If Snellen's chapter in the book is indicative, then technological change may preclude any atavistic return to the ways of the past.

The alternative manner of thinking about institutional change is to think of it as a more circular process. Rather than there being any linear progress, change may simply be moving governments back and forth along a number of different continua that define political and administrative life. Herbert Simon (1947) argued that most of our understanding of public administration was in terms of pairs of contradictory "proverbs," and that reform also moved back and forth between the two poles (see also Peters, 1998; Hood, 1998). In this view there is less real progress, and more simple alternation, and attempts to correct the actions taken during the last round of reform. In this view reform may simply be correcting what appear to be the errors from the last round of reform, a process that will set the stage for the subsequent round. Of course, there is some truth to both views of change, and change in the public sector displays some of both characteristics. Some of the changes that have occurred in the public sector may be irreversible, and represent real progress; one might mention the greater attention given to quality and service (Bouckaert and Pollitt, 1995; Pollitt, this volume) as well as the enhanced capacity to create, manage, and utilize information. Social change may also mean that the role of the public servant, and especially the senior public servant, has been changed in some fundamental ways (Bourgault and Savoie; Ingraham, Moynihan, and Peters, both this volume).

On the other hand, one thing the future reforms may hold for government is correcting some of the apparent excesses from the last round of reform. In the process of attempting to make government more efficient and effective it appears that some important public service values (see below) have been denigrated. Those values may well have to be revived and reinforced during the next round of change. Perhaps the most important of these values is the manner in which accountability is exercised within the public sector and the relationship between elective and permanent officials (Aucoin and Heintzman, this volume). As well as accountability, these relationships also appear to have changed with respect to the tasks of managers and the "bargain" they work under (Hood, this volume).

And there will be a next round. Almost all the reforms we have been discussing in these three books were undertaken by people of goodwill attempting to create an optimal government for their own country, or for the governments they were advising. Even those change agents who have been successful in creating the type of system of governing they had intended at the outset almost certainly will not satisfy the next group of political leaders to come to power, nor meet the standards proposed by the next wave of administrative "gurus" (Huczynski, 1993). This process of administrative change is almost certain to be continuous; perhaps not continuing with the intensity observed over the past two decades, but certainly continuing.

THE FUTURE OF GOVERNMENT

We have a difficult time envisioning a future in which national governments, in some form or another, are not major actors in governance (see Peters and Wright articles, this volume; see also Pierre and Peters, 2000). This assumption may reflect in part the difficulty in getting outside several centuries of history and our own experience, but it appears that there still will be a role for these governments. That having been said, there are real challenges to the central position of these players in governance. We discussed the impact of globalization (Savoie, 1996) explicitly in the first book, but that force continues to exert pressures that may diminish the capacity of national governments to control their economy and society (Strange, 1996). In Europe a good deal of governance activity has been moving to the level of the European Union, creating a system of "multi-level governance." There are also pressures to move governing downward to lower levels, and allow most governing to take place at the regional, local, or even community level (Etzioni, 1996; Tam, 1997), and to use non-governmental actors to do a number of things that governments at one time would have done (Rhodes, 1998). If all these forecasts were to come to pass it seems that there might be little left for national governments to do.

We would argue that most of the doom and gloom statements prophesying the end of the state are overstated at best, and ignore a good deal of evidence about the need for national governments in a more globalized and decentralized world (Hirst and Thompson, 1996; Scharpf, 1998). Most importantly, the simplistic view of a declining nation state appears to assume that political power is a zero-sum game, whereas in reality many governments have found that the international environment can actually enhance their own power vis-à-vis domestic economic forces.[1] In addition, the real power of international markets, especially the capital market, may mean that governments will have to be stronger rather than simply abdicate their responsibilities to the market.

The above general statement may require substantial nuancing. Almost all of our discussion has been concerned with industrialized countries, but the less-developed countries may be more subject to the control of the international market. On the other hand, however, the more developed countries may be more subject to pressures for community control over policies. Likewise, some policy areas may be more subject to international pressures than are others. Financial policy will be more subject to these pressures than would education or social welfare policies, so any generalizations about these influences are subject to real question.

Even if the nation state is to continue to exert substantial influence over a variety of policy areas, it almost certainly will not be able to do so in the manner to which governments have been accustomed in the past. The public no longer has sufficient confidence in their governments – a lack of confidence that appears to be shared by government itself – for the public sector to engage in the conventional pattern of "top-down" command and control regulation of economy and society. This means that governments will continue to intervene, but may do so in less intrusive manners. This will be true in part in the choice of policy instruments used by national governments (see Salamon, forthcoming), as well as in the increasing use of subnational governments and third party actors.

HOW WILL GOVERNMENT INTERVENE?

The future of government intervention appears to lie in the use of a wide variety of mechanisms to achieve public purposes. The principal task of governments, especially national governments, therefore becomes one of setting the goals for society rather than directly implementing the policies to achieve those goals. Certainly there will be some policies that these governments will have to implement, given their sensitive nature or the need to ensure rights and equality, but those may be fewer than is sometimes assumed.

The need to manage policy through networks and cooperative relationships with subnational governments will mean that government may appear to have lost some of its power to influence its society. The opposite may be the case, however, and government may actually be stronger than in the past. In the first place government may be able to enhance its own legitimacy by borrowing some from the groups that it uses to implement its programs. Further, by cooperating with individuals and organizations who understand the clients of programs well, and by taking into account more of the views of those clients, government organizations may be able to make public programs attain more of their desired goals, and perhaps at less cost.

THE FUTURE OF THE PUBLIC SERVICE

The final question is what the role of the public service will be in the future of governing. The various descriptions of reform contained in these three books have pointed to the changing composition of the public service, and the changing conception of their role in the process of providing governance in industrialized democracies. The general observation has been that the career public service is not valued as it once was, and that an increasing proportion of public employees are coming from the private sector, having had little or no prior experience in government.

For many advocates of change these reforms in the public service were needed to bring government into closer touch with society. Further, the assumption has been that the private sector management experience possessed by most of these new employees will improve the efficiency of government and, in the words of Vice President Gore, "make government work better and cost less." In the process of imposing these changes in the public sector, political leaders often have denigrated the values and contributions of the career public service, and in the process they have fostered the view that public and private sector careers are essentially interchangeable; "management is management" is often heard as a statement justifying this view.

Some of the changes in public sector employment have come about through less purposive policy choices. One of the more important of these less direct changes has been through the gradual erosion of public sector pay and perquisites. As compensation has remained stagnant, or grown more slowly than pay in the private sector, many of the most qualified civil servants in countries such as Canada and the United States have resigned. Even in countries where pay for chief executives has grown dramatically the public sector in general has been squeezed, forcing many long-term employees out of public employment. It is difficult to deny that there has been a brain-drain in the public sector.

The question then is whether this trend of declining public employment can continue, or whether there is not some value to (more or less) permanent government employment, and the values that such employment has tended to inculcate in members of the public service. Further, if government is to remain a central player, especially in areas such as science, technology, and regulation, it will need the high-quality personnel that are being deterred from entering, or remaining in, public employment. In several countries there have been reports of government no longer having the capacity to perform essential regulatory functions that depend upon those qualified personnel.

It is clear that governments will continue to need to be capable of providing essential scientific, technical, and regulatory functions, and that there will be a continuing social need for those types of employees. But what about the more general managerial functions of government; will there still be a need for the generalists who have tended to predominate in the upper echelons of government organizations? Also, will those generalists be primarily managers or will they also have important policy advice functions? There appear to be several possible answers to those interrelated questions.

One possible scenario attaches a high degree of importance to the role of generalists, and especially generalists in central management positions. In one view the central problem for the future of governments like that of Canada will be the capacity to coordinate programs and to manage the "horizontal" element of governing (Peters, 1996). If that is true then generalists are crucial in the centre of the public sector. There is a need for individuals who have experience in a number of different departments or agencies, and who can understand a variety of conceptions about good policy and priorities, to coordinate. Expertise and commitment may be important, but a broader view may also be important. This generalist role also implies that insiders rather than outsiders will be more valuable, given their capacity to accumulate experience and alternative conceptions of "good" public policy.

Further, one of the alternative scenarios mentioned above may become even more relevant than it already is, and subnational governments and third-party actors may be assigned an even greater role in the implementation of national policies. If that does come to pass, then some of the same skills appropriate for managing horizontal government may also become relevant for managing a new set of vertical and network relationships. As well as seeing policy from the perspective of other departments, these managers will need to be able to see policy from the perspective of other levels of government, and from contractors who may have their own policy objectives. Skills in bargaining and negotiation, rather than more conventional management, will be essential for ensuring implementation in such a setting.[2]

An alternative scenario argues that coordination is less a job for the centre than it is for the bottom of public organizations. Rather than attempting to impose coordination from above (generally a difficult task), a more decentralized system of governing would permit employees at the lowest echelons to coordinate programs, often on a case by case method. In this view, the future of the public service (again largely at the top) might be more specialized, with each organization being content to do its own job well and to permit coordination to occur far from Ottawa or Washington. In this view the policy, rather than management, skills of public servants may be most relevant.

Then there is the question of the policy role for the civil service. This role has been de-emphasized for much of the last several decades, as the emphasis within government has been on management and, secondly, on having individuals committed to the program of the government, rather than neutral careerists, render the policy advice. It may be that the policy role for public servants is being reinvigorated, and that there is a growing sense that some detachment from partisan politics. There may also be some attempt to foster a longer-term view on the consequences of public policy, rather than just looking at the political advantages of the government of the day. The policy advisory role of public servants may be more constrained – concentrating perhaps on the more technical issues rather than on broader issues like economic management – but there does appear to be some reassertion of this role for the public service.

Also, at least in some countries, there may be some fiscal latitude for increased public sector activity. We have all grown accustomed to government being under pressure to reduce rather than increase its taxes and expenditures, but the generally good economic conditions in the late 1990s have generated sufficient income to permit some thinking about new or enhanced programs. The economic (and revenue) growth, combined with the increasing number of active governments of the political left would, in turn, require more capacity to analyze policy, coming perhaps from the senior public service. This economic windfall may be short-lived, but the possibility of thinking about program change may provoke a revival of interest in the public service.

At this point we should also ask if the emphasis in reform of the public sector has not been too much on the public service. The reforms of the past several decades have tended to have an unstated assumption that the problem in government lay in public administration and the public service. If that assumption about the causes were correct then certainly there have been remedies proposed and implemented. The public service has been subject to a range of deinstitutionalizing reforms, with civil service rules and regulations being loosened or abolished, a number of jobs opened to external competition, and private sector management techniques imposed.

The most important problems in government now may reside in the other components of the governing machinery. If governments find that the public does not trust them, or respect them, then at least part of the blame must reside with elected officials and their behaviour.[3] It may be convenient to displace the blame for failures onto the public service, but it is not always fully correct to do so, and the next round of reform should perhaps be in the elective components of the system. In fairness, some governments have begun to recognize this problem and to implement major reforms of the political as well as administrative components of the system.

There are numerous alternative futures for the public service, all of which are possible. Picking which one will be the actual outcome of the contemporary process of change is difficult, and indeed no one simple scenario may be the result; there may be mixtures and different "models" may be dominant in different countries and even within different policy areas. The general conclusion we have reached from the investigations reported in these volumes is, however, that a well-educated and widely trained public service will remain an essential element in good government. The task facing national governments then is to create the conditions that will maintain and foster such public service. That may be easier said than done, however, given the widespread misunderstanding of the sources and solutions of problems within the public sector.

CONCLUSION

As Yogi Berra once said, the future hasn't happened yet. That astounding insight is as true for the public sector as it is for baseball games. The only problem is that much more is riding on the future of government than on the outcome of any baseball game. The fates not only of nations as entities but also of the individual citizens who comprise those nations rest to some degree on making the correct choices about governing. The rather individualistic assumptions guiding much of the retreat from the state assume that individual actors have much more capacity to shape their own futures outside of the public sector than may be reasonable in a complex, interdependent world.[4]

The good news is that the future of governing may be more controllable than the outcome of a sporting event. There is an opportunity to shape the nature of governments and its interventions and to shape the nature of the personnel who will be responsible for government. That future is not, however, fully controllable. Changes in social, economic, and political variables are themselves unpredictable and will have important consequences for governing. Perhaps the clearest advice that would arise from the contents of the articles in this book is that any future government, and the people within in it, will need to be flexible and adaptive. The pace of technological and social change will likely be no less than it has in the past, and citizens are likely to be even more skeptical of public policies, and public servants, than they have in the past. The task will be challenging and ever-changing, and it will indeed require some of the best and brightest in each society if it is to be successful.

NOTES

1 This is most clear for European governments that have been able to use the requirements of the Maastricht Treaty and the EMU to reign in unions and other powerful actors that were placing upward pressures on spending and budget deficits (Scharpf, 1998).

2 Of course, some analysts (both public and private sector) conceptualize management as employing just those types of skills of team-building and negotiation.

3 In many countries the public bureaucracy, if far from widely loved, is still more respected than parliaments.

4 The paradox is that many of the same analysts who argue that governments have in essence become powerless against global forces somehow assume that the individual can be more successful in mastering and taming those forces. This appears to be at best hubris.

BIBLIOGRAPHY

Bouckaert, G., and C. Pollitt. 1995. Quality in European Public Services. London: Sage.

Etzioni, A. 1995. *New Communitarian Thinking*. Charlottesville: University of Virginia Press.

Hirst, P., and G. Thompson. 1996. *Globalization in Question*. Oxford: Polity.

Hood, C. 1998. *The Art of the State: Culture, Rhetoric and Public Management*. Oxford: Clarendon Press.

Huczynski, A. A. 1993. *Management Gurus*. London: Routledge.

Peters, B. G. 1996. *Managing Horizontal Government*. Ottawa: Canadian Centre for Management Development.

_____ 1998. What works? The antiphons of administrative reform. In *Taking Stock*, eds. B. G. Peters and D. J. Savoie. Montreal: McGill-Queen's University Press.

Pierre, J., and B. G. Peters. 2000. *Governance, Politics and the State*. Basingstoke: Macmillan.

Rhodes, R. A. W. 1996. The new governance: governing without government. *Political Studies* Vol. XLIV, 4 (September).

Salamon, L. M. Forthcoming. *Understanding the Tools of Government*. New York: Oxford University Press.

Savoie, D. J. 1995. Globalization and Governance. In *Governance in a Changing Environment*, eds. B. G. Peters and D. J. Savoie. Montreal & Kingston: McGill-Queen's University Press.

Scharpf, F. W. 1998. Globablization: the limitation of state capacity. *Swiss Political Science Review* 4: 91-116.

Simon, H. A. 1947. *Administrative Behavior*. New York: Free Press.

Strange, S. 1996. *The Retreat of the State*. Cambridge: Cambridge University Press.

Tam, H. 1998. *Communitarianism: A New Agenda for Politics and Citizenship*. New York: New York University Press.

The Contributors

Peter Aucoin
McCullough Professor in Political Science
Department of Political Science
Dalhousie University
Halifax, Nova Scotia

Jonathan Boston
Professor of Commerce and Administration
Public Policy Group
Victoria University
Wellington, New Zealand

Jacques Bourgault
Associate Professor
École nationale d'administration publique
Montreal, P.Q.

David R. Cameron
Professor, Department of Political Science
University of Toronto
Toronto, Ontario

Ralph Heintzman
Assistant Secretary, Service and Innovation
Treasury Board Secretariat of Canada
Ottawa, Ontario

Christopher Hood
Professor, London School of Economics and Political Science
Department of Government
London, England

Patricia Ingraham
Professor, The Maxwell School of Citizenship & Public Affairs
Syracuse University
Syracuse, New York

Donald P. Moynihan
Professor, The Maxwell School of Citizenship & Public Affairs
Syracuse University
Syracuse, New York

B. Guy Peters
Maurice Falk Professor of American Government
Department of Political Science
University of Pittsburgh
Pittsburgh, Pennsylvania

Jon Pierre
Professor, Department of Political Science
Göteborg University
Göteborg, Sweden

Christopher Pollitt
Professor of Public Management
Erasmus University,
Rotterdam, The Netherlands

Donald J. Savoie
Clément-Cormier Chair in Economic Development
Université de Moncton
Moncton, New Brunswick

Richard Simeon
Professor of Political Science and Law
University of Toronto
Toronto, Ontario

Ignace Snellen
Professor of Social Science
Department of Public Administration
Erasmus University
Rotterdam, The Netherlands

Vincent Wright
Professor of Politics
Oxford University
Oxford, England